VIVE LE ROI!

. . . .

VIVE LE ROI!

A HISTORY OF THE FRENCH

CORONATION FROM CHARLES V

TO CHARLES X

RICHARD A. JACKSON

University of North Carolina Press

Chapel Hill and London

© 1984 The University of North Carolina Press

All rights reserved

Manufactured in the United States of America

Library of Congress Cataloging in Publication Data

Jackson, Richard A., 1937–

Vive le roi! : a history of the French coronation
from Charles V to Charles X.

Translation of: Vivat rex.

Bibliography: p.

1. Coronations—France—History.   2. France—Kings
and rulers.   I. Title.

DC33.15.J3213   1984   944   83-25896

ISBN 0-8078-1602-7

IN MEMORIAM

Andrew Matthew Jackson
(1873–1958)

William Robert Craig
(1889–1973)

Albert Ralph Jackson
(1907–1970)

CONTENTS

PREFACE

The present work is the English-language version of a book published in French under the title *Vivat rex: Histoire des sacres et couronnements en France, 1364–1825* (Strasbourg, 1984). The study is not so much a complete history of the French coronation ceremony from Charles V to Charles X as it is a series of studies derived from that history. To have written just the history of the ceremony itself, to have described the manifold—and often minor—changes that took place over the centuries, for example, to have determined and listed what official or noble did what on the occasion of crowning each of France's kings, would have done little more than satisfy a certain idle curiosity that, although it might have solved some historical problems, would hardly have warranted the expenditure of effort. I have been more interested in seeking in the ceremony suggestions as to what topics, hitherto either neglected or in need of reinterpretation, should be pursued as possibly adding to our understanding of conceptions of French kingship or as illustrative of the transition from medieval to modern monarchy. Consequently, I have deleted most of what may be considered purely antiquarian, retaining only what contributes to the whole without, I hope, badly misinterpreting the history of the subject. I should also note that I have rather severely limited the notes either to what is absolutely necessary, or to what seemed to me most useful—potential digressions could be found everywhere.

It would have been easy to have written a much longer book, to have added material that would probably be of value within other contexts. The amount of manuscript and printed material on the coronation ceremony is astounding, particularly as one approaches the present. The recent bibliography of Gaston Saffroy (*Bibliographie généalogique, héraldique et nobiliare de la France*, 4 vols. [Paris, 1968–78], 1:679–719) lists over 650 works dealing with the French coronation—83 of them concerning that of Napoleon alone—and the bibliography hardly comprehends all of the relevant materials. There are at least one hundred manuscripts containing medieval coronation *ordines*, and there are scores of printed editions of individual *ordines* in collections of sources or in

variously scattered articles. Saffroy almost totally ignores everything written in German, and he lists little in English. He fails to
include dozens of articles, and much of the literature that treats
peripherally of the coronation is absent. Saffroy's bibliography,
lengthy and useful though it is, could probably be doubled in
length without exhausting all the materials for a history of the
French coronation ceremony.

These materials are extremely varied. There are studies of all or
part of the ceremony like the excellent ones by Marcel David and
Percy Ernst Schramm on the coronation oaths and the history of
the medieval kingship (see the bibliography for these and the other
works here noted); they have numerous eighteenth- and nineteenth-century predecessors that tend to restrict themselves more
narrowly to the ceremony itself. Works like Ralph E. Giesey's studies of the royal funeral ceremony and the juristic basis of dynastic
right and Ernst H. Kantorowicz's explications of the royal *laudes*
and the king's two bodies have obvious application even though
written within much broader or different frameworks. There are
many descriptions of the ceremonies; although some were composed on the basis of secondhand information, some were written
by those who were present. There are expense accounts, plans,
magnificent commemorative volumes, memoirs, chronicles, letters,
papers of officials, printed programs, music, and miscellaneous
physical remains of the coronations. The latter include the
churches in which the ceremonies took place and—despite the dis-
persion of much of the treasuries of the cathedral church of Reims
and of the royal abbey of Saint-Denis—crowns, swords, scepters,
offerings, the new Holy Ampulla in its reliquary, garments, and
tapestries, among other things. (Many of these objects are now on
display in the Musée du Sacre in the Palais de Tau—the former
archiepiscopal palace in Reims whose name comes from its T-
shaped ground plan—and others are occasionally on display in the
Galerie d'Apollon in the Louvre.)

The studies written in the eighteenth and nineteenth centuries
occupy a place of their own among the sources for a study of the
coronation. Eighteenth-century books like those of Pons Augustin
Alletz, Dom Charles Joseph de Bévy, and Nicolas Menin are not
just serious attempts to write a history of the coronation; they are
also useful for the information they give on contemporary conceptions of kingship. This is true also, albeit to a lesser extent, of

the early nineteenth-century works of men like J. C. Clausel de Coussergues, Félix Lacointa, and Alexandre LeNoble. All of these studies tend towards a more or less slavish imitation of each other, though, and the only one that still has real merit as an imaginative, critical attempt to unravel the problems involved is the work of J. M. C. Leber, whose results suffer from his not having had the knowledge acquired by the succeeding century and one-half of scholarship. (This excuse cannot be made for an odd book by Jean Pierre Bayard published in 1964; Bayard caters to the current fad for the supernatural, mixing James G. Frazer, Marcel Eliäde, magic, astrology, alchemy, and Christianity in a study quite devoid of any serious scholarly results.)

Two works deserve special recognition. The first is Sarah Hanley's learned study of the development and significance of the ceremony of the *lit de justice*, which is being published at nearly the same time as the present work. If I have not cited it as often as I should have, that is only because I did not have a printed copy available as my final copy was prepared. I can only suggest that anyone who is interested in the transition from one reign to another must read Hanley's book. The other is the doctoral thesis of a Swiss scholar, Anton Haueter, *Die Krönungen der französischen Könige im Zeitalter des Absolutismus und in der Restauration*, which was published after I had finished the research and most of the writing of my study. Haueter has assembled a great mass of information about the coronations from 1654 to 1825, and it is partially on that account that my treatment of those ceremonies is as brief as it is. Haueter's work and mine have different aims, however, and they must be regarded as complementing each other. I did not think it useful in the present context to present the wealth of details that Haueter does, but I believe that the way in which I trace the ceremony over a longer period enables me to offer explanations that Haueter could not give. My notes refer to his work only at crucial points, but the reader who wishes more detail cannot avoid consulting what is clearly the most thorough study of the modern ceremony.

It is my pleasant duty to express my grateful thanks to the many individuals and institutions who have made this work possible. The University of Houston has thoughtfully provided a subvention that makes this edition possible, and it has been generous with three separate grants (including a Faculty Development Leave) and willing to allow me several leaves of absence over the past few years. The American Council of Learned Societies kindly accorded me a Study Fellowship that made it possible to study Byzantine ceremonial in the gracious surroundings of the University of Wisconsin's Institute for Research in the Humanities. I was able to pursue particular aspects of the problems discussed here owing to subsidies provided on two separate occasions by the American Philosophical Society from its Penrose Fund. Invaluable aid was given by the libraries of several universities (Houston, Illinois, Minnesota, the Bodleian at Oxford, Princeton, Strasbourg, Texas, Wisconsin), public libraries both in the United States and abroad (the British Library, the New York Public Library), archives (Archives de la Marne et de la province de Champagne, Archives Departementales d'Eure et Loire, Archives Nationales), French municipal libraries (Arras, Auxerre, Laon, Reims, Rouen, Saint-Omer, Sens, Troyes), the Musée Condé in Chantilly, and, of course, the libraries in Paris (the Bibliothèques de l'Assemblée Nationale, de l'Arsenal, de l'Institut de France, Mazarine, Nationale, and de Sainte-Geneviève); without the help of the considerate curators and staffs of such institutions, historical studies would be impossible. I have obtained information concerning a number of critical points from the *Nachlaß* of the late Ernst H. Kantorowicz, which I have been privileged to examine, but in accordance with the wishes of his literary executors I have not made specific attributions.

Chapters 8 ("Election and Consent of the People"), 9 ("The Sleeping King"), and 10 ("Peers of France and Princes of the Blood") were previously published in somewhat different forms in (respectively) the *Journal of Modern History, Bibliothèque d'Humanisme et Renaissance*, and *French Historical Studies.* I should like to thank those periodicals for permission to republish these chapters.

Simply to name the individuals who have helped me over the years would require a lengthy list, for it would include my fellow students from university days, my own students who often posed provocative questions, and many colleagues, friends, and acquaintances within and without the historical profession and widely scattered over two continents. To all of them I express my deepest gratitude, but most of all to two individuals who must be named. The first is Ruth Ann Traver, who was a most helpful critic in matters of grammar and style, and who dedicated many long hours to typing the early drafts of my text, often under considerable pressure. The second is Ralph E. Giesey, in whose seminar at the University of Minnesota I became interested in the coronation ceremony, and who taught me to read and to interpret history. I have not always followed advice given to me, perhaps to the detriment of my work, and I claim all responsibility for whatever errors remain. I do not see them myself, or I would correct them, but I take some comfort in my increasing awareness that the only way to avoid making mistakes in print is not to publish. There is doubtless not a chapter that follows that is not amenable to amplification and correction; if such be stimulated by what I have written, I shall be satisfied that my work has served a useful function.

This book is dedicated to the memory of three men, none of whom had time to be much concerned with history. My grandfathers and my father were all farmers, and people who spend their lives coaxing food and fiber from a recalcitrant soil under harsh climatic conditions do not have the leisure to pursue historical studies. I suspect that my paternal grandfather's disinterest in the past was deliberate as he turned away from the difficult life of his youth in the Lofoten Islands and assumed a family name that he conceived to accord with the new land in which he chose to spend over three-fourths of his life. In his adopted home, though, he developed an interest in, and knowledge of, current events which few I have since met have been able to equal, and, since I believe that a good knowledge of the present is a *conditio sine qua non* for understanding the past, he possessed one of the basic requisites of the historian. My father was more interested in history, both of the United States and of Europe, but he had decided to devote his life to carving a farm out of the woods and swamps of North Central Minnesota and to caring for a large family, activities that left neither time nor energy for more intellectual pursuits; a farming accident damaged his eyesight toward the end of his life, and he finally had to forego what reading he had previously done. My maternal grandfather's interest in the past was more personal, and he spent much time in the last years of his life traveling up and down and across the central United States seeking out relatives, searching for the tombs of his forebears, and trying, without any formal training, to establish the family genealogy. Instead of being cultured, these three men cultivated, and it is the fruit of their efforts and that of the unnamed millions like them over the centuries that enabled kings to be and that allows us to undertake historical studies. They are the salt of the earth, and may their kind endure to the end of time!

PART ONE

THE HISTORY OF THE CORONATION

.   .   .   .

1

INTRODUCTION

· · · · · · · · · ·

A nation's history is often mirrored in its vocabulary, and the French language has one usage that is sharply divergent from the English. The French tend to speak of the consecration, the *sacre*, of a king, while the English usually refer to the coronation, as do the Germans (*die Krönung*, although the Germans are more likely to refer to *die Weihe* than the English to the consecration or the sacring). This is interesting, for the French and English coronation ceremonies had so much in common that they were able to borrow freely from each other over the ages, and in each country the kings were both consecrated and crowned. The French thus emphasize the ecclesiastical and liturgical aspects of the ceremony, and the English emphasize the constitutional aspects.[1] In both countries, though, the coronation had lost most of its constitutive importance long before the end of the Middle Ages, but England's monarchs have continued to be crowned, whereas France's became ever more closely bound to the Church since the Carolingian Age, thus bringing about a union of throne and altar that made the coronation ceremony improbable even when last performed, in 1825. The French Kingship also made itself dependent upon absolutist doctrine, whereas England's did not. Our task in studying the coronation ceremony since Charles V's coronation in 1364 is, in part, to explain how and why this happened (following English usage, I ordinarily use the word "coronation" except when directly translating the French *sacre*).

The French monarchy since the Middle Ages developed numerous ceremonies that became ever grander and more carefully circumscribed as the royal and aristocratic elements of the monarchy became increasingly rigid. There were ceremonies for the birth of a prince or princess, for marriages and baptisms in the royal family, for formal entries, for *lits de justice*, for the *lever* and the *coucher*

of the king (after the mid-sixteenth century), for the coronation of
the queen (until 1610), and for the royal funerals and coronations.
The last two were intimately connected, marking as they did the
transfer of power from one king to another, but in terms of sheer
time involved, the royal funeral ceremony of the Renaissance was
the longest of the monarchy's ceremonies. Even it ceased to be
practiced after the death of Henry IV in 1610. It was the coronation ceremony that, eventually drawing 50,000 or more to the city
of coronation, remained the grandest and most noted of the royal
ceremonies.[2]

The coronation of the French kings was normally carried out
in the cathedral church of Notre Dame in Reims by its archbishop.
Surviving depictions of the coronation show much of the church
hung with tapestries that concealed some—but not all—of its
Gothic forms, and the other incidental decorations reflected the
artistic taste of the times; the decorations for the coronations of
Napoleon in Paris and Charles X in Reims, for example, were executed under the direction of Charles Percier, Jean Le Cointe, and
Jacques Ignace Hittorff, the creators of the Empire style. All who
participated in the ceremony or who were simply present were clad
in their most impressive costumes, which, when the ecclesiastical
vestments are taken into account, reflected the styles of several
centuries. The most magnificent ceremony of the king's life was
also the most expensive. The coronation of Saint Louis in 1226
cost over 9,000 livres, while Napoleon's coronation officially cost
some 4 million francs; the *grand écuyer* alone budgeted over 660,-
000 francs for Charles X's coronation, and the total cost of the
ceremony in 1825 amounted to more than a staggering 6 million
francs. These costs reflect the increasing complexity of the ceremony with the passage of time.[3]

The remotest origins of the coronation lead back to the legendary history of the Middle East, to the anointing of Moses by Aaron
and of the Hebrew kings by the high priest. These became the
models for Christian ceremonies of anointing that came to be devised upon the succession of some of the kings of Visigothic Spain.
Only later was the consecration introduced into Frankish lands
with the anointing of Pepin the Short in 751 upon the foundation
of the Carolingian dynasty. Thereafter, the practice of consecrating
the monarch spread to England and the remainder of western Europe, even finding its way to Byzantium, where the consecration of

the *basileus* was not known before about 1200. As time went on, the ceremony of consecration, accompanied perhaps at its very beginning by a mass, was lengthened by the addition of prayers that became a traditional part of the internationalized ceremony.[4]

As distinct from the consecration, the coronation had more recent origins that may date no further back than Constantine's wearing of the diadem (itself, though, perhaps a borrowing from the East and a modified version of the earlier laurel crown occasionally worn by the Roman emperors) and the subsequent development of a coronation ceremony in the Eastern Roman Empire. Not until the famous Christmas of 800 was there a coronation in the West, when Charlemagne somewhat imprudently had himself crowned by Leo III. There was no consecration accompanying Charlemagne's coronation, but the two ceremonies were shortly thereafter combined at the coronation of Louis the Pious in 816, and the basic elements of the ceremony quickly coalesced into the form they retained until the end of the West Frankish and French monarchy.[5]

The succeeding coronation *ordines* altered the order of the constituent parts of the developing ceremony, and, above all, they added to it. In France the most important medieval addition, apart from the various insignia, most of which were provided for by the end of the tenth century, consisted of the incorporation of knightly practices and of legendary and supernatural elements that had the effect of creating the *religion royale*: the Holy Ampulla, the thaumaturgic power, and the king's supra-lay characteristics.

By modern times the *religion royale* was the primary ground for performing the coronation ritual, but there had been a time in the High Middle Ages when the coronation had had a supreme constitutive importance. As the Carolingian monarchy collapsed in the ninth and tenth centuries, the West Frankish monarchs came to their position only after they were "elected" by the great barons of the kingdom. Much ink has been spilled over the meaning of the Carolingian election, and the subject became one of the greatest political moment in the second half of the sixteenth century (see chapter 8). The Germanic elective principle seems not to have been an absolute right, but quite simply the right of choosing the most able—or most desirable—member of the royal family, the *stirps regiae*. To see the right as more than that is seemingly to attribute to a comparatively unsophisticated intellectual milieu a depth of governmental and legal conceptions that did not exist before the twelfth-century revival of Roman law. However, to say even this much is probably unhistorical, for in the long struggle between the Carolingians and the Robertians for the West Frankish throne, there is the selection of one family or the other as the *stirps regiae* in addition to the choice of a member of a family. Any theoretical concept of the elective principle and its limitations must therefore be very fully tempered by the political, social, and ecclesiastical realities that existed at the time of any particular "election."[6] The failure to recognize that the Carolingian barons and prelates were not exactly jurists and political theorists has led to much historical anachronism (an interesting subject in its own right, historical anachronism, as we shall see, could make its own contribution to historical change).[7]

The election (the term is thus used in a limited sense) was not complete without the coronation: a West Frankish or French monarch was not king until he had been crowned, and he did not date his reign from his election, but from his coronation. (In modern democracies also the head of state does not assume office immediately after the election—in the United States, for example, the inauguration some two months later provides the crucial date.) The election and coronation of Hugh Capet in 987 was not in itself particularly significant; its importance became clear only much later, when the French monarchy had truly become successive to the nearest male heir.

The transition from the elective to the hereditary monarchy was made possible primarily by the biological ability of Hugh Capet and his successors to provide comparatively healthy male heirs who had often reached maturity by the time their fathers died. The incidents that caused the early Capetians to crown their successors as co-kings also had the effect of bringing about an instantaneous transmission of power upon the old king's death, for France already had a crowned king who dated his reign either from his coronation or from his predecessor's death. Both kinds of dating were used, leading to considerable confusion in the royal acts of the eleventh and twelfth centuries. Philip Augustus, the last king to be crowned during his father's lifetime, dated his reign exclusively from his coronation, a practice followed by his two successors. This was the source of a problem because for two centuries the kings had been crowned during their fathers' lifetimes, and in the thirteenth century if one were not fully king before the coronation there existed an awkward interregnum. This difficulty became truly serious when Louis IX died in Tunis in 1270, and it was clear that several months would lapse before his son could be crowned; in fact, over a year passed before the coronation of Philip III. An interim solution to the problem was found: the military leaders of the French army in Tunis were required to swear oaths of loyalty to the new monarch; Philip dated his documents from that event. The events in Tunis were too unusual to establish a general rule, however, and the problem of the interregnum was eventually solved by means of one of the most interesting juristic fictions ever devised, the notion of the king's two bodies.[8]

The fiction had its origin in a complicated interplay of canon law and ecclesiastical practice, the revived Roman law, and purely fortuitous circumstances like the death of Louis IX while on crusade. In its most fully developed form in late sixteenth-century England and France, the theory urged that the king had two bodies: one, the body of the king, was like that of any other man, physical, mortal, subject to aches and pains and illness, and certain finally to decay; the other body, that of the King, was immortal (or at least sempiternal), liable to neither illness nor death nor decay. The English conceived of the King as a corporation sole, a corporation represented at any moment by only one living member, but nonetheless arising always phoenix-like and, like the phoenix and other corporations, immortal. This was carefully expressed when the English asserted that "the king, as king, never dies," and Shakespeare could write a complicated pun on the bodies of Polonius and the king when he had Hamlet say, "The body is with the King, but the King is not with the body. The King is a thing . . . of nothing" (Act IV, scene ii).[9]

The fiction was graphically portrayed in bi-level ecclesiastical and lay tombal monuments. The upper level portrayed the dead person in all his glory with all the insignia of office, while the lower one was as faithful a depiction of the actual dead body as it was possible to make—the reality here might become a bit stretched, as in the case of Catherine de Médicis, who found her lower effigy (completed before her death) so ugly that she forbade its use on her tomb.[10]

Several French kings were buried under such bi-level monuments, the remnants of which may still be seen in the royal necropolis in the basilica of the former abbey of Saint-Denis (now the cathedral church of Saint-Denis). This is a most fitting location, for the fiction of the king's two bodies was most extensively acted out in the French Renaissance funeral ceremony at Saint-Denis and in Paris. By the fifteenth century it had become the practice to place a waxen effigy of the king on top of his casket; the effigy was adorned with the insignia of kingship so that the appearance was of one alive rather than of one dead. In the early sixteenth century the physical body of the king came to assume a place quite clearly subordinate to the effigy of the king as King. The sixteenth-century effigies were treated as though actually living, even to the extent of being served ceremonial meals as they surveyed their chamber from a bed of state. After a specified period of days, the funeral service was held in the cathedral church of Notre Dame in Paris, from which the funeral procession—following at least partly the same route the kings had taken on the occasion of their first formal entry into their capital—wended its way some six miles to the north. Further ceremonies in the basilica of Saint-Denis culminated with the lowering of the dead king's body into the grave. Then, attending officials placed the regalia of kingship upon the coffin, and stewards of the household threw their batons into the grave, signifying that their term of office came to an end with the death of the king. Last, the banner of France was lowered to the coffin, and through the basilica rang the funerary cry, "Le roi est mort!" followed almost immediately by the raising of the banner and the triumphal shout "Vive le roi!" The acclamation led directly to the coronation ceremony, which usually took place within a few weeks, with its own cry of "Vivat rex in aeternum."[11]

France could have but one king at a time by the end of the Middle Ages, and the treatment of the funeral effigy as king alive meant that the actual successor to the throne had to remain quasi-secreted for the duration of the funeral ceremony. Henry II, for example, could not attend his father's funeral but had to content himself with observing the passing cortege from behind curtained windows. The fiction that imposed this kind of restriction was a juristic one that was most likely to have been acted out in an age of lawyers like the sixteenth century. The mid-seventeenth century was more prosaic—if we note that Louis XIV's coronation was postponed for more than a decade after his accession, we may partly understand why Henry IV's was the last royal funeral to act out the fiction of the king's two bodies.[12]

The Renaissance funeral ceremony had continued to enfeeble the constitutive aspect of the coronation: the acclamation of the king as King at Saint-Denis seemed to make the coronation redundant. Also undermining the requirement for a coronation was the acceptance of a general dynastic right of succession to the throne. This was an automatic process, and by the fourteenth century hereditary succession had become so entrenched that Philip the Fair's three sons were able to succeed each other; the crown passed without serious internal difficulty from the last of the direct Capetians to Philip VI, the first of the Valois monarchs—the dynastic claims of Edward III, must, it seems, be seen as pretention and an auxiliary to more fundamental issues having to do with the feudal past of the French and English monarchies.[13] Other failures to provide direct heirs to the throne led to further familial (though not dynastic) changes in the late fifteenth and early sixteenth centuries. Even Henry of Navarre would undoubtedly have had little difficulty had it not been for the religious troubles and the fact that Henry was a Huguenot.

The right of dynastic succession came to be hammered out over a period of decades, and when Henry finally succeeded, it became impossible to doubt that the eldest surviving son of the nearest cadet line should be king if the direct royal line should die out. If the king should produce a direct heir, the matter was all the easier. In one of the descriptions of the coronation of Louis XIII in 1610, it was reported that in a friendly gesture the child-king boxed the duke of Elbeuf (also a child) on the ear, an act that caused the writer to exclaim that this was "a streak of the cheerfulness and of the living image [*la vive image*] of Henry the Great."[14] The context makes this appear a casual comment by the writer, but it was more than that. Charles de Remond, writing shortly after the coronation, could speak often of "that living image" (*cette vivante image*), and he urged that all France would echo the words "Long live LOUIS, long live the image of my HENRY in the Image of the nascent King [*du Roy naissant*], and in the honor of the son the memory of the father."[15] At a *lit de justice* held in 1614 Louis was again called the living image of his father.[16] This living-image metaphor destroyed any further need to maintain the fiction of the king's two bodies.

The King was now represented fully in the person of the individual who became king solely by the biological accident of birth and the right of succession. There was no longer a need for a funeral ceremony to prevent a theoretical interregnum, and there was no longer a need for a coronation to make the king.

It is clear that one would seek in vain to find a late medieval, Renaissance, or modern French king constituted by his coronation. Nevertheless, the coronation did have a constitutional role to play: if nothing else it imposed theoretical limitations upon the king that will have to be examined in some detail.[17] Furthermore, the coronation had a popular importance that may hardly be overestimated.

Two coronations show this popular element most clearly: those of Charles VII in 1429 and Henry IV in 1594. In both cases France was at war; in both there was a mixture of civil and foreign war. Only when the civil war was more or less successfully brought to an end did the foreign war cease, and in both cases a major turning point in the civil war was the coronation of the king. In 1429 Joan of Arc considered it her mission to raise the seige of Orléans and lead Charles to Reims for his coronation, after which the consecrated king of France would be able to drive the *godons* from his kingdom. Joan never referred to Charles as anything but the dauphin before his coronation (which followed his father's death by seven years), and when at her trial she was asked why she persisted in doing so, she replied that he was not king until he had been consecrated and crowned at Reims.[18] Only after the coronation did Joan address Charles as *Gentil roy*. The Maid's knowledge of the French constitution and law may have been weak, but she certainly was representative of the vast majority's belief that a coronation was necessary to make a king, and the triumphal journey from Tours to Troyes to Châlons-sur-Marne to Reims was followed by the even quicker capitulation of Laon, Soissons, Château-Thierry, and Provins. In the popular mind the coronation made the king.

The same was apparently true a century and one-half later, although it is difficult to determine whether the success of Henry IV was due more to his conversion or to his coronation. Both undoubtedly played a role in the minds of Henry's contemporaries, and at the very least the coronation—even though it differed in some important respects from that of his predecessors—capped the process of legitimization that for many began with the public conversion at Saint-Denis in 1593.[19]

The longest period between an accession and a coronation occurred after the death of Louis XIII in 1643; only after eleven years and two revolts of the Fronde did the coronation take place. One cannot help but wonder whether one or both of the Fronde revolts would have taken place had Louis XIV been crowned at a younger age; Mazarin, at least, seems to have thought not.[20] Perhaps they would have, and the coronation would have meant nothing. Certainly it was not even a popular necessity after Waterloo: Louis XVIII was not crowned, and nobody seems to have denied that he was king for want of a coronation. Louis did wish to be crowned, though, and there were at least two projects for his coronation: one for a ceremony in Reims (1814), and the other at the church of Sainte-Geneviève (now the Panthéon) in Paris (1819).[21] The proposed ceremony on at least one of these occasions reflects a new conception of kingship that contained many elements of the old. The ceremony of the Old Regime was altered to make it similar to the royal-imperial ceremony of Napoleon's coronation in 1804, and the king was to swear to uphold the Constitutional Charter, but the legend of the Holy Ampulla was revived and was to serve the Restoration monarchy as it had its medieval and early-modern predecessor. The grandiose ceremony prepared for Charles X in 1825 showed as clearly as possible that king's desire to return to the norms of the past, and the final French coronation ceremony differed from its early-modern counterparts only to the extent made necessary by the events that had intervened after the previous royal coronation in 1775.[22]

Although some individual ceremonies do demonstrate unambiguously that there was a need for the royal coronation, although some do show us what conceptions of kingship obtained at the beginning of certain reigns, others are not as informative. As we move back into the High Middle Ages we find that only rarely are we able to draw assured conclusions about French kingship from the coronation ceremony. We are often hard-pressed to know just what conceptions of kingship obtained in France before the thirteenth century because our sources are so few and so laconic. That may well be why the medieval coronation texts have long been considered of prime importance for the study of the subject—the late Percy Ernst Schramm founded his study of the king of France, the only good study of its sort in any language, primarily upon the texts of the medieval coronation *ordines*.[23] Schramm's intention of writing a history of the cult of kingship was a laudable one, but the history suffers faults that make some of Schramm's asseverations debatable. Schramm tended to believe, like his predecessors, that a coronation text, once it began to be used, served as the basis for the ceremony until it came to be replaced by another text. This was not always true, as we shall see (below, chapter 3), and it is incautious to extrapolate ideas written down in one period into a succeeding age. In fact, it appears, the coronation ceremony contributes very little to our knowledge of the cult of kingship between the late tenth century and the early thirteenth century. We do have three texts from the thirteenth century—they probably all date from the reign of Louis IX—but each of them suffers dating or other problems that impose caution when it comes to interpreting them.[24] Beginning with the text composed for the coronation of Charles V in 1364, we enter new territory, for from that date we can establish with a fair degree of certitude the basic order of the ceremony on each occasion.[25] Beginning with 1364, therefore, the coronation ceremony becomes a rather reliable and fairly precise source for investigation of the conceptions of the cult of rulership; more than that, though, it enables us to observe some of the inner workings of the transition of French kingship from the Middle Ages to the nineteenth century.

A single ceremony, even one repeated sporadically with the passage of the ages, can tell us only part of what kingship is. The medieval ceremony says next to nothing about feudalistic kingship until it assigned a role to the twelve Peers of France at a time when the monarchy was ceasing to be primarily feudal. It is largely silent on such matters as the administration of justice, royal military activities, the king's financial systems, or the acquisition and care of the royal domain, in short, about the monarch's myriad preoccupations that eventually led to the creation of the state. Even if the subject be more narrowly defined as the cult of kingship, the coronation provides but partial information that must be supplemented with the writings of lawyers, political theorists, pamphleteers, and poets. Nonetheless, the coronation ceremony remains one of the historian's mines of information, one that must be exploited to produce a durable alloy. We shall have numerous occasions to see ways in which the coronation does yield useful knowledge about the French royal cult over the centuries.

Equally interesting is the way in which ceremonial changes inform us about the stages and means by which the kingship made the transition from medieval to modern. It would be hazardous to offer a definition of medieval kingship because the institution changed so much after the tenth century, but, nevertheless, in the fourteenth century, when this study begins, there are still many aspects of that kingship that most people would recognize as typically medieval. The kings had been breaking away from their feudal past since the days of Philip Augustus, but that past was still sufficiently alive to determine to a large degree the composition and activities of the French hosts during the Hundred Years' War. The royal domain had increased greatly since the twelfth century, but important parts of France still remained outside the king's direct control, and even the domain tended still to be conceived in terms of personal property, despite the development of the Chambre des Comptes and other administrative institutions. Permanent royal courts, above all the Parlement of Paris, had been created, but it was still the king, not the state, who was the source of justice and the kingdom's final arbiter. The cult of kingship was pervaded with beliefs in the efficacy of the king's thaumaturgic power, the sanctity of the Holy Ampulla, or the miraculous origin of the fleurs-de-lys, beliefs inherited from an earlier, more primitive age but retained in a period in which superstitious credulity had hardly diminished. The consecrating activity of the Church was still necessary to make a king, as it had been ever since the days when Hincmar of Reims had succeeded in transforming the coronation ceremony from the secular one it had previously been. During the last five hundred or so years of the monarchy each of these traits suffered mutations that are illuminated by the study of the coronations.

Charles X was crowned in 1825 in accordance with a ceremony that had had its origins in the Early Middle Ages, at a time when there was not yet a France and when no one could possibly have predicted that the modern state would be born of the monarchy. Owing at least in part to the role played by the coronation during the first half of the Capetian period, the kingship had managed to free itself from whatever elective element had originally helped to make the king. Beginning with the thirteenth century, other methods of ensuring a smooth succession were devised, and in 1610 the ceremony became largely a display of royal grandeur and of dynastic succession, which it remained to the end. Medieval texts had often spoken of the *consecratio* and *coronatio*, and whereas the popular mind failed to make a clear distinction between the two and apparently continued to believe the ceremony a useful, even necessary one, there was little of the *coronatio* as a secular constitutive act in the ceremony we are here studying. How little is strikingly portrayed by the painting Hyacinthe Rigaud did in 1715, seven years before the coronation, of the young Louis XV already bearing his crown, scepter, and other regalia.[26] The *consecratio* retained its full value, on the other hand, and the survival of the ceremony as a *sacre* is of supreme importance for interpreting the modern cult of kingship, including that of Charles X.

A brief description of a well-documented and fully developed ceremony that stands at the end of the Renaissance and the beginning of the modern age, the coronation of Louis XIII, may serve as a useful introduction to the structure of the ceremony. Resolution of particular problems presented by the late medieval coronations and by ceremonial innovation and its significance will be necessary before we can proceed to an examination of theoretical or real limitations upon the king. These latter are exemplified by the coronation oaths, the law of inalienability, restrictions upon the royal right of pardon, and the development in the sixteenth century of the theory that the monarchy was still elective. Such limitations were hardly beloved by proponents of the royal cult, which expressed its absolutistic tendencies by means of the fiction of the sleeping king and by the complementary rise of the Princes of the Blood at the expense of the medieval Peers of France. The kings' connection with the legendary and miraculous past was underlined by the precoronation entries into Reims, which, in addition, depicted something of France's increasing imperial aspirations in the age of absolutism. The French Empire was finally realized by Napoleon, whose own coronation in 1804 paved the way for the temporary return of the coronation ceremony in the Restoration. By turning our attention successively to each of these topics, we will be able to demarcate the medieval from the modern and to essay an evaluation of the coronation in history and its significance.

2

THE CORONATION OF LOUIS XIII

.   .   .   .

The year 1610 was a pivotal one in the history of French royal ceremonial. The coronation of Marie de Médicis at Saint-Denis on Thursday, 13 May, was to have been followed three days later by her formal *entrée* into Paris, but the death of Henry IV at the hands of Ravaillac on Friday postponed the *entrée* forever, and Henry's second wife was the last French queen to be crowned.[1] Instead of enjoying the spectacle of a formal entry into Paris, the new queen mother made her initial ceremonial appearance after her coronation on Saturday, 15 May, in what was to become the first of a series of inaugural *lits de justice* that preempted any constitutive value that either the funeral of the late king or the coronation of the new king might still have had.[2] The funeral of Henry IV was consequently the last of the Renaissance funeral ceremonies, but the queen mother did decide in the course of that summer to proceed immediately with the coronation of her young son, without waiting until he should reach his majority—thus following in the footsteps of a distant relative, Catherine de Médicis, who had had her son, Charles IX, crowned on 15 May 1561, two years before his majority.[3]

The departure of Louis and his mother from Paris on Saturday, 2 October 1610, was the beginning of a round-trip journey that was to last exactly three weeks. The royal party did not reach Reims until Thursday, 14 October, when the city of Louis's coronation greeted him with speeches and numerous officials and thousands of troops and citizens on parade. After Louis had been presented with the keys to the city, the royal entourage passed through several triumphal arches on its route to the cathedral church of Notre Dame, where a *Te Deum* was sung in the king's honor; Louis was then conducted to the neighboring Palais de Tau, the archiepiscopal palace that was to be Louis's residence during the following days.[4] On Friday, Louis visited the basilica of Saint-Remi, where he saw the Holy Ampulla and the body of Saint Remigius,[5] and in the afternoon he visited the neighboring convent of Saint-Pierre, whose nuns sang another *Te Deum*. On Saturday the king visited still another church in the city, Saint-Nicaise, where he viewed the reliquary head of Saint Sixtus, thought to have been the first bishop of Reims. At four in the afternoon Louis returned to the cathedral church for his confirmation by Cardinal Joyeuse, who was to crown him the next day. Unlike many of his predecessors, Louis XIII did not hold a vigil of knighthood during part of the evening before his coronation.[6]

By October of 1610 five months had lapsed since the death of Henry IV, enabling all preparations to be completed for Louis's coronation. Ample time had not always been available; the preparations for Charles VII's ceremony had had to be carried out particularly hastily, in less than twenty-four hours, whereas a lapse of six weeks between accession and coronation was normal. At Louis XIV's coronation in 1654 the king was to enter the church unceremoniously from the side because the covered walkway from the archiepiscopal palace was not completed, despite the passage of eleven years since his accession and the unaccountable last-minute postponement of the ceremony by a week.[7] In 1610, though, there were no obstacles to the smooth performance of the ceremony, and by the time Louis entered the church for his confirmation on Saturday everything was properly disposed. Much of the cathedral was covered with tapestries and precious cloths, the necessary platforms and oratories were in place, and temporary seating had been constructed for those fortunate thousands who were admitted to the building the next morning.

1. The Beginning of the Ceremony

The ceremonies began early on the day of coronation, Sunday, 17 October. The canons of the cathedral chanted matins before the break of day, and the various officials arrived to ensure that the spectators should be directed to the seats reserved for them. The officiating Cardinal Joyeuse (who had crowned Marie de Médicis a few months before) and the remaining five ecclesiastical Peers of France (Joyeuse represented the archbishop of Reims) arrived at the sanctuary before 7:00 A.M. These were soon followed by the representatives of the six lay Peers of France, who carried the coronation regalia with them from the archiepiscopal palace. The twelve peers then held a convocation to delegate the bishops of Laon and of Beauvais "to go and seek the king" in his lodging in the archiepiscopal palace, where the precoronation ritual of the sleeping king was enacted.[8]

When the king in procession arrived at the entrance of the church, the bishop of Beauvais said a prayer, and the cantor and musicians sang Psalm 20 (*Domine, in virtute tua laetabitur rex*); while the psalm was being sung, the king and his retinue approached the altar, where the bishops of Laon and of Beauvais presented him to the officiating cardinal.[9] After another prayer the king was led to his raised dais facing the officiant's chair (i.e., his back was to the nave as he faced the altar), and the other participants took their places. Joyeuse presented holy water to the king, and the choir began to sing tierce.

Just before the king was sought by the two episcopal peers, he had delegated four barons to go to the abbey of Saint-Remi to accompany the Holy Ampulla from its repository there to the cathedral church. When the four (and their extensive retinue) arrived at the abbey, its grand prior mounted a white horse (*haquenée*) that the barons had brought with them for the purpose.[10] The grand prior, carrying the Holy Ampulla in its reliquary on a chain around his neck, accompanied by the singing of the monks of the abbey, and covered by a canopy carried by four monks, moved in procession through the tapestry-bedecked streets of the city to the main portal of the cathedral.

As the last psalm of tierce was concluded, the procession of the Holy Ampulla arrived at the church, and Cardinal Joyeuse, notified of its arrival, went with a number of clerics to the portal of the church to meet the grand prior waiting under his canopy. The grand prior presented the Holy Ampulla to the officiant, but not before he had extracted from the cardinal a notarized promise that he would return it to the monks of the abbey at the conclusion of the coronation ceremony.[11] As the relic was placed in the hands of the cardinal, the cathedral choir began to sing a hymn to the ampulla, *O pretiosum munus*. During the singing of the hymn the clergy returned to the altar, the cardinal displayed the ampulla to the audience—whereupon the king and congregation respectfully rose in reverence of the object—and placed it upon the altar, and the grand prior took his place at the right side of the altar, where he remained on guard throughout the ceremony. The grand commander of Saint-Denis, who had accompanied the coronation insignia—the closed "imperial crown," the smaller crown, the scepter, the *main de justice*, the royal mantle, the sandals, the spurs, the sword, the tunic, and the dalmatic—from the royal abbey north of Paris, took up his position on the left side of the altar.[12] The cardinal recited another prayer and retired to a sacristy near the altar to put on his chasuble and other garments for mass, while the choir sang sixte. The cardinal and assisting bishops returned to the altar, and the cardinal did reverence to the altar and saluted the king.

Joyeuse then approached the king and solemnly asked him to protect the canonical privilege, due law, and justice of the bishops and of the churches committed to them. Louis, who remained seated, promised to do so, after which he was raised from his chair by the bishops of Laon and of Beauvais, who asked the assembled people whether they would accept Louis XIII as their king—one description says that all approved "by their tacit consent." The king then swore the oath of the kingdom: that his Christian populace would preserve peace for the Church, that he would prohibit all sorts of violence, that he would be just and merciful in his judgments, and that he would attempt to expel all identified heretics from his land and jurisdiction. After swearing the oath Louis kissed the Gospels, upon which he had placed his hands while swearing the oath.[13] Joyeuse returned to the altar, whither Louis was conducted by Laon and Beauvais. The first gentleman of the chamber removed the king's long robe of silver-colored linen, leaving him in a camisole of crimson satin over a chemise, and the cardinal recited more prayers.[14]

The next stage in the ceremony was the investiture with the symbols of knighthood. The grand chamberlain of France placed slippers on the king's feet, and Monsieur (Louis's brother), who represented the duke of Burgundy, invested the king with golden spurs that he immediately removed.[15] The cardinal next blessed the "sword of Charlemagne" in its scabbard, girt Louis over his camisole with the sword and immediately removed it, drew the sword from the scabbard (which he laid on the altar), kissed and placed the naked sword in the hands of the king, and recited a traditional prayer. After the choir had finished chanting an antiphon, Louis held the sword with the point upright while the cardinal said another prayer. When this was ended, Louis in turn kissed the sword and offered it to God by placing it upon the altar; from there the cardinal took it up and again placed it in the hands of the now-kneeling king, who handed it to the marshal of La Châtre, who represented the constable of France. The marshal carried the sword upright before Louis during the remainder of the coronation ceremony and the postcoronation banquet.[16]

The king remained on his knees while Joyeuse recited three rather long prayers and proceeded to prepare the Holy Balm for the king's consecration. Using a golden needle, he withdrew a small amount of the congealed balm from the narrow-necked Holy Ampulla. He scraped the balm onto the paten of the chalice of Saint-Remi, poured some chrism from the chalice onto the balm, and mixed the balm and the chrism. While he did this, the choir sang a response (*Gentem Francorum inclitam*) and versicle; the cardinal then said another prayer.[17]

A long series of liturgical acts now followed. Laon and Beauvais conducted Louis to the altar, and king and cardinal prostrated themselves on pillows for the next half-hour while the choir sang the coronation litany, a litany distinguished by its inclusion of a number of local saints and a triple invocation to Saint Remigius. The litany was interrupted when Joyeuse stood up, faced the prostrate monarch, and pronounced a threefold benediction; he then returned to his place beside the king until the completion of the litany. The cardinal then arose, removed his miter, and said a series of versicles and responses and two prayers. He proceeded to sit with his back to the altar and to recite three additional orisons, during which the king knelt before the officiant. Louis remained on his knees after Joyeuse had finished these; the ties holding the king's camisole and the chemise beneath it were opened so that his back and breast were bared, and all was ready for the consecration.[18]

2. The Consecration and Coronation

The officiant sat before the kneeling king for the consecration of France's new monarch, which began when the cardinal raised his voice slightly to utter a long prayer of extraordinary grandeur.[19] When the narrator had finished the orison, he smeared a small amount of the Holy Balm on his thumb and, making the sign of the cross on the top of Louis's head, said, "I anoint you king with sanctified oil. In the name of the Father, and of the Son, and of the Holy Ghost. Amen." Repeating this procedure, he anointed the king on the chest, between the shoulders, on each of the shoulders, and at the bend of each arm.[20] While Louis was being anointed the choir sang an antiphon, and when the anointing and antiphon were completed Joyeuse recited three prayers. The first of these (*Christe, perunge hunc regem in regimen*) is significant in that the monarch was called "king" for the first time in the liturgy of the ceremony, that is, in the liturgical sense Louis was king of France only after he was consecrated. Louis's camisole and chemise were closed, and the grand chamberlain dressed him in a tunicle (which represented that of a subdeacon), a dalmatic (which represented that of a deacon), and the royal mantle (which represented the chasuble of a priest). The king then knelt before the cardinal, who anointed him on the palms of the hands with the words "Ungantur manus istae de oleo sanctificato." The king remained on his knees, his hands clasped before his chest, while Joyeuse stood up, removed his miter, and said another prayer.[21]

The officiant blessed the coronation gloves and placed them on the king's hands,[22] and he was handed the royal ring, which he blessed and placed on the fourth finger of the king's right hand.[23] This was followed by another prayer and the presentation of the royal scepter and the hand of justice (*main de justice*, a short scepter surmounted by an ivory hand), each with prayers.[24] The chancellor of France went to the altar and, facing the king, called the representatives of each of the Peers of France to present themselves for the coronation.[25]

After the peers had taken their places at the altar, Joyeuse used both hands to lift the heavy crown from the altar and to place it over, but not on, the head of the king. The other eleven peers immediately stretched out their hands to aid the officiant in supporting the crown while he recited a prayer; when it was finished he alone placed it upon the king's head.[26] After five additional prayers and benedictions were read—most of the length of the ceremony was caused by the large number of prayers and benedictions and the litany, which was itself very long—Louis was conducted to the royal throne on its platform on the rood-loft. He was preceded by the marshal of La Châtre, who, as representative of the constable of France, carried the coronation sword, and followed by most of the other great officers of the household. During the procession the twelve Peers of France continued to support the crown on Louis's head "as much as they were able," an extremely awkward practice inherited from past coronation ceremonies. When all had arrived at the throne, the cardinal said the formula of enthronement, "Sta, et retine," and seated the king with the words "in hoc regni solio confirmet te," which were followed by other liturgical texts.[27]

The cardinal next removed his miter, bowed before and kissed the king, and cried in a loud voice, "Vivat Rex in aeternum!" Each of the Peers of France followed suit, but as soon as the officiant had uttered the *Vivat Rex* the people within the church picked up the cry of "Vive le Roi!" Musicians sounded their instruments at random "with such a noise that no one could hear oneself speak," and heralds threw a number of commemorative coronation jettons about; also, some "seven or eight hundred sparrows, goldfinches, and other small birds" were released from their cages within the choir—"The king took great pleasure in seeing these small animals flying and singing around His Majesty."[28] Outside the church the Regiment of the Guards fired many salutes. Confusion and noise, a sonorous expression of relief by the bored spectators, reigned supreme for a short time, but the ceremony soon took a more pedestrian turn when Joyeuse began the *Te Deum*.

3. The Mass and Postcoronation Ceremonies

During the mass that followed (the ordinary mass for the day) the Evangel was brought to the king by the assisting Cardinal Gondi, who bowed before the monarch three times as he approached him; after the king had kissed the text, it was taken to the officiating cardinal, who did likewise. When the time for the offering arrived, Louis presented to the cathedral church of Reims a chased golden vase, a silver and a gold "loaf of bread," and a purse containing thirteen pieces of gold (each worth thirteen *écus*) similar to the coronation jettons.[29] The king, carrying his scepter and *main de justice*, descended to the altar to make the offering in person; as he returned to the throne the people resumed their acclamation, "Vive le Roi!" Joyeuse said the *Pax Domini*, which concluded the mass, and handed the pax to Cardinal Gondi with a kiss; Gondi carried the object to the king, to whom he in turn gave the kiss of peace; the ecclesiastical peers, followed by the lay peers, also then gave Louis the kiss of peace. Louis was conducted from the throne to a small oratory near the altar, where his crown was removed for his confession and absolution by Joyeuse. Going to the altar, he knelt and publicly recited his confiteor, and he received communion in both species, the host and the wine, an unusual practice that was a sign that the king of France was something more than an ordinary layman. The coronation crown was again set on Louis's head and then removed to be replaced by a smaller and lighter crown, which Louis wore during the festivities that followed.

The ceremony in the church was now completed. Louis retrieved his scepter and *main de justice* and departed in procession for the archiepiscopal palace while the Holy Ampulla was returned to the abbey of Saint-Remi. Once he had reached his room, Louis's hands were washed and his chemise and gloves were removed and given to the first almoner of France to be burned, for they could not be worn again because they had touched the Holy Balm.[30] Louis was dressed in new garments (except the royal mantle) and led to an elevated table at one end of the great hall of the palace, where he was joined by the Peers of France and other great dignitaries for the coronation banquet (*festin royal*).

The ceremony of consecration and coronation had ended with the king's departure from the church, and the coronation banquet was only the first of several attendant ceremonies that had yet to be observed. Louis retired to his chamber for the night after the banquet; he returned to the church the next afternoon to receive from Cardinal Joyeuse the collar of the Order of the Holy Spirit, which had been founded by Henry III, but before the collar was placed around his neck he swore and signed the oath of the order.[31] On Tuesday, Louis again returned to the church, this time to assist at a baptism. On Wednesday the royal cortege left Reims to go to the shrine of Saint Marcoul at Corbeny, where Louis touched eight or nine hundred sufferers of the king's evil.[32] On Saturday, 23 October, he reached Paris, where he was greeted officially (but without the benefit of a formal *entrée*) and returned home to the Louvre.

3

THE ORDER OF THE MEDIEVAL CEREMONY

. . . .

The coronation of Louis XIII occupies almost exactly the chronological middle point between the coronations of Charles V and Charles X, although that was the reason neither for its selection as our model ceremony nor for the choice of the other two coronations as the terminal points of this study. The coronation of Charles X in 1825 is obvious, of course, because it was the last coronation ceremony in France. The grounds for selecting the coronation of Charles V, on the other hand, are much less clear, for they are closely related to the development of the medieval *ordines*, the history of which must be briefly recapitulated.

1. The Coronation *Ordines*

The word *ordo* has a fairly precise liturgical connotation: it is a compilation of the prayers, hymns, and anthems used in a religious ceremony; almost exclusively liturgical, its rubrics are as brief as possible, and it is usually prescriptive: it prescribes what should be done in the future rather than describes what has been done in the past. An *ordo* may be distinguished from a directory or a description. A directory is composed exclusively—or nearly so—of the directions for the application of an *ordo*; hence, it is composed mainly of rubrics, it is intended to be used in conjunction with an *ordo*, and it is normally prescriptive. A description, on the other hand, is often a combination of an *ordo* and a directory, although it does not necessarily spell out in detail the liturgical parts of a ceremony; it is characterized by having been written after the ceremony has taken place, it describes that particular ceremony, and it may or may not be prescriptive.[1]

Each of these has its examples. The description of Charles VIII's coronation is clearly intended to be prescriptive, as is Nicolas de Thou's description of Henry IV's coronation in 1594.[2] Some parts of the official description of Louis XVI's coronation in 1775 are copied so exactly from the official description of Louis XV's coronation in 1722 as to render the later one quite useless; in this case the prescriptive character of the earlier description is as important as its descriptive character.[3] The *ordo* of Reims (we shall return to this and other specific texts in a moment) is the only medieval French example of a directory, and, because it does not give even the incipits of the prayers, it should not be called an *ordo*; usage, however, styles it an *ordo*, and we shall leave it at that.[4] Before the end of the thirteenth century the distinction between an *ordo* and a directory was becoming blurred, and the last Capetian *ordo*, which was truly prescriptive, combined an *ordo* and a directory in one text, which thereafter was the norm.[5] We shall use the term *ordo* to refer to any liturgical text composed for a coronation, no matter how long the rubrics, distinguishing it only from a description that throws additional light upon a particular ceremony.

The modern ceremony grew out of the medieval ceremony, and the basic problem in the study of the latter has been the dating of the medieval *ordines*. Much of the work of an author who wrote as recently as 1953 is of little utility because he was unaware of the dates of the medieval *ordines*.[6] When Théodore and Denis Godefroy made their outstanding collection of materials relevant to the French ceremonial (published in 1619 and 1649), they often assigned incorrect dates to the *ordines*, partly because they could not conceive of *ordines* not written for some specific coronation, and partly because they copied dates assigned by other authors (Jean du Tillet, for example).[7] The Godefroy compilation was (and is) so important that its dates became almost canonical. Not until the first years of the twentieth century was a new attempt to assign proper dates to the *ordines* undertaken. The dates were argued in a well-known controversy between two German scholars, Hans Schreuer and Max Büchner, and a few years later Marc Bloch entered the discussion briefly in his excellent study of the thaumaturgic powers of kings.[8] Finally, in the 1930s Percy Ernst Schramm published a series of studies of the medieval *ordines* of England, Germany, France, and other countries, and by taking such an international approach, he was able to provide dates that are usually persuasive.[9]

Schramm's work suffered one major shortcoming: Schramm, who was an outstanding historian otherwise, actually examined very few of the relevant manuscripts. He had to content himself with photocopies or printed editions, and in doing so he committed errors because some of the French *ordines*, the Fulrad *ordo* for example, had never been published in full. In perusing the manuscripts, I have had to revise some of Schramm's dates and to assign new appellations to some of the *ordines*.[10] We may note here six *ordines* that probably served at coronations of the Capetians and the Valois: (1) the Erdmann (or West Frankish) *ordo* of about 900; (2) the Fulrad *ordo* (ca. 980); (3) the *ordo* of Reims (ca. 1230); (4) the *ordo* of 1250; (5) the last Capetian *ordo* (1250–70); and (6) the *ordo* of Charles V (1364). To these may be added two medieval texts that are not *ordines*, Jean Golein's *Traité du sacre* (1374) and Jean Foulquart's tract on the coronation and its costs (1478). It would be well to keep these medieval texts in mind because we shall refer to them repeatedly in the course of this study.

2. The *Ordo* of Charles V

The *ordo* of Charles V occupies a special place in the above list because it is the point of departure for the late medieval ceremony. A manuscript of the *ordo*, completed and added to the royal library in 1365 (i.e., between 13 April 1365 and 4 April 1366), was soon assumed to have been the *ordo* used at Charles's own coronation on 19 May 1364. This manuscript is adorned with about forty miniatures that illustrate many details of the ceremony, and Percy Ernst Schramm, although recognizing that the text itself may not have been used in 1364, thought that the miniatures might preserve certain details of Charles's coronation. Nonetheless, the miniatures, though very fine, do not attempt to present an actual picture of the setting of the ceremony, and only six of them are concerned with aspects of the ceremony that are in Charles's *ordo* but not in its predecessor, the last Capetian *ordo*.[11]

The earlier *ordo* was composed shortly after the middle of the thirteenth century. Contrary to long-held belief, though, it is dangerous to assume that an *ordo* like this one was used for a given coronation simply because it was already in existence; as we shall see, one must examine whatever sources are available for information that might enable one to identify an *ordo* with a coronation.[12] We do know, nonetheless, that the coronation oath that Philip VI swore in 1328 was the one that first appeared in the last Capetian *ordo*, and we may assume that the *ordo* was used then. Owing to its rapid diffusion (at least five manuscripts date from the first half of the fourteenth century), we would probably not be far wrong in assuming it to have provided the basic outline of the ceremony in 1271 (Philip III), 1285 (Philip IV), 1314 (Louis X), 1317 (Philip V), and 1322 (Charles IV). Furthermore, because it was used in 1328, it was undoubtedly consulted for the coronation of John in 1350.[13]

A long coronation *ordo* is not produced quickly, and one might ask whether there was sufficient time to prepare the *ordo* of Charles V between the death of John in England on 8 April 1364 and the coronation of Charles in Reims on 19 May, only six weeks later; that hardly seems enough time to produce the longest and most complete *ordo* of the French Middle Ages, especially so because preparations for the ceremony were not begun until 20 April (several months were available for the preparation of Charles VIII's ceremony in 1484).[14] If used, and if it took more than a month to prepare the *ordo*, it was composed (or at least begun) during John's reign, in which case the *ordo* is misnamed. On the other hand, Charles's autograph inscription when he entered the completed manuscript in the library with the words "We have had it corrected, edited, copied, and illuminated in the year 1365" may imply that the *ordo* was written after the coronation and that Charles was crowned in accordance with the last Capetian *ordo*.[15] The question as to whether Charles was crowned in accordance with the *ordo* that bears his name may be answered by examination of its content.

The new *ordo* differs from the old in some interesting ways—and we need not consider here the new text's clause of inalienability, which was added later.[16] Because most of the additions—and particularly the prayers and benedictions—were not composed specifically for this *ordo* but were copied from other texts, it is impossible to determine with certitude what was in the mind of the compiler or compilers of the *ordo*. Nonetheless, the adaptation of certain formulae and the disregard of others surely gives some hint at the frame of mind of those who worked in Charles V's circle.

The most immediately striking characteristic of the new *ordo* is its expansion of the ceremonial, and this is evident at the very beginning of the *ordo*. The last Capetian *ordo* had provided simply that the king should enter the church with the archbishop, bishops, barons, and others before the blessing of the holy water. The new *ordo* introduced the procession of the bishops of Laon and Beauvais to the archiepiscopal palace to raise the king from his bed of state and to lead him to the church to the accompaniment of hymns and prayers; this new ceremony, which became the foundation for the later fiction of the sleeping king, was to take place after the other participants in the ceremony had taken up their places in the church.[17] The new prayers consisted of *Omnipotens sempiterne Deus, qui famulum tuum*, which asserts God to have elevated the king to the throne and implores His help in securing the well-being of the monarch's subjects; *Deus, qui scis humanum genus*, which likewise calls upon divine aid in protecting the subjects; and *Omnipotens Deus, caelestium moderator*, which again asserts the king to be raised to the throne by God, who is also asked to fortify him with ecclesiastical peace. The response, *Ecce mitto angelum meum, qui praecedat te*, and versicle, *Israël, si me audieris*, both promise that for the king who harkens to God's words the king's enemies will also be God's enemies; Psalm 21, which is also chanted, promises that the king's enemies will be swallowed up in the wrath of God.

The political implications of these liturgical additions are not difficult to find. The first phase of the Hundred Years' War had ended shortly before with the disastrous Treaty of Brétigny of 1360; the English held a large portion of France, and their king laid claim to the French throne. The repeated identification of the enemies of the king with the enemies of God could have but a single clear reference in the mid-1360s, and the claims that God raised the king to his position—Psalm 21 says that "thou hast placed a crown of precious stone upon his head"—clearly provided the king with a claim that not even Edward III was capable of bettering. Such a political interpretation is substantiated by the addition of another prayer, *Deus, inenarrabilis auctor mundi*, which immediately preceded the investiture of the sandals and the spurs. This prayer asserts that God had preelected the king, and it calls for God's benediction upon the king and his army (*cum exercitu suo*), while God is to be "a breastwork against the troops of the enemies, a helmet in adversity, endurance in good fortune, an eternal defence in protection," and the source of the king's men's fidelity and his commanders' peace.

Given the political nature of the new *ordo*, one would naturally expect a new emphasis to be placed upon the bestowal of the sword, which was obviously crucial to the monarchy after Brétigny. Whereas the last Capetian *ordo* had provided for an investiture formula, an antiphon, and a prayer for a total of three elements, Charles V's *ordo* provided for eight elements: two benedictions, two investiture formulae, the antiphon, and three prayers. One of the benedictions, *Exaudi, Domine, quaesumus preces nostras*, requests that the sword strike dread, fear, and terror into those who lie in wait for the king, and one of the prayers, *Prospice, omnipotens Deus*, solicits inviolate peace in the kingdom and prays that the king be "the strongest protector of the country [*patria*] and comfort of the churches and holy monks" and "the strongest vanquisher of enemy kings by overwhelming rebels and pagan nations." *Deus, Pater aeternae gloriae*, the last of the prayers that accompanied the bestowal of the sword, beseeches God to cover the king's enemies with confusion. Other liturgical additions to the ceremony make similar references, either to the God-given kingship, as in *Ungantur manus istae de oleo sanctificato*, which accompanied the anointing of the hands, or to a hopeful triumph over the enemy, as in the succeeding prayer (*Deus, qui es justorum gloria*), as in two of the new benedictions that followed the coronation (*Tibi cum timore* and *Honorifica eum*), and as in two of the three special prayers added to the mass (*Quaesumus, omnipotens Deus* and *Haec, Domine, oratio salutaris*). The second part of the new coronation formulary, *Accipe coronam regni*, refers both to God-given kingship and to defense of the Church.

These additions to the liturgy of the ceremony make overwhelmingly clear the obsessive concern with the divine source of kingship, triumph over enemies, and peace, dominant thoughts of those who compiled the *ordo* in the 1360s. Defense of the realm was, of course, a crucial element in later medieval kingship,[18] and it is obviously so in the last Capetian *ordo*, but that consideration does not prevent Charles V's *ordo* from assuming the appearance of extreme bellicosity. Taken in and of itself, the *ordo* furthermore demonstrates that in the minds of its compilers the struggle we know as the Hundred Years' War was anything but ended in 1364.

These considerations make it most likely that Charles V's *ordo* was used at his own coronation in 1364. We have already noted the arguments that might make one think that it was not, but the arguments for its use are more potent. The major objection, that the time between the beginning of preparations for the coronation and the ceremony itself was insufficient to produce the *ordo*, is not a strong one. While it is true that Charles's *ordo* is the longest one of the Middle Ages, it must also be recognized that it closely follows the order of the last Capetian *ordo*, which, practically unchanged, provided the basic structure of the new composition, so that the latter was perhaps three-fourths completed before it was begun. The old *ordo* suffered few structural alterations, and they are not extensive. The novelties consist primarily of additions that tend to be grouped in blocks composed of several elements, and this work could have been completed fairly quickly. It would not have been necessary to go far to seek the sources: there were copies of the last Capetian *ordo* in both Paris and Reims; there was a copy of the Fulrad *ordo* (with important variations from the original of about 980) in Reims and probably also in the royal library; the *ordo* of Pedro IV of Aragon was probably in Paris, although it could have found its way to Reims; the German *ordo* could have been found in both Reims and Paris, and the same was undoubtedly true of the very popular pontifical of William Durandus; copies of the Reims liturgy could easily have gone to Paris.[19] In brief, the *ordo* could have been written in either city, and it is not yet possible to decide which it might have been. That the *ordo* was completed quickly is shown by some internal contradictions, particularly at the beginning, where the older arrival of the king at the church was not deleted when the new *ordo* introduced the processional seeking of the king in the archiepiscopal palace. The emphasis of the *ordo* on matters of current political interest—victory, peace, the kingdom's well-being, and the divine origin of the kingship—is a powerful argument for its composition in late April and May 1364 and for its use at Charles V's coronation.

That probability becomes a near certainty when we take into consideration the portion of the *ordo* that concerns the coronation of the queen. This was very considerably lengthened over its predecessor in the last Capetian *ordo*. Here, too, the additions reflect current concerns. Charles and his queen, Jeanne de Bourbon, the last French queen to be crowned at the same time as her husband, still had no male heirs in 1364, after several years of marriage. The new prayers insistently implore the queen's fecundity, citing the examples of biblical women who had borne children after years of fruitless marriage. From its very origins in the ninth century the liturgy for the coronation of a queen had had something of the nature of a fertility charm, and at no time was this more clearly expressed than in the *ordo* used at the coronation of Charles V and Jeanne de Bourbon in the fourteenth century.[20] The last medieval French text that, despite its lengthy rubrics, was an *ordo* in a strict sense is also, therefore, the first one that can be attached with a fair degree of certitude to a particular coronation, and the coronation of Charles V is the logical starting point of this study.

Before turning to the coronations of Charles's successors, a few words must be said about the other liturgical novelties in the *ordo* of 1364. The additions so far discussed are relatively restricted temporally in that they reflect particular concerns of the monarchy at the time of Charles's coronation. Less so restricted is a second major concern of the new liturgy, justice, which was the primary subject matter of the first part of the new coronation formula and of two of the new benedictions that followed, and it was the secondary subject of the prayer *Deus, qui es justorum gloria*, which followed the unction of the hands. Two new orations, *Deus, totius creaturae* and *Deus, qui victrices Moïsi*, are concerned with the defense of the faith, which must be distinguished from the defense of the churches, which falls within the general heading of defense of the realm. Finally, there is a new responsory beginning with *Gentem Francorum inclitam* and a prayer, *Deus, qui populo tuo*, both of which are devoted to the legend of Saint Remigius and the Holy Ampulla.

The last two additions carry on a French tradition that had its earliest manifestation in the coronation *ordines* in the *ordo* of Reims, and that was shortly thereafter fairly fully developed in the last Capetian *ordo*. This tradition dealt with the French mythology of kingship, which was adhered to from the thirteenth to the nineteenth century. The foremost characteristic of the mythology is the legend of Clovis and Remigius and the Holy Ampulla.

The legend was given concrete form in the ninth century by the powerful and influential Hincmar, archbishop of Reims, who himself did not originate the story, which was at least slightly older.[21] According to Hincmar's version, Saint Remigius, archbishop of

Reims, found himself facing a serious difficulty when baptizing the Frankish king Clovis to Christianity in 496—that traditional date is wrong, but we do not need to concern ourselves with it here. The cleric who was to bring Remigius the consecrated chrism was prevented from doing so on account of the crowd in the church, and Remigius turned his eyes toward heaven to pray for help. His prayer was answered, and a dove descended from heaven bearing in its beak a small ampulla of chrism; Remigius baptized Clovis with this sacred balm. The legend was one that could obviously be turned to the use of Reims, and Hincmar did just that. Nevertheless, the story was more or less forgotten outside of Reims, and not until the reign of Saint Louis did it resurface to make its impact upon the coronation ceremony. None of the West Frankish or French *ordines* contain any hint of the legend before the composition of the *ordo* of Reims.[22] This *ordo* has the monks of the abbey of Saint-Remi processionally march to the cathedral church "with the sacrosanct ampulla," and the abbot, who carried the ampulla, was to walk under a silken canopy carried by four monks. The archbishop and bishops were to go to the door of the church to take the ampulla with the promise of returning it in good faith. In preparing the chrism for the unction, the archbishop was to add to the already consecrated chrism a small part of "the oil sent from heaven," and the French king, consequently, "alone among all the kings of earth enjoys the glorious privilege of being anointed with oil sent from heaven."[23] The emphasis of the *ordo* on the ampulla and its contents points to the abbey of Saint-Remi as the place in which the *ordo* was composed, but it would hardly have triumphed as completely as it did—the handling of the ampulla did not greatly differ as late as 1775—if the legend it publicized had not served the interests of the kingship.

Other legends likewise came to be attached to the French kingship and the coronation. As a part of what must be termed a thirteenth-century reconceiving of the kingship, the French kings came to "acquire" the power to touch for scrofula, to cure what in England was called the "king's evil." The Fourth Lateran Council of 1215 strictly defined the Church's sacraments and limited their number to seven, but the French continued to insist that the consecration of their king was an eighth sacrament. The quasi-sacred French banner, the *oriflamme*, was credited with a miraculous origin, and already the Fulrad *ordo*, which dated from the tenth century, had provided for a benediction of the banner, although there is no evidence that that was ever done at a coronation ceremony. The fleurs-de-lys were also said, like the Holy Ampulla, to be sent from heaven and to be a special mark of God's care for France. Finally, as a result of the consecration, the king and queen were given the right to communicate in both species, like the priesthood; this privilege, which first appeared in the *ordo* of Reims, gave strength to the belief that the consecration was an eighth sacrament.[24]

Despite the extensive mythicizing of the kingship in the thirteenth century, only the legend of the Holy Ampulla remained crucial to the coronation ceremony. Within a lifetime of the composition of the *ordo* of Reims, the last Capetian *ordo* furthered its program and gave detailed instructions for the handling of the ampulla and the role to be played by the clerics of the abbey of Saint-Remi; this material forms so extensive a part of the last Capetian *ordo* that it would be difficult to believe that the *ordo* was composed anywhere but at the abbey itself. A modern scholar has commented that "the text was richer, more exact, better organized than the preceding one,"[25] and thus it apparently very quickly supplanted all previous *ordines*. In this way Saint Remigius, who had previously been little more than a fairly local saint, was launched upon a path that made him nearly a national saint. This is evident in Charles V's *ordo*, which adopted a versicle modified from a very old hymn from the local liturgy for the feast of Saint Remigius and made it into a response with a national—and nationalist—implication: "St. Remigius, having received the chrism from heaven, consecrated with a holy flood the illustrious nation of the French together with their noble king and enriched them with the fullness of the Holy Spirit,"[26] an appropriate passage to be chanted while the consecrating bishop prepared the chrism. The *ordo* retained the reference of the last Capetian *ordo* to the French king as the only one among all kings to be consecrated with a heaven-sent oil, which in turn had been copied from the *ordo* of Reims.[27]

The only surviving contemporary copy of Charles V's *ordo* is the British Library's Cottonian manuscript Tiberius B.viii. The manuscript is clearly commemorative in its lavish illumination, and it is also quite official, both in the sense that the manuscript is a collection of coronation materials from one of the oldest registers of the Chambre des Comptes, and in the prescriptive nature of Charles's *ordo*, which was obviously intended to be used in the future. This official character was emphasized on 7 May 1380, when, shortly before his death, Charles deposited a copy of the *ordo*, along with other objects specifically prepared for the coronations of his successors, in a long box in the coronation treasury of the abbey of Saint-Denis. Charles's intent was fulfilled before the end of the year at the coronation of Charles VI on 4 November. At the same time the new king "took" the manuscript now in the British Library for his coronation, as we are informed by a contemporary marginal note in one of the inventories of the royal library.[28] However, the renewal of the Hundred Years' War in the fifteenth century and the consequent dispersal of the royal library halted what might otherwise have been a straightforward development of the coronation ceremony, with significant implications for the development of the French ceremony and French constitutional thought and practice.

3. The Ceremonies of Charles VII and Louis XI

By 1424, Paris and the royal library in the Louvre were in English hands, and none of the manuscripts there could be obtained for the coronation of Charles VII in 1429. Because the treasury at Saint-Denis with its copy of Charles V's *ordo* was also under English control, Charles VII had to content himself with what was located in Reims. There is another copy of Charles V's *ordo* in a pontifical copied for Jean, duke of Berry (copied from Tiberius B.viii), but it had passed to the Sainte-Chapelle in Bourges upon the duke's death; there its presence was apparently forgotten, so it was likewise not available for Charles VII's coronation. There was a copy of the *ordo* in the cathedral treasury at Reims from the late sixteenth through the eighteenth century, but, although it appears to have been a fourteenth-century copy, there is no evidence that it was in Reims in the fifteenth century, and it is possible that it was the Saint-Denis manuscript, which disappeared from the monastery's treasury between 1581 and 1598. Nothing has been found to demonstrate that there was a copy of Charles V's *ordo* in Reims in 1429. On the other hand, one—and possibly two—manuscripts of the last Capetian *ordo* existed in Reims. It is quite certain that the abbey of Saint-Remi had a copy of this *ordo* from the later thirteenth century, which accords with what is now known of its date of composition. The existence of another copy of the *ordo* in the cathedral treasury of Reims is less certain. This was an early four-teenth-century manuscript (ca. 1330) that was in the treasury from at least about 1590 to 1793; its date makes it quite possible that it was in Reims already in the early fifteenth century.[29] The writings of Jean Juvenal des Ursins, archbishop of Reims, prove that he knew the coronation oaths only in the form they had in the last Capetian *ordo*, and if he consulted a manuscript in Reims it is more likely to have been one in the cathedral church than one in the abbey.[30] That, nonetheless, is still speculative, but there is evidence that Charles VII was crowned in accordance with a manuscript of the last Capetian *ordo* rather than the *ordo* of Charles V, as would normally have been expected.

None of the records of the ceremony is detailed, and together they produce only three hints as to the *ordo* used. The anonymous *Histoire et discours*, after describing in detail the ceremonies surrounding the bringing of the Holy Ampulla to the cathedral, says simply that the king came before the archbishop for his consecration "dressed as was proper," without any allusion to the seeking of the king, consequently pointing to the last Capetian *ordo* rather than to the newer *ordo*. The remainder of the description is so brief, though, that this amounts only to very weak evidence.[31]

Much stronger support for the thesis that the last Capetian *ordo* was used is given in a letter, written by three Angevin gentlemen on the day of the ceremony, addressed to Charles's wife and mother-in-law. According to the letter, the ceremony lasted from 9:00 A.M. to 2:00 P.M.[32] No information on the amount of time required for previous coronations survives, and later records tend to be open-ended, that is, to say when the ceremony began but not to give the time of its conclusion. When times are specified, preparations are said to have begun in the church at 4:30 or 5:00 A.M., the king is said to have dispatched four barons to the abbey of Saint-Remi for the Holy Ampulla at 6:00 A.M., and the two bishops are said to have departed from the church to seek the king at 7:00 A.M. Such was the timetable for the coronation of Charles VIII in 1484 and of Louis XIV in 1654. We also know that some ceremonies were not completed until 2:00 or 3:00 P.M. On the other hand, Charles IX's coronation in 1561 is reported to have lasted from 8:00 A.M. to 1:00 P.M., which would have made it no longer than Charles VII's even though the more recent ceremony introduced the ceremonial fiction of the sleeping king. However, the five hours of Charles IX's ceremony include only the time that the king was absent from the archiepiscopal palace, whereas the five hours of Charles VII's ceremony seem to refer to the whole service.[33] The late beginning in 1429 is easily explained: the archbishop of Reims did not take possession of his office until 16 July (the day before the ceremony), the king did not enter the city until that evening, and the whole night was spent in feverish preparation for the coronation on Sunday, 17 July, preparations that probably could hardly have been completed by 5:00 or 6:00 A.M. The brevity of the following ceremony points to the use of the last Capetian *ordo* rather than the longer *ordo* of Charles V.

Additional light is thrown on the matter by the records of the trial of Joan of Arc, who stood beside the altar during the coronation. Joan's interrogators, who suspected her of witchery among other things, had heard that she had used supernatural means to discover the royal gloves after they had been mislaid before the coronation. When they questioned her closely on the matter, she professed complete ignorance of the matter and stated only that everyone present wore gloves and that those of the king were in no way peculiar. Whatever one may think of Joan, she strikes one as a veracious person who was completely baffled by the drift of the questions, and her puzzlement is understandable if the last Capetian *ordo* was used because, unlike the *ordo* of Charles V, it did not provide for any investiture with gloves.[34] The interrogators, on the other hand, had access to the more recent manuscript of Charles V's *ordo* in the treasury at Saint-Denis and perhaps also the manuscript from the royal library (Tiberius B.viii), and they would have assumed quite naturally that a (nonexistent) copy of that *ordo* at Reims would have been used in 1429. Joan's bafflement is explicable only in terms of their error. Furthermore, the peculiar *ordo* used at the coronation of Louis XI in 1461 may be explained by assuming that the last Capetian *ordo* had been consulted for Charles VII's coronation.

In 1478 Jean Foulquart wrote his treatise on the obligations of the city of Reims at a coronation. The work contains numerous details of the coronation in 1461. After discussing the city's preparation for a coming ceremony, it proceeds to a translation of a coronation *ordo* that was neither the last Capetian *ordo* nor the

ordo of Charles V, but a mixture of the two; this mixture was undoubtedly the text used at Louis XI's coronation. Although both of
the previous *ordines* affected the new *ordo* throughout its whole
length, the first part tends to follow the *ordo* of Charles V as far as
concerns the ceremonies preceding the king's arrival at the church,
but the second part closely follows the last Capetian *ordo*: thus, as
presumably in the *ordo* used at Charles VII's coronation, there is
no unction of the hands and no bestowal of the gloves.[35] Finally,
the new *ordo* carefully arranges the postenthronement ceremonies—coronation of the queen, mass, offerings, departure from the
church, return of the Holy Ampulla—into their proper chronological sequence, which no previous *ordo* had done. The queen's coronation *ordo* is that of the last Capetian *ordo* rather than of the
longer *ordo* of Charles V. The dominance of the last Capetian *ordo*
in the *ordo* of Louis XI is understandable only if the older work
achieved renewed vitality at the coronation in 1429, and Louis XI's
ordo marks a new trend to reintroduce parts of the *ordo* of Charles
V, which may be considered to have reached its fulfillment at the
coronation of Charles VIII in 1484.

If, nonetheless, we take one of our sources at face value, the *ordo*
translated by Foulquart was not used in 1461, and the coronation
of Louis XI was the most curious one in the whole history of the
ceremony. Most astounding is the behavior of the king as reported
by Georges Chastellain.

> Now the king, knowing that the Holy Ampulla had arrived at
> the church, and leaving his position near the high altar at
> the choir, quickly went to it immediately upon its entry;
> there he reverently flung himself down upon his knees and
> adored it with joined hands; then the Bishop of Laon took
> him by the hand and raised him, and those who carried the
> Holy Ampulla went on to the high altar, upon which they
> placed it. The king followed closely with his peers and ap-
> proached the high altar, then he thrice threw himself upon
> his knees before the holy vessel. Then the third time the
> Bishop of Laon, who was behind him, took him by the hand,
> raised him, and had him kiss the Holy Ampulla. Then the
> king, again moved by devotion, remained on his knees for a
> long time, apparently engaged in very devout prayer, and
> gazed fixedly at the Holy Ampulla.

Chastellain then describes the partial disrobing of the king in preparation for his unction: they "rendered him completely nude down to below the belt [*ceinture*] and in this state led him up in front of the altar."[36]

Louis did have a particular veneration for the Holy Ampulla, and as he approached the end of his life he fell increasingly victim to superstition and neuropathy. These attitudes combined and induced him to have the Holy Ampulla brought from its repository in the abbey of Saint-Remi to what became his deathbed in 1483 in the hope that the miraculous nature of the ampulla would somehow restore him to health. Although he wanted to be anointed again, he was informed that that was impossible, but he was allowed to have the object in his presence during the last weeks of his life. He went to considerable trouble to obtain even this, for it was necessary to obtain papal approval for the temporary removal of the ampulla from the abbey.[37] Chastellain's report of Louis's coronation completes the story of his veneration, which must have extended through the whole of the reign. It is, however, impossible to believe that Louis was as abject as Chastellain reports, and the extensive adoration in 1461 may be reduced to more probable terms. Chastellain, who was in the retinue of Philip the Good, duke of Burgundy, was present at the ceremony, but he was not a very important personage, and that is most significant. The cathedral church of Reims is a wonderful structure, one of the crowning glories of medieval thought and architecture, but it is a Gothic building with aisles, chapels, ambulatory, and arcades, and it is a poor place to display a ceremony to a large number of people, particularly since the rood screen (*jubé*) constructed early in the fifteenth century (and removed in 1744) almost completely cut off any view of the altar from the nave. Thousands of people attended a coronation ceremony, but not many of them could see what was happening. A seat behind a pillar, for example, enabled one only to be present. The events before the high altar could have been viewed by only a few. The major portion of the ceremony took place in secret as far as most spectators were concerned. The sudden appearance of the crowned king upon the platform as he was conducted to his enthronement marked for the majority the monarch's first appearance since his entry into the church, which may explain why the ensuing acclamations seemed so sincere. Chastellain obviously could not observe the ceremony continuously, and his description of what happened is necessarily based upon occasional glimpses of the event. It is probable that Louis did go to the door of the church to meet the ampulla; this was not provided for by the *ordo* translated by Foulquart or by any other *ordo*, but, given Louis's attitude, it seems likely. The triple kneeling by the king probably took place during the kissing of the Gospels after swearing the coronation oaths (if the king knelt for that), during the singing of the *Te deum* (for which the king was led to the altar by two bishops, who presumably also raised him), and when the sword was offered upon the altar (as stipulated by Charles V's *ordo*). The long, "very devout prayer" was simply the kneeling of the king during the litany. The fact that Chastellain then discusses the disrobing of the king and refers to the swordbelt (*ceinture*) proves that these previous ceremonies had already taken place.

Chastellain's poor observation point also explains what would otherwise be a most vexing novelty:

> . . . the prelates and princes led the [royally robed] king by hand to his royal chair . . . ; there he was seated in glory and majesty, and the prelates and princes retired behind him a little, excepting only the Duke of Burgundy, first peer, who placed his bonnet upon his head and then took the precious and rich crown and, raising it high with both hands so that everyone could see it, held it for some time above the head of the king; and after that was done, he placed it very gently upon the head, crying in a loud voice, "Vive le roi! Montjoye Saint-Denis!" at which all the crowd, at the sound of his cry, cried after him the same words and "Noel!" and bells, trumpets, and clarions sounded so loudly that all ears were deaf from it.[38]

This coronation by the duke runs counter to all tradition, not only in France but also everywhere else in Europe, and even though we know that the duke of Burgundy played a larger role than normal in 1461, Chastellain's description simply is not convincing. The account is garbled by a faulty memory. Louis was undoubtedly crowned by the archbishop before being led to the throne by the twelve Peers of France, as was customary. It was also customary for the peers to utter the acclamation as they gave the king the kiss of homage. Chastellain's chronicle was a highly laudable account of its author's patron, and Chastellain, ignoring the activities of all the other peers, selected the role of the Burgundian duke alone for his story. It is possible, nevertheless, that Burgundy did place the crown upon Louis's head at some point in the ceremony; Foulquart's *ordo* provides that the crown be removed during the mass at the reading of the Gospel, and it must have been removed also during the king's communion—at either one of these times the crown could have been held by the duke of Burgundy, who might thereafter have placed it upon the monarch's head, giving rise to Chastellain's odd description. The chronicle provides some interesting details, but, *mutatis mutandis*, it does not detract from the view that Foulquart's *ordo* was operative in 1461.

Three separate *ordines* were used at three separate coronations, and this fluctuation created a terrible confusion that found partial expression in the bastard *ordo* of Louis XI. The detailed description of Charles VIII's coronation in 1484 noted the uncertainty and described what steps were taken to terminate it.

> Before the king's arrival in Reims his throne and the chairs for the peers had been prepared, as had been the old books and ordinaries of the mystery of the consecration, which tell what ought to be done at each coronation; these were seen and collated by Monseigneur the Archbishop of Reims, by the other ecclesiastical peers, and by others with them; and that that concerns the mystery and the ceremonies of the consecration and coronation had been revised and completely perfected in accordance with the stipulations of the said books and ordinaries. For that reason it will no longer be necessary to seek or to search in order to know what one ought to do in such a case because everything has been accomplished in this work.[39]

This description marks a new departure in the history of the French ceremony: it is the first work to describe in detail what happened and also to include the liturgy, and, because it was the firm foundation for all future development, it finally made Charles V's *ordo* a permanent part of the ceremony. Thereafter liturgical novelties largely cease to be very interesting in their own right, and it is the nonliturgical innovations that are the vehicle for conveying new conceptions. The medieval liturgy does have something to contribute, nevertheless, to our knowledge of ceremonial change and the modern conception of kingship.

THE MECHANICS OF CHANGE

· · · · · · · · · · ·

One cannot assert that all aspects of the ceremony are of equal interest. Some of them are slavish imitations of previous ceremonies, the original meaning of which often had been forgotten, and which no one attempted to evaluate within a new context. Reinterpretation of others enabled the continued use of old elements to provide a means for modifying the sense, if not the performance, of the ceremony. Some additions or alterations were made only because the past was not always well known or because it was misconstrued. Others are unique events, explainable within the context of contemporary history but with no particular import either at the moment or in the future. Some had a significant message to convey only at the time of their introduction, but came to be retained and altered over the course of the ages. The development and interpretation of some (the ritual of the sleeping king, for example) are so complicated that they require whole chapters, whereas others may be treated more or less summarily. One aspect of the ceremony, the liturgy, suffered suprisingly little change after 1364, and the novelties that were introduced tended to be so before the end of the fifteenth century. In the modern age, therefore, the liturgy is worthy of our attention primarily as reflective of the continuity between the medieval and the modern age and as a support for arguments developed by one writer or another. A brief discussion of the liturgy, as well as of a series of miscellaneous novelties, will aid in comprehending why alterations did or did not take place.

1. The Liturgy

Through the liturgy we may trace the progressive development and refinement of the ceremony from the Carolingians to the end of the fifteenth century. Some of the prayers that were said at the coronation of Charles II in 869 and almost all of the prayers in the *ordo* for the coronation of Louis the Stammerer in 877 were still in the ceremony in the nineteenth century. Even when new prayers were introduced into the French ceremony, there was a kind of continuity with the past to the extent that many of them were adopted from English, German, Spanish, or imperial *ordines*, so that by the end of the Middle Ages there were significant similarities between the coronation ceremonies of France and of the other western European countries.[1]

The ceremony's importance in the Middle Ages lay in the ritual acts of consecration and coronation. Robert Fawtier believed that a study of the coronation in the earlier Middle Ages "would certainly show that the Capetians—during the tenth and eleventh centuries at least—held the coronation rite to be the strongest possible guarantee of their position."[2] Although the sacral character of the French kingship certainly came to it by means of the ceremony, Fawtier's thesis can no longer be fully sustained. We have all been taught that the Capetian monarchs to Philip II Augustus owed their very position on the throne to the fact that they were crowned co-kings during their fathers' lifetimes, and thus the elective principle of kingship, which threatened to prevail in the West Frankish kingdom in the tenth century, came to be replaced by the hereditary principle in the course of the two hundred years after the selection of Hugh Capet.[3] A recent article has shown, nonetheless, that the Capetians did not normally create co-kings as a means of assuring the succession, but as an instrument of anticipatory association of the heir. Arising from particular needs at a given time, such associations were not peculiar to the monarchs; there was nothing particularly royal in elevating a successor to an incumbent's office, and the long series of such elevations has masked the largely fortuitous nature of what had appeared to us to have been a constitutional act.[4]

The kings did differ from other French noble families in one crucial respect, nevertheless: they were anointed. Once anointed, the king was set apart from other men by his special consecration, as was the bishop, after whose consecration the king's tended to be patterned, thus implying that the king had at least a quasi-sacerdotal character. The *ordo* of Charles V continued this tradition by adding a benediction of the ring before its bestowal. The ring had long been one of the royal regalia, but the blessing was patterned after the episcopal practice: the royal benediction, *Deus totius creaturae*, was a modified form of the benediction of the episcopal ring.[5] The similarity between the bishop and the king was further emphasized in this *ordo* by the introduction of an unction of the hands. It is possible that this was copied from a German (not an imperial) *ordo*, in which there had been a long tradition of anointing the hands, but it was as likely to have been borrowed from the episcopal ordination rite, particularly since Charles V's *ordo* also added an investiture with gloves after the hands were anointed— there was no model for this practice in the German *ordines*, but there was in the episcopal ones. Charles's *ordo* adds that the purpose of the gloves was to keep the anointed hands from becoming tainted through touching vulgar objects, a logical continuation of the last Capetian *ordo*'s injunction to burn the chrism-soaked shirt of the king upon the completion of the ceremony.[6]

The special aura surrounding the anointing of the French kings was given particular emphasis in several additions to the liturgy in the fourteenth and fifteenth centuries. Two of them have already been noted: the *Gentem francorum inclitam* response and the *Deus, qui populo tuo* prayer, which treated Saint Remigius not as a local saint but as a national intercessor.[7] Two more such additions, referring specifically to the Holy Ampulla as well as to Saint Remigius, were made in 1484. The first, *O pretiosum munus*, was a processional hymn chanted as the ampulla was borne from the cathedral portal to the altar: "O precious gift, O precious gem, which was heaven-sent by the ministry of an angel for the unction of the kings of the Francs."[8] The second 1484 addition, *Omnipotens sempiterne Deus, qui pietatis tuae dono*, said after the ampulla had been placed upon the altar, referred to the unction sent to Saint Remigius.[9] Until the Revolution, the legend of Remigius and the Holy Ampulla continued to be embedded at the heart of the coronation liturgy, where it had been placed in the late Middle Ages after completing its rise from the centuries-long obscurity in which it had lain before the early thirteenth century had brought it back to light.

The numerous liturgical changes after 1484 do not mask the rite's continuity as the most striking trait of the French ceremony since the fifteenth century. This meant that the liturgy was not only not forgotten, but also that it became a treasury from which ideas and arguments could be drawn. It is impossible here to examine in detail the uses to which the coronation rite could be put from the sixteenth century on, but a single example is instructive. Sometime between the coronations of Louis XIII and Louis XIV an anonymous author wrote a brief treatise on the coronation—from the drift of the argument one has the impression that it was written after the death of Louis XIII. The author cites two prayers to prove that the king was recognized as such before the coronation: *Omnipotens sempiterne Deus, qui famulum tuum*, which says that God "has deigned to elevate your [i.e., God's] servant N. to the highest rank in the kingdom," and *Omnipotens Deus, caelestium moderator*, which likewise addresses God as having "deigned to promote your servant N. to the kingdom's highest rank." The coronation, therefore, did not give the king "any new authority"; it is "only a holy ceremony to proclaim the kingship solemnly and to consecrate it to God with the person of the king upon whom one beseeches the effects of the interior unction of God by means of the public prayers and by the symbol of exterior unction. . . ."[10]

The ceremony as such may not have been superfluous in the writer's mind, but it certainly was not necessary to make the king, and he quoted in support of his view a passage from the *Sta et retine* formula of enthronement: "Stand firm and maintain yourself in the place that you have held until now by paternal succession, which has been delegated to you by hereditary right by the authority of omnipotent God." (The author ignores the passage immediately following, which adds "and by our [the consecrator's] present delivery of authority.") Consequently,

> the king possesses the kingship by paternal succession before the unction and the coronation; . . . in virtue of the unction and the coronation he possesses it by the authority of God. . . . In a word, it is that that I have already observed, the renewal of the kingship (to use the phrase of the Holy Scripture), and if we wish to explain it in the context of the whole ceremony, it is the renewal and the conservation of the king-

ship, which is also called election. One can also call it, like the ancient French, the confirmation of the kingship. . . .[11]

Our anonymous writer gives us a good example of how the liturgy could be used and abused in the postmedieval period. His interpretation of the rite carries on a tradition that, though undoubtedly unknown to him, had begun in the fourteenth century when Jean Golein, in writing his *Traité du sacre*, had assigned symbolic meaning to various acts of the ceremony.

2. Unique Events

Only to be expected in such a long and complicated ceremony are certain discontinuities, events that are unique to a particular coronation; some may be worth extensive study, others do not signify anything of particular interest. This is true of liturgical and nonliturgical innovations alike. It would be very misleading to give the impression that a liturgical innovation, once introduced, remained a permanent part of the ceremony, even though it might have been intended to accomplish a certain design. For example, one of the seventeen prayers and benedictions recited after the coronation and before the inthronization was *Benedic, Domine, hunc praeelectum principem.* Charles V's *ordo* altered this to *hunc regem nostrum,* but Charles VIII's *ordo* restored the older form while retaining the newer one (*hunc regem nostrum praeelectum principem*).[12]

The most anomolous of coronation rites was clearly that of Henry IV in 1594. His conversion at Saint-Denis on 25 July 1593 could have been only part of a program to be completed by his consecration and coronation, but there was a major hindrance to the latter: Reims was in the hands of the Catholic League, to which its archbishop, a Guise, was wholly beholden. Henry decided, therefore, to have himself crowned at Chartres by its bishop, Nicolas de Thou. There was a medieval tradition for the coronation at Chartres, although it had been suppressed by the success of Reims, and the right to officiate was also claimed by the archbishop of Sens, one of whose predecessors had crowned Louis VI at Orléans in 1108.[13] The selection of a locus and an officiant was not the only hurdle to be surmounted, though, for the French kings had been anointed with the Holy Balm since the early thirteenth century (or from the baptism of Clovis, as was commonly believed), and that was in Reims. The solution to the problem was to resort to another holy oil, the oil that legend asserted to have been given by the Virgin to Saint Martin of Tours, an oil preserved at his monastery at Marmoutier near Tours. Some alterations to the ceremony were required by the circumstances—none of the ecclesiastical peers of France was present, and all had to be represented—but the changes were minimized as much as possible, and the coronation seems to have taken place without any hitch. Belief in the efficacy of the oil of Saint Martin seems to have overcome any doubts raised by the fact that it was the wrong oil for consecrating a French king, for no one seems to have denied the validity of Henry's coronation for that reason. After all, Louis XI had arranged that not only the Holy Ampulla from Reims but also the ampulla from Marmoutier should be brought to him as he lay upon his deathbed in 1483.[14] The oddities of Henry's ceremony, in short, wrought no permanent change, although the ceremony did provoke in the mind of Henry's consecrator some ideas that remained alive until the end of the Old Regime.

Innovations originally unique and unimportant could become elevated even in the modern period, nevertheless, into the complicated framework of political thought. When Charles IX was crowned in 1561, he was only ten years old. His three royal garments so weighted him that he had to be supported; the crown was held near (instead of on) his head as he was conducted to his throne; and he was unable to descend from the throne in order to make his offering. One's sympathy for the child-king unable to walk on account of the burden of his regalia extends to Louis XIII, who was two years younger than Charles IX at his coronation. An attempt was made to take the young Bourbon's age into account, for a small sword was used during the ceremony of investiture (it was replaced by the "sword of Charlemagne" when handed to the Constable of France), and a small crown was substituted for the "crown of Charlemagne" before the king was led to the throne, rather than at the conclusion of the mass, as was customary. Even these precautions were insufficient to prevent an embarrassing situation, however, for both the king and the chevalier de Vendôme, who carried the queue of the royal mantle, had to be bodily carried up the steps to the throne. The newly crowned king gave expression to his extreme youth when the fourteen-year-old duke of Elbeuf, who represented one of the lay peers, a playmate of the young king, approached to deliver the kiss of homage; Louis then "struck him with a friendly blow while beginning to laugh gently and with modesty."[15] Children who may be pitied for the rituals they had to endure, young lads who became the titular heads of state? Charles and Louis were that, but they were more; they were the objects of a royal cult and a crucial guarantee of a degree of peace and public order, of smooth transition from reign to reign. This must have been in the mind of one writer who described Louis XIII's buffet of the duke of Elbeuf: "I shall note in passing a streak of the cheerfulness and of the living image of Henry the Great [*de la vive image de Henry le Grand*]; when Monsieur the Duke of Elbeuf (who was almost the same size as His Majesty) came to kiss him, out of fondness he [the king] thwacked him and kissed him at the same time. We did not see anything so cheerful during the nearly seven hours that the ceremony lasted."[16] The wording and context of this passage do not lead one to suspect that the event was anything more than a pleasantry of a child, but the living-image metaphor, used at a critical time in French history, was fraught with deep implications for the succeeding history of the kingship, and the seemingly insignificant could shroud a weighty constitutional cargo, as we have seen.[17]

Numerous oddities were neither as explicable nor as significant as the living-image metaphor. Louis XIV was crowned on 7 June 1654, although the ceremony had been planned for 31 May, and the coronation jettons that were thrown out with the acclamation bore the original date. It now is impossible to know why the ceremony was postponed a week at the last moment; the consecrator himself, the bishop of Soissons, later wrote that even he did not know why the delay took place.[18] Potentially even more puzzling is the date of Francis II's coronation. That was planned for Sunday, 17 September 1559, but the ceremony took place on the following day; Francis was, therefore, the only French king to have been crowned on a day that was neither a Sunday nor an important feast day. We might suspect that the ceremony was put off on astrological grounds—astrology was popular among all classes in the sixteenth century, and we know that in England the dates of both the Catholic Mary's and the Protestant Elizabeth's coronations were selected by the astrologer John Dee. No such consideration was at work in the French ceremony, though, and we are forced to accept a much more banal explanation. An addition to a sixteenth-century manuscript copy of Charles V's coronation *ordo* informs us that on the planned day of coronation the duke of Savoy, one of the highest ranking spectators of the event, had fallen victim to a fever and that it was on his account that Francis II was crowned on an otherwise very ordinary Monday. Just as what at first appears pica-yune may be notable, so what originally appears remarkable may be only trivial. The major result of the duke's illness has been to cause some dispute among scholars as to the date of the corona-tion, for the jettons had already been struck with the anticipated date.[19]

Whatever may have been thought at the time, innovations, if they were retained, were later almost always thought to have been practiced for centuries, and several hundred years of modern scholarship, often repetitious, have confused and complicated the study of the coronation ceremony and made to appear ancient that which was not. Modern cities, for example, still make a practice of presenting to important personages the symbolic keys to the city. The symbolism implies that the city is always open to those per-sons—despite the failure of any major modern city to possess walls that would enable it to keep out strangers. In the Middle Ages, on the other hand, such a presentation was a token of submission, clearly so on two separate occasions in the *Chanson de Roland*. There is no evidence that this symbolism appeared at the corona-tion ceremony before Reims submitted to Charles VII at the con-clusion of his triumphal journey to the city for his coronation; only thereafter did the presentation of the keys of Reims to the new king remain an important feature of the precoronation entry.[20] Like-wise, the royal largesse, expressed at the coronation with the distri-bution of jettons upon the utterance of the cry "Vivat rex!" and during the singing of the *Te Deum*, cannot be older than the coro-nation of Henry II in 1547, despite dozens of assertions to the contrary.

3. The Royal Largesse

During the reign of Louis XIII, Jacques de Bie's *La France métallique* portrayed coronation medals or jettons for Pepin, Louis II, Hugh Capet, and (with the exceptions of Charles IV and Louis XII) every French king from Louis VI on; all those before Henry II are spurious. Henry II's jettons set the style for the later ones: a portrait of the king and the date of his coronation on the obverse, and on the reverse a hand reaching from the clouds or a dove coming from heaven with the Holy Ampulla over the city of Reims and a device. The jettons were of varying sizes and could be either gold or silver.[21]

At the same time that the jettons were introduced into the ceremony, the thirteen pieces of gold that were part of the king's offering were altered to match the style of the jettons. Prior to 1547 the coins had been described only as thirteen pieces of gold, although Charles VIII's *ordo* had styled them "thirteen gold *écus* for bezants" in 1484,[22] and the medieval *ordines* had called them bezants. The origin of the thirteen bezants had until recently escaped detection; it had been suggested that they were part of the offering from the earliest times of the monarchy, which is not at all convincing, or that they were somehow related to the marriage ceremony, which does not make any sense given the time of their introduction.[23] The first *ordo* to mention coins as part of the offering was the *ordo* of Reims (ca. 1230), which added "thirteen gold coins" (*XIII aureos*) to the offering of bread and wine in a silver ewer. The last Capetian *ordo* (from the later part of Louis IX's reign) changed that to "thirteen gold bezants" (*tredecim bisantios aureos*), which was repeated in Charles V's *ordo* (*tresdecim bisantos aureos*).[24] The bezants, in other words, were substituted after the number of coins had been set at thirteen. If, as may be the case but is by no means certain, the number thirteen was selected to represent the king and the twelve Peers of France, the *ordo* of Reims must have been composed after 1225, the earliest date at which, as far as we know, the number of peers was raised to twelve, although the last Capetian *ordo* is the first coronation document to list all twelve peers with their names.[25]

Why should the latter *ordo* have replaced the unspecified gold coins with bezants? To say that it was the result of some sort of Byzantine influence upon the French ceremony, perhaps in the light of Louis IX's crusades, would be not just imprecise, for there is no evidence to support such a view. It would make more sense to have named the bezant because it was still a kind of international monetary standard, a coin of known value circulated in France as well as elsewhere; such an explanation would be less factitious, but there is a better one, one that can be given in light of what we know of the contemporary rivalry between the abbeys of Saint-Denis and of Saint-Remi. It is quite simple: Louis IX evolved the custom of annually placing four bezants on the altar of Saint-Denis as a token of his homage; the practice could hardly have been pleasing to Reims, and the substitution of the explicit "thirteen gold bezants" for the coronation offering of an indefinite "thirteen gold coins" effectively preempted any offering which a king might later make at Saint-Denis, thereby establishing the priority of the city in Champagne over the monastery in the Île-de-France.[26]

We may demonstrate, on the other hand, that a Byzantine example was operative in the case of the jettons to which the offering's coins became assimilated in the sixteenth century. It is a very precise example that is useful for showing how cautious one must be in seeking foreign influence on French innovation. Because French ceremonial came in the modern period to be increasingly complicated and carefully circumscribed, we are ever more strongly tempted to seek in the East Roman Empire the sources of contributions to French ceremonial. It even seems that sometimes Byzantium provided the only viable examples for France. A recent writer fell prey to this tendency when he referred to Louis XIV's "vision of kingship which had made the old king so cleverly insist on the exact observance of a quasi-byzantine ceremonial."[27] Another scholar described in detail the Byzantine imperial *Anateilon* before skipping, without any demonstration of continuity, to be sure, but with an implication of similarity at least, to the French ceremonial *lever du roi*.[28] This is not the place to investigate the possibilities of Byzantine origins of all French ceremonial, but as far as the coronation ceremony is concerned, that influence was very limited. The genesis of numerous aspects of French practices can indeed be traced to Byzantium, but the trail to France is long and circuitous because it tended to pass in the Early and High Middle Ages via the occidental empire, and that is not the same as a direct later medieval influence, which in any case would have to have been rather limited before the discovery in the eighteenth century of the unique manuscript of our most important source for Byzantine practice, Constantine Porphyrogenitus's *De ceremoniis*.[29] The jettons are another matter.

When the jettons were thrown out in the nave of the church and in the square before the church at Henry II's coronation, they were but part of a larger congeries: the description of the ceremony speaks of "about one thousand pieces of gold and ten thousand silver pieces [the coronation jettons] . . . and of another large quantity of *écus* and common money."[30] Such largesse was unprecedented in the French ceremony, but not in the Byzantine coronation ceremony. Pseudo-Codinos's *De officiis* describes two separate acts of largesse. The first took place at the beginning of the ceremony of inauguration, after the emperor had signed his profession of faith but before his first public appearance (for elevation upon the buckler and for the acclamations): ". . . one of the senators [*synkletikos*], to whom the emperor gave the task, throws to the crowd things that are called *epikombia*. It is done in this way. One cuts pieces of cloth and wraps each piece around three *nomismata* of gold, the same number of silver ones, and three obols, and one throws them to the crowd. They throw out thousands of these little bandages, as many as the emperor orders. It is customary to throw these *epikombia* in the square before the shrine, the great church [Hagia Sophia]. . . ."[31] On the day after the coronation ceremony, the emperors go to the other palaces,

> where the *epikombia* are again thrown out to the crowd by a *synkletikos*. On the same day the emperor himself goes to the courtyard in which the statue of the great martyr [Saint] George is located; the chief of the *vestiarion*, who has a large number of loose gold *nomismata* in his robe, remains at the emperor's side; the emperor takes the *nomismata* and distributes as many of them as he sees fit to the surrounding *archontes* and sons of *archontes*. The cause of this distribution of the *nomismata* is the desire of the emperor for all the *archontes*, the sons of *archontes*, the army, and the people (*ton demon*) to rejoice with him, eating and drinking at the emperor's expense.[32]

The fact that the *editio princeps* of *De officiis* was published only in 1588 does not hinder the work from having provided the model for Henry's largesse. The Bibliothèque Nationale's manuscript *grec* 1786 was copied about 1540 for Guillaume Pélicier, Francis I's ambassador to Venice from 1539 to 1542. The manuscript was listed in the inventory of the royal library at Fontainebleau in 1550, and there is no reason to believe that it was not consulted in the preparation of Henry II's coronation ceremony—it was the right manuscript in the right place at the right time.[33] We know that Henry personally saw to it that the royal insignia at Saint-Denis were refurbished for his coronation; he probably expended similar care on the order of the ceremony.[34]

The true importance of the introduction of the coronation largesse is not that it is Byzantine in origin—although it is always a pleasure to determine the genesis of a practice—but that it is the only innovation after 1350 that is demonstrably based upon a precedent from the East Roman Empire. The other novelties in the ceremony must be sought in French political life and French thought; one might say that with the passage of time the French coronation ceremony, whatever the sources for its earlier development, became increasingly French. French political circumstances alone make sense of the innovations in Charles V's *ordo*: the emphasis on victory, peace, justice, and the divine origin of kingship; the addition to the liturgy of passages referring to Saint Remigius and the Holy Ampulla; and the inconsistencies in the *ordo*. Only political circumstances and their effects on the coronation manuscripts may account for the peculiar oscillations of the *ordines* used in the later fourteenth and fifteenth centuries until the creation of the modern ceremony with the *ordo* of Charles VIII in 1484. The abnormality of Henry IV's coronation resulted from the current political situation, as did certain idiosyncracies of Francis II's and Louis XIII's coronations.[35] The rise of Remigius to a quasi-national sainthood had its roots in France alone, and even the introduction of the largesse in 1547, despite its Byzantine origin, must be viewed within the context of increasing French interest in Greek studies during the reign of Francis I.

At every stage in the history of the ceremony there is no evidence of a conscious, determined development, but rather of a response to contemporary needs and conceptions: "changes in the institutions of society occur slowly and subtly, the transformations often less a result of conscious innovation than of adaptation to the exigencies of the moment."[36] To this comment by a recent writer, one must add that the ceremony was considered at every performance essentially the continuation of a long historical custom, and, in consequence, the past was repeatedly investigated in order to bring the present into accord with it. Because the sources that survived did so in such an incomplete fashion that their survival must be regarded as fortuitous, many of the innovations themselves came into being as the result of what for all practical purposes must be called chance. Two factors, therefore—contemporary adaptation and chance—combined to alter the ceremony with almost every coronation, despite the high degree of continuity given to it by the liturgy. Even when chance played a significant role, nevertheless, one can sometimes determine why a given practice was revived after having fallen into desuetude, and the innovations can deepen our knowledge of how the kingship departed its medieval form to take its modern guise and why it did so. By seeking to distinguish the haphazard from the purposeful and by dissecting congeries of opinions, one may prevent the study of the ceremony from being just entertainment. These general reflections on the mechanics of ceremonial change are nicely illustrated by some aspects of the ceremony that may be construed as limiting the king; of these, the most obvious are the coronation oaths.

PART TWO

THE LIMITS OF KINGSHIP

· · · · · · · · · · ·

THE CORONATION OATHS AND DUELING

· · · · · · · · · · ·

1. The Coronation Oaths

By the later Middle Ages the French coronation oath consisted of two parts, both of which were sworn in Latin. The first of these, the ecclesiastical oath, concerned the bishops and the Church; it was almost exactly a repetition of a request (*petitio*) made by the consecrating bishop, normally the archbishop of Reims. This oath was in the form of a *promissio*, but Marcel David has shown that it had the validity of an oath (*juramentum*).[1] The king swore, "I promise to all of you [i.e., the bishops of the realm] and grant that to each of you and to the churches entrusted to you I shall protect the canonical privilege, due law, and justice, and I shall exercise defense of each bishop and of each church committed to him, as much as I am able—with God's help—just as a king ought properly to do in his kingdom."[2]

The second part of the coronation oath—perhaps one should rather say the second coronation oath—came to be commonly called the oath of the kingdom. In the later Middle Ages it was taken immediately after the ecclesiastical oath, but beginning with the coronation of Henry II in 1547 the taking of the two oaths came to be separated by the ceremonial *consensus* (or *assensus*) *populi*.[3] The oath of the kingdom was sworn by the king with his hands placed upon the Gospels, and afterward he kissed the Gospels:

> To this Christian populace subject to me, I promise in the name of Christ:
> First, that by our authority the whole Christian populace will preserve at all times true peace for the Church of God;

Also, that I shall forbid all rapacities and all iniquities of
all degrees;

Also, that I shall enjoin justice and mercy in all judgments
in order that a clement and merciful God may grant his
mercy to me and to you;

Also, that in good faith to all men I shall be diligent to expel from my land and also from the jurisdiction subject to
me all heretics designated by the Church. I affirm by oath all
this said above.[4]

Both oaths have a distinguished history, but that of the ecclesiastical oath is somewhat longer.[5] It first appears in a West Frankish
ordo for the coronation of Charles the Bald as king of Lotharingia
in 869. The use of the oath spread outside the West Frankish kingdoms, and it became standard in the coronation *ordines* of several
European countries. In France it was used, basically unchanged, at
the coronation of Louis XVI nine hundred years after it had first
been formulated.[6] The ecclesiastical oath has a peculiar distinction: in France it came to be repeated at the cathedral church of
Notre Dame in Paris when, after the development of formal entries
into the city in the fourteenth century, the king made his postcoronation entry there. The king was required not only to retake the
oath but also to sign it, which had not been the case at his coronation. Presumably, the fact that the oath was in the form of a promise rather than a *juramentum* enabled it to be taken a second time.
The practice seems to be new in the fourteenth century, and at
least one king was sufficiently astounded by the bishop of Paris's
petitio to take the oath that he asked whether this were normal
under the circumstances.[7]

Unlike the ecclesiastical oath, the oath of the kingdom was
sworn only in France during the period under study, although the
oldest parts of it are not French. The first three clauses of the
oath were copied from an Anglo-Saxon *ordo* for the late tenth-
century French Fulrad *ordo*, which may have been used in France
as early as the coronation of Philip I in 1059. The clause concerning heretics (the fourth clause of the oath) was added after 1215; it
is nearly a verbatim implementation of a decision made by the
Fourth Lateran Council.[8] All four clauses are referred to in the
ordo of Reims, although this *ordo* does not actually quote the oath.
It is quoted, however, in the numerous manuscripts of the last

Capetian *ordo*, which was compiled toward the end of the reign of Louis IX, and the complete oath as given above remained standard in France until the end of the Old Regime. Neither this nor the ecclesiastical oath was sworn by Charles X at his coronation in 1825.[9]

A significant addition was made to the oath of the kingdom in the *ordo* of Charles V, when a clause of inalienability was added. This clause exists only in two manuscripts of the *ordo*, however, and one is demonstrably copied from the other. The matter of inalienability and the coronation ceremony is such a complicated one that it will be necessary to examine it alone at length in another chapter (below, chapter 6).

There is intriguing evidence that the oath of the kingdom sworn by Henry II in 1547 did not include the clause to expel heretics from the kingdom,[10] but apart from that no changes were made in the coronation oaths between the thirteenth century and the coronation of Louis XIV in 1654, when a new oath was added to the ceremony. The rule of the Order of the Holy Spirit that the king, as grand master of the order, should swear at his coronation to uphold the order's statutes was observed by both Henry IV and Louis XIII, but both kings swore that oath only on the day after their coronation, when they were formally received into the order. In 1654, on the other hand, the oath of the order was taken during the coronation ceremony itself, immediately after the oath of the kingdom, even though Louis XIV was not to be received into the order until the following day. The effect of inserting this oath into the coronation ceremony was not so much to elevate the prestige of the modern knightly order as to begin a process of demeaning[11] the old coronation oaths; this trend continued at the eighteenth-century coronations. Both Louis XV and Louis XVI took the two medieval oaths and the oath of the Order of the Holy Spirit, but they also swore an oath as grand master of the Order of Saint Louis (which had been founded by Louis XIV in 1693 for military merit) to obey the rules of that order.[12]

2. The Antidueling Oath

The final accretion to (and debasement of) the oaths took place at the coronation of Louis XV in 1722, when the king swore:

> We, in consequence of the kings' our predecessors' edicts against duels, registered in our court of Parlement, pending the time when we shall be able to renew them when we arrive at our majority, and wanting to follow above all the example of Louis XIV of glorious memory, our great-grandfather, who on the day of his consecration and coronation solemnly swore the execution of his preceding declaration, given in the *lit de justice* that he held on the seventh day of September 1651 at his majority.
>
> To this end we swear and promise in witness and word of a king [*en foi et parole de Roy*] not to exempt in the future, for whatever reason or consideration there might be, any person from the rigor of the edicts given by Louis XIV, our great-grandfather, in 1651, 1669, and 1679; that no pardon or amnesty will be accorded by us to those who find themselves charged with the crimes of duels or premeditated encounters; that we shall not consider the solicitations of any prince or lord who intercedes for those guilty of the said crimes; affirming that neither in honor of any marriage of Prince or Princess of our Blood, nor for the births of a Dauphin and princes who might arrive during our reign, nor for any other general or particular consideration, whatever it be, shall we knowingly permit any letters of pardon to be drawn up contrary to the above said declarations of edicts, in order to maintain inviolably a law so Christian, so just, and so necessary. So may God and his Holy Gospels aid me in this.[13]

Louis XVI swore the same oath, *mutatis mutandis*, at his coronation, but Charles X did not because dueling as such was not illegal after the Revolution.

The medieval coronation oaths spoke in lofty and general terms of protection of the Church and of peace and justice in the kingdom. Although the promise to expel heretics was more specific than the remainder of the medieval oaths, even that was couched in rather general terms. The new oath to observe the edicts against duels, on the other hand, was specific, and even at that it was at first only provisional until the king could renew the edicts at his majority. (At Louis XVI's coronation this provisional clause was struck out of the oath, thus making the oath valid for the lifetime of the king.)[14]

Louis XV's oath against dueling shows clearly that by the eighteenth century the oath of the kingdom had lost most of its value. Certainly that was the case with the fourth clause, which no king since the Middle Ages could enforce—even Louis XIV, when he revoked the Edict of Nantes in 1685, did not expel the heretics from the kingdom, but instead forbade them to depart, while making the practice of their religion illegal, and upon the conquest of Alsace he granted that area's Lutherans special status, allowing them to retain their religious beliefs and practices. Theoretically, the last monarchs of the Old Regime could have prevented duels by right of the first clause of the oath of the kingdom: "by our authority the whole Christian populace will preserve true peace." In fact, by the eighteenth century the general terms of the medieval oath seem to have been no longer efficacious, and the edicts against duels were given greater prestige by their incorporation into a special coronation oath. At the same time, the whole ceremony of oath-taking at the coronation was vulgarized by the addition of an oath that referred to only one type of peace in the kingdom. Government and law had both changed drastically since the final for-mulation of the oath of the kingdom in the thirteenth century.

3. The Problem of Dueling

The addition of the new oath is, however, a measure of the seriousness of dueling, which was a significant problem in France in the seventeenth and eighteenth centuries. It had not always been so. Dueling between individuals—as distinguished from private warfare—was hardly a notable problem in the Middle Ages, partially because there were more serious disturbers of the peace than duelers. Judicial duels ceased to be practiced in France after the famous one in July 1547, which turned out to be so unfortunately bloody that Henry II decided not to sanction any more such duels.[15] In the long run the most important source of the early modern problem of dueling was the increasingly strict ordering of the higher levels of French society, leading to numerous disputes over prerogative and struggles for precedence.[16] The lengthy contest between the duke of Montpensier and the dukes of Guise is one of the most notable examples of these (see below, chapter 10), although it was different from many other feuds in that it did not end in bloodshed.

The magnitude of the problem was becoming apparent already in 1566 when, under the instigation of Chancellor Michel de l'Hôpital, Charles IX published an ordinance that made him the first French king to prohibit dueling. During the next three-quarters of a century extensive legislation declared duelers to be guilty of lese majesty and made the punishments for dueling increasingly harsh —capital punishment became the penalty for infractions of the edicts, partially because duels were "veritable revolts against the authority of the king."[17] Because some duelers pretended that their battle resulted from a chance encounter rather than from premeditation, the government provided in 1611 (and again in 1644) that every encounter leading to a combat should be considered a duel. During the minority of Louis XIV the incidence of dueling became such a serious problem of state, owing largely to the troubles of the Fronde, that the laws against dueling were codified in an important piece of legislation promulgated at the *lit de justice* at which Louis was declared major (7 September 1651); those provisions were amplified in 1679 in the Sun King's final decree on the matter. Louis XV published the last edict against dueling upon reaching his majority in February 1723, thus fulfilling the intention of the first part of his coronation oath a few months before.[18]

Although many historians have commented on the seriousness of dueling during the first half of the seventeenth century—and particularly during the minority of Louis XIV—their statements have lacked conviction for want of supporting documentary and statistical evidence. Louis XIV's coronation ceremony provides such evidence, however, because at least part of the depositions and records of the prisoners freed and pardoned at his coronation survive in five large volumes of bound manuscripts in the Bibliothèque Nationale.[19]

A random sampling of cases from the first volume of these manuscripts produced eight cases of dueling and eleven cases of other crimes (one case was deleted because it involved both dueling and homicide in self-defense).[20] Projecting from this—and assuming to be accurate the statement that Louis pardoned some 6,000 prisoners at his coronation—Louis must have pardoned about

2,500 duelers in 1654.[21] Some of the cases in the manuscripts date as far back as 1639, but most of them date from 1648 or 1650. If we assume the French population to have been twenty million in the mid-seventeenth century,[22] that amounts to one case per 8,000 of the general population, or, over a period of six years, 2.085 per 100,000 of the population per year. This by itself would not seem to demonstrate that dueling was a very serious problem. In 1609, however, Pierre de l'Estoile had claimed that Henry IV had accorded 7,000 pardons for dueling in less than nineteen years.[23] If L'Estoile's figure is accurate and if most duelers applied for pardon (admittedly somewhat risky assumptions), that would indicate an incidence of 1.84 duels per 100,000 of general population per year. Dueling was thus clearly a more serious problem in the middle than at the beginning of the seventeenth century, particularly considering the unlikelihood that even the majority of duelers presented themselves to the prisons at Reims in order to seek pardon on the occasion of Louis XIV's coronation.

These figures for the incidence of dueling in the mid-seventeenth century are subject to refinement and correction. They are based upon a very small sampling (19 cases) of perhaps 1,000 cases detailed in the first four manuscript volumes of the records of the pardons granted by Louis XIV. This is not the place, though, to undertake an extensive statistical and historical study of dueling in the seventeenth century. Suffice it to say that paging through the manuscripts gives the impression that the incidence of dueling was higher than the figures suggest, an impression that is supported by another set of figures. In 1819 Baron (later Duke) Etienne Denis Pasquier reported to the Chamber of Deputies that during the eight years of Louis XIV's minority more than 4,000 persons lost their lives in individual combats.[24] This figure gives an incidence of 2.5 duels per 100,000 of the general population per year (as compared with my 2.085). Pasquier's figure does not take into account the duels that did not end in homicide; therefore, the incidence of dueling was much higher than Pasquier's figure alone indicates.[25]

These figures are not sufficiently large to measure the incidence of dueling among the noble classes, which, despite the spread of dueling to the bourgeoisie, bore the brunt of the evils of personal encounters. If we use Pasquier's figure, and if we assume the noble classes to have numbered about 300,000 in the mid-seventeenth century, the incidence of homicides by duels could have been as high as 167 per 100,000 per year. The edicts against dueling were manifestly necessary, and it is perhaps understandable why an oath to uphold the edicts should have found its way into the coronation ceremony.

In any case, such an oath was prescribed by Louis XIV's lengthy edict of 7 September 1651, which concluded with the statement that the king had resolved "expressly and solemnly to swear the observation [of the edict] on the day of our proximate consecration and coronation," and the edict of 1679 states that "we have expressly and solemnly sworn the execution [of the edict] on the day of our consecration and coronation."[26] That—contrary to the edict—Louis XIV did pardon hundreds, if not thousands, of duelers at his coronation is proven by surviving documentation. The *Roi Soleil* was therefore either a liar in his edict of 1679—he cannot be held fully responsible for failing to keep his resolution in the edict of 1651, for the coronation was postponed for another three years—or he was a perjurer for pardoning duelers at his coronation. Because we do have quite extensive records of Louis's coronation, we know that, despite the declaration in the edict of 1679 and the statement in Louis XV's oath against dueling, Louis XIV did not swear at his coronation to uphold the edicts against dueling.[27] He can be acquitted of the charge of perjuring himself immediately after swearing his coronation oath.

Louis XV and Louis XVI were, therefore, the only two kings to swear an oath against dueling. The introduction of the oath in 1722 is easily understandable, for it seemed, owing to the declarations in the edicts of 1651 and 1679, that Louis XIV had sworn such an oath. It must have been rather a shock, therefore, to those responsible for Louis XV's coronation ceremonial when they could not find Louis XIV's oath. They had to produce a new oath quickly, as is demonstrated by the finished result. The oath is not only by far the longest of the coronation oaths, it is also the most awkward and poorly conceived. The first paragraph does not even form a complete sentence, and the sentence of the second paragraph is marred by anacoluthon. Furthermore, the substantive portion of the oath was copied almost verbatim from the concluding passages of the edict of 1651 (but not from the nearly similar passage of the edict of 1679). When the government's records failed to provide a copy of the nonexistent oath of Louis XIV, it was probably hoped that a copy had been preserved at Reims; when the officials arrived there, they again failed in their quest, but in order to model the ceremony as much as possible after its presumed predecessor they produced the ad hoc result.[28] Awkward though it was, this oath was repeated five decades later at the last coronation of the Old Regime.

4. The Efficacy of the Oath

In a way it is fortunate that Louis XV and Louis XVI did swear such a specific oath at their coronations, for the oath makes possible an easily verifiable measurement of the validity of the coronation oaths and the extent of royal absolutism, if we take absolutism to mean the lack of restrictions on the king's power to act. At best, the kings enforced the edicts only partially; there is only one well-known case of the full death penalty having been visited upon someone guilty of dueling, and that sentence resulted more from a blatant defiance of royal authority than from the simple act of dueling.[29] Even when the king's officials and courts did sentence duelers to the full extent of the rigors of the edicts, the sentences were simply not carried out. Jacques de Bane, for example, one of the prisoners pardoned at Louis XIV's coronation, was still free over two years after the deadline had passed for the confirmation of his letter of pardon, and Roger de Raymond, one of the prisoners who sought pardon at Louis XV's coronation, had been condemned to death for dueling in 1698, twenty-four years before the coronation.[30] The pardons were granted, and the delays took place, despite the fact that the kings, when they promulgated their edicts, said that "we swear and promise in witness and word of a king" (*nous jurons et promettons, en foi et parole de Roi*) not to exempt anyone from the rigors of the edicts; such was the wording of the edicts of 1651 and 1679.[31] On that basis alone one must conclude not only that the word of the king meant little, but also that the king was not bound by his oath.

This lack of stricture on the king's actions is evident in 1722. Louis XV accorded nearly 600 pardons at his coronation, and a two-volume manuscript of the proceedings (*procès-verbal*) survives.[32] Of the 258 cases in volume I, twenty-seven were not accorded pardon, and two of these cases were clearly duelers even though they were not called such. On the other hand, a random sampling of six prisoners accorded pardon turned up one who had wounded someone else with a pistol, one who had killed someone with a sword in a spontaneous fight, and one who had killed someone in a sword fight that apparently was not spontaneous. All three of these cases were interpretable as duels under the terms of the royal edicts.[33] To the three we might add a fourth case that involved a gun battle between several antagonists on each side; the battle evolved in the course of a hunt and resulted in one death.[34] It appears, therefore, that at least half of the prisoners pardoned in 1722 were duelers even though they were careful to avoid calling themselves such. In this respect there is a vast difference between 1722 and 1654, when the prisoners did not hesitate to admit that they were guilty of homicide by dueling. Louis XIV and the Regency may not have stopped dueling, but they did make it socially less acceptable than it had been, a conclusion borne out by a recent brief study of dueling in the early seventeenth and in the early eighteenth century.[35] Nonetheless, by failing to identify duelers as such Louis XV failed to uphold the spirit of either the edicts or his coronation oath, and although the king was legally bound by his oath, he was de facto free to do as he wished, and hence, absolute.

This practical absolutism must be tempered by another consideration, though: the king's officials and the king's courts, including the *parlements*, acting for and in the name of the king, served as the normal extensions of the king's administration of justice. These institutions did in fact pass sentence on those found guilty of dueling, often to the full extent of the rigors of the edicts. Although few or only part of the sentences were executed, those upon whom the sentences were passed suffered disgrace, financial loss, and even voluntary exile in order to avoid the (feared) execution of the sentence.[36] For practical purposes and in normal times the king, acting through his institutions, was in consequence limited by his own institutions, and he did not appear to his subjects as an absolutistic ruler. Whatever the caprices of an individual king, the very fact that he passed edicts against dueling or swore at his coronation to uphold those edicts was used by his government to offset some of the effects of the monarch's capriciousness.

The whole question of absolutism is a thorny one, the discussion of which has been unnecessarily muddled by failure to make essential distinctions. Before this issue can be fully assessed, it is important to see what other limitations there were on the king's power of acting. The oldest of them, one juridically more important than the oath to uphold the edicts against duels, was the prohibition of alienation of the royal domain. Here, as with Louis XIV's oath against dueling, there is an interesting case of a spurious coronation oath.

6

THE CORONATION AND INALIENABILITY

• • • • • • • • • •

"And I shall preserve inviolably the sovereignty, rights, and nobility of the crown of France, and shall neither transfer nor alienate them."[1] So reads the clause that was inserted after the first part of the oath of the kingdom in Charles V's coronation *ordo* of 1365. It has the distinction of marking the first appearance of inalienability in the French ceremony, and its presence there can in a sense be traced until the disappearance of the principle from the ceremony after the early seventeenth century. "In a sense," it must be said, because, as we shall see, the received historical opinions about inalienability and the coronation must be considerably altered.

The addition of inalienability to the coronation oaths gives the impression of introducing the principle into the sphere of French public law in what was probably the quickest fashion possible. Although it is generally recognized that French public law was vague and uncertain in the later Middle Ages, all who study it agree that the doctrine of inalienability played a crucial role in French political history on several occasions, and those scholars who have written on the development of the French law of inalienability have agreed that one of the basic sources of that law was the oath that Charles V and his immediate successors swore at their coronations. Théodore and Denis Godefroy had come to that conclusion in the seventeenth century, and their great authority has been relied upon by many since then. Peter N. Riesenberg, the author of the most detailed work on inalienability, and, more recently, Hartmut Hoffmann both emphasized the role of the coronation oath in the development of inalienability in France.[2] They have done so because there is no convincing evidence that the French royal rights were considered generally inalienable until after the appearance of the clause in Charles V's *ordo*.

As a theoretical issue, inalienability became significant only after the middle of the sixteenth century. France was then without any clearly defined constitution, which preyed upon the minds of those scholars who concerned themselves with the underlying conceptions of what we know as the developing nation-state. Believing that there were certain fundamental principles underlying the state as they knew it, but not having a terminology to apply to those principles, the writers of the second half of the century began to define their conceptions in terms of "fundamental laws," laws that, they believed, formed the very foundation of the monarchy. They generally posited at least two such laws.[3] The first was that of succession to the throne by the nearest male heir whose descent could be traced through the male line alone, and the second was inalienability. That the first was not universally accepted led to severe political problems before the end of the century.[4] That the second was elevated to such a high status explains the importance in the theoreticians' minds of the coronation oath of inalienability, and the scholars' attitude then has been maintained ever since— the French still distinguish between their constitutional history, which begins only with the Revolution, and the fundamental laws that formed the constitution of the monarchy. The sixteenth century and its successors have tended to look upon the development of inalienability ahistorically, however, failing to emphasize that the principle was not at first the result of theoretical considerations, but of practical needs.

1. The Origins of Inalienability

Why inalienability came to France as late as it did, and why it came when it did, are two questions that need to be answered, although in neither case is the answer easy. By 1365 the principle of inalienability was at least two hundred years old, for it had been developed for the empire already during the second quarter of the twelfth century. By the end of that century an oath of inalienability was introduced into certain episcopal ordination ceremonies in Italy, and in the 1230s this oath probably was required of many bishops and archbishops even outside of Italy, a practice that may be attributable to Gregory IX. Whereas episcopal ordinations provide the first concrete evidence for an oath of inalienability, such oaths quickly spread to the secular domain. There is strong evidence that Henry III of England swore inalienability, as did Edward I, although it is likely that the oath was appended to the English monarchs' oaths of fealty to the pope rather than incorporated into their coronation oaths. In 1222 Andrew II of Hungary promised in his Golden Bull to bind himself and his successors to maintenance of the principle of inalienability, a promise that the papal curia interpreted to mean that Andrew had sworn inalienability at his coronation. When Honorius III wrote to Hungary about the matter in 1225 he referred to the supposed coronation oath of inalienability taken by the king; this letter became the decretal *Intellecto*, which in turn was the primary instrument through which inalienability was generally adopted, as is demonstrated in the case of the Spanish kingdoms, which saw the introduction of inalienability in the second half of the thirteenth century.[5] Why, then, did France refrain so long from following the widespread custom?

The answer must be sought, it seems, in the Capetian conception of kingship. Without going into the details of a vast and still obscure subject, it is clear that at least the early Capetians did not apply a concept of territoriality to their kingdom; there was no national state or suprapersonal political unit of any other sort. Their kingdom was conceived of only as a collection of discrete holdings and rights belonging to a group of feudal lords. Their own patrimony, consisting of personal and familial properties and rights, was likewise not thought of as forming a unity, but as a congeries of real estate and rights. It may be that there was some conception of a royal domain early in the thirteenth century, but that was quite different from any modern conception, and in any case, despite the centralizing tendencies of Philip the Fair, the kings of the fourteenth century tended to revert to a personal interpretation of their possessions, which still remained conceptually little more than a collection.[6] This is apparent from an instruction drawn up for two royal investigators by Philip IV's government in 1305; the instruction lists under the heading of various types of jurisdiction, not general rights to blocks of territory, but individual villages, castles, monasteries, etc., with a summary of the number of hearths subject to the king under each type of jurisdiction (and also, not incidentally, with a notation of the monetary sums owed to the king).[7]

It may well be that the French did not develop a clear conception of suprapersonal royal rights, prerogatives, and domain until they were forced to do so by the pressure of events during the first phase of the Hundred Years' War, when the process of developing abstract concepts was aided by the simultaneous introduction of the theory of inalienability. By the time the war broke out the European background for inalienability was sufficient to provide France with its model, and even in France the government had been slowly moving in the direction of inalienability for some time. There were two types of fourteenth-century sources for this tendency. The first, which was highly theoretical and legal, is exemplified by an episode in the dispute with Aragon over the Val d'Aran in 1308, when it was argued that the French claim descended from the Carolingians, that the French king had the right of the empire in his kingdom, and that, because prescription of time could not run against the king, the king could not diminish the borders of the kingdom.[8] The second type of source was practical, for it consisted of a series of revocations of alienations made by previous kings. On 29 July 1318, Philip V revoked royal gifts granted since the death of Saint Louis in 1270, and Charles IV published a similar ordinance on 5 April 1322, a few weeks after his coronation (21 February 1322). These were followed in the next few decades by a number of like attempts to revoke grants that had been made for financial or other reasons. Because it became customary for a new king to declare such revocations near the beginning of his reign—Charles V's revocation, for example, was made just two months after his coronation—the association of revocations with the assumption of royal authority was natural.[9] Revocations of alienations previously made was not nearly the same thing as forbidding alienations in the first place, though, and not until the time of John and Charles V did prohibitions of alienations come to be generally expressed. Also, general arguments like those presented in 1308 did not do more than provide only a broad intellectual milieu within which a more legally precise conception of inalienability could develop.

The defeat of the French at Poitiers in 1356 and the subsequent Treaty of Brétigny did much to aid in introducing inalienability, but only in a manner quite indirect. The first general prohibition of alienations is found in the famous ordinance that the Estates General forced upon Charles as lieutenant general of the kingdom in 1357. The ordinance temporarily revolutionized the government of France and stripped the dauphin of most of his powers; among other things, Charles promised "that with all our power we shall hold, guard and defend the *hautesses, noblesses, dignités,* and *franchises* of the crown, and all the *demaines* that do and can belong to it, and that we shall not alienate the said domain nor suffer any of it to be alienated or estranged or put beyond our authority. . . ."[10] This prohibition, be it noted, had nothing to do with France's recent military defeat, but only with what the Estates General felt to be squandering of royal rights by an excessively munificent prince.

The next prohibition of alienation came four years later, after the deliberate failure of the French to ratify two clauses of the Treaty of Brétigny. In November 1361, John issued a charter reuniting Burgundy, Champagne, Toulouse, and Normandy to the crown. Of these four Normandy was a special case, for article 12 of the Treaty of Brétigny had provided that the French king should renounce "l'omage, souveraineté et demein" of the duchy of Normandy (among other territories). In the final negotiations prior to the ratification of the treaty at Calais on 24 October 1360 this was one of the clauses that the French managed to have removed from the main body of the treaty. It was agreed, however, that the two clauses would be implemented by 29 September 1361 at the latest, although negotiations between John and Edward III set the date of 15 August for the final renunciation, with 1 and 30 November as alternate dates in case the August deadline was not met.[11] The deadlines passed, and with almost indecent haste the French took advantage of the English failure to sign the articles by reuniting Normandy to the crown in November. Because Normandy alone of the four territories mentioned in the charter of 1361 did thus occupy a special position, the charter prescribed a special coronation oath for the duchy, which in 1355 had been given as an appanage to Charles as dauphin. The charter stated that if John were to die and Charles to become king, the latter should swear an oath not to alienate the duchy, or if Charles should die first, then John and his successors would swear the oath upon reception of the insignia of the coronation.[12]

2. Charles V's *Ordo* and Inalienability

The alienations required by the Treaty of Brétigny and the provision for a limited coronation oath of inalienability by the 1361 charter would seem to have provided sufficient grounds for the addition of the clause of inalienability to the coronation oath in Charles V's *ordo*. The *ordo* containing the clause survives in two contemporary copies. Paris Bibliothèque Nationale latin 8886 is a sumptuous manuscript copied for Charles's brother, Jean, duke of Berry. Donated to the Sainte-Chapelle at Bourges after the duke's death in 1404, it was subsequently forgotten, and it played no role in the further development of the coronation ceremony.[13] In any case it was demonstrably copied from the other manuscript, London, British Library Cotton Tiberius B.viii, which bears the king's autograph note, date, and signature.[14] Because this manuscript is the only contemporary one to contain the clause of inalienability, because it has been since its rediscovery and publication in the seventeenth century the primary source for belief in the presence of a French coronation oath of inalienability, and because it has certain problematical features, it merits closer examination.[15]

The nonalienation clause appears twice in the manuscript, which is a collection of coronation materials (of which Charles V's *ordo* is the most important) drawn primarily from the *Libri Memoriales*, the oldest registers of the Chambre des Comptes.[16] The most significant location of the clause in the manuscript (in which the clause appears twice) is in the oath in Charles V's *ordo*, but there is an important feature of the manuscript at that point: after the words "nostro arbitrio in omni" in the first part of the oath of the kingdom, the whole of the oath (some nine and one-half lines) has been erased, and the oath as it now stands has been fitted into the erased space by ample use of abbreviations and by crowding the script together. Therefore the first part of the oath of the kingdom now reads: "Hec populo christiano et michi subdito in Christi nomine promitto: In primis, ut ecclesie Dei omnis populus christianus veram pacem nostro arbitrio in omni tempore servet, et superioritatem, jura et nobilitates corone Francie inviolabiliter custodiam, et illa nec transportabo nec alienabo."[17]

Something was obviously inserted into the oath of the kingdom after the manuscript was transcribed, perhaps soon thereafter. A detailed examination of the manuscript enables one to assert with

reasonable confidence that the addition was the clause of inalienability, which did not figure in the original version of Charles V's
coronation oath.[18] If that were all we had to deal with, the problem
posed by the clause of inalienability would be less difficult to solve
than it in fact is. As noted, Tiberius B.viii is a collection of materials. In order of appearance these are: (1) a French translation of
the *ordo* of Reims; (2) the texts of the coronation oaths; (3) lists of
the old and the new Peers of France;[19] (4) the *ordo* of Charles V;
and (5) sundry oaths for royal officials. The oath of the kingdom in
(2) contains the clause of nonalienation without erasure or correction, but that oath does not contain the clause to expel heretics;
these facts led one scholar to argue that the clause of inalienability
was originally in (4), Charles V's *ordo*, and that the erasure was
made in order to insert the missing antiheretic clause. The evidence of the manuscript at the erasure does not support this contention, and the argument fails to recognize an essential feature of
the oath in (2): it was a superseded form of the oath of the kingdom; copied either directly or indirectly from a marginal addition
in a twelfth-century copy of the Fulrad *ordo* at Reims, it had not
been used at the French coronations since at least 1328, and perhaps not since 1226.[20] This oath, in short, may not be used as
evidence for what took place in 1364, and its clause of inalienability is an addition made outside the context of any particular coronation ceremony. As a result of all this, the manuscript must fail to
convince us that Charles himself swore the clause of inalienability
even though it appears twice in Tiberius B.viii.

A manuscript tradition of Charles's *ordo* that is independent of
Tiberius B.viii provides further evidence that the clause did not
exist in the original version of the *ordo*. Shortly before his death in
1380 Charles deposited in a box in the abbey of Saint-Denis a copy
of the *ordo* (with a preceding translation of the *ordo* of Reims, just
as in Tiberius B.viii) together with other objects (crowns, scepters,
etc.) prepared for the coronations of his successors. The Saint-
Denis manuscript has since disappeared, but it has been possible to
trace its history until the end of the sixteenth century and to recon-
stitute the most important parts of its text, which does not contain
the clause of inalienability found in Tiberius B.viii. Both manuscripts were probably copied from a common source, the text used
at Charles's coronation, but only Tiberius B.viii shows proof that it
was examined and corrected by the king himself.[21] The royal scru-

tiny would seem to have been the logical cause of the erasure and correction made in the oath, although we do not have enough information to enable us to know why the clause was given its particular wording.

The presence of the clause in Tiberius B.viii led, after publication of the manuscript, to the historical error that the kings from Charles V to Louis XI swore inalienability at their coronations. This conclusion was not warranted, however, for Tiberius B.viii, the sole manuscript containing the clause that could have been used at French coronations, was not available to the French in the fifteenth century because the duke of Bedford took it to England after acquiring it and numerous other manuscripts from the royal library in the 1420s. Charles VI, crowned before this, was therefore the only king who could have used Tiberius B.viii at his coronation and who could have sworn the nonalienation clause, but whether or not he did so remains to be seen.[22]

The whole story of inalienability in the coronation ceremony has been considerably muddled by the fact that, whereas the coronation records (except for Tiberius B.viii) consistently fail to include an oath of inalienability, there is a variety of literary evidence that has been interpreted to show that the kings from Charles V even to Henry IV swore at their coronations not to alienate their rights. Examination of this evidence will show that it does not prove that a coronation oath of inalienability was sworn. We shall attempt to bring into accord the literary (and legal) assertions and the records of the coronation ceremonies.

Space does not here permit the discussion of more than one or two examples from each reign, but in every case those that are the most convincing have been selected for discussion. Even negative evidence, by itself weak, may bear some weight when coupled with positive arguments. Charles V, for example, is said to have sworn inalienability in 1364. When, however, he revoked alienations from the domain on 24 July 1364, just two months after his coronation, the letters of revocation made no reference to any coronation oath: instead, the document refers only to the letters of December 1360 by which John had revoked alienations made since the time of Philip the Fair.[23] If Charles had sworn a clause of inalienability, and if he had been the first king to do so, he would surely have invoked the oath to justify his revocation. We should therefore assume that the clause of inalienability had yet to be formulated. This argument by itself would be insufficient to deny the oath to Charles, but when coupled with the problems surrounding the clause in Tiberius B.viii and the absence of the clause in the Saint-Denis manuscript of Charles's *ordo*, it contributes to but a sole conclusion. Also, the doctors of Bologna who in 1369 wrote a brief on the legality of the alienations required by the Treaty of Brétigny failed to refer to any oath of inalienability.[24] The only explicit reference during Charles V's reign to any such oath was made by the French royal representative at the Anglo-French negotiations at Bruges in 1376 when he urged that "the king at his accession and consecration [*nouvelleté et consecration*] swore in the presence of his people not to alienate the rights of his crown [*drois de sa couronne*]" and that if the king were to alienate his rights he would perjure himself.[25] Such a statement could easily have been based upon the corrected oath in Tiberius B.viii (which, as we have seen, provides but weak evidence for what actually happened), and the argument of perjury was an old one that had turned up already at Vincennes in 1329. It is striking that when the author (or authors) of the *Somnium viridarii* (and its French translation, *Le songe du vergier*, which must also be consulted) turned to the issue of inalienability, he cited canon and feudal law only, not a coronation oath, as forbidding alienations of royal rights.[26]

The proofs that Charles V did swear his clause of inalienability fail to convince, but the evidence concerning Charles VI is more ambiguous. On the one hand a contemporary note in one of the inventories of the royal library remarks (of the manuscript we now know as Tiberius B.viii) that "the king took it for his consecration, 5 [*sic* for 4] October 1380."[27] This statement does not tell us whether the manuscript was actually consulted by those who drew up the ceremony for Charles's coronation—who therefore might have included the clause of inalienability in the ceremony—or whether the king simply took with him to Reims the most magnificent exemplar of the coronation texts in the royal collection. The latter possibility—the method of preparing the library's inventory and other arguments taken into account—is more probable, in which case the manuscript had no influence whatsoever upon the ceremony. The strongest evidence that Charles VI took an oath of inalienability is found in an ordinance of 1402 that revoked previous alienations: "Considering also that when our predecessors and also we were consecrated and anointed kings, they and we too swore most solemnly in the presence of the peers, several prelates, and other princes of our kingdom to maintain the rights of our crown as well as of the entire domain, and we also swore not to alienate or separate them in any manner and to readmit, rejoin, and reunite that which would be alienated. . . ."[28]

At this point we must emphasize the major weakness of this statement, a fault that applies to most of the later evidence for an oath of inalienability. Charles VI's ordinance says unambiguously that the king swore not to alienate and also to revoke alienations made. The clause of inalienability in Tiberius B.viii makes absolutely no reference to revocation. If, therefore, Charles VI swore something relating to the maintenance of royal rights, it was not the clause inserted in Tiberius B.viii's oaths of the kingdom. The only possible source in France for coupling an oath of inalienability to an oath of revocation is found in the canon law, in the decretal *Intellecto, de jurejurando*, which, as noted, was the primary authority for inalienability in western Europe in the later Middle Ages.[29] There is not the slightest shred of direct evidence, though, that any French king swore an oath similar to that required by *Intellecto*. Consequently, however explicit the statement of 1402 may be, it is based to such an extent upon a general rule of canon law that it is impossible to believe that Charles VI swore the explicit oath apparently described in the ordinance. The other evidence for Charles's oath of inalienability is as weak as that of 1402, and it all dates from the fifteenth century only;[30] in other words, twenty-two years passed after the coronation before any reference was made to Charles's coronation oath of inalienability. The evidence is not strong enough to make it seem likely that Charles VI swore such an oath, even though he did take Tiberius B.viii with him to Reims.

In 1444, Charles VII claimed that he had sworn at his coronation not to alienate "the domain, lordship, and prerogatives" of the crown of France, but because he added that he had also sworn to recover that that had been alienated, his statement suffers the same want of conviction as Charles VI's similar remark in the ordinance of 1402.[31] Nonetheless, given the nature of the Treaty of Troyes, it was only natural that the issue of inalienability should arise during Charles's reign. Jean Juvénal des Ursins, bishop of Laon and later archbishop of Reims, one of France's leading politi-

cal and intellectual figures, referred to the king's oath of inalienability on several occasions, and the weight of his evidence has
been emphasized by more than one historian. In the mid-1430s he
wrote a tract on the Anglo-French struggle in which he claimed
that "the king expressly swears at his coronation that he will not
alienate any of his inheritance" and that "royal ordinances have
been kept and observed in this matter for so long that memory
does not run to the contrary."[32] Thus does Juvénal des Ursins demonstrate that there was a tradition of such a coronation oath even
though the sources we have so far examined fail to prove that the
oath had ever been actually sworn by a king. In 1444–45 he wrote
another treatise on the French conflict with the English in which he
argued, "And it would be a very wondrous matter if the king could
not validly alienate a part of his inheritance, and swore not to do so
at his coronation, but could alienate his crown and his kingdom"
(referring to the Treaty of Troyes). Later in this same work he said
that King John "swore at his coronation not to alienate anything"
and that "if anything had been alienated, he would recover it."[33]
This last statement begins to make us doubtful of Juvénal des
Ursins' accuracy because no other reference to John's coronation
oath of inalienability has ever turned up. Finally the whole edifice
of Juvénal des Ursins' evidence proves to be a house of cards that
collapses completely when he quotes the coronation oath, which he
does in a treatise on justice and the office of the chancellor (addressed to his brother, Guillaume Juvénal des Ursins, chancellor of
France): "And as far as the people are concerned, the king promises and swears the following: *Hec populo christiano et michi subdito in Christi nomine promitto: In primis, ut ecclesie Dei omnis
populus christianus veram pacem in omni tempore servet. Item ut
omnes rapacitates et omnes iniquitates omnibus gradibus interdicam. . . .*"[34] The text is that of the oath of the kingdom as we have
already seen it, but it does not contain the clause of inalienability
found in Charles V's Tiberius B.viii manuscript. Apart from the
king himself the two people in France who should have known
what the king swore at his coronation were the archbishop of
Reims and the chancellor of France. Given Jean Juvénal des Ursins'
emphasis upon a coronation oath of inalienability, his inability to
quote it verbatim is the clearest possible demonstration that it simply did not exist, that Charles VII did not swear it.

One should not be surprised at the conclusion that Charles VII did not swear the clause of inalienability or at Jean Juvénal des Ursins' inability to quote the coronation oath with the clause. Because there was no copy of the *ordo* of Charles V in Reims in 1429 it is likely, as we have seen, that the last Capetian *ordo* was used on that occasion, and the latter *ordo* had no clause of inalienability. By the time Louis XI was crowned in 1461, on the other hand, at least one copy of Charles V's *ordo* was available for consultation, and it was instrumental in devising the new ceremony, although this ceremony still lacked an oath of inalienability.[35]

It is true that less than a month after the ceremony at Reims Louis XI informed the Parlement of Paris that "we swore and promised at our consecration to defend the domain of our kingdom and of the Crown of France, that we would care for and augment it, and that we would reunite and return to our authority that that previously had been separated, alienated, and dismembered," and he made a similar assertion two years later.[36] Again we are faced with the problem of an oath that provides for both inalienation and revocation of alienations already made, and the king's statements, if true, lead to the conclusion that there was either some sort of suppressed oath or (as we shall see) an implied oath. We may delete from consideration the former possibility because the oath that Louis XI actually did swear survives in two separate sources, and neither of them contains an oath that differs in any significant respect from the oath of the last Capetian *ordo*. One source is the unusually credible work—one which can be described as a protocol ex post facto—of Jean Foulquart,[37] and the other is a document in the records of the Parlement of Paris. In 1482 Louis sent a copy of his oath to be registered by the Parlement, and through this act the oath has been preserved; Louis almost certainly did not swear inalienability at his coronation, probably because the copy (or copies) of Charles V's *ordo* available to him did not contain the clause of Tiberius B.viii.[38] It is a bit difficult to believe, nevertheless, that Louis was deliberately prevaricating in 1461, and after briefly glancing at the later coronations, we shall have to return in order to see just where in the coronation ceremony the principles of inalienability and revocation might have been hidden.

Throughout the sixteenth and the first half of the seventeenth centuries there are repeated allusions to the royal oath of inalienability. Hardly a reign passed but that someone, either officially or unofficially, declared that the king regnant had sworn inalienability. The coronation records, nonetheless, preserved through this whole time their stubborn silence on the matter, and on occasion they could be overwhelmingly persuasive. This is particularly true of Henry IV's oath because the careful description of, and commentary on, his coronation was impeccably composed by his coronator, Nicolas de Thou, bishop of Chartres. De Thou's description does not show any trace of an oath of inalienability, but it does contain the suggestive statement that Henry signed and deposited a copy of his oath with the Bishop of Chartres for conservation in the treasury of the cathedral church and in the archives of the cathedral chapter and the city hall.[39] The original with Henry's signature does not appear to be extant, but there is an eighteenth-century copy of the city's *registre de chartres* that, under the date of 16 March 1594 (Henry was crowned on 27 February), contains a copy in French of Henry's oath as taken from the original signed by the king and countersigned by one of his secretaries, just as Nicolas de Thou had claimed.[40] It hardly needs to be said that the manuscript does not contain the clause of inalienability. This evidence is as convincing as any might possibly be, and statements to the contrary by the *érudits*—which includes outstanding scholars like Pierre Dupuy—can only make one mistrust the latter. With possible exceptions, the scholars and royal officials did not deliberately falsify the evidence, but by the sixteenth century the notion of an oath of nonalienation and revocation had become so entrenched in the French public mind that it had become almost impossible to suppose that the oath had not contributed materially to the fabric of the Renaissance French constitution. Perhaps, however, that is doing an injustice to the Renaissance monarchy, and it may be that it is the modern scholars (from the seventeenth century on) who have been blinded by their own conception of oaths and their contents. If so, sixteenth- (and probably fifteenth-) century views of the coronation oath were quite different from what we have believed them to have been, and we must attempt to delineate those conceptions.

Modern scholars are not solely to blame if they have viewed the fifteenth- and sixteenth-century coronation oaths ahistorically, for part of the blame lies with Charles V and the clause he caused to be inserted into the manuscript of his *ordo*, Tiberius B.viii. By altering the oath as he did, Charles surely intended his change to be prescriptive; the clause of nonalienation seems appropriate in light of the Treaty of Brétigny. After the rediscovery of Tiberius B.viii in the seventeenth century, scholars finally had a specific clause of non-alienation to which they could point, and they confidently settled upon that clause as the text to which many late-medieval and six-teenth-century witnesses to the royal coronation oath of inalien-ability referred. The difficulty with the received view is that there is a complete absence of evidence for such an oath in the corona-tion records; Tiberius B.viii is, as far as can be now determined, the sole evidence for such an oath,[41] and it could not possibly have been used in France after 1424. Unless a whole host of capable people from Charles V's time on were blackguards and liars, they must have had something other than Charles V's clause of inalien-ability in mind when they referred to an oath of inalienability.

3. Inalienability in the Coronation Oaths

By eschewing the consideration of a specific clause of inalienability in the coronation oaths, we arrive at a completely different picture of the rise of the principle of inalienability in France. Almost from the very beginning of French interest in the subject the proponents of inalienability had urged general considerations rather than spe-cific words in support of their opinions. When Philip VI called an assembly to meet at Vincennes in 1329, the question of the alien-ation of some royal rights to the Church arose. Arguing for the royal party, Pierre de Cuignières urged that the king's coronation oath was one of the grounds for the monarch's inability to make the alienation: "Also, the king cannot relieve himself of such rights as is proven by numerous chapters in Distinction 10 [of Gratian's *Decretum*]. Just as the king swore at his coronation not to alienate the rights of the kingdom and to revoke alienations already made, so is he required by oath to revoke alienated rights whether they were in any way usurped by the Church or anyone else."[42] Cuigni-ères's allegation of canon-law principles, rather than of specific coronation oaths, is significant, for he thereby implied the general validity of the canonistic principles of inalienability in France.

Not all at Vincennes agreed with Cuignières, though, and the opposing view of the Church was ably presented by Pierre Roger (later Pope Clement VI), whose arguments were supported by Ber-

trand, cardinal of Saint-Clément. Again and again Roger attacked
Cuignières's assertion that the king had taken an oath of inalienability, and at one point, addressing the king, he very nearly
quoted the coronation oath as we know it from the last Capetian
ordo:

> . . . you swore only this and no more at your coronation, that
> is to say, that to the bishops and churches committed to
> them you would preserve the canonical privilege and due law
> and justice and that you would defend them as much as you
> were able.
>
> Also, that by your authority the whole Christian populace
> would preserve true peace for the Church of God at all times.
>
> Also, that you would forbid all rapacities and all iniquities
> of all degrees.
>
> Also, that you would enjoin justice and mercy in all
> judgments.
>
> Also, that in good faith you would be diligent in expelling
> from your land and jurisdiction the heretics damned by the
> Church.
>
> This you swore and no more, with due respect to lord Peter
> [de Cuignières], who has said that you swore one other
> thing.[43]

Through his precise identification of inalienability with a specific coronation oath, Roger would appear to have been on solid
ground, and if we had had similarly precise quotations of the coronation oaths of later kings—it must be remembered that Roger's
quotation dates from only a year after Philip's coronation—the
whole history of inalienability in France would undoubtedly have
long since been resolved more satisfactorily than has been the case.
Nevertheless, Roger and Saint-Clément could be just as general in
their argument as Cuignières, and both men denied that canon law
forbade alienations to the Church, citing not only canon but also
Roman law in support of their view.[44] This turned out to be highly
ironic, for, whereas there was no specific oath of inalienability
in France, it was canon and Roman law, to which feudal law was
sometimes added, that created the legal basis for making the royal
domain inalienable.

The essential step toward a generally applicable law of inalienability was taken late in Charles V's reign by the compiler of the

Somnium viridarii, which is so important for our knowledge of French political thought in the latter part of the fourteenth century. In claiming that there is a French oath of inalienability the author has the knight say that there are certain rights that, according to Roman law, are imprescriptible and that the regalian rights (*jura regalia*) are among them. Therefore, "the prince may not renounce such rights because he swears at his coronation not to alienate the rights of the kingdom (*jura regni*) and to revoke those alienated," according to the decretal *Constitutiones* and the following decretal "and the notes there [i.e., the glosses]" (*Decretum*, dist. 10, c. 4–5). The knight also urged that feudal law forbade alienations and that the canon law has a *casus expressus* on the matter, *Intellecto, de jurejurando*. In short, the knight argued that canon law not only forbade alienations but also that it required the revocation of previous alienations. Furthermore, citing the Romano-canonistic principle that *quod omnes tangit, ab omnibus debet approbari* (X.1.33.13), he says that a lord's subjects cannot be forced to accept a new lord unless they consent to him, and, turning to the *Libri feudorum*, he argues that feudal law expressly prohibits a lord from transferring a vassal's fief to another lord without the vassal's consent.[45]

When the French translation of the work, *Le songe du vergier* (which dates from ca. 1378), added a new chapter attacking the English claims to Guyenne, the text continued to rely on canon law for its opinions.[46] The opposing view, that is, that certain alienations were permissible, was presented by the cleric, who, like Pierre Roger half a century earlier, said that alienations to the Church were legal. The cleric cited Roman law and the example of the Donation of Constantine, but then he virtually nullified the legal value of his citations by saying that (1) the king cannot alienate his highest jurisdiction (*le ressort*), although *le ressort* could be lost by prescription of time, and that (2) the Donation of Constantine was not valid as a donation, but rather as "a form of remission or statement of good faith [*elle vault bien en forme de remission ou de recongnoissance de bonne foy*]."[47]

That the *Somnium viridarii* cited a coronation oath in support of inalienability, but did not quote precise words, is not surprising in view of what we now know about the inalienability clause in Charles V's *ordo*, and the work's legal argument for inalienability was anything but original. Not only was it preceded by Cuignières's argument half a century earlier, but also it was foreshadowed in a recent legal opinion. After his accession Charles V had taken the precaution of inquiring of the jurisprudents of Bologna as to whether Aquitaine could lawfully be separated from France. The Bolognese reply, favorable to Charles's cause, was delivered in 1369. Its arguments were based upon Roman and canon law, and it did not mention any coronation oath of either King John or Charles. This opinion of the Bolognese jurists, rather than the king's coronation oath, appears to have provided the specific legal evidence cited by the writer of the *Somnium viridarii* in arguing that the king had sworn an oath of inalienability.[48] Thereby at the end of Charles V's reign a legend began, a myth had its inception, and the myth was to grow into one of the strongest pillars of the developing French nation-state.

Inalienability, as discussed and defined in the *Somnium viridarii*, suffered remarkably little change in the following century and one-half. The theory became in all essential respects customary law by virtue of the long-held belief that the kings swore at their coronations not to alienate rights and to revoke those alienated. If the question was ever raised—but it does not seem to have been—as to where in the ceremony the king swore to maintain the Roman and canon law on inalienability, one had only to refer to the first of the royal oaths, the ecclesiastical oath with its promise to the bishops that the king would "protect the canonical privilege, due law, and justice" and that he "would defend each bishop and each church committed to him as much as [he was] able." That is what Louis XII had in mind in a letter he wrote in 1506: ". . . furthermore, that would be for me to contravene the first solemn oath I took at Reims when I was consecrated and crowned, which is to do everything that I can know to be for the good, the safety, and the conservation of my kingdom, without consenting to or directly permitting its diminution."[49]

Louis's use of the word *kingdom* had the sanction of long use in France, but it was still a rather vague word. After Louis XII, on the other hand, the monarchy began to use more specific concepts that were in accordance with the developing characteristics of the nation-state. In an ordinance of 1517 that revoked previous alienations, Francis I declared: "We are obligated, however, by constitution [*par constitution*] to protect and maintain our domain, as much as we are able and without alienation, in accordance with the oath to that effect that we took at our coronation and in accordance with the said constitution [*par ceste dite constitution*], which prohibits alienation; any transferral of this domain is forbidden and may not take place and should be revoked. . . ."[50] Medieval references to inalienability had tended to refer to rights; although the word *domain* was occasionally used, its sense seems to have been restricted to specific blocks of territory of usually no great extent or at least to those territories and rights that could be thought of as belonging personally to the king. When Francis referred to the domain he appears to have had the whole territory of the kingdom in mind, and the government of this whole territory was limited in some degree by a constitution, a "setting together" of certain implied laws, one of which was expressly said to be the law of inalienability of the domain. We would not normally expect to find the word *constitution* used in the sixteenth century, and in fact it had only a limited usage then, but its appearance in 1517 may hint at the underlying structure of the legal fiction we call the state, which, in turn, we cannot conceive of without the accompanying notion of territoriality. Territoriality, in its turn, implies some degree of inalienability, for if the whole of the territory of a state could be alienated, the state would necessarily cease to exist.

4. The Marriage of King and Kingdom

None of this was clear during the reign of Francis I, of course, and two further steps had to be taken before inalienability of the domain became sharply defined law. The first of these occurred at the coronation of Henry II in 1547, when, according to the description of the ceremony, the archbishop of Reims "blessed a ring (which had a singularly beautiful and rich diamond) with which the king married the kingdom, receiving it from the hand of the Archbishop of Reims on the medicinal finger of the right hand."[51] The marriage of the king and kingdom at the coronation was not just a play with words, symbols, and concepts, for the coronation was a deadly serious ceremony, and the fictional marriage directly brought Roman law to bear upon the French monarchy's prohibition of alienation.

The bestowal of the ring after the king's hands had been anointed and the gloves placed on them, and before the king was invested with the scepter, had been a part of the French ceremony since the mid-thirteenth century, when the bestowal was accompanied and followed by two prayers. In the *ordo* of Charles V the ring was also blessed before it was placed on the monarch's ring finger. Some scholars have seen in the fourteenth-century benediction the implication that already then the king was considered to be married to his kingdom.[52] Ernst H. Kantorowicz has demonstrated, however, that although the benediction was taken from the episcopal ceremony, and that although the bishop was considered to be married to the Church at his ordination, the benediction of the royal ring did not imply a marriage between the king and the kingdom. Kantorowicz argued convincingly that the fourteenth-century text did not have the marriage metaphor in mind because the decisive words of the episcopal bestowal were not borrowed for the royal ceremony.[53]

The marriage metaphor first appeared in a coronation ceremony, not for a king, but for a queen. The description of Anne of Brittany's coronation at Saint-Denis in 1504 says that when the consecrator placed the ring on her "first finger of the right hand, the said marriage ring signified and denoted that she married and took possession . . . of the kingdom of France. . . ."[54] It is difficult to know what sort of interpretation one should apply to the metaphor on this occasion. The idea of the ring as a symbol of the marriage bond is, of course, an old one,[55] and it would naturally have come to mind only two months after the wedding of Anne and Louis XII. The statement in 1504 may have meant no more than that the queen was elevated to a royal dignity through her marriage to the king and through her subsequent coronation, in which case the king and the kingdom would have been identical. The metaphorical marriage of the bishop to the Church may well have lurked in the background, but Anne's marriage to the kingdom does not appear to have possessed juristic content. All that we can say with confidence about the statement is that it introduced the marriage metaphor into the milieu of the coronation ceremony.

A decade later another Breton associated the marriage metaphor specifically with the king and by implication with his coronation oath. Alain Bouchart wrote in his *Grandes chroniques de Bretaigne* (1514) that "I have found in the sources six special insignia with which the kings ought to be adorned. First, there is given to the king a royal ring which signifies the faith that he promises to preserve properly for the commonweal of his kingdom as does the spouse for his wife [*qu'il promect droit garder à la chose publicque de son royaulme comme l'espoux à son espouse*], for the ring signifies faith and affection, which qualities ought not in any way be lacking in a king."[56] The promise Bouchart referred to is the ecclesiastical oath, which contains the phrase "just as a king ought properly to do in his kingdom." The marriage metaphor having thus been connected with the coronation oaths, the next step in casting the web interwove the idea of royal marriage to the kingdom with the concept of episcopal marriage to the Church.

This was done in 1538 by one of the best-known legal theorists of the first half of the century, Charles de Grassaille, in his *Regalian Rights of France*, which is rightly viewed as one of the main sources of French absolutistic thought. Grassaille wrote, "The king is said to be the spouse of the republic. . . . And it is said to be a moral and political matrimony, just as a spiritual matrimony is contracted between the Church and a prelate. . . . And just as a husband is the head of the wife and the wife is truly the body of the husband, so is the king the head of the republic and the republic is his body."[57] Grassaille's argument was not new, although it seems previously to have been ignored in France. Kantorowicz has shown that it was almost a verbatim quotation of parts of the argument of Lucas de Penna, a fourteenth-century Italian jurist whom Grassaille cited: ". . . a moral and political matrimony is contracted between a prince and the republic. Also, just as a spiritual and divine matrimony is contracted between the Church and a prelate, . . . so a temporal and terrestrial marriage is contracted between a prince and the republic. . . . Also, just as a husband is the head of the wife and the wife truly the body of the husband, . . . so the prince is the head of the republic, and the republic his body."[58] Grassaille's study was popular enough to be republished in 1545, just two years before Henry II's coronation, and the various strands were succinctly drawn together in the ring rubric in 1547.[59] Kantorowicz called that an "almost juristic rubric," a characterization that is particularly apposite.[60]

The juristic interpretation of the marriage metaphor had been provided in 1537 in a brief by Jacques Cappel, who argued before the Parlement of Paris that Francis I's alienation of Flanders to Charles V was illegal. Like the *Somnium viridarii*, Cappel referred specifically to Honorius III's decretal, and, again like the *Somnium viridarii,* he drew arguments from Roman law, although these were much more extensive in Cappel's brief than they had been in the earlier work.

> For, according to the Salic law and to customary, divine and positive laws, the holy patrimony of the crown and the old domain of the prince do not fall within the realm of the commerce of nations . . . and they are not transferable to any but the king, who is the husband and the political spouse of the commonwealth [*mary et espoux politique de la chose publicque*]; the commonwealth transfers the domain to the king at his consecration and coronation as a dowry of the crown; the kings solemnly swear at their consecration and coronation never to alienate this domain for any reason whatsoever, for it is inalienable according to *Intellecto, de jurejurando.*[61]

During the reigns of Henry II's sons numerous jurists picked up Cappel's views and supported them with additional evidence drawn mainly from Roman law (with a smattering of references to canon, feudal, and Salic law). In 1565 Jean Papon wrote, "The domain of the king is the true dowry that the commonwealth transfers to the king, its spouse in a political marriage."[62] Jean Bodin used the same terminology in his *Republic* (1576), and he reported an extensive use of the metaphor by a president of the Parlement at the Estates General of 1576 when he (the president) argued that alienation was forbidden.[63] The metaphor became a commonplace and appears many times in works published in the last quarter of the century and in the first half of the seventeenth century.[64]

The clearest association of the marriage metaphor with inalienability was made by Réné Choppin in his *Treatise on the domain of the crown of France* (1572), for Choppin associated marriage and inalienability with a specific Roman law, the Lex Julia. According to the Justinian interpretation of the Lex Julia, a husband did not have the right to dispose of his wife's dowry without her consent, and he could not mortgage it even with her consent. This law had become widely adopted in France in the Middle Ages before it was called into the service of French political thought in the sixteenth century. A principle of private law, it came, like other principles of private law, to be applied to public law, and for Choppin the king, as spouse of the kingdom, could not legally alienate the royal domain, his dowry: "For just as according to the Lex Julia the dowry that a woman brings to her husband in marriage is inalienable, so the patrimony and domain of the crown is like the inseparable dowry of the Republic."[65]

French interest in inalienability had first become intense during the first phase of the Hundred Years' War, when the principle had been formulated and commonly accepted. The reign of Francis I saw a renewal of that interest in the wake of military defeat by Charles V at Pavia and the subsequent Treaty of Madrid (1526). When the Parlement of Paris was asked in 1527 to register the treaty, by which Flanders, Artois, and Burgundy were to be "returned" to the emperor, it refused to do so, arguing that the royal domain was inalienable.[66] The treaty was not observed, but Francis again renounced his claims to Flanders and Artois in the Treaty of Crépy (1544). We know that Henry (II), by then dauphin, protested this treaty, and it is quite possible that, just as he was concerned with the condition of the coronation regalia and vestments,[67] he personally was responsible for the introduction of the marriage rubric into his *ordo*, which amounted already in 1547 to a declaration of inalienability.

Descriptions of the coronations of the three successors of Henry II either do not survive, or if they do they are so brief that we have no evidence that the marriage rubric was part of the ceremony in 1559, 1561, and 1575. Not until 1594 and the publication of Nicolas de Thou's description of Henry IV's coronation at Chartres did the ring and marriage rubric reappear, and then it was presented in its most elaborate form: "Because the king solemnly married his kingdom on the day of his coronation and was as if inseparably united with his subjects by the gentle, gracious, and loving bond of marriage, in order that they love one another mutually like spouses he was presented with a ring by the Bishop of Chartres as a token of that reciprocal conjunction. . . . [T]he Bishop of Chartres placed the ring, by which the king married his kingdom, on the fourth finger of his right hand, from which a particular vein proceeds to the heart."[68] In this passage De Thou strengthened the juristic implications of the marriage rubric, for the last sentence is almost a direct quotation from Gratian's *Decretum* (C.30.5.7), in which the canonist discussed the customs connected with matrimony.

We have good proof that the marriage rubric in the coronation ceremony of Henry IV had considerable juristic impact during the reign. When Henry became king of France he brought his patrimonial possessions in the Kingdom of Navarre with him. In 1590 Henry had published letters patent that provided that his patrimonial lands would not be united with the crown of France. The Parlement of Bordeaux registered the letters without difficulty, but the Parlement of Paris—then located at Tours—refused to do so. Jacques de la Guesle, the attorney general of the Parlement of Paris, invoked in his remonstrances the juristic fiction of a holy and political marriage at the accession of a king of France; therefore, he asserted, the patrimonial lands of the monarch became indivisibly united with the royal domain, and the king was bound to transmit to his successor all that he himself had received.[69] This argument did not please Henry, and he initiated a judicial discussion of the question. The Parlement of Paris still had refused to register the letters patent, and Henry was still administering his domain in Navarre as a separate domain when he was crowned in February 1594. Even after that date Henry continued to assert the separateness of his Navarrese domain, and in 1596 he published new letters patent renewing those of 1590. He did not give way until 1607, when he published an edict expressly revoking the letters patent of 1590 and uniting his patrimony with the royal domain. The intellectual antecedents of Henry's capitulation were clearly expressed in the edict's statement that Henry's predecessors "have contracted with their crown a sort of marriage commonly called holy and political, by which they have dowered the crown with all the lands that might belong to them."[70]

The rubric that claimed that the king married his kingdom when he received the ring did not remain long in the French coronation ceremony. Introduced at the coronation of Henry II in 1547 and expanded in 1594, it was mentioned again only in connection with the coronation of Louis XIII in 1610,[71] after which it dropped out of all *ordines* and descriptions of the coronation, although the ring itself continued to be blessed and bestowed until the end of the monarchy.

5. From Principle to Statute

The juristic fictions of the sixteenth century did not appeal to the seventeenth century—the Renaissance funeral ceremony with the effigy also disappeared after 1610[72]—and, in any case, the marriage metaphor as a source for inalienability had become redundant by the time the first Bourbon was crowned. Inalienability was manifestly acquiring increasing precision in the sixteenth century. When introduced in the Middle Ages, it had been rather nebulously based upon canonistic maxims that were equally vaguely associated with the coronation oaths. The ring-marriage rubric of 1547, on the other hand, carried a precise connotation that was carefully delineated by the lawyers of the second half of the century. The narrowing of general principles into specific law was completed by an edict promulgated at Moulins in 1566. The preamble to the edict recognized the uncertainty of inalienability up to that point and explains the grounds for the publication of the edict: "Since we promised and swore among other things at our consecration to protect and maintain the domain and royal patrimony of our crown, one of the principal nerves of our state, and to recover the portions and parts of it that had been alienated, . . . and since the rules and old maxims concerning the union and conservation of our domain are thought by some to be bad and are little known to others, we think it very necessary to collect and to organize them by articles and to confirm these to be general and irrevocable so that no one after this may doubt them."[73] The edict allows alienation in only two cases: (1) to create appanages for the eldest males of the royal house, and (2) on account of necessity of war, but then only after letters patent have been read and published in the parlements, and with the reservation of perpetual right of recovery. The edict of Moulins was followed a few years later by similar provisions in the edict published at Blois (1579) in response to a request of the Estates General of 1576.[74] These two edicts transformed the general principles of inalienability into positive law, and there could no longer be any doubt whatsoever that the royal domain was inalienable. Just as the legal implications of the ring-marriage rubric took precedence over the medieval conceptions of inalienability, so after 1566 positive statute took precedence over the ring-marriage rubric. The latter was a part of French political thought for a few more decades, but its symbolism and artificiality did not appeal to the modern world, and it disappeared from the political scene. Modern governments tend to appeal to specific laws rather than to general law, and the edict of Moulins is in that respect characteristic of a modern state.

It is a long way from the first appearance of inalienability of certain royal rights in France in the first part of the fourteenth century to the inalienability of the domain in the modern state. The development was a long, slow process reflective of the medieval monarchy's gradual metamorphosis into a modern state, and it was curiously inseparable from the coronation ceremony. Coronation evidence was invoked as early as 1329 by Pierre de Cuignières and as late as 1655 by Pierre Dupuy,[75] and coronation documents like Tiberius B.viii have caused the last several centuries of scholarship to misinterpret the origins of inalienability and its presence in the coronation ceremony.

A further source of modern misinterpretation may be proposed: the modern reliance upon maps. We are so accustomed to maps—of the Carolingian Empire, of the consequences of the Treaty of Verdun, of the Hundred Years' War—that we fail to realize that these maps would have meant little if anything to contemporaries. Cartography did not develop until the later fifteenth and sixteenth centuries, not because medieval man was incapable of producing maps, but because they were meaningless within the context of medieval government.[76] It is certainly a simplification to say that the medieval monarchs did not conceive of their kingdoms as the large blocks of territory we associate with the nation-state, but there is enough truth in the statement to warrant emphasizing it. Charles V's clause of inalienability, the clause that no king appears to have sworn, does not speak of the kingdom or of the domain, but of "sovereignty, rights, and nobility," or however one wishes to translate those vague, overlapping, partially redundant terms. The sixteenth century, on the other hand, spoke of "the domain of the king" or "of the crown," and it implied territorial extent and specific borders.[77] A modern historian has remarked that the political history of modern Europe is essentially a history of borders, and it is hard to imagine that having been the case before the genesis of the modern state with its presupposed territoriality and inalienability.

Throughout the early modern period the French government tended toward what we call absolutism, but the law of inalienability would seem to have limited the power of the king. This appearance of confinement may even have been partly what caused the deletion of the marriage metaphor from the coronation ceremony at Louis XIV's coronation in 1654. There were, nevertheless, other limitations upon royal power, limitations that were either potential or actual, and we could hardly begin to find the boundaries of French royal absolutism unless they too are examined. The confines imposed upon the royal right of pardon as exercised at the modern coronations show that the Bourbon kings of France were not as absolute as we might think.

THE RIGHT OF PARDON

· · · · · · · · · ·

The coronation ceremony must be regarded as more than the single ceremony that took place in the cathedral church of Reims (or Chartres in the case of Henry IV) on the day of the consecration and coronation. It was rather a whole series of ceremonies that extended over several days beginning with the king's arrival at Reims and concluding with the formal postcoronation entry into Paris. Although the freeing and pardoning of the prisoners in the prisons at Reims was visually one of the least spectacular of these ceremonies, it was one of the most impressive in view of the number of people involved, which at Louis XIV's coronation amounted to perhaps as many as 6,000 prisoners. Moreover, the freeing of the prisoners has its own contribution to make to an understanding of the conceptions of kingship and the nature of absolutism.

1. The Ceremony and Its Beginning

Owing to the length of the descriptions of the freeing of prisoners at Louis XV's coronation and to the survival of a manuscript copy of the records of that freeing in 1722, we are very well informed about the ceremony on that occasion. On 23 September 1722, over a month before Louis's coronation on 25 October, the king commissioned four nobles (among them, two counselors of the king) to examine the prisoners so that pardon would not be granted to those "unworthy of all pardon." On the next day a detailed instruction was drawn up for the commissioners; it noted, among other things, the crimes for which pardon was not to be given. The commissioners were to travel the projected route of the king from Versailles to Reims several days before the coronation, sending on to Reims the prisoners who had voluntarily entered the prisons in the cities along the route, and forbidding the jailors of the prisons in those cities to send on—and the jailors of the prisons in Reims to accept—any prisoners who might present themselves after the commissioners' passage.[1]

The commissioners left Paris on 5 October and traveled to—and visited the prisons in—Daumartin, Villers-Cotterêts (where there were no prisoners), Soissons (where they visited several prisons), and Fismes, arriving in Reims on 7 October (i.e., they traveled along the modern routes N2 and N31). After a delay of several days the commissioners began their interrogation of the prisoners in the presence of the grand almoner of France. The interrogations began on 16 October, but they were not completed until 28 October, three days after the coronation of the king. In each case the commissioners were to determine the names and surnames of the prisoners, their estate (*état exact*), the cause of detention, and the crimes for which they sought pardon, but, judging from the surviving copy of the *procès-verbaux*, not all of this information was obtained in every case. Those prisoners who were not qualified for pardon were to be sent to other prisons, but each of these was to be provided by the secretary of state with a safe conduct sufficient to enable the prisoner "to withdraw to wherever seems good to them," although the safe conduct could not be valid for more than three months. Lists (*rolles*) were made of the prisoners to be pardoned and of those to whom pardon was refused.[2] Of the 588 prisoners thus examined, 511 were granted pardon and 77 were refused pardon. Of those pardoned, three were charged with service in the king's troops.

On 29 October, Cardinal de Rohan, grand almoner of France, clad in his cape and rochet and accompanied by two of the king's almoners, went to the prisons of Reims to free the criminals granted pardon. He had the prisoners assemble, and then he "talked to them in a very touching fashion in order to urge them to merit by their conduct the pardon that the king had accorded them." He also apprised them of the king's orders to expedite their pardons without cost (they had already been warned by the examining commissioners to register their letters of pardon within three months) and to give to those who needed it the money to return home. When the cardinal left the prisons to return to the archiepiscopal palace, he "was followed by all these prisoners, who went to give the first testimonies of their acknowledgement by acclamations of 'Vive le Roi,' with which they made the whole neighborhood of His Majesty's apartment resound," a conclusion to the ceremony which certainly gives the impression of having been anything but spontaneous.[3]

Some writers have asserted that the freeing of prisoners at the coronation was very old, even as old as the monarchy, but in this they are mistaken.[4] Records of the coronation do not speak of the practice before the coronation of Louis XIII in 1610, and we know of it then only through a remark made by Charles de Remond, abbé de la Froenade, in his explication of the release of birds after the enthronement.[5] None of the other descriptions of Louis XIII's coronation speak of the prisoners. Although previous writers' silence on the subject does not prove that Louis's predecessors had not pardoned prisoners at their coronations, the probability that they did so is not high. One eighteenth-century writer, Nicolas Menin, did declare that at the coronation of Henry II in 1547 Philbert de Cossé, grand almoner of France, released all in the prisons of Reims, 445 prisoners.[6] Menin's statement has a ring of truth on account of the exact number he gives. Nevertheless, it has not been possible to find a source to verify his statement, and Menin errs in giving the wrong first name (which should be Philippe instead of Philbert) of the bishop of Coutances. Apart from the silence of the descriptions of Henry's coronation, the release of birds within the church after the enthronement in 1610 provides one other reason for doubting that Henry freed prisoners, as we shall see.[7] All in all, therefore, the pardoning of prisoners at the coronation seems to be a seventeenth-century development.

We know no more of the event in 1610 than that Louis did pardon criminals, but we are extensively informed about the pardoning at Louis XIV's coronation in 1654. As we have already seen, five volumes of manuscripts dealing with the subject survive. Although they do not give the details of the machinery for pardoning that the two volumes on Louis XV's pardoning give, they include many depositions written by the prisoners themselves and thus impart a much greater sense of spontaneity. It has been claimed that the grand almoner of France counted 10,000 prisoners released, but this is certainly an inflated figure.[8] The printed description of the coronation says that Louis released "more than six thousand" prisoners, but even this may be too high.[9] Volume 5 of the manuscript on the subject lists (and sometimes briefly notes the cases) of about 2,500 prisoners, while volumes 1 through 4 consist of depositions and *procès-verbaux* of about 1,000 prisoners.[10] Without going to the time-consuming and comparatively unrewarding effort of determining whether the 1,000 cases in the first four volumes are included in the lists in volume 5 (none of the volumes has indexes or even tables of contents), it is impossible to know how many prisoners are listed, but 3,500 would not be an inflated figure; nevertheless, since the records are incomplete, it is possible that as many as 6,000 prisoners were actually given pardons in 1654.

In terms of the sheer numbers involved, Louis XIV's coronation marks the zenith of the ceremonial pardoning. Louis XV freed fewer than 600 prisoners, and the number continued to fall at the last coronation of the Old Regime: the commissioners in 1775 examined 150 prisoners, of whom only 112 were considered worthy of the royal pardon.[11]

After the enthronement of Louis XVI, and accompanying the *Vivat rex*, the largesse, and the fanfares, there was another symbolic act, interpreted for us by one of the descriptions of the ceremony: "The fowlers thereafter released a large number of small birds, which by the recovery of their liberty signified the effusion of the sovereign's favors (*grâces*) over his people and that men are never more truly free than under the reign of an enlightened, just, and beneficent prince."[12] The author's explanation makes sense within the context of the ceremony—or at least within the context of the Enlightenment—but the liberation of birds within the church, a kind of subceremony within the subceremony of acclamation, had been practiced at every coronation since 1610, when, despite assertions to the contrary, it had first been introduced. Although at first glance little could seem more remote from pardoning of prisoners than the freeing of birds, such immediate impressions are often deceiving.

At Louis XIII's coronation some "seven or eight hundred sparrows, goldfinches, and other small birds that had been carried into the choir in cages and baskets" were let loose as the coronation jettons were distributed.[13] A contemporary eyewitness, the abbé de la Froenade, who appears to have been in the entourage of Marie de Médicis, interpreted the scene. "During these acclamations several birds were let go free in the church in order to testify to liberty and also to the mercy of the king, which was later extended to several criminals who owe their freedom only to his clemency. I was assured that the fowlers of Paris are required to furnish a certain number of birds for each coronation and that before the arrival of the king a single one is freed . . ., representing the dove which bore the Holy Ampulla to Clovis."[14] The abbé's informant was apparently misinformed himself, for there is no evidence for the freeing of the birds before 1610 (and nowhere is there any record that a single bird was released in memory of the fifth-century dove), and the introduction of the ceremony of the birds at the same time as the first pardon of prisoners at a coronation serves as reasonable proof of the correctness of the abbé's interpretation. At the succeeding coronations, although birds were released during the acclamations, the meaning of the practice had been forgotten, as in the case of Louis XVI's ceremony.[15] Here as elsewhere, most people quickly forgot the original meaning of a ceremonial innovation, which in this case had had the effect of tying into the ritual of the coronation itself the postcoronation demonstration of the king's mercy and power when he pardoned those in the prisons of Reims.

2. The History of the Pardoning Right

Of course one should not think that the king's power to pardon was new in 1610 or even that the ceremonial freeing of prisoners was a novelty then. Apart from the normal exercise of the royal power by the machinery of government in the course of a reign, the right of pardon was generally exercised on certain important occasions like Good Friday, the birth of a prince or princess, the marriage of the queen, or the first formal entry into a city.[16] In January 1456 François Villon, for example, requested pardon on the occasion of the birth of the princess Marie d'Orléans, and in order to be sure of obtaining it he made the request under two different names. A few years later, during the reign of Louis XI, the bishop of Orléans had Villon, by then a recidivist, imprisoned for theft; when at his accession Louis decided to travel through Meung-sur-Loire he freed all the prisoners in the city (including Villon) because it was his first *entrée* there.[17] This granting of pardon on the occasion of the first entry into a city is crucial to the introduction of the practice into the coronation ceremony. As early as 1223 Louis VIII is reported to have freed prisoners when he made his postcoronation entry into

Paris.[18] When Louis XIII freed prisoners in Reims in 1610 he did so presumably because he was making his first entry as king into the city on that occasion. At the same time, though, the practice of freeing birds was introduced into the coronation ceremony in order to symbolize the monarch's indulgence, and the consequent association of the liberation of those in the prisons of Reims with the coronation ceremony made the practice thereafter standard.

On the other hand, neither the power of the king to grant a general pardon, nor the interdiction against any but the king's granting pardon, nor perhaps even the right of the king as such to grant pardon appears to be very ancient in France. It has been argued that the Merovingian kings did not have the power of pardon and that the same is true of the Carolingian rulers (at least before 829). Even among the early Capetian monarchs the right of pardon was severely limited by the feudal system, for each lord possessed the right of pardon as one of his feudal rights, and the king's right was limited to his own domain.[19] This should in no way cause surprise when we take into account the fact that the early Capetians treated their domain more or less as a private patrimony in a way hardly distinguishable from the way in which other feudal lords treated their territories.[20] As the kings struggled with the feudal nobility they acquired the latter's rights, and during the captivity of John after Poitiers, when the regent Charles (V) apparently believed that he could exercise the right of pardon to the fullest extent, he found imposed upon himself three ordinances (dating from 1357, 1358, and 1360) that declared that the regent could not exercise pardon until after the Great Conseil had deliberated on the matter and two or three of its members had verified the fact by their signatures; the chancellor of France, the maîtres des Requêtes, and other officials were to swear that they would not seek any pardon outside the council.[21] That this series of ordinances was a deliberate attempt to control the regency and perhaps to limit the power of the crown is of no concern to us here; what is significant is that by then the regent believed that he possessed extensive powers of pardon.

Charles (V) may well have had legal grounds for believing that he possessed such powers. As early as 1308, Philip IV had granted a general pardon, perhaps the first instance of such clemency on the part of a French king. The *Grand coutumier de France*, compiled by Jacques d'Ableiges in the fourteenth century, said in a chapter on royal rights that to the king alone belonged the right of verifying and registering all pardons granted by him for any crimes or excesses.[22] This was not, be it noted, a claim for the exclusiveness of a royal right of pardon, which only gradually gained widespread acceptance. Charles, as regent, took a step in that direction in May 1359, when he forbade the great officers of the king to accord letters of pardon, and Charles VII went so far as to nullify all letters of pardon even if granted by the royal chancelleries, a provision which was part of the reform of the judicial system in 1454.[23] Nonetheless, at the beginning of the reign of Charles VI the duke of Berry was given the right to grant letters of pardon even to those guilty of lese majesty; in 1477, Louis XI accorded to the count of Angoulême the right to pardon the prisoners (with a few exceptions) in the cities in his domain upon the occasion of his first entry into them; and during the reign of Charles VIII, Anne of Brittany had the right to absolve ten persons of her choice on no fewer than forty-eight feasts.[24] The final step in the limitation of pardon to the king alone was not taken until Louis XII promulgated his reforming edict of March 1499. The ordinance limited to the king and his successors the right to grant pardons, and it revoked in perpetuity any such rights that anyone might have from him or his predecessors, a restriction that was repeated in the even longer reform edict of November 1507.[25] Louis's legislation was efficacious, and when Francis I wanted to accord the right to his mother, the Parlement of Paris, in the sixteenth century the zealous defender of royal prerogatives, protested and argued that the right was one of the best marks of sovereignty.[26] This did not prevent Francis from granting to Emperor Charles V the right to exercise pardon in France, and the emperor did use this power before the end of the year (1539), an episode that is no less unusual than the permission given to Charles to move his troops through French territory, and that does not detract from the rule that by the reign of Francis I it was possible to say truly that "the right of pardon belongs only to the king."[27]

Historians have been little concerned with the origin of the French right of pardon, particularly as it relates to the coronation. In 1615 Laurens Bouchel thought that its inspiration was partly biblical, and he cited the passage in which David says, ". . . shall there any man be put to death this day in Israel? for do not I know that I am this day king over Israel" (II Samuel 19:22). This rather farfetched derivation of the French practice from the clemency of David on the day of Absalom's death was only slightly improved upon by Nicolas Menin in 1723 when he cited Saul's words on the day of his accession ("There shall not a man be put to death this day: for today the Lord hath wrought salvation in Israel" [I Samuel 11:13]) as the source of the French right.[28] Those who saw the origins of the right in the Roman Empire may have been in some ways a bit closer to the truth. They often cited two classical literary sources: Seneca, who discussed pardon and clemency and the difference between the two, but who did not describe the Roman practice;[29] and Suetonius, who said that the emperors sold pardons (Vespasian, 16) and that Claudius ordered an amnesty for all (except for a few tribunes and centurians) for everything done during the first two confused days of his reign (Claudius, 11). Comparatively recent scholarship has not been too persuasive in its survey of the Roman development of the pardoning right. One writer believed that the emperors exercised the right by virtue of their office of Pontifex Maximus, and another that it was by virtue of the *lex regia* (he cited Ulpian on Codex 1.4.4 in support of his contention).[30] Another scholar said that the first emperors often accorded a general pardon (*lex oblivionis*) at the beginning of their reigns, but that this was not practiced after Diocletian; furthermore, he notes, the laws under the title *de generali abolitione* in the Justinian corpus (Codex 9.43), which were the Roman law sources most often cited for the French practice, do not provide for a true pardon, but only an *indulgentia generalis* in that they grant but a thirty-day delay of the processes against guilty senators.[31] None of these scholars attempts to do more than to show a certain similarity between ancient Roman and French practices, so their work is of little use to the historian.

In all this presumed derivation of the French law from the Roman, modern historical research has taken its cue from the incredibly influential—and often incorrect—views expressed by Jean Bodin in the *Republic*. In Book I,10, Bodin discussed at length pardon as the fifth mark of sovereignty; seeing the right of pardon as associated with sovereign authority in all times and all places, he devoted little space to the development of the right in France except to give a few scattered examples from French history. Instead, he adduced Roman law as the source of the French right, and in this he was followed by numerous seventeenth- and eighteenth-

century authors.[32] When Laurens Bouchel published his reference
work on French laws in 1615, he cited Justinian's Codex 9.42–43
and Digest 48.16 for the source of the right of pardon in general
and Digest 48.16.12 as the source of the general pardon given
at the coronation. A few years later Cardin Le Bret likewise cited
the Digest as the source for the Roman—and presumably for the
French—practice. Jacques Godefroy, reputedly the most learned
jurist of the first half of the seventeenth century, traced the freeing
of prisoners at the time of the coronation at Reims back to a law of
Constantine that had been put into effect (supposedly) in France
by Clovis. Even as recently as 1893 a student of legal history tried
to argue that the French right was derived from Roman law.[33] The
Roman law milieu in which French law often developed does make
it possible that Romanistic studies changed the course of French
development even though they may not have originated that development, if not for the whole right of pardon, at least for the kind of
general pardon granted on public occasions. For such general pardon there is no evidence before 1308,[34] by which time the Justinian corpus was widely known and used in French legal and royal
circles. It is undeniable that Roman law determined in part the
kinds of crimes that could or could not be pardoned by the monarch, but before that issue can be addressed, something must be
said about the machinery of the royal pardon.

3. The Judicial Treatment of Pardons

By the time the kings began to exercise a general pardon at their
coronations (1610) the administrative machinery of pardoning
had become quite well developed. The Old Regime distinguished
between seven types of letters of pardon (*lettres de grâce*). The one
that was accorded at a coronation was the *lettre d'abolition*, which
took its name from *abolitio* in Roman law. Such a letter, which
corresponded to the modern amnesty, might be accorded either
before or after a condemnation and sentencing, and it might apply
either generally or to an individual.[35]

A person who had obtained a *lettre d'abolition* was not thereby a
free man, though. The letter had first to be presented to and ratified (*entérinée*) by the proper tribunal, and in the case of a pardon
granted at a coronation, this had to be done within three months of

the date of the letter (up to six months could be allowed for other pardons). The bearer of the letter (nobles included) had to present his document while bareheaded and on his knees, and he had to swear under oath that the information contained therein was correct. He then returned to prison until proper inquiries as to the veracity of his statements were made and until the letter was ratified; in the eighteenth century at least three judges had to pronounce on the confirmation of the letter, after which its bearer would be released from prison. If the information in the letter was incomplete, or if the crime was worse than indicated, extraordinary proceedings were to be started on the basis of subreption or obreption of the letter. With the kinds of fees required by the monarchy's judicial and penal systems, a criminal who had been granted a letter of pardon could thus find himself heavily burdened financially, but in the case of the coronations that cost was relieved by the royal provision that the pardons were to be expedited without cost and that the prisoners who needed money should be given enough to enable them to return home.[36]

Owing to this judicial procedure and a peculiarity of the pardons granted at the coronations, a person who had not previously been apprehended or imprisoned might actually be incarcerated after having obtained the king's pardon. As a coronation approached, royal officials advertised throughout the kingdom that the king would grant pardons at his coronation (this may not have been the case in 1610, about which we have no details), and criminals from both within and without (i.e., those in exile) the kingdom voluntarily admitted themselves to the prisons of Reims (or of several other cities on the route to Reims in the case of Louis XV).[37] In some cases these people had never been prosecuted, and in a few instances their crimes had not even come to the attention of the authorities. All prisoners were liberated at the coronation, but since they had to remain in prison from the time they presented their letters of pardon until the letters were ratified by the tribunals, the royal pardon did sometimes lead to a novel experience. Even then, not every prisoner who had received a letter of pardon could be assured of his subsequent freedom, for the king's power of pardon did not extend to all crimes.

4. Restrictions upon the Right

The exclusion of certain types of criminal behavior from the pardoning right is a most interesting limitation upon the authority of
the king. There is no particular reason to believe that the monarchs themselves willingly allowed their power thus to be circumscribed, and this is clearly true of the first general law of the sort,
the ordinance that was wrested from the Dauphin Charles as lieutenant general of the kingdom by the Estates General in March
1357.[38] In that ordinance Charles promised not to grant pardons
for a whole host of serious crimes: premeditated murder and muti-
lation of members; rape or abduction of women whether nuns,
married women, or maidens; arson of churches or premeditated
arson elsewhere; violation of truces, safe-conducts (*asseuremens*),
or sworn peaces; and transgression of safeguards (granted to monasteries, etc.). Charles furthermore promised that if by importunity
pardons had been received for such crimes, they were to be null
and void.[39] The kinds of crimes listed clearly show the Estates'
intent to bring some sort of security to the troubled countryside,
but the dauphin could hardly have been happy with the resulting
limitation of his freedom of action. A few years later (March 1360)
Charles appeared to place a vaguer limitation upon himself and his
government by forbidding the presidents of the Parlement of Paris
to honor all pardons given by him or his "lieutenants, constables,
marshals, masters of the crossbow, or captains" if such pardons
were given "without just and reasonable cause or against the well-
being of justice or to the prejudice and damage of mylord the king,
of us [Charles], or of anyone else whomsoever."[40] This mandate
was general enough not particularly to limit the king, and Charles's
intent was obviously to discourage the granting of pardons in the
king's name. The royal reaction was to prove effective until the
sixteenth century, when a new set of circumstances began to elicit
the emplacement of permanent boundaries around the royal pardoning right.

The first limitation of this novel type dates from February 1566
in an ordinance on judicial reform promulgated by Charles IX at
Moulins during the early stages of the Wars of Religion when the
judicial system was beginning to break down. The ordinance provided that anyone who resisted or hindered (*outrager ou exceder*)
a judicial officer in the execution of his duty should be punished by

death, that he should not be given a letter of pardon (*grâce ou rémission*), and that, if he did manage to obtain such a letter, it should be disregarded, stipulations that were repeated a few years later, in 1572.[41] They were again repeated in May 1579 in the administrative ordinance drawn up for Henry III in response to the complaints of the Estates General that had met at Blois in 1576. The ordinance made the crime more serious than before by providing that "those guilty of such crimes shall be rigorously punished without hope of mercy as having directly attacked our authority and power," which had the effect of assimilating the crime to lese majesty. Unfortunately for his own reputation, the last of the Valois kings aroused such passions and dislikes in his own time that even today the positive merits of his legislative action are hardly appreciated. In fact, his treatment of the pardoning right was to be greatly influential upon later legislation. Not only did this ordinance follow its predecessors in making obstruction of justice an irremissible crime, but also it forbade all princes and other lords to intervene with the king to be lenient in such matters, and, highly significantly, it provided that any letters of pardon that might be extracted from the king by importunity should be disregarded, as should be any jussive or derogation (*jussion ou dérogation*) that the ruler might later grant contrary to the present ordinance.[42] The edicts of Charles IX had prevented the royal officials from granting pardons in such cases, but Henry III's ordinance was the first to extend that limitation to the king himself and to protect it against future royal transgressions of the limitation, a voluntary restriction of the royal power that remained in effect throughout the Old Regime. Such had not been the case during the reign of Francis I when he forbade his courts to give letters of pardon to homicides but reserved the right of pardon to himself: "the offenders may and ought to have recourse to the sovereign prince in order to receive pardon."[43]

The ordinance of 1579 began to curtail even this royal reservation with its provision that premeditated murders (*pour les meurtres de guet-apens*), whether avenging themselves for quarrels or otherwise murdering, should not be granted pardon, a restriction that was extended to anyone who accompanied such murderers; if letters of pardon were granted to these, they were to be ignored even if signed by the king and countersigned by the secretaries of state. The ordinance furthermore forbade that letters of pardon, though signed by the secretaries of state, should be valid if granted to assassins or to those who hired assassins whether or not the crime was successfully completed; the king did not attempt to strip himself of the right to pardon these latter crimes, however.[44]

The novelty of the restriction upon the king's pardoning right is clear despite Jean Bodin's recent (1576) discussion of pardon as one of the marks of sovereignty. Bodin's argument at first appears, as usual, to be rather confusing. At the beginning of his discourse he wrote, "From this marke of Majestie, and benefit of supreame Appeale, dependeth also the power to grant grace and pardon unto the condemned . . . be it for life, be it for goods," etc., and he further wrote that kings have "thought nothing more royall, than to deliver the condemned from death," implying that the royal pardoning right was indeed unlimited. It certainly included lese majesty, a capital crime (as are all the crimes we have discussed so far): "But of all the graces and pardons that a prince can give, there is none more commendable than when he pardoneth the injurie done against his owne person: and of all capitall punishments none is more acceptable unto God, than that which with most severitie is executed, for the wrong done unto the majestie of himselfe." At one point, nonetheless, Bodin had urged that the sovereign's pardoning right is limited: "But I am of opinion (saving alwaies the better judgement) that no soveraigne Prince, nether yet any man a live can pardon the punishment due unto the offence which is by the law of God death, no more then he can dispence with the law of God, whereunto he is himselfe subject," which might seem to contradict what he otherwise said, but which should in no way surprise those who are aware of the basic assumptions underlying—and basic limitations applying to—the great compiler's concept of sovereignty.[45] Exactly what Bodin meant by the "law of God," a phrase that he often employed, is difficult to know, for, like his conception of natural law, his definition of divine law was nowhere clearly spelled out.[46] It appears, though, to refer to the Pentateuchal legislation as, for example, in his discussion of premeditated murder: ". . . how can he [the prince] then pardon the wrong done unto almightie God? or the murther wilfully committed; which by the law of God is death, for all the pardon he can give. . . . Or whereas by the law the punishment for theft is death, the good prince may convert that punishment into the restitution of foure fold, which is the punishment by the law of God appointed" (cf. Exodus 22:1). He then quotes the Deuteronomic law as preventing pardon of a premeditated murderer: "But the wilfull murderer *You shall take him* (saith the law) *from my sacred altar, neither shalt thou have pitie on him, but cause him to dye the death: and afterwards I will stretch forth my great mercies upon you*" (with a marginal reference to Deuteronomy 19 and 21).[47] Bodin's derivation of limitations from the Old Testament was not adopted by other writers, despite the popularity of the *Republic*. As additional crimes were made irremissible, the sources cited for them were normally the Roman law.

At the beginning of the seventeenth century there was some doubt as to whether certain crimes were indeed irremissible. In 1615, Laurens Bouchel, who knew his legal material well, noted that there were irremissible crimes mentioned in the Roman law but that some of these were sometimes remitted by the "pleine puissance du Roy" and that these abolitions emanated from the "pleine souveraineté, et propre mouvement du Roy." Nonetheless, he remarked, the authors of the Roman law saw otherwise, and the Greeks disagreed among themselves, although he finds evidence for the French practice in the example of a letter of pardon that had been granted for a homicide.[48] Only two years later Bouchel's dilemma was more or less officially solved by Bernard de la Roche-Flavin. Since the latter was a practicing judge—he had been counselor of the king in the Privy Council and in the Council of State, counselor in the Parlement of Paris, and for thirty-six years first president of the Chambre des Requêtes of the Parlement of Toulouse—his opinions on legal matters carry a great deal of weight for early seventeenth-century opinion. La Roche-Flavin cited three royal ordinances as evidence for the irremissibility of two crimes: Charles IX's edicts of 1566 and 1572 concerning those who hindered the officers of justice, and Henry III's edict of 1579 concerning assassins. The fifteenth-century civilian, Andreas Barbatia, was cited as the source for the general rule that those guilty of capital crimes might not be pardoned, but when La Roche-Flavin turned to a listing of individual capital crimes, he extracted every one of them from the Justinian corpus.[49] Even the greatest apologist for absolutism in the first half of the century, Cardin le Bret, admitted that the Roman law had declared certain crimes to be irremissible.[50]

The most flexible of the Roman laws cited by La Roche-Flavin was *Nemo deinceps* (Codex 1.4.3), which declared irremissible the crimes of divine lese majesty, the rape of virgins, parricide, homicide, and sacrilege. Parricide was also irremissible by virtue of the law *Si quis in parentis* (Codex 9.17.1), but La Roche-Flavin cited Digest 48.9.1 to show that this crime included the murder of brothers, sisters, uncles, aunts, and a number of other relatives. Codex 9.9.31 made sodomy a capital and irremissible crime, as was counterfeiting by virtue of Codex 9.24.2, which also declared the latter crime to be lese majesty. Lese majesty in general was made irremissible by Codex 9.8.5.

None of these crimes that had their basis in Roman law was listed in the great criminal edict of 1670, which determined the system of French criminal justice until the end of the Old Regime. That edict declared that only involuntary homicides should be pardoned, and that no letters of pardon should be given for duels, premeditated assassination (including anyone involved in any way with the assassination), forced abduction, or the obstruction of officers of justice.[51] Nonetheless, all of the crimes that La Roche-Flavin said the Roman law declared irremissible were listed in 1722 among the crimes that Louis XV would not pardon at his coronation (with the exceptions of parricide and sodomy, which were considered so serious that it was probably thought unnecessary to list them).[52] The Roman law has long been considered to have provided an essential element in the rise of absolutist monarchy, but it was not generally recognized until recently that that same law, which had become in the Justinian corpus a tolerably equitable result of a millenium of legal development, could provide some of the principles that could limit the authority of the king; we have already seen one example of this in the development of the inalienability of the domain. The limitations on the king's pardoning right provide another example, the efficacy of which may be tested by means of individual cases of prisoners granted or refused pardon at the coronations of Louis XIV and Louis XV.

5. Application of the Restrictions

The first four volumes of the records of 1654 contain more or less extensive descriptions of around 1,000 cases (actually 1,513 cases are numbered, but a fair number of them are duplicate or triplicate depositions of a single case).[53] Some of the cases date as far back as 1639 (V, 166), but most of them date from 1648 or 1650 or later, that is, to the period of the Fronde with its general growth of violence throughout French society and its weakening of governmental authority. Crimes pardoned in 1654 included many cases of duels and unpremeditated encounters leading to homicide (e.g., I, 1–2, 6–7, 34, 88, 251), as well as numerous tavern brawls resulting in death (e.g., I, 95); because the edicts against dueling treated chance encounters leading to death as duels, we must conclude that the king considered his pardoning right to extend to dueling despite the fact that duelers had been declared by royal edict to be guilty of lese majesty.[54] Other crimes pardoned were involuntary manslaughter—whether in self-defense (I, 83), which is only to be expected, or accidental (I, 136)—and at least one case of horse theft (I, 154). Some were pardoned who had committed crimes that to us might seem relatively mild; one poor man had been sentenced to a fine and life service in the galleys for diverting water for his parents from a meadow that belonged to them (I, 16). Others seem to have been only partially pardoned; a seventeen-year-old youth in Reims had been sentenced to make a due apology (*amende honorable*) and to pay a pecuniary fine for having sworn and blasphemed the name of God; *accordée* was usually noted for those prisoners granted pardon, but in this case *gratis* was written instead, meaning, presumably, that the monetary fine was remitted, but that the youth still had to perform the *amende honorable* (V, 169). As far as the more serious crimes were concerned, at least one recidivist was pardoned (V, 166^v–167), as was at least one case of first- or second-degree murder (I, 186), but the descriptions of the cases are often so brief that it is impossible to determine whether there might have been mitigating circumstances that made it possible to accord a pardon.

The examining officials themselves had difficulty determining the severity of some crimes. For example, in 1648 a certain Pierre Coulourna was traveling a high road with a friend when a dispute arose with a local type named Jean Bedrene, who struck Coulourna's friend twice with a knife, which caused the latter's death soon thereafter. Coulourna then got a gun with which he killed Bedrene; for that Coulourna was condemned to death, but because he had just served six years in the army he had apparently used that means of avoiding the execution of the sentence. There are three depositions of the case: the first noted "accordé à servir," that is, the pardon should be granted provided that Coulourna continue his military service; the second denied the pardon but allowed Coulourna to be released from prison; and the third noted "accordé à la charge de servir pendant deux ans," coming to the same decision as the first but limiting the required service to two years (II, 363–64, 366). The requirement of military service for a prisoner accorded pardon was not at all uncommon (e.g., I, 181, 194, 273; II, 317), but it seems to have been demanded primarily of those who were homicides and enlisted in the military.

That the king's pardoning right was limited is shown by a number of criminals to whom pardon was not granted. One was a case of incest between a woman and her stepfather, for which she was sentenced to perpetual imprisonment in a convent and he to nine years in the galleys; her request that she be given her liberty was refused (I, 40). Another was a case of fratricide: Denis Comine was condemned to death for having killed his brother after the latter had beaten him with a club (*baston*) (II, 352). Alexandre François de Chalus at the age of sixteen had killed the second wife of his now-dead maternal grandfather because she had said repeatedly that his mother was a whore and because she had refused to give him his money so that he could serve the king; Chalus was not accorded pardon, probably either because the murder was premeditated or, more likely, because it came under the prohibition of familial homicide (I, 275). Denys Joly, who had counterfeited several letters and seals of the Petite Chancellerie, for which he had been condemned in perpetuity to the galleys, did not receive a pardon for a crime that was lese majesty (III, 833).[55] Finally we may note the case of Jacques de Bane, who wanted the confirmation of a letter of pardon that he had been given in December 1651 for participating in a duel of four against four; the refusal to confirm it probably resulted from Bane's failure to present the letter for confirmation until 19 July 1652, after the six-month limit had passed (II, 411).

The inability of a prisoner to obtain a pardon at a coronation did not mean that he was forced to remain in prison. The Tournelle (the criminal court of the Parlement of Paris) had long held that anyone who voluntarily rendered himself prisoner in the hope of obtaining the king's pardon at his first *entrée* into a city, but who was not pardoned, could require that he be released from the prison. That right could not be exercised, though, if the criminal had already presented a letter of pardon for ratification, in which case he was considered to have voluntarily made himself subject to the jurisdiction in which the court was located until such time as the decision was made as to whether or not the letter of pardon should be ratified.[56] The same rules were maintained at the coronations after the freeing of prisoners had been introduced there, and all of the prisoners who were not accorded pardon (whether full pardon or limited by the obligation to serve in the army) were freed (*eslargi*) from the prisons.

A detailed examination of the cases in 1654, which is not possible here, would doubtless give an exact idea of the limitations upon the royal pardoning right then. In general, though, it seems that the most serious crimes—lese majesty, incest, and fratricide and other familial homicides—were in fact unpardonable. On the other hand, some premeditated murderers and duelers, who were supposed to be unpardonable, were pardoned. By the time Louis XV was crowned in 1722 the limitations on the king's right were more exactly observed.

The instructions for those commissioned to examine the prisoners in 1722 carefully excluded from the king's pardon those "who are charged with the crimes of divine and human lese majesty, dueling, counterfeiting, abduction, rape, desertion, premeditated murder [*assassinat de guet-apens*], highway robbery, premeditated arson, fraud [*faussetés*] committed by public officials in the exercise of their duties, and armed and organized commerce in illegal salt or contraband, as well as those condemned to prison by order of the Marshals of France."[57] The records of the pardoning in 1722 were much better kept and summarized than those of 1654, and of 588 prisoners examined, 511 were given a pardon and 77 were refused. A random sampling of twenty-three cases of those refused pardon (i.e., all those refused pardon in the first of the two volumes of the records) does not provide examples of every one of these crimes, although it does for most of them. There are three cases of human lese majesty: a goldsmith who bought goods stolen by an officer of the king (and presumably from the king) (no. 47); disobeying a *lettre de cachet* (no. 249); and escape from prison (no. 63).[58] There were three cases of counterfeiting (nos. 53, 140, and 229), two cases of dueling (nos. 134 and 204), one case of desertion (no. 12), two to five cases of premeditated murder (nos.

205 and 215, and probably nos. 74, 176, and 208), and one case
of probable highway robbery (no. 174, which is described only as a
nocturnal theft with murder of the victim). Also not pardoned were
one case of fratricide or familial homicide (no. 221), one case of
recidivism (no. 159), one case of piracy (?—no. 187—the criminal
had stolen a salt-ship belonging to a *fermier général,* so the crime
might have been considered lese majesty), and one case of sodomy
engaged in upon several occasions (no. 56—the criminal was sentenced to twenty years in prison and to death, which was presumably to follow the imprisonment). One priest was refused pardon
for having attempted to seduce a girl in his parish (no. 185), as
was another priest who had been condemned at the age of fifty-
four to be hanged and burned for having used the confessional to
seduce and have sexual relations with several women and girls of
the village (no. 183). One person's request for the repeal of the
lettre de cachet that forbade him from returning to Paris was denied (no. 221), and, finally, pardon was refused to a man who had
gotten a number of soldiers of the guards to extract by force some
money that belonged to him (no. 255).

It is impossible to say why pardon should have been denied to
some of these criminals, and it is also impossible to determine why
pardon should have been granted to some others. There were at
least two cases of pardons granted to men who had killed in sword
fights (nos. 28 and 241). The first was a spontaneous fight, but the
edicts against duels made that sort of combat punishable as a duel;
the second was never tried for his homicide, which may account for
the pardon granted four years later in 1722. All in all, though, the
impression that one gets from the records of 1722 is that few, if
any, serious crimes were pardoned unless there were clearly mitigating circumstances (and not always even then), that the administration of criminal justice was much more strict than it had been
three-quarters of a century earlier, and that the king's pardoning
power was much more severely restricted than it had been at the
end of the struggles of the Fronde.

That the king's power of pardon was not complete might seem
surprising in the light of the normal custom in the modern nation-
state for the chief executive officer to exercise that power without
any legal limitation. Certainly the apologists for absolutist government, men like Bodin or Le Bret or Bouchel, argued that the king's
pardon resulted from his full power, and La Roche-Flavin quoted

Seneca to the effect that the power to save men from death was such an excellent gift that the gods granted it only to kings and sovereign princes.[59] Nevertheless, the concepts of *pleine puissance* and sovereignty must be interpreted within their early modern context and not confused with the political thought associated with the contemporary nation-state—however absolute the monarchy of the seventeenth and eighteenth centuries might seem, it was an institution very different from the totalitarian horrors of the twentieth century and even from the less capricious forms of modern government.

The French monarchy was limited by its customs and by its own legal system. In defining absolutistic kingship we must distinguish between the king who was theoretically absolute in the thought of the political theorists, the king who was de jure absolute (which he was not, because he was limited by laws), and the king who was de facto absolute (which he was to the extent that he could normally intervene with impunity into many matters of government, but which he was not in that he usually allowed his government to take its own course and in that he was bound by those social constrictions—both noble and popular—that survived whatever attempts he might make to mold and modify public opinion and practices). The very existence of a complicated and carefully conceived legal and administrative machinery could not help but reduce the monarch's sphere of action.

Despite its limitations, the freeing of prisoners at the coronation was a symbolic act with certain constitutive implications. The coronation may not have been, strictly speaking, constitutionally necessary, but by virtue of his coronation the king entered into possession of his full authority and made flesh the principle of dynastic succession. The proof of the latter lay in the king's ability to touch for scrofula after his coronation, and the royal thaumaturgic power demonstrated the legitimacy of the monarch. The proof of the former lay in the king's pardon of prisoners after his coronation, and this postcoronation ceremony was both a demonstration and a proof of the ruler's power and authority. It is assuredly no accident that this demonstration was introduced into the coronation ceremony in 1610, the year that may be taken as marking the final transition from the medieval, feudal monarchy toward the modern, dynastic monarchy, as was manifested in the ceremony of the sleeping king's emphasis on the kingship given by God.

The ceremonial pardoning of prisoners did not cease with the disappearance of the monarchy. To note the most recent examples, the first official act of the presidents of the Fifth Republic is usually to declare an amnesty,[60] thus continuing the practice introduced at the royal coronation in 1610, and in a certain sense the French presidents of the Fifth Republic are, in a state avowedly democratic, the successors of the Bourbon kings of a state supposedly absolutistic. Despite revolutions, constitutional vicissitudes, legal reforms, and a succession of presumably contrasting governments, there is more continuity to French history than people are often willing to admit. This does not mean that one should confuse republican presidents with their royal predecessors, for the presidents govern, at least in theory, "in the name of the people." Even the kings, though, had "the people" to contend with, and the revival in the sixteenth century of a high medieval element of election by the people created a problem that contributed to the near destruction of the kingdom after the assassination of Henry III in 1589.

8

ELECTION AND CONSENT OF THE PEOPLE

. . . .

Early in 1589, not long after the duke of Guise was murdered, the Catholic League named the duke of Mayenne "lieutenant general of the royal state and crown of France" until an Estates General, which was called for July, could meet. This meeting of the Estates General, as well as others called for 1590 and 1591, failed to take place, and only in early 1593 was the League able to have its adherents gather in Paris for an Estates General. The letter that Mayenne sent out calling for the election of deputies carefully avoided saying that the main purpose of the assembly was to elect a king, and in his public declaration of December 1592 Mayenne had been equally cautious. Nonetheless, there was no doubt in anyone's mind as to why the Estates were called to Paris. As soon as the deputies arrived, the partisans of the various candidates for the throne—the young duke of Guise, Mayenne, the duke of Nemours, the marquis of Pont, the duke of Savoy, even the king of Spain— worked for the election of their particular candidate.[1] But did the Estates General have the right to elect a king?

It would hardly occur to modern historians to think that the French monarchy was elective, certainly not in the way that the Holy Roman Empire was. From Hugh Capet to Henry III the nearest surviving male heir had succeeded his predecessor. That there was a "juristic basis of dynastic right to the French throne" has been demonstrated by Ralph E. Giesey in his work of that title, although Giesey's study also shows how complicated the law of royal succession was in France.[2] How then did some in the sixteenth century come to believe that it was legal to elect a king in France? That a theory of election was propounded in the sixteenth century is fairly well known, but the development of that theory, its arguments, the sources upon which it was based, and the role of the coronation ceremony are little known, as are the extent to which and the ways in which the theory was attacked. Upon examination, these problems provide some interesting examples of the reciprocal influences of political thought and political action, and they show how far attempts to limit the king could go.

1. The Theory of Election

A number of scholars and apologists developed the theory of elective kingship over the course of several decades. As early as 1484, Philippe Pot, sieur de la Roche, had suggested vaguely in his speech before the Estates General that the monarchy formerly was elective, and he had argued specifically that the people were above the king. Statements like that were rare, though, and even the somewhat radical sieur de la Roche quickly admitted that the law of succession had changed since ancient times.[3] There is some evidence that election of the king was a topic of debate at the University of Paris in the 1550s, but unfortunately we do not know the content of those discussions.[4] What appears to be the first full-fledged exposition of royal election appeared only in 1573 in one of the best-known works of the sixteenth century, the *Francogallia* of François Hotman.

Hotman, who was an *historiograph du roi* for a time, focused his attention upon the history of Frankish institutions, which he thought showed an active participation of the people in the government. This participation, which had since disappeared, had shown itself particularly in the creation of a king. Hotman quoted the tenth-century chronicler Aimoin in support of his contention: "The Franks elected a king according to the custom of other nations, and they placed Pharamond upon the royal throne." Additional evidence was provided for Hotman by the ancient method of inauguration: the king was raised on a shield and carried thrice around the camp "amid universal applause and shouts of acclamation." Pepin, who began the Carolingian dynasty, was also created king by the people; Pope Zacharias only gave his advice on the matter.[5] Even as late as 1328 the people in a sense participated in the elevation of Philip VI to the throne in that he "succeeded to the French crown . . . with the consent and the approbation of the twelve Peers of France." Hotman was too astute a lawyer to believe that the Frankish practices had continued to the sixteenth century,

however, and he had already agreed with a passage from Jean de
Terre Rouge to the effect that the kings succeeded in France "by the
force of custom . . . ; established custom alone confers the kingdom on the successor."[6]

Hotman's approach to the subject was primarily historical
and legal. He did not apply Frankish practices to the present—
although he may have implied that they ought to be, as, indeed, his
contemporaries thought in the aftermath of Saint Bartholomew's
massacre. The results of Hotman's attempt to write objective history were mirrored in the work of another royal historiographer,
Bernard du Haillan, whose *History of France* was first published in
1576. Du Haillan's influential study said, "It is necessary to note
that until Hugh Capet all the kings of France were elected by the
French, who retained this power of electing and banishing and
driving out their kings. And although sons sometimes succeeded
their fathers, and brothers their brothers, that was not by hereditary right, but by the election and consent of the French."[7] Further
on Du Haillan wrote, "One reads that the kings of France were
formerly elective and not hereditary, and, although they since have
attributed to themselves the hereditary possession of it [the king-
dom], rejecting the election which the people performed in this
matter, there still remains a form of election that is performed at
their consecration and coronation at Reims, at which the Peers of
France, in the name of the Church, and the nobility, and the people, elect the king there present. But this form of election is only a
shadow of the old one."[8]

Du Haillan raised an interesting point—the remainder of elective elements in the sixteenth-century coronation ceremony. The
description of Henry II's coronation in 1547 reads, "And after the
said Seigneur had taken the oath *Promitto* [i.e., the ecclesiastical
oath], he was raised from his chair by the Bishops of Langres and
of Beauvais. The three persons thus standing, they made a show
(*firent contenance*) of asking the people and entourage if they
accepted him as king. And as though having received the consent
of the people (*comme ayans receu le consentement dudit peuple*),
my lord of Reims had him take the oath to the kingdom, which
begins *Haec tria promitto*, with his hand on the text of the Holy
Gospels, which he kissed."[9] This was the first time in the Renaissance period that any sort of consent of the people at the coronation was mentioned, but it was not the first time that a *consensus*

populi had appeared in the French coronation *ordines*. We need only note here that the *consensus populi* in Henry's coronation ceremony was borrowed from the *ordo* of 1250, and that that in turn had been based upon a tradition of other *ordines*—Frankish, German, and English —that also included such consent.[10]

The addition of the *consensus populi* to the coronation ceremony of the sixteenth century came about as a result of the conflation of older *ordines*, leading to an almost adventitious archaizing of the ceremony.[11] This accident led to a revised ceremony that the kings of France soon had occasion to rue, for even before the publication of Du Haillan's *History*, the evidence of the coronation ceremony was applied by Théodore Beza in the formulation of his theory of resistance.[12]

Beza, unlike Hotman, was writing a *livre de circonstance*; consequently he carried Hotman's arguments one step further. Like Hotman and Du Haillan, Beza contended that the Merovingian and Carolingian monarchs were chosen and elected, and he quoted for evidence the coronation oath that the continuator of Aimoin had attributed to Charles the Bald. From that he concluded, "I say therefore that the French, though they had chosen their kings first from the race of Meroveg, then from the posterity of Charlemagne, and finally from the descendants of Hugh Capet, nonetheless so arranged their monarchy from the beginning that their kings did not at all reign by right of succession alone, but were elected by the consent of the Estates of the kingdom. . . . In brief, if the kingdom was not elective, Pepin did not have the right to it, nor Hugh Capet either, since there was no default of succession of the male heirs of Meroveg when Pepin became king, nor of the male heirs of Charlemagne when Capet took possession of the crown."[13] Beza furthermore implied that the kingship might still be elective—in this he differed from Hotman—when he said tellingly, "Peoples and nations have ordinarily retained the power of restraining sovereigns, which reservation can be prejudiced neither by great age nor by prescription of time."[14] According to Beza, who was given to using examples from the history of Israel, even the kingdom of David and his successors was elective: "The kingdom was indeed successive as far as race was concerned because God had so ordained, but it was elective as far as the individual was concerned." This seemingly sophistic argument was picked up by at least one other Huguenot writer of the 1570s,[15] but Beza's exegesis was not publicly carried further until the appearance of the *Vindiciae, contra tyrannos* in Latin in 1579 and in French in 1581.

The *Vindiciae* presented the most highly developed theory of elective kingship that the Huguenots put forth. This work posed a conundrum when it said that "God appoints kings, gives kingdoms to the kings, and elects kings. Now we say that the people establish kings, transmit kingdoms, and confirm the election by their vote."[16] As the writer developed this thesis in the third question of the *Vindiciae*, it became clear that God plays little role in the establishment of kings—the people actually control the situation. More than any other Huguenot tract, the *Vindiciae* explained, repeatedly, who the people were. The people as a whole were represented by the officers of the kingdom or the crown (but not the officers of the king), and what may be said of the whole people may be said of these representatives.[17] For France, therefore, the people, as represented, were the great officers of the crown (the constable, the chancellor, the admiral, etc.), the Peers of France, the Estates General. The peers play a particularly important role, for it is to them "as though to the whole kingdom [that] the king about to be consecrated is accustomed to give his promise [i.e., his coronation oath]."[18] At one point the *Vindiciae* almost quoted the coronation ceremony: "When the king of France is consecrated, the Bishops of Laon and Beauvais, ecclesiastical peers, first ask the whole people present whether they wish and command that he be king, whence it is said even in the formula of consecration itself that he is thereupon elected by the people. As soon as the people are perceived to have consented, the king swears that he will maintain the laws and privileges of France and all rights in general, that he will not alienate the domain, etc."[19] To this powerful argument the *Vindiciae* added what by now had become the usual recitation of the election and deposition of kings of the first and second races. Like Beza, the author of the *Vindiciae*, in replying to the assertion that the kingdom had become hereditary, contended that prescription of time does not run against the people. The author proceeded to turn the tables on the proponents of hereditary monarchy by using their own catch phrases, emphatically denying that "le roi ne meurt jamais": "If you should charge that kings have been established by the people who were living perhaps five hundred years ago, not by those who live today, I, on the other hand, say that, although kings die, a people, like any other corporation, in the meantime never dies."[20]

However, by the time the *Vindiciae* was published in 1579, the Huguenots hardly had the power to put the program of the *Vindiciae* into effect. That was left to the supporters of the Catholic League after the situation had dramatically shifted with the death of the duke of Anjou in 1584, after which the Huguenots lost all reason to want to change dynastic succession, for their leader, Henry of Navarre, was now the heir apparent to the throne by legitimate succession according to the "Salic law." The decisiveness of this about-face was intensified with the assassination of Henry III in 1589.

Also in 1589 the League preacher Jean Boucher anonymously published his rather scurrilous *On the Just Renunciation of Henry III*, which was an ad hominem attack on the monarch who had engineered the assassination of the duke of Guise. Boucher's allegations that the kingship was elective sound familiar, for they were drawn almost verbatim from the *Vindiciae*.[21] In tract after tract other League writers also repeated the arguments, asserting that the kingship was still elective. The author of *On the Just Authority of the Republic over Impious Kings* did so in 1590, using historical examples and evidence from the coronation ceremony to prove his allegations; the author furthermore declared that the coronation was necessary (which obviously would have made things difficult for a Huguenot king, who would have to be "elected" at his coronation).[22] Finally, in 1591 a tract devoted wholly to the subject of election was printed anonymously under the title *Discourse by Which It Will Appear That the Kingdom of France Is Elective and Not Hereditary*.

The *Discourse* may have been written by a lawyer, but it did not add much that was new to the theory of election. There was the normal catalog of Merovingians and Carolingians who were elected, and Philip of Valois was said to have been elected; to these was added the striking assertion that "Louis XII, feeling that he would not have any son, convoked the Estates General, which assembled at Tours in the year 1506. There Francis, Duke of Valois and of Angoulême, was named and elected to be king after the said King Louis."[23] No other writer had found an "election" so recent, and the consequences of the election of Francis I were obvious. The writer, in addition, denied that the Salic law had any validity, and he urged that the nearest male relative was not always elected.[24] At the coronation ceremony the Peers of France elected the king, and the people approved their choice: "Moreover, the election has always been held so necessary in France that, even though five of the six lay peerages have been reunited with the Crown, it has been observed and carefully guarded that to complete the old ceremony certain of the principal seigneurs of France, representing the Peers, perform at the consecration of the king the duties and functions of those whom they represent."[25] The *Discourse* concluded by saying that if the reign had degenerated into tyranny the Estates might bring order. The Crown of France is like a minor, and if prescription of time does not run against the king, still less can it run against the Crown or public law.[26] The *Discourse* may not have been original or even very carefully argued, but it did epitomize the thoughts of many of the League's writers. In addition it pointed out what had to be done, and a year later steps were taken to put its program into effect when the duke of Mayenne sent out letters calling for a meeting of the Estates General in Paris.

Little need be said here of the Estates General of 1593. The moderate deputies were won over to the "legitimist" cause when Henry of Navarre announced his intent to change his religion, and the French never seriously considered the candidature of Philip II of Spain. The Estates General did contemplate electing Isabelle, the eldest daughter of Philip II and of Elizabeth of Valois, but when the negotiations with Spain broke down, the Parlement of Paris declared that the fundamental laws of the kingdom, including the Salic law, must be obeyed.[27] The meeting of the Estates General gradually drifted out of existence, and the French increasingly accepted Henry IV as their king. When in 1610 Henry met the fate of his predecessor, the loss was mourned by the French with a depth of feeling that amply demonstrated his popularity. Had Henry not been so successful, it is questionable whether the dynastic succession of the Bourbon kings would have been effectively legitimized.

2. The Denial of Electiveness

The juristic basis of dynastic succession, which did much to bring Henry to the throne, was strengthened by the reinterpretation of that very evidence that the advocates of elective kingship had used to support their opinions. The potential danger of the elective arguments had been recognized almost from the beginning, and some of the same people who had helped to develop the theory of election also provided some of the arguments for the attack on the theory. The interpretation of the evidence by these men and their successors led to two basic positions: the first allowed that the kingship had been elective but had ceased to be so; the second denied that the kingship had ever been elective.

Major proponents of the former position included, as we have seen, the Hotman of the *Francogallia* and Du Haillan, who agreed with Hotman that all the kings to Hugh Capet were elected, but who said that the kingship had since become successive; in other words, Du Haillan accepted the historical evidence at face value but explained away the evidence of the coronation ceremony by calling it a shadowy remnant of the past.[28] This position was held as late as 1587, when the able lawyer Louis Charondas Le Caron first published his *Pandectes ou digestes du droit françois*. According to Le Caron, "The three orders and estates of France conferred [the kingdom] with a certain ceremony and law; and afterwards it was made an inheritance passed on by succession . . . to the nearest male of the royal blood, which is still the case at the present."[29] A modified view of early medieval succession was presented in Matteo Zampini's *De gli stati de Francia*. For Zampini, Pharamond was elected, but then the kingdom immediately became successive. As far as the elections of Pepin and Eudes were concerned, Zampini thought that they "ought to be called declarations, and not elections, inasmuch as Pepin and Eudes came from a very distant line of the Merovingians."[30] Zampini's attack on the historical elections was carried on in various ways by other writers, who denied that the kingship had ever been elective.

Some of these people were not truly impartial scholars, but only what one might call apologists of monarchism. For example, Louis Le Roy, taking up his pen against the *Francogallia* in his *De l'excellence du gouvernement royal*, dismissed the ceremony of the shield (which Hotman had thought to be a form of election) with the assertion that this and other ceremonies had been changed because they were ridiculous; such ceremonies did nothing but "satiate the desire of the curious researchers of antiquities," and they most certainly could not replace the more civil customs of more recent times.[31] Le Roy did not directly attack the authenticity of the chronicles but only cast doubt on the veracity of the chroniclers, whose works, he said, were "written for the most part by ignorant monks or envious strangers." Contrary to what they had reported, "the kingdom of France, without form of election, goes always from male to male to the nearest of the lineage in such a way that the king never dies, as is said."[32]

Le Roy was a *politique*, an advocate of moderation, as was his great contempory Bodin, whose *Republic* was published the next year. Bodin's discussion of the evidence was novel, to say the least. Ignoring the historical evidence for election, Bodin concentrated on the *consensus populi* in the coronation ceremony, arguing that it was not a true form of election and that those who had seen it as such had ignored that it was given only after the archbishop of Reims had performed his own manner of electing the king. Bodin discussed a number of examples of election and concluded that the word *elect* was used only by the archbishop of Reims, who pretended to have from the pope the right to elect the king. This was easy for Bodin to deny, and he concluded that the king "takes his scepter neither from the pope, nor from the Archbishop of Reims, nor from the people, but from God alone."[33]

Supporting Bodin's antielective position were two influential works published in 1578 and 1579, Jean du Tillet's *Les memoires et recherches* and François de Belleforest's *Les grandes annales, et histoire générale de France*. Du Tillet explained the elements of election in the coronation ceremony by saying that they ought to be understood as acceptance and submission to the king elected by God, "not as any right of the subjects to give the kingdom by voice or election. For it has always been hereditary."[34] Du Tillet did not attempt to explain the use of the word *elect* in reference to the succession of the early medieval kings, but when Belleforest turned his attention to the evidence, both in history and in the coronation ceremony, he did so at greater length than any other sixteenth-century proponent of successive kingship. Belleforest studied the supposed elections of the past in great detail. Pharamond, he said, was not elected, but was the nearest surviving heir of his predecessor. If, he claimed, "the people and seigneurs assisted and used some ceremonies having the appearance of election, that was in order better to approve and confirm that succession and to do homage to him who succeeded their late prince."[35] Plunging into an attack on Hotman, Belleforest said that the author of the *Francogallia* wanted to make the kings elective like the duke of Venice or the emperor of Germany. Strongly stating absolutist doctrine, Belleforest asserted that the kingship was granted by God and that the king was not actually bound by the laws, but that if he did submit to the laws, that was only for his grandeur and honor. None of the kings of the first two races, not even Pharamond, was elected, because in every case the new king had royal blood. What the chroniclers seemed to call an election in such cases was not, but was only an approval of him who had become king. Belleforest wrote, "[N]ot that I wish to deny completely that election was enjoyed by the people, but I say that that was only to authorize the blood of the royal princes, inasmuch as they alone were chosen to come to the throne." In this sense the coronation ceremony in the sixteenth century must be understood: when the people were asked if they wished that he who was being consecrated command them, that was done "more to keep that form of consent than of necessity."[36] In this fashion Belleforest nullified all the historical and ceremonial evidence that the proponents of election had used to support their theory. After this, little more needed to be said to defend successive kingship—which did not, as we have seen, prevent the Catholic League from taking the elective position.

The question certainly remained very much alive; Belleforest published his work in 1579, in the same year that the first edition of the *Vindiciae* appeared and argued the elective position. When in 1585 the League was making its influence felt, the able Pierre de Belloy felt constrained to publish his *Apologie catholique*, in which he used legal evidence to argue that the kingship was successive and in which he further disarmed the coronation evidence for election by asserting the coronation to be unnecessary since it was only a public declaration of the king's power of governance. In support of his contention, he urged the juristic formula *le mort saisit le vif*.[37] Belloy continued his argument in his *Examen du discours publié contre la maison royalle de France*. Here he said that the Merovingians were successive, so that when Childeric was deposed, that did not indicate that the law of succession was condemned, but only that the individual was replaced by someone more capable, and that the kings of the second race were always successive. Since Pepin there had been no interruption of succession. As far as Gregory of Tours, Aimoin, Ado of Vienne, and others were concerned, when they said that the French had "proclaimed, elevated, and established a king," that was not to be understood as simply election, for at the coronation the seigneurs, nobles, and barons of the kingdom were accustomed only "to take the public oath to him, to greet and welcome him on his accession to the Crown, just as we still see in our days." Even if the old histories said accurately that the kings were "received with the consent, favor, pleasure, content, and will of all," nonetheless the kings "were called to the Crown by succession and as though into their fathers' inheritance, [which was] continued without interruption in those three lines for one thousand two hundred years or thereabouts." Even if the kingdom had been elective, Belloy concluded, one could not claim without being guilty of lese majesty that for six hundred years and more "only natural succession by blood makes our kings legitimate."[38]

Seven years after Belloy's explication, Nicolas de Thou raised the antielective position to official doctrine in his description of, and commentary on, the first Bourbon's coronation. Immediately after describing the ceremony of the *consensus populi*, De Thou added, "Not that this acceptance is to be taken for election, the kingdom having always been hereditary and successive to the nearest male, but as a declaration of the submission, obedience, and fidelity that they [those assisting at the coronation] owe to him as to their sovereign lord by the express order of God."[39]

After De Thou's assertion it was anticlimactic for a League pamphleteer to repeat all the old elective arguments in his anonymous *Dialogue d'entre le Maheustre et le Manant*. This writer, however, was more moderate than some of his predecessors in that he thought that the candidates had to be found among the members of the royal house.[40] On the other hand, Jean Boucher did not change his opinion after Henry IV's success, and he wrote in his *Apologie pour Jehan Chastel* (1595): "Among the ceremonies of which [i.e., the contemporary coronations] this one is express, that asks the people three times if they will have such and such a person as king (which represents the form of a true election); one infers from all this that by this means the title of king is deferred to the consecration and to the consent of the people."[41]

Such views became rare, though, and they died out with the general decline of French resistance theory after 1594. The writers of the early seventeenth century tended solely to the position that the kingship was successive. This was true of lawyers like Guy Coquille, who came down squarely on the side of succession, and it was equally true of absolutist apologists like André Duchesne, whose *Les antiquitez, et recherches de la grandeur et majesté des roys de France* urged that the kings were "elected and designated" by God alone. Finally, a new argument against elective kingship was presented by Jean Baricave in 1614; his *La defence de la monarchie françoise* urged that if the monarchy were elective "it would have been necessary to convoke the three estates of the kingdom, which has never been done at the consecration of the kings of France."[42] And, one might add, it was not to be done during the next two centuries either. Nevertheless, ideas, once born, die with great difficulty, if at all, and some writers again picked up the theme of election during the revolts of the Fronde.[43] The ceremony of the *consensus populi* was also cited as evidence for the elective nature of French kingship over a century later by some writers of the Enlightenment.[44] All these late appearances of the theory could not mask the fact, however, that, from Henry IV on, the proponents of election had been defeated and that France continued to enjoy a succession of absolutist kings by dynastic right until the end of the monarchy.

From a twentieth-century point of view, the theory of election might seem to have been historically insignificant, for the modern French did not in fact elect a king. Nonetheless, the modern success of dynastic absolutism could not have been foreseen in 1593, when the possibility of an elective kingship was of importance not only theoretically but also practically: supporters of the Catholic League, absolutely opposed to the accession of a heretic to the position of Most Christian King, had to decide what to do.

Historical events often happen as a result of fortuitous circumstances. Henry of Navarre was brought to the throne by a series of such: the premature death of the duke of Anjou, the failure of Henry III to provide heirs, and then the assassination of the last Valois king. If we add to these another circumstance not at all implausible, if Henry of Navarre had remained faithful to Calvinism, then the theory of election might have been completely implemented in Paris in 1593, and the history of modern France might have been much different than it was: two Frances might have resulted, or, at the very least, the civil wars would have been prolonged. These are not idle speculations, for they were possibilities that had to be considered at the time.

To us it might seem doubtful that the League's Estates General ever came close to electing a successor to Henry III, for Henry of Navarre had closely followed the events from Chartres, and he had shown himself conciliatory from the very beginning of the meeting. Individuals can sometimes influence the course of history, and Henry did so when, with one of the most consummate senses of timing in the history of politics, he had his intention to be converted announced to the Estates General in Paris just when the negotiations with Spain were beginning to break down. This action—coupled with the obtuseness and delay of the Spaniards—turned the tide for Henry, and it was his subsequent success that made the theory of election seem counterhistorical. In itself and at the time, though, the theory was not, and the attempt to apply it at the meeting of the Estates strikingly exemplifies the way in which political thought could lead to political action.[45]

The writers who stripped the *consensus populi* and elective kingship of any contemporary validity thereby destroyed one of the theoretical limitations upon the monarch. In so doing they made a major contribution to the edifice of absolutism, which, as the coronation ceremony shows in various other ways, was constructed but gradually and as though by chance. How gradually and haphazardly is shown by the origin of the fiction of the sleeping king and the rise of the Princes of the Blood.

PART THREE

STRIVING TOWARD ABSOLUTISM

. . . .

9

THE SLEEPING KING

· · · · · · · · · ·

1. Louis XIII's Ceremony

On the morning of the coronation of Louis XIII the twelve Peers of France gathered in the cathedral church, and they delegated two of their number, the bishops of Laon and of Beauvais, "to go and seek the king in his lodging."[1] Accompanied by two crosses, candles, and holy water, the canons, vicars, and chaplains of the church preceded the bishops in the procession to the king's chamber in the archiepiscopal palace. The bishops wore pontifical habits, and relics of saints dangled from their necks.[2] When they arrived at the chamber of the king and found it closed, the bishop of Laon knocked on the chamber door.

"Whom do you want?" asked the duke of Esguillon, grand chamberlain of France, from within.

"Louis XIII, son of Henry the Great," responded the bishop.

"He is sleeping," replied the grand chamberlain.

The sequence of knocking, question, and reply was exactly repeated a second time. The bishop knocked a third time, and again the grand chamberlain asked, "Whom do you want?"

"Louis XIII, whom God has given us for king," replied the bishop this time.[3]

Thereupon the door was opened and the two bishops and the grand cantor of Reims entered the room to find the king lying on a richly decorated bed of state (*lit de parade*).[4] Louis was wearing a sleeveless chemise of Holland linen and a camisole with sleeves. Both garments were parted in front and rear so that they could be opened for the sacring; until that time, though, each of the garments was held closed by means of buttons or loops.[5] The king wore over these garments a long robe, with sleeves, of silver cloth; one source says that the cloth was linen, another says that the robe was in the form of a nightshirt.[6] When the bishops saw the king, the bishop of Laon said a prayer beginning *Omnipotens sempiterne Deus, qui famulum tuum.*[7] Then the bishops kissed their own hands and raised the king from his bed, each raising the king by one arm "with every exhibition of honor as due to their sovereign prince, who represents on earth divine majesty and sovereign power."[8] While the king was led processionally to the church, the clergy of the church chanted a response and a versicle.[9]

It would hardly occur to us to believe that Louis XIII was actually sleeping when the two bishops arrived at his chamber on the morning of the most important ceremony of the monarch's life. To be sure, one scholar has argued that the kings of France were in fact sleeping on several occasions prior to their coronations on account of the rigors of the preceding night vigil. However, the night vigil had been ameliorated at least by 1364 (and probably even earlier), so this argument does not convince us.[10] This little ritual was patently too contrived to be accidental: the monarch was fully dressed and ready to be led to the church for his coronation, and the exact repetition of questions and responses shows that we are here dealing with a ceremonial fiction of some sort.

What is the meaning of this strange ceremony? What are its antecedents? The ritual is reminiscent of several previous practices: the role of the bishops in medieval coronation *ordines*; the night vigil of knightly candidates and their repose on a bed; assertions that the kingship was God-given; the curious thrice-knocking at the door in certain liturgical ceremonies. To understand the ritual in 1610, it will therefore be necessary first to investigate the medieval liturgical origins and knightly background of what took place at Louis XIII's coronation. The sixteenth century must then be studied for the further development of the ceremony and the role played by the religious and political difficulties of the France of Catherine de Médicis. When the origins of Louis XIII's ritual have thus been sought, it will be possible to reexamine the ritual and its meaning within the conceptual framework of early seventeenth-century monarchical ideas. Finally, there is the possibility that the 1610 ritual anticipates the much better-known conceit that resulted from the fusion of royal and solar symbolism under Bourbon absolutism, so it will be necessary to look again at the sixteenth century for examples of solar symbolism and to see how such symbolism was expressed at the coronations of the Bourbon kings of France.

2. The Medieval Background

The remote origins of the ritual of the sleeping king go back to an early medieval German *ordo*, that of Mainz (ca. 961). It provided that the king should come to the church from his chamber, that a bishop should say a prayer (*Omnipotens sempiterne Deus, qui famulum tuum*), and that two bishops, one on each side of the king, should lead him to the church while singing a response and a versicle.[11] This part of the *ordo* of Mainz did not affect the French coronation ceremony even as late as 1230, the probable date of the influential *ordo* of Reims. It did, however, enter the English ceremony, and the weight of the English example was apparently felt when the French consulted English *ordines* and a basically German text to compose a new *ordo*, the *ordo* of 1250. The provision of that *ordo* for the procession from the king's chamber to the church was copied by the *ordo* of Charles V.[12]

Charles V's *ordo* was the first to prescribe the procession of peers and clerics to seek the king in his chamber, and it added a number of elements not found in any previous French *ordo*:

> And the canons of the church of Reims, accompanied by two crosses, wax candles, and a censer with incense, shall go to the archiepiscopal palace. And the Bishops of Laon and of Beauvais (who are the first of the episcopal peers), with relics of the saints hanging from their necks, shall be in the said procession. And in the great chamber (*in camera magna*) they shall seek the prince who is to be consecrated king sitting and half-lying on a bed (*sedentem et quasi jacentem supra thalamum*) properly appointed. When they arrive in the presence of the prince, the Bishop of Laon shall say this prayer:
>
> *Omnipotens sempiterne Deus. . . .*
>
> When this prayer is finished, the two bishops shall immediately and honorably support him on the left and the right and shall lead him reverently to the church, singing this re-

sponse with the canons previously mentioned:
  Ecce mitto angelum meum. . . .
  When this response is finished, the versicle shall be sung:
  Israel, si me audieris. . . .[13]

With this *ordo* the role of the bishops of Laon and Beauvais in this part of the ceremony was defined as it was to remain until the end of the Old Regime.

The *ordo* of Charles V presented for the first time the king's repose on a bed. The *ordo* of Mainz did not, however, serve as the model for this. In fact, no coronation ceremonial before the *ordo* of Charles V contains any hint of a bed.

There is little doubt that the bed was adopted from the ceremony of initiation into knighthood. Our knowledge of knightly initiation ceremonies before the twelfth century is fragmentary, but we know that by 1100 they were accompanied by a number of religious elements. One of these was the vigil that the knightly candidates were beginning to keep in the night preceding the dubbing. Although it seems not always to have been so, the night vigil could be either preceded or followed by a purificatory bath; after the bath the candidate was placed in a bed that acted as a ceremonial towel to dry him. One French formula for the creation of new knights in times of peace, described as an *ordo* "according to the custom of England," directs that "two esquires of honor grave and well seen in courtship and nurture and also in the feats of chivalry" were to have the care of the knightly candidate. A bath, covered to protect against the coldness of the night, was to be prepared. Then the king commanded his chamberlain to choose "the most noble and wise knights" present to go and instruct the candidate as he bathed. After the candidate left the bath, he was placed on a bed until dry, whereupon he was removed from the bed and warmly dressed for the night vigil. In the early morning he heard matins and the mass and communicated if he wished, and he went to bed again until the day was fully broken. The two knights aiding the candidate next were to go to the king and say, "Sire, when it pleases you, our master will awaken." At that, the king was to command the wise knights, esquires, and minstrels to go to the chamber of the candidate in order to awaken and dress him and to precede him to the hall where the ceremony was to be completed.[14]

Some of these aspects of the ceremonial of knighting first appeared in coronation ceremonies in the thirteenth century or perhaps already in the twelfth century. An *ordo* drawn up for the kingdom of Burgundy contains the first known reference to a bath in connection with a coronation. The English Westminster directory of 1273 said, "Also, on the said day of the coronation, the prince who is to be crowned shall be raised in the aforesaid royal seat in the said hall, after he has first bathed. And after the bath a tunic and a silk shirt shall be prepared for him. . . ."[15] H. G. Richardson has argued that this directory was based to a large extent on the older *ordo* of Reims, the first French *ordo* to mention the vigil. A late thirteenth-century French translation of the *ordo* of Reims and the last Capetian *ordo* both mentioned the night vigil, but not the bath.[16] On these bases one may safely say that the night vigil became a part of the French coronation ceremony at least by the end of the thirteenth century. The ceremonial bath, on the other hand, was not mentioned in any of the French *ordines*, so we may conclude that the French kings never took the bath as a part of their coronation ceremony. Despite the absence of a ceremonial bath from the French coronation, nonetheless, its auxiliary, the bed, was borrowed by the *ordo* of Charles V.

A bit of reflection reveals reasonable grounds for introducing parts of the ceremony of knightly initiation into the French coronation ceremony. It is quite possible that in the *ordo* of Mainz and in all *ordines* based upon it (including that of Charles V), the bishops acted as sponsors of the king prior to the coronation, just as one has sponsors when baptized. In the same fashion the candidate for knighthood was instructed and led to the chapel by the two knights.[17] The role played by the bishops in the French coronation ceremony from the time of Charles V thus has the appearance of having resulted from a combination of three ceremonies: coronation, baptism, and knighting. The bed, then, would have been introduced as a result of the same sort of combination of two ceremonies: coronation and knighting.

The first detailed French text that was undoubtedly a narration of a coronation after the event was the description of Charles VIII's ceremony in 1484. The night vigil was still found at this coronation, albeit in a truncated, symbolic form. Charles heard vespers and later returned to the church for a short time to say his prayers—the description says that he did this "because the *ordo* of consecration provides that during the night the king must go in great silence and without fanfare to the church to make his orison and to keep vigil there for a period of time in prayers and orisons, if it pleases him."[18] After that he returned to the archiepiscopal palace, where he remained the whole night until sought by the bishops delegated by the Peers of France. When the bishops of Laon and Langres—the bishop of Beauvais was ill—arrived at the king's chamber, they found him "seated or leaning on one elbow, and half-lying on a parade bed." When the bishops saw the king, the bishop of Laon said the *Omnipotens sempiterne Deus* prayer. "After this prayer was finished, the Bishops of Laon, on the right, and of Langres, on the left, reverently raised the king from the bed and led him in procession to the church to be consecrated and crowned king of France."[19] One cannot suggest that any hidden symbolism was intended when Charles VIII was raised from his bed in 1484; the raising of the king appears to have been no more than an act of respect on the part of the bishops.

In the sixteenth century Francis I was lying—or at least leaning on his elbow—on a bed from which he was raised by the two bishops, and Henry II was raised from the bed upon which he was lying. Each monarch was then led to the church by the two bishops who had been dispatched to seek him.[20] No reliable description of the coronation of Francis II in 1559 survives, but the following coronation—that of Charles IX in 1561—added to the ceremony the ultimate fiction: that the king was asleep.

3. The Sleep of Charles IX

Charles IX was the first king to sleep fictitiously. Prior to his coronation he lay on a bed (*lict de parade*), dressed as his predecessors were, and ready for his coronation. All twelve of the Peers of France went together "to knock on the door of the chamber of the king, asking in these words:"

"Where is our new king, whom God has given us to rule and govern us?"

"He is within," replied the prince de Joinville, who was serving as grand chamberlain for his father (the duke of Guise, who represented one of the lay peers), from within the chamber.

"What is he doing?" asked the peers.

"He is reposing."

At this reply the peers requested, "Awaken him in order that we may salute him and do reverence to him."[21]

After this dialogue the peers waited a little while at the door; then the grand chamberlain opened it to them saying that the king had awakened. The peers did obeisance to the king, and the cardinal of Lorraine, speaking for all the peers, said to the young king "that they, knowing that he was in the city, had not wanted to fail to come to him to render him the obeisance, faith, and homage that they owed him, promising him to be always faithful and obedient subjects. And so that the people might know most assuredly that he was their true and natural lord and king, they petitioned him to come to the great temple and church, where he would find the preparations that they had caused to be made in order to consecrate and crown him king."[22] All the peers then returned to the church and after a little while sent the cardinal of Bourbon (Charles, archbishop of Rouen) and the cardinal of Guise (Louis, archbishop of Sens) to conduct the king by his arms to the church, where the king said a prayer.

Several aspects of this ritual at Charles IX's coronation lend the ceremony a peculiar awkwardness: the procession of all twelve peers to the king's chamber, the maladroit dialogue, and the infelicitous wait at the closed door before the peers were allowed to enter the room to perform obeisance and make their speech. This awkwardness has not been particularly noticed by historians, nor have they noted one very important fact about the ceremony in 1561: it was unique in the history of the French ceremony. On this occasion only did all the Peers of France go to the king's chamber and use this particular form of dialogue.[23] Also unique was the time of the visitation. It took place before the peers held their usual consultation to delegate the two episcopal peers to seek the king in his lodging. Only when all twelve peers had returned to the church after awakening Charles did they delegate the cardinals of Bourbon and of Guise to seek the king and bring him to the church. What we have here, therefore, is the first instance of the sleeping king, but we still do not have the ritual of the sleeping king as performed at the coronation of Louis XIII. The latter, which became the norm for future coronations, was a quite different ceremony even though based upon Charles IX's ritual.

Charles IX's ceremony invites several possible explanations, but the description is so ambiguous that it would be difficult to choose

among them. Fortunately though, there are two other descriptions
of the ceremony. One of them says: "First, after the king had arisen
for the day, he was led to a royal bed and was made to seem to
sleep thereon; Monsieur the Constable came to him, carrying his
naked constable's sword, and said to the king, 'Sire, awaken, for
it is today that God has elected you king,' and other customary
words; and from there he was led to the church in great triumph,
dressed completely in white in a great mantle of silver cloth, a cap
of white velvet with a white plume, and flesh-colored half-boots
that made the legs and feet appear nude."[24] The third description
of the ceremony comes from an unpublished manuscript history by
the president de Montagne; it corroborates to a high degree the
anonymous description just quoted:

> In the first place, as soon as the king had arisen from his
> ordinary bed, he was placed in a royal bed, in which he was
> made to appear to be sleeping. The Sieur de Montmorency,
> Constable of France, came to him, carrying the naked royal
> sword in his hand. And he said to the king, "Sire, awaken. It
> is not longer time to sleep because God has elected you king
> to command the great and excellent monarchy that is the
> kingdom of France and has called you today to receive the
> sacred signs of his mercies. And divine favors are promised
> to you by God so that you may worthily acquit yourself of
> such a heavy and important charge," and other customary
> words. These gave him [the king] occasion to arise suddenly,
> and he was quickly dressed completely in white, that is to
> say in a great mantle of silver cloth, a white velvet cap with
> a white plume, and half-boots flesh-colored in such a way
> that they made the legs and feet appear nude. In this cos-
> tume he was led to the church of Notre Dame with great
> magnificance and in triumph.[25]

These passages have the appearance of having been based on a
description by someone who was within the king's chamber at the
time, whereas the first description appears to have been written by
someone outside the chamber, perhaps by one of the clerics. By
interweaving three accounts, we can get a fairly full picture of what
probably happened in 1561. The events would have taken place in
the following order: the peers gathered in the church and the king
arose and dressed for the day; Charles was put on a bed and made

to appear to be sleeping, and the peers all went to the door of the king's chamber; the peers asked for the new king "whom God has given us"; they learned that he was "sleeping," and they asked that he be awakened; the constable next "awakened" the king, saying that it was the day that God had elected him king; the grand chamberlain opened the door of the chamber and said that the king had awakened; the peers entered the chamber, did obeisance to Charles, and delivered their address; as the king was being dressed in his overgarments (mantle, cap, and boots), the peers returned to the church and delegated two of their number to go seek the king and bring him to the church, probably in the time-honored fashion.

There seem to have been two factors that played a role in this ceremony, one political, the other theoretical. We must look at each in some detail.

The political situation of France was tense in 1561. Shortly before the death of Francis II in December 1560, his mother, Catherine de Médicis, had induced Antoine de Bourbon, king of Navarre, to renounce the regency in her favor. After Francis's death the house of Guise lost power temporarily, and Catherine attempted a reconciliation between the staunchly Catholic house of Guise and the house of Bourbon, which was leaning strongly toward the reformed religion. She also attempted to bring about a certain amount of ecclesiastical and judicial reform, hoping to attenuate the influence of the reformers, but it was easier to legislate reform of the most glaring abuses than to abolish them. More than once during the first few months of 1561 the rivalry between Guise and Bourbon nearly precipitated France into civil war. Added to this was Catholic violence, on the one hand, and Protestant disobedience on the other. Catherine desired the maintenance of civil order more than the triumph of Catholicism, and on 19 April she promulgated an edict (in her son's name, of course) allowing all subjects of the king to pray freely in their lodgings behind closed doors. Such provisions did not calm France, nonetheless. Radicals on either side were interested in neither compromise nor toleration. In the words of the Venetian ambassador to France in a report of 2 May, ". . . each day witnesses greater confusion and disorder . . . [and] this kingdom, of yore most flourishing and most obedient to its King . . . has quite changed, so that by the disunion of the people, and by that of the Princes of the Government, it has become so weak and infirm that friends have not much to hope nor foes to fear from it."[26]

While civil and religious strife was coming to a head, preparations were being made for the coronation, which had to be postponed to 15 May (Feast of the Ascension) for want of funds. On 3 May the court departed for Reims; its departure, according to the Venetian ambassador,

> was delayed by want of money, and by reports spread through the Court against the Cardinal of Lorraine and the Duke of Guise, to render the King of Navarre suspicious. Many writings were also scattered about, telling the King of Navarre to beware of proceeding to Rheims, as he was going into the house of his enemies, who intended to injure him. Cardinal Châtillon, the Prince of Condé, and the Admiral did everything to hinder this journey, endeavouring to persuade the King of Navarre that the sole reason for the consecration of his most Christian Majesty was to give him additional authority to command as King, in order that . . . he may some day dismiss the King of Navarre and his dependents. . . .[27]

On Tuesday, 14 May, the court arrived in Reims. That same day the Venetian ambassador reported that new edicts published in Paris forbade holding conventicles and private congregations in new houses to preach new doctrines, under penalty of rebellion, and that all persons of every rank were held to observe the Catholic religion and rites, under the same penalty. He also reported that Antoine de Bourbon had exhorted his brother (the prince of Condé), the admiral (Gaspard de Coligny), and other adherents of the reformed religion to return to the Catholic religion and not to foster disturbances in France.[28]

Such was the political and religious situation on the eve of Charles's coronation. A result of this state of affairs is evident in the list of the men chosen to represent the twelve Peers of France at the coronation. Nine of them were Catholic and were to remain so until their deaths; included among these were Charles, cardinal of Bourbon (brother of Antoine de Bourbon and later the League's "Charles X") and four sons of Claude de Lorraine, the first duke of Guise.[29] Antoine de Bourbon, whose religious position was somewhat uncertain at this time but who was a staunch enemy of the house of Lorraine, represented the duke of Burgundy. Odet de

Coligny, cardinal Châtillon, served in his capacity as bishop of Beauvais; he was, along with his brothers Gaspard and François de Coligny, to be one of the leaders of the Huguenot movement (see the genealogical table, p. 142).[30]

The peers at this coronation were a diverse group that included four members of the house of Guise, two members of the house of Bourbon (three, if we include the duke of Nevers), and Odet de Coligny. We are well aware of the conflict of interests and opinions among these men, and it might well be suspected that some would withhold their full allegiance to the king if he (or his mother, who ruled in his name) should seem to favor one religion or party over another. Thus, the dangerous political situation in France may well have prompted Catherine de Médicis to carry out a prudent political maneuver in sending the twelve Peers of France to the king in his chamber in the archiepiscopal palace, where they did obeisance to him. She may have been attempting to prevent the outbreak of the civil war. Although it is true that there is an element of election of the king by the peers when they petitioned Charles to go to the church to be crowned, the speech by the cardinal of Lorraine definitely emphasized the obedience of the peers to their king.

The second factor that apparently played a role in the precoronation ritual in 1561 was theoretical; it stressed the election of the king by God. The important words are, "Where is our new king, whom God has given us to rule and govern us?" These words were taken from one of the old coronation prayers, *Ungantur manus istae de oleo sanctificato*, which was said by the officiant as he anointed the king's hands: "May these hands be anointed with the sanctified oil with which the kings and prophets are anointed, just as Samuel anointed David king, in order that you may be blessed and constituted king in this kingdom, which God our Lord has given you to rule and govern. . . ."[31] When the constable awakened Charles with the admonition that God had elected him, he was simply reaffirming the verity of the old prayer.

The emphasis on God-given kingship in 1561 is not to be wondered at, particularly considering the reintroduction into the French ceremony of the archaic elective element in 1547. By 1561 it was becoming evident to all that France's religious difficulties would soon create internal problems the like of which had not been experienced for generations. Those who composed the coronation ceremonial surely did not want to take the chance that the king's

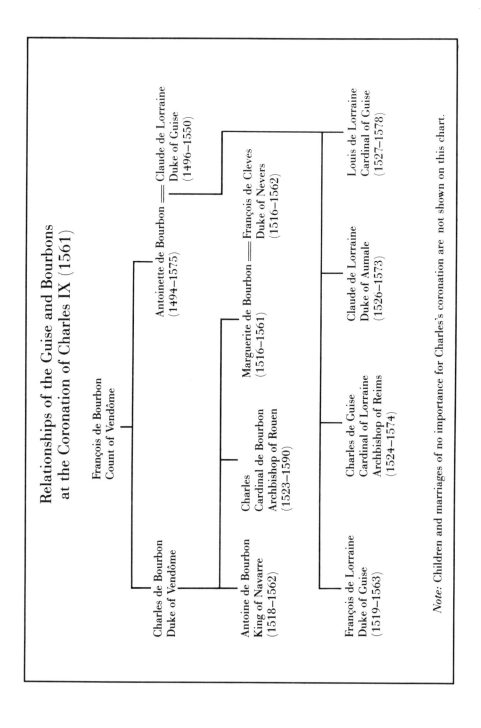

Relationships of the Guise and Bourbons
at the Coronation of Charles IX (1561)

François de Bourbon
Count of Vendôme

Charles de Bourbon
Duke of Vendôme

Antoine de Bourbon
King of Navarre
(1518–1562)

Charles
Cardinal de Bourbon
Archbishop of Rouen
(1523–1590)

Marguerite de Bourbon == François de Cleves
(1516–1561)   Duke of Nevers
                    (1516–1562)

Antoinette de Bourbon == Claude de Lorraine
(1494–1575)   Duke of Guise
                       (1496–1550)

François de Lorraine
Duke of Guise
(1519–1563)

Charles de Guise
Cardinal of Lorraine
Archbishop of Reims
(1524–1574)

Claude de Lorraine
Duke of Aumale
(1526–1573)

Louis de Lorraine
Cardinal of Guise
(1527–1578)

Note: Children and marriages of no importance for Charles's coronation are not shown on this chart.

opponents would use this elective element to argue that the French kingship was elective, so a deliberate affirmation that the king was constituted in France by God could almost have been predicted.

It has not been possible to find the exact model for the staging of the fictional sleep at this coronation, but it was undoubtedly thought to have been a normal part of the ceremony in the past— certainly the fact that the king was traditionally found lying on a bed would easily lead one to such a conclusion. There may also have been a biblical model for the fictional sleep in a verse like Isaiah 60:1 ("Arise, shine; for thy light is come, and the glory of the Lord is risen upon thee") or Isaiah 60:3 ("And the Gentiles shall come to thy light, and kings to the brightness of thy rising").

On the basis of available evidence, it would be hazardous to advance assured explanations of the meaning of the king's fictional sleep in 1561. It has been suggested that the sleep was meant to symbolize the minority of Charles IX at his accession (he was born on 27 June 1550, he acceded to the throne on 5 December 1560, and he was crowned on 15 May 1561) and that, consequently, the king's authority lay in abeyance until his majority.[32] The explanation is attractive, especially when we consider that the ritual of the sleeping king came to be fully developed at the coronation of Louis XIII, who was also a minor (Louis was born on 27 September 1601, he acceded to the throne on 14 May 1610, and he was crowned on 17 October 1610). Nonetheless, the explanation belongs to the realm of speculation, and the fictional sleep in 1561 remains an enigma that cannot now be penetrated, although the role of the Peers of France at this precoronation ritual may well be explained by political circumstances surrounding the coronation.

In one way or another Charles IX's ceremony contained all of the elements of the fully developed ceremony of Louis XIII—with the exception of the thrice-knocking at the door and the accompanying dialogue. The most important addition at Charles's coronation was the fiction that the king was sleeping, which did not appear at the coronations of Henry III in 1575 and Henry IV in 1594. When the fiction appeared again, the ritual reached its final form with the sleeping king, the thrice-knocking at the door, and the dialogue, but without the procession of all the peers to the king's chamber as at Charles IX's ceremony.[33]

4. The God-given King

The historical development of the fiction of the sleeping king may not help us much in explaining the meaning of the ritual at Louis XIII's coronation, but it does show how the ceremony came into being over the course of several centuries. It is necessary to seek the sources of only two more elements of the ritual—the thrice-knocking and the particular sequence of questions and replies.

The thrice-knocking at the door was most likely derived from liturgical ceremonies. A common Palm Sunday procession had a dialogue and knocking similar to those of Louis XIII's coronation ceremony. One that was used in France gives the instruction that, after the singing of the Palm Sunday hymn *Gloria, laus et honor*, "the bishop . . . struck the door [of the church], saying, 'Lift up your heads, O ye gates; and be ye lift up, ye everlasting doors; and the King of glory shall come in' [Psalm 23:7; Psalm 24:7 in the AV]. Those within the church replied, 'Who is this king of glory' [Psalm 23:8; 24:8 in the AV]? When [the bishop] had said, 'Lift up your heads,' for the third time to them [within the church], and the latter had given the same response, he finally shouted, 'The Lord of hosts, he is the King of glory' [Psalm 23:10; 24:10 in the AV]. Then the closed doors were opened."[34] This passage does not say clearly that the bishop knocked at the door each time he made his request, but that such knocking was usual is shown by a similar description in the Mozarabic *Missale Mixtum* (edited under the auspices of Cardinal Ximenes at the beginning of the sixteenth century) as well as by numerous *ordines* for the dedication of a church, which contain a similar dialogue.[35] Otherwise, we have here a number of the elements found in the sleeping king ritual in 1610: the thrice-repeated request and the answering question; the twice-repeated reply and the different reply given the third time; and then the opening of the closed doors.

A quite different sequence of questions used in the Navarrese coronation ceremony in 1490 might have also provided a model for the French practice in 1610. In 1490 the prior of Roncevaux (acting for the bishop of Pampaluna, Caesar Borgia) advanced toward the king and queen (Jean d'Albret and Catherine) on their chairs in the church and asked in a loud voice, "Excellent Prince and Princess, powerful Lord and Lady, do you want to be our kings and lords?"

"Yes," replied the king and queen, "for such is our pleasure and our will."

The question was repeated three times, and the same response was given to each question. Then the prior asked them whether they would take the customary coronation oath; when they answered affirmatively, the oath was administered.[36]

The liturgical ceremonies for Palm Sunday and the dedication of a church and the Navarrese coronation ceremony may have been models for the questions and answers used in 1610, but they did not give the ritual its meaning. The sense of the ceremony was embodied in the dialogue. Twice the bishop of Laon knocked on the door of the king's chamber and asked for "Louys XIII, fils de Henry le Grand." Both times he was told, "He is sleeping." The third time, the bishop asked for "Louys XIII, que Dieu nous a donné pour Roy." Only then was the door opened to reveal the young monarch ready to be led to his coronation. In other words, the young Louis, the descendant of Henry IV as a man, was sleeping. The King, however, was not sleeping, and he was represented as ready for his coronation the moment he was called. The dialogue made a distinction between the corporeal king (the person of Louis XIII) and the abstract King, which was embodied by Louis.[37]

The burial cry at the Renaissance royal funeral, "Le roi est mort! Vive le roi!" proclaimed to all that France was never without kingship, that it was never without a king.[38] Another way of describing monarchial continuity was formulated by Chancellor Michel de l'Hôpital on the occasion of Charles IX's declaration of majority: ". . . the kingdom is never vacant, but there is a continuation from king to king, and as soon as the king has closed his eyes we immediately have a king, we have a lord and master, without waiting for a coronation, unction, or sacring, without waiting for all other solemnities."[39] Charles Loyseau expressed the same fiction when he wrote in his *Du droit des offices* toward the end of Henry IV's reign, ". . . the first maxim of our French law, that *le mort saisit le vif*, which makes it so that at the same instant that the defunct king expires his last breath, his successor is perfect king, by an immediate continuation of the right and of the possession from one to the other, without there being imaginable any interval of interregnum. . . . This is why we say vulgarly, that *le Roi ne meurt point*, that is to say, that royalty is always filled, and never vacant."[40] The maxim that "the king never dies" (which came to be considered as meaning essentially the same thing as the funerary cry) described the sempiternity of the King and was the closest that the French came to a direct assertion of the juristic fiction of the King's superhumanity.[41]

Le roi ne meurt jamais also shows the growing dynastic bias of the French monarchy. The maxim was the French version of the Romano-canonical *dignitas [qui] non moritur*. Instead of the abstract *dignitas* of the Latin dictum, the French maxim speaks of the *roi*, the King who does not die but who is represented by the kings who succeed each other by right of dynastic succession. In this way the French blurred the distinction that the English were careful to make when they said that the king, as King, never dies.[42]

Can it be doubted that these ideas found expression in the ritual of the sleeping king at Louis XIII's coronation? Both times that the bishop of Laon asked for Louis, the son of Henry the Great, the king was said to be sleeping. Then the bishop called for Louis the God-given King, and the door was opened to show that the King never sleeps, the King never dies. The ritual ceremonially enacted Loyseau's words when he wrote that Louis XIII was perfect king, without awaiting his consecration, from the moment of his father's death.[43]

Intellectually satisfying though this explanation of the ritual of the sleeping king in 1610 may be, it has one major drawback—later writers did not interpret the ritual in this way, but offered other explanations. The original sense of the ceremony was quickly forgotten, and there was neither commentary nor explanation when it was performed in 1654. Antoine Aubery, for example, contented himself with simply a brief description of it in his history of Cardinal Mazarin.[44] The first interpretation of the ceremony seems to be that given by Saint-Simon in 1712:

> This choice [of a successor] and the part that the great
> feudatories, later called peers, have in it may be found in the
> survival to our days of the method of going to the king's
> chamber. . . . What can such a singular ceremony signify if
> not that the peers assembled all together have resolved to
> consecrate a king; that his closed chamber and the response
> that he is sleeping show that he who is sleeping does not

dream at all of such an immediate assumption of the crown; and the opening of the chamber when he is called king by the peers at the door [shows] that they are adjudged by the Grand Chamberlain (who holds and is an officer of the Crown) to be competent judges either to choose him (as was formerly said) or to declare him king (since the time when choice ceased to be mentioned). The remainder of the action is in conformity with that interpretation. The Prince, completely lying down and found as though sleeping on his bed behind closed curtains, as though nude because he wears only a simple satin camisole over his shirt, as unshod because he wears neither boots nor spurs, is raised by the two prelates-peers . . . ; all that can only mark a man who thinks of nothing, who is enveloped in a very deep sleep . . . , who allows himself to be raised . . . and to be conducted, still groggy and poorly awakened, whither the peers wish to lead him. Nothing smacks more of an election, free on the one hand but unexpected on the other, of a Prince, not less eligible because there is nothing to show that he was not so, an election made by those who have the right and are the only ones who have this right because the Grand Chamberlain does not recognize election except by them, and because he immediately submits to them on the matter, not by word, but by deed . . . ; all this emphasizes that the authority and action belong to the peers alone.[45]

Saint-Simon's views do not go far toward explaining the original meaning of the ritual. They do not closely follow the ceremony as performed at any time during its history, they are clearly fanciful and biased so as to support the writer's high opinion of the authority of the dukes and peers of France. Even worse, they do not accord with another contemporary interpretation, an official one that saw the raising of the king from his bed by the two bishops as somehow analogous to the rising of the sun. It may indeed be that Louis XIII's ceremony did imply something that was made clear only a century later at the coronation of Louis XV in 1722, when the ritual of the sleeping king was called the *lever du roi*, thus conjuring up the image of the daily ceremony in the Sun King's bedchamber. Although it would seem to be an anachronistic approach to the problem to seek this sort of imagery in 1610, the ritual does merit consideration in connection with solar symbolism, an entrancing problem in its own right.

5. Solar Symbolism

There are numerous sixteenth-century examples of the equation of the king of France with the sun. In 1538 already the French monarch was called a second sun by Charles de Grassaille. An epithalamium written for the occasion of the coronation and marriage of Henry III in 1575 contains several solar allusions:

> Qu'est que Phoebus ne dore
> Qu'est ce qu'il ne colore?
> Qui ignore des Roys
> Le Roy cette journee
> De ton filz Hymenee
> Plier dessoublz les lois?
>
> Qui ignore les fleches
> Couvertes des flammeches
> De ton filz amoureus,
> S'estre en forme de flamme
> Cachees dedans l'ame
> De ce Roy genereus?
>
> .   .   .   .
>
> Qu'on porte ses louanges
> Par les terres estranges
> Et son los qui reluit
> Comme fait par la plaine
> Du desert de Cyreine
> Le Soleil chasse-nuict.
> O heureux journee
> Hymen ô hymenee.[46]

Perhaps the best-known sixteenth-century examples of the comparison between king and sun were two poems written by Pierre de Ronsard for a carnival at Fontainebleau in 1565, at which Charles IX was costumed as the sun. One of them has the king mount to the heavens "where I have taken the garb of the Sun in order to make my virtues manifest to the stars as well as to mortals." The poem goes on to assert that one would search in vain, "not finding my equal in the universe," and concludes with the rhetorical question, "What could surpass the virtue of the Sun?" The second poem is, if possible, even more explicit. It asserts that the sun and the king are similar in power: "The one governs the Heaven beneath it, and the other, France." The one takes its primeval light from the milieu of the stars, and the other gives light to the earth "like a great God." The single difference between the two evokes the astonishing image of a royal apotheosis: ". . . the Sun will die after a period of time, and Charles will go to the Heaven to take its place."[47]

These examples of sixteenth-century solar imagery (to which many more could probably be added) certainly show that Louis XIV was no innovator when he chose and used the sun as his personal symbol. Their purpose here is not to detract from *le Roi Soleil*, however, but to demonstrate that the sun image was common before the coronation of Louis XIII in 1610. Keeping the sixteenth-century images in mind, it is possible to see solar imagery in the ritual of the sleeping king in 1610.

There is ample evidence that Louis XIII—or, rather, those who directed his ceremonial—drew a strong parallel between the new king of France and the rising of the sun. One of the tableaux at Louis's coronation entry into Reims was centered on a young arbor that had been growing for some time from the jointure of two stones connected by a bit of cement. The plant was nourished only by the water lapping at its base, and it had "a trunk as straight as if it were planted on real earth." The artist attributed to the arbor the verse:

> Assis sur cette pierre dure,
> Je vis de la fraicheur des eaux;
> Et Phebus nuit à ma verdure
> Quand il prend ses plus chauds flambeaux.
> Mais aujourd'huy j'ay d'avanture
> Un heureux change à ma nature:
> Car si la trop cruelle ardeur
> De Phebus me tuë, et m'offence:
> Je revis voyant la splendeur
> De *LOUŸS*, Soleil de la France.[48]

On one of the triumphal arches at this entry was a representation of the device of Louis. This was described as "a rising Sun that, in the luster of its first rays, dissipated some large dense clouds on the opposite side of the arch"; it bore the device OCCASUM GALLIA NESCIT, "France does not know the sunset."[49] Another of the triumphal arches carried out the rising-sun theme with the verse:

> Déjà mes beaux jours éclaircis
> Semblaient devenir obscurcis,
> Retombant dans leur nuit première:
> Mais le lever de mon soleil
> Astre d'un aspect non pareil
> Change cette nuit en lumière.[50]

Ten years after the coronation of Louis XIII, André Favyn published his *Theatre d'honneur*, which discussed not only knighthood but also coronations. Favyn's work is highly speculative and unreliable as an historical work, but some of the author's conceptions of kingship are informative. For example, in discussing the Assyrians and Persians, he asserted that "those Nations of the East, judging the Sunne to be the author of that perpetuall fire: tooke it for God himselfe, and for an assured Symbole of Divinitie. The Throane whereof they beleeved to be seated, and planted justly in the midst of the Sunne, entrusted by the Jewes to such beleeving, and the saying of the royall Psalmist. *In Sole posuit Tabernaculum suum* [with a marginal reference to Psalm 18:6; 19:5 in the AV]."[51] Further on, Favyn wrote:

> Now, concerning the French, they honour their Kings and call them Sires, of the auncient Gaulish word Σειρ, Σείρος which signifieth the Sunne: because those Monarchs have bin said to be truely the Suns, not onely of France, but of all Christendome. . . .
> His [the Prince's] very name onely stifleth troubles and seditions. But so soone as this bright Lampe is extinguished the Land seeth it self obscured with darknesse, and pitchie cloudes. As the Eclipse of the Sunne happening by little and little the Ayre is darkened, altred into sullen lookes; and the Subjects troubled, being (without a guide) exposed to the windes of ambition, of all disorder and disobedience.[52]

The products of Favyn's imagination do not bear directly on the coronation of Louis XIII, but they do tell us something of what early seventeenth-century French officials thought about the kingship and the sun.[53]

Ernst H. Kantorowicz has written an engrossing study of the use of sun symbolism. He traces the classical Greek and Roman *Oriens Augusti* theme (the identification of the emperor with the rising sun-god), then investigates the early Christian identification of the sun with the Christ by means of the word *oriens*. Kantorowicz shows how these two streams merged in Byzantine imperial theology to bring about the appearance of the emperor as a sort of Sun-Christ and to symbolize the rising of two suns: Christ as the Sun of Justice and the emperor as the giver of light. Without attempting to trace the details of the interim development, Kantorowicz finally turns to the sun kingship of Louis XIV. In 1653 the French monarch chose the sun as his personal symbol; the subsequent plenitude of sun symbolism staggers the imagination. The sun's face peers at us from books, monuments, medallic histories of the reign, and *ballets de cour*. The great palace at Versailles was oriented so that the king's bedroom looked down the Avenue de Paris toward the rising sun. The identification of the king with the sun was made complete with Louis's daily *lever* and *coucher*, ceremonies by which the king mimicked the rising and setting of the sun. The origin of this ceremonial, diurnal *lever* has yet to be traced fully, and it certainly does not seem to be found in Byzantium, but Kantorowicz may have shown one of his characteristic flashes of inspiration when he suggested that knightly and coronation ceremonials—he had in mind particularly the precoronation ritual of the sleeping king—provided the antecedents for Louis XIV's ceremony.[54]

Although the influence of the coronation ceremony on the *lever du roi* may be questioned, the *lever du roi* undeniably affected the coronation ceremony of the eighteenth century. The daily *lever* of the Roi-Soleil was a propaganda device that was certainly on the minds of those who prescribed the ceremonial for the coronation of Louis XV in 1722. The fictional sleep of the king at his coronation and his rising from his bed forcibly struck at least one person, Antoine Danchet, who shortly after Louis's coronation gave us the first official explanation of the ritual of the sleeping king.

Danchet's *Le sacre du roy*, a very large folio volume of beautifully executed plates, was an officially commissioned commemorative work on the coronation. Among its contents is a series of more or less realistic depictions of significant parts of the ceremony, each of which is accompanied by an allegorical engraving. One plate shows the raising of Louis XV from his bed of state by the bishops of Laon and Beauvais. The engraving is entitled "Lever du Roy," and its accompanying allegory is entitled "Explication des figures allégoriques qui répondent au Tableau de Lever du Roy." The allegorical engraving portrays *la France* in a chariot being drawn upward by four horses, just as in the representations of the *Oriens Augusti* theme in classical antiquity. The explanation of the allegory says:

> *La France*, adorned with her crown and dressed in the royal mantle, is seated in a luminous chariot of the sort that the poets attribute to the sun beginning its course; in place of the Horae who ordinarily accompany it, we see in the air several genii carrying the royal insignia; at the approach of the chariot, night is dispelled and light appears again.
>
> These figures, which denote the *Lever du Roy*, have, moreover, a precise relation to the beginning of the king's reign.
>
> After having mourned a great number of princes, the hope and ornament of the throne, we came to lose a king who had marked the longest reign of the French monarchy by a thousand deeds forever memorable, and this loss seemed to plunge into the most frightful night a nation always distinguished by the love that it bears its sovereigns. But, among such just causes of tears, the new Star that was to restore benign days to us began to diffuse its tender light; its first gleams soothed our sorrows and were the portents of our good fortune.
>
> The device placed at the bottom of the cartouche has as its design a young lily that is rising up and that is beginning to blossom out in the first rays of the sun; the core of the device is these words:
>
> SURGENS CORUSCAT
> He sparkles as soon as he rises up.[55]

We may note how fitting a counterpart Danchet's explanation is to the sun symbolism at Louis XIII's coronation, when the new king dissipated the darkness, and when the France that "does not know the sunset" received Louis, her splendorous new sun.[56] It cannot be doubted that the solar symbolism at Louis XIII's coronation was analogous to that of Louis XV's coronation as explained by Danchet. Nonetheless, any argument that the fiction of the sleeping king in 1610 was intended to symbolize the king as the sun would be quite tentative. Danchet produced his work more than a century after the appearance of the fully developed ritual, and his explanation lacks the support of any seventeenth-century interpretation. What is certain is that in 1722 the sleeping king was associated with the sun, and one cannot help but think that the interpretation of the ceremony was different on the two occasions. Consequently, the fiction of the sleeping king gives the impression of meaning quite different things in 1561, 1610, and 1722.

Though its roots lay far back in the Middle Ages, only in the sixteenth century did the fictional sleep enter the coronation ceremony, initially as a means of assuring peace in the kingdom through a declaration of obedience and an emphasis on the God-given kingship. When the ceremony came to be fully developed in 1610, it was used primarily to express the fiction of the king's two bodies, the physical body that is mortal, and the spiritual body that never dies and is immediately ready for the coronation upon the evocation of the God-given king. When Louis XV was crowned seven years after the conclusion of his predecessor's long reign, France was accustomed to the spectacle of Louis XIV's daily *lever* and *coucher*, the emulation of the sunrise and sunset. The sun had been made Louis XIV's personal symbol, and it remained the personal symbol of the Bourbon kings, so Louis XV's fictional awakening was explained in terms of solar imagery, an exegesis which was repeated at Louis XVI's coronation in 1775.[57]

Monarchical France experienced one last reinterpretation of the ritual of the sleeping king at Charles X's coronation, when the modifications of the ceremony were so extensive that it lost much of what it had in common with the rituals of the Old Regime; the changes in 1825 were construed to mean that the old ceremony implied a subservience of the king to the priest.[58] By 1825, in other words, the old ceremony was totally misunderstood, and no one realized that in one way or another the old monarchy had used the ritual as one of several ways of expressing its tendency toward dynastic absolutism, which was exactly contrary to the thesis presented by Saint-Simon in 1712. Further dynastic bias may be discerned in the fascinating rise of the group known collectively as the Princes of the Blood.

PEERS OF FRANCE AND PRINCES

OF THE BLOOD

. . . .

1. The Duke of Montpensier's Claim

The eve of Henry II's coronation in 1547 was marred by the appearance of a serious dispute over precedence. It had been decided that three of the "old" Peers of France (the duke of Guyenne, the count of Flanders, and the count of Champagne) were to be represented respectively by the dukes of Guise (Claude de Lorraine), of Nevers (François de Cleves), and of Montpensier (Louis II de Bourbon). Because the peers-dukes normally preceded the peers-counts, and because Flanders preceded Champagne, Montpensier found himself in a subordinate position. All three men had the honor of being among France's "new" peers, but Montpensier claimed that, as a Prince of the Blood (*prince du sang*), he should have precedence over both Guise and Nevers, who were not Princes of the Blood. On the other hand, the latter two claimed that they ought to take precedence over Montpensier because their peerages were older than his. On 25 July 1547, the day before his coronation, Henry II published a provisional ordinance temporarily regulating the matter of precedence between Montpensier and his two opponents.

> We make known that, having put this matter to the deliberation of some princes and seigneurs as well as the other lay and ecclesiastical Peers of France assembled here, these were of the opinion with us that on account of the brevity of time before our consecration and coronation it would be very difficult to be able to decide the matter at present. For this rea-

son, and considering that in this solemn act of our consecration and coronation there is no question of anything that touches in any way the honor and preeminence of the royal blood [*il n'est question de chose qui touche en rien l'honneur et préeminence du Sang Royal*], . . . we have ordained by this present ordinance—in a provisory manner, owing to the brevity of time, and until it has been otherwise decided—that our cousins the Dukes of Guise and of Nevers (Count of Eu), created and received as Peers of France before our cousin the Duke of Montpensier, shall precede—in this act alone—this our cousin the Duke of Montpensier, but that, nonetheless, this may not in any way prejudice him afterwards [*sans ce que cela luy puisse toutesfois aucunement prejudicier par cy-aprés*], whether in similar acts, or in any other of honor and preeminence, whatever they be. . . .[1]

In short, the king refrained from directly meeting the issue by resorting to a vague reassurance to Montpensier and by using the rank of the person represented—rather than the rank of the person representing—as the basis of precedence in his coronation ceremony.[2]

This episode dramatizes a crucial phase of the struggle between the Peers of France and the Princes of the Blood. The Peers of France, second only to the king in prestige, represented the medieval principle of a ruling consortium of king and great barons. The Princes of the Blood—male members of a ruling dynasty and its cadet lines, and capable of becoming king of France if the present king or his direct line should die out[3]—represented royal absolutism's dynastic principle. The prestige of the Princes of the Blood was rising in the sixteenth century, and Montpensier as one of them could assert his claim to preeminence in 1547, but the peers were still able to maintain their rights. At this point the Princes of the Blood had been growing in importance for about a century, and Henry II's ordinance specifically stated that his decision did not endanger "in any way the honor and preeminence of the royal blood"; in the half-century after this, the princes would win complete precedence. Thus the quarrel at Henry's coronation marks a kind of equilibrium between the two forces.

Although the story of the rise of the Princes of the Blood has been largely neglected by modern historians, practically every sixteenth-century writer on the institutions of the French monarchy thought the princes' struggle for supremacy of sufficient importance to warrant discussion. Two of the most able of them, Jean du Tillet and Charles Loyseau, even devoted major portions of whole books to the issue of precedence.[4] Upon examination, the history of the struggle shows that it does indeed have its own story to tell of the rise of French royal absolutism.

2. The Peers of France

It was most natural that the dispute should have broken out within the context of a coronation ceremony. One of the main functions of the Peers of France was to act at the coronation, and the peers played a commanding role in the ceremony throughout late medieval and modern times. The most important of the peers in the ceremony was, of course, the archbishop of Reims, who normally officiated. However, the other peers also played prominent roles, either singly, in groups, or in toto. Some of the peers were occasionally entrusted with carrying the regalia,[5] and the duke of Burgundy placed the royal spurs upon the king and then removed them. The bishops of Laon and of Beauvais were entrusted with the task of going to seek the king in the archiepiscopal palace and of leading him to the cathedral church to be consecrated and crowned. All the peers stretched forth their hands to support the crown after it had been placed upon the king's head by the officiant, and all participated in the enthronement of the king. It was even asserted that the king took his coronation oath "in the hands of the peers," who thus served as the recipients of the oath.[6]

The late Percy Ernst Schramm, employing an argument that was developed in sixteenth-century France, averred that the support of the crown by the peers was a symbolic expression of the origin of the kingship, which came not from God alone, but also from the people, who were acting through the hands of the peers. It is doubtful, though, that Schramm's statement fits the sixteenth century, and it most certainly is not applicable to any previous period. The coronation *ordines* emphasize that the crown was placed upon the head of the king by the archbishop alone; only then did the peers support it. By this the peers were pledging support to the crowned king rather than expressing any elective principle—they were acting as vassals. Likewise, after the king had been seated upon his throne by the archbishop, the peers all gave him a kiss of homage. Both the coronation and the enthronement were thus but different aspects of an expression of the feudal relationship between the king and the Peers of France. At least one early seventeenth-century scholar clearly recognized this feudal relationship when he called the peers "the first vassals of the kingdom."[7]

The twelve Peers of France had not always been so important for the coronation of the French king. While theoretically all vassals of the king were peers, the terms *par regni* and *par Franciae* were first used toward the end of the twelfth century to distinguish the greater from the lesser of those vassals who held immediately of the king, the greater being the ones with the title of count or duke. By 1216 there were nine peers: the archbishop of Reims, the bishops of Langres, Beauvais, Châlons, and Noyon, the dukes of Burgundy, Normandy, and Guyenne, and the count of Champagne. About 1225 the bishop of Laon, the count of Flanders, and the count of Toulouse were added, to bring the number up to twelve. These later additions may have resulted from a very conscious imitation of the *chansons de geste*, which speak of the twelve paladins (also called peers) of Charlemagne; the propaganda inherent in this archaizing was so effective that there were some who believed even in the eighteenth century that the origin of the twelve peers was to be found in the reign of Charlemagne.[8]

It is impossible to tell when the Peers of France first began to participate in the coronation ceremony. The *ordo* of Reims (ca. 1230), the first surviving coronation *ordo* to be written after the formation of the college of peers, definitely assigned functions to the Peers of France. In this *ordo*, the duke of Burgundy, who was the only peer named, placed the spurs on the king and removed them. The peers—it was not said how many—immediately stretched forth their hands to support the crown when it had been placed upon the king's head by the archbishop. They also supported the crown while the king was being led to his elevated throne; after the enthronement the episcopal and lay peers alike kissed the king, and the archbishop then returned to the altar. We do not know which peers were to carry out the stipulations of the *ordo*, and we do not know whether any provision was made for the representation of the duke of Normandy, whose duchy had been confiscated by Philip Augustus. We may assume no more than that the ecclesiastical peers and the lay peers whose territories had not reverted were to be present.[9]

By the Renaissance the peers had important rights and prerogatives in addition to their crucial functions at the coronation ceremony, for they had come to occupy a very special position in the French hierarchy. They had always acted as judges in the so-called *cour des pairs*, which eventually came to be confused with the *cour du roi* so that they acquired deliberative voices in the Parlement of Paris. Within their peerages they possessed a type of superior jurisdiction that otherwise was limited to appanages and royal dowries. By the early seventeenth century a new awareness of institutions led to the assertion that the peerages were offices like other offices in that they could not be exercised by third parties.[10] By then, though, the nature of the peerage had changed drastically from its original form.

The college of the twelve peers had always been more ideal than real. With the judgment against John Lackland in 1202, Normandy reverted to the crown. Thus by the time the number of peers was set at twelve there were no longer twelve peers. This process continued during the thirteenth century: Toulouse reverted to the crown in 1271, and Champagne was added to the crown lands with the accession of Philip the Fair in 1285. Three new peerages were created in 1297 to replace the old; in 1315 a thirteenth was created; and eventually there were to be twenty-six Peers of France. A distinction first seems to have been made between the original twelve Peers of France and the newer peers sometime in the latter half of the fourteenth century. The former came to be called the "old" peers, and it was their roles that were played at the coronation until the end of the Old Regime.[11]

In the course of the fourteenth and fifteenth centuries the last three of the old lay peerages reverted to the crown or were lost to the crown. Some of them were given out again as appanages, but these also reverted from time to time. Burgundy fell to the crown in 1361 with the death of Philippe de Rouvres, the last Capetian duke of Burgundy. It was given as an appanage to King John's son Philip in 1363, but the Valois dukes of Burgundy became extinct with the death of Charles the Bold in 1477, in which year Louis XI managed to get himself recognized in the duchy. The county of Flanders, however, had passed into the hands of the dukes of Burgundy in 1384, and it disappeared as a peerage because it was not recov-

ered by Louis XI when he reacquired Burgundy. The Treaty of Brétigny recognized the English sovereignty over the duchy of Guyenne in 1360, and the duchy was not to return to French possession
until 1451 (although it was given to Charles VI's son Louis as an
appanage in 1401). Guyenne remained with the crown after the
death of Charles, duke of Berry (brother of Louis XI) in 1472.
Thus, ever since the number of the Peers of France had been set at
twelve, there were some of the old lay peerages that no longer
existed, and none of them survived after 1477. Because it had
become obligatory for twelve peers to act at the ceremonies of the
monarchy, it was also necessary that someone represent those old
peerages that no longer existed. This representation set the scene
for the struggle between the peers and the Princes of the Blood in
1547.

3. The Princes of the Blood

The phrase "Princes of the Blood" has been—and is—often
abused, for, like most such expressions (and concepts which they
convey), it came into being gradually. At least as early as the reign
of King John phrases such as "nobles of our blood" or "nobles of
our lineage" were being used in a restrictive sense to refer to those
who were later to be called the Princes of the Blood, and during the
first half of the fifteenth century the most common term came to
be "nobles of our blood and lineage"; these nobles were given special consideration in many matters. Nevertheless, the earliest use
(that I have been able to find) of the phrase "Princes of the Blood"
dates only from 1441, when it was used in a complaint of the Estates; strictly speaking, it would therefore seem inappropriate to
apply it to earlier times. The addition of the word *prince* was an
essential step in the development of the concept, not only because
it implied a separation of the Princes of the Blood from the other
nobles of France, but also because it shared something of medieval
political thought's concept of the *princeps* with his implied power
to rule.[12] By increasingly enriching the connotations of the term,
the French monarchy subsequently completed the outline that had
been sketched by the mid-fifteenth century.

Although "Princes of the Blood" had been coined by 1450, the
phrase was not yet in common use, and the accompanying notion

was not yet clearly defined. The emphasis on royal consanguinity had begun, it is true, but its importance had yet to be established. Already during the reign of Charles VI the Princes of the Blood (i.e., those who later would have been so called) were disputing precedence among themselves, and they supported their respective contentions by means of noble titles as well as by degrees of relationship to the king.[13] Furthermore, the princes' relative position in the noble hierarchy was still indefinite. In 1458 the Parlement of Paris decided, in response to a royal query, that those Princes of the Blood (the term used was *seigneurs du sang*) who were also peers should be present and called to the trial of John, duke of Alençon (a Prince of the Blood and a new peer) "comme les anciens Pairs." On the other hand, the Parlement refused to decide whether the Princes of the Blood who were not Peers of France should enjoy the same prerogatives as the peers in judgments concerning their persons, positions, and estates. The Parlement's hesitation may be explained by the fact that it was then trying the duke of Alençon for treason and did not want to confuse the trial.[14] Nevertheless, the Parlement's evasion of the issue is a measure of the distance the Princes of the Blood had risen in the French hierarchy.

The growing significance of royal blood probably resulted from the disaster of the Hundred Years' War, for blood became one of the weapons taken from the French intellectual arsenal to combat the English pretensions to the French throne. Perhaps the war even contributed a specific event that did much to raise the Princes of the Blood above other nobles—the anomalous circumstances surrounding the coronation of Charles VII. The six men chosen to represent the old lay Peers of France were an interesting group: John, duke of Alençon (he who was to be tried for treason in 1458), represented the duke of Burgundy; Charles de Bourbon, count of Clermont (whose father, the duke of Bourbon, had been a prisoner of the English for ten years, and who himself was to lead the revolt known as the Pragerie in 1440), represented the duke of Normandy; Louis de Bourbon, count of Vendôme (who had made a rather astonishing escape from the Tower of London after he had been captured at Agincourt), represented the duke of Guyenne; Guy, seigneur de Laval (brother-in-law of the count of Vendôme and member of the king's council), represented the count of Toulouse; Raoul, seigneur de Gaucourt (who apparently played an important role in reorganizing the French military system later in Charles's reign), represented the count of Flanders; and Hardouin, seigneur de Maillé (one of the three governors of the young Charles), represented the count of Champagne.[15] The first three of these men were Princes of the Blood (to use the later terminology), and the fact that they were chosen to represent the old dukes-peers would not have gone unnoticed in later times. By selecting them as he did, Charles emphasized both royal blood and loyalty to the throne, for there were no less than twelve (and possibly eighteen) adult nobles of the royal blood alive at the time; although some, like the duke of Bourbon, were prevented from attending the coronation by the exigencies of the struggle with England, others had cast their lots with the English and Burgundians.

The role of the Princes of the Blood continued to be augmented at the coronations of Louis XI in 1461 and Charles VIII in 1484. On both of these occasions nobles who were Princes of the Blood represented five of the six old lay peers (the duke of Burgundy was present in 1461, but he was represented by Louis, duke of Orléans, in 1484). This trend was reversed at the coronation of Louis XII in 1498, when only two Princes of the Blood represented the old lay Peers of France.[16] Nonetheless, the concept of Princes of the Blood had continued to develop, and the records of the Estates General held at Tours early in 1484 demonstrate amply that "Princes of the Blood" had almost completely supplanted the older terminology.[17]

From the middle of the sixteenth century there was a second reversal of the trend for Princes of the Blood to represent peers, but princes did represent four of the old peers at the coronation of Francis I in 1515. Although the sixteenth century was not at that time as strict about rankings in the noble hierarchy as it was to become, the relative importance of the royal blood certainly seemed to be emphasized at Francis's postcoronation entry into Paris in 1515, when the duke of Alençon, the duke of Bourbon, and the count of Vendôme—all Princes of the Blood—immediately followed the king and preceded the duke of Lorraine and other members of the nobility. In other words, by 1515 a count of the royal blood could take precedence over a duke in whose veins the blood of kings did not flow. A single event did not provide a sufficient precedent for all time, though, and at the dinner on the evening following the entry the duke of Lorraine sat above the count of Vendôme (but below the first two Princes of the Blood).[18]

The equivocal situation at Francis I's coronation entry was entirely appropriate: during the first half of the century the peers and the Princes of the Blood constantly exchanged positions, and a lengthy series of rather distasteful disputes was the natural consequence. The first of these occurred in 1506, when, at a meeting of the Parlement, the peer-bishop of Laon refused to cede to Louis de Bourbon, prince of La Roche-sur-Yon, a Prince of the Blood but not a peer; the Parlement ordered both to retire with the understanding that their disagreement would be settled, but nothing was done. There were times when the matter of precedence was comparatively easy to resolve. One such case occurred in 1517, when the cardinal of Vendôme, a Prince of the Blood and Peer of France, was allowed to precede the peer-duke of Nevers, who had claimed that the lay peers preceded the ecclesiastical peers.[19] In 1521 and again in 1523 the double dignity of peer and prince allowed the duke of Alençon to precede the bishop-duke of Langres, one of the ecclesiastical peers. Nevertheless, to be a Prince of the Blood alone was not sufficient to warrant precedence, and the importance of the peerage was recognized at a *lit de justice* in 1527, when Francis I created the count of Saint-Paul (a Prince of the Blood) peer solely for the judgment of Charles de Bourbon, constable of France. A decade later that seemed no longer necessary, and, at the trial of Emperor Charles V as count of Flanders, two Princes of the Blood who were not peers sat above one of the peers. On that occasion, nonetheless, the basic ambiguity of the situation was emphasized by the fact that the cardinal of Lorraine, archbishop and duke of Reims, sat above the cardinal of Bourbon, Prince of the Blood and bishop-duke of Laon; the fact that the former was the most important ecclesiastical figure in France could not help but cloud the issue.[20]

4. Montpensier's Suit

Two individuals played a central role in resolving the dispute to the advantage of the Princes of the Blood: Louis II, duke of Montpensier (1513–1582), and Catherine de Médicis, who as queen mother eventually came to his aid. The duke of Montpensier was a man extremely jealous of his rights, which is understandable if we realize that the Capetian dynasty was experiencing a tremendous contraction. By 1550 many of the branches of the dynasty had died out: the direct Valois line; the Angevin line; the dukes of Burgundy; the Valois counts of Alençon; the Valois counts of Nevers; the counts of Evreux; the Bourbon counts of Clermont; the Bourbon counts of Montpensier; the Bourbon counts of Saint-Pol; and the Bourbon seigneurs of Carency. The Valois-Orléans kings (Francis I and his successors) and the descendants of the Bourbon Charles, duke of Vendôme (e.g., Antoine, king of Navarre, and Louis, prince of Condé), and the Bourbon princes of La Roche-sur-Yon, dukes of Montpensier, were the only descendants of Saint Louis still alive. In 1550 there were only ten princes of the Blood descended from Saint Louis (not including the king, Henry II), whereas in 1450, for example, there had been at least twenty-three Princes of the Blood. Of course, the situation was to become even more serious before the end of the century, and the desperate danger of the total demise of Louis IX's progeny contributed much to the rise of the Princes of the Blood, of dynastic kingship, and of French royal absolutism, which all must be seen as at least partly the chance result of a number of historical accidents (e.g., the death of Henry II in 1559 after his fatal joust).[21]

Under these circumstances it is no wonder that the Princes of the Blood should establish themselves as a group set apart from the other nobles of France in the sixteenth century. Even those who were Peers of France came to be distinguished from the other peers by virtue of their direct descent from a royal progenitor, and, at the same time, they assumed—or were given—the rights and prerogatives of the peers. Before the end of the century they were often called "born counselors of the king" (a phrase originally applied to the peers) or a part of the royal dignity, and they were even referred to "as a ray of royal majesty."[22] Like the peers they were granted the right to wear their swords in the Parlement, and the prince closest to the king (but who was not the son of the king) was granted special privileges.[23] Charles Loyseau said that they were true princes (even though there was only one prince, in the sense of the Latin *princeps*) "because they alone are capable of true Principality and sovereignty."[24] Although some of these attributes date only from the latter part of the century and thus postdate the resolution of the struggle between the princes and the peers, it is not inaccurate to note that as the Princes of the Blood acted for the old Peers of France at various ceremonies—particularly the coronation ceremony—those ceremonies themselves came to be an expression of the dynastic principle of absolutism. In the sixteenth century the coronation became constitutive of dynasticism, not of the man entering into an office. It was for this reason that, at the coronation of Henry II in 1547, the nasty argument between the duke of Montpensier, on the one hand, and the dukes of Guise and of Nevers, on the other, was of such great importance.[25]

The eve of Henry's coronation was not the first time that Montpensier had gotten himself involved in a dispute with the peers. In 1541, at the presentation of roses to the Parlement, Montpensier claimed that, because he was a Prince of the Blood as well as a peer, he should present the roses before the duke of Nevers, whose peerage was older, but who was not a Prince of the Blood. Each protagonist argued his case, and the court decided in favor of Montpensier.[26]

Montpensier was not to be so fortunate in 1547, though. Henry II settled the dispute for his coronation ceremony by temporarily giving precedence to the older peers rather than to a Prince of the Blood. The provisional character of the charter by which Henry arranged this is very explicit, and the outcome of the struggle might have been quite obvious had it not been for one important factor: one of the men over whom Montpensier claimed precedence at Henry's coronation was Claude de Lorraine, duke of Guise; given the power of the house of Lorraine in sixteenth-century France, the outcome was anything but a foregone conclusion.

At first, matters went quite well for Montpensier and his fellow Princes of the Blood, despite Henry's indecision in 1547. At the royal supper following Henry's entry into Paris in June 1549 only Princes of the Blood sat at the table with the king: two cardinals on the king's right and four lay princes on his left. In the Parlement two weeks later three Princes of the Blood sat above the dukes of Guise and of Nevers (although the cardinal of Lorraine, as archbishop-duke of Reims and first Peer of France, sat first on the king's left). Then the winds began to blow in favor of the peers, especially of the duke of Guise. At a *lit de justice* held in November 1551 Guise sat immediately on the king's right, and when he was preceded by Montpensier in February 1552, he apparently created a considerable row. As a result Henry II wrote letters patent to the Parlement ordering it "to correct and rewrite the register which was made and kept for the day of that sitting and assembly of the peers, where by inadvertence, as is said, our cousin [the duke of

Guise] allowed himself to be preceded."[27] Henry's changed attitude toward the Princes of the Blood was illustrated by his decision in August 1551 that the princes could not take part in some judgments if they were not peers, and the king placed the duke of Lorraine and the duke of Nevers immediately on his left in a meeting in 1557. Three Princes of the Blood were given the first three positions on the king's left in Parlement in June 1559 (only a few weeks before Henry's accident), but it was the duke of Guise as grand chamberlain who was granted the position of honor at the king's feet. Of course, the decision that the ecclesiastical officials should be ranked in the order of their ecclesiastical offices (rather than their other titles or blood relationships) worked to the advantage of the cardinal of Lorraine, archbishop of Reims, throughout the last decade of Henry's life.[28]

Montpensier as representative of the Princes of the Blood continued to fare badly during the first years after Henry II's death. The duke of Guise preceded him at the coronations of Francis II and Charles IX, and it may be that Montpensier was preceded even by the duke of Nevers in 1561. Each time, though, Antoine de Bourbon, as king of Navarre, preceded Guise. Furthermore, Catherine de Médicis intervened on both occasions; she placed the monarch's oldest surviving brother immediately after the king and before Navarre in 1559 and 1561, and at Francis's coronation she had all three of the king's brothers (nine, eight, and five years of age) dressed as peers so that they could march before Guise.[29]

Catherine was probably responsible for placing Guise after the Princes of the Blood in the summer of 1561 and again in 1563,[30] and she was certainly responsible for arranging a significant meeting of the Princes of the Blood in 1573 after the election of her son (the future Henry III) to the Polish throne. Present at the meeting were the king and the two other Valois princes (his brothers) and seven of the eight (or nine) Bourbon Princes of the Blood. The members of this assemblage signed a statement to the effect that Henry's rights to the French throne would be recognized by all after his acquisition of the Polish crown and that Henry (III's) heirs would be considered the legitimate successors to the French throne even though they might be born outside the kingdom. This compact of the Princes of the Blood marked the penultimate stage in the feud between the royal blood and the antiquity of the peerage—by the agreement of 1573 the princes closed their ranks for a single positive act; from there it was but a short step to concerted action against a general class of acts, that is, against the claims of the Peers of France.[31]

Although the feud may not have broken out again until after Henry III's coronation early in 1575 because Montpensier did not represent one of the old Peers of France at this coronation, it was Henry who finally settled the dispute in 1576. Sometime in the first part of 1575 Montpensier requested Henry to resolve the affair. In his request he argued that "in your kingdom the lay peerages are fused in your person, Sire, and that none of your subjects can represent them except abstractly or by imagination." He continued by asserting, "Monsieur de Guise . . . , under the pretext that his predecessors had led themselves to believe that they represented the peers of the Duchy of Burgundy. . . at the coronations of Henry II, Francis II, and Charles IX . . . , wants at the present by such means to deduce a consequence . . . detrimental to the suppliant. . . ."[32] On 17 April 1575, Henry III ordered the Parlement to investigate the issue and to be prepared to render a decision within a month. On 15 March 1576 Montpensier appeared before the Parlement to present his case verbally, and the Parlement apparently reported favorably to his cause. Henry discussed the matter with his mother, the Princes of the Blood, the duke of Guise, and other great nobles, and at Blois in December 1576 Henry promulgated an edict designed to settle the dispute once and for all: ". . . henceforth the Princes of our Blood, Peers of France, shall precede and hold rank according to their degree of consanguinity over the other princes and seigneurs, Peers of France, no matter what title they may have, just as much at the consecrations and coronations of kings as at the sessions of the courts of Parlement and any other solemnities, assemblies, and public ceremonies."[33] When this edict was registered by the Parlement of Paris on 8 January 1577, it became a part of French public law. Royal blood had triumphed over its feudalistic opponents—more completely than the edict might lead one to believe.

5. The Result of the Verdict

Literally interpreted, the edict of 1576 had a rather confined character. It only settled the rank of those princes who were also peers; it did not say anything about those princes who were not peers, and it did not establish rank among the princes themselves. Nonetheless, the edict was construed to give the princes absolute precedence over the peers. Charles Loyseau wrote with characteristic succinctness in the early seventeenth century:

> . . . now that the rank of the Princes of the Blood is better established than ever, even though they be neither dukes nor counts, one no longer doubts that they should march in all places before the dukes and the counts, that is to say, before the peers, and that among themselves they ought similarly to rank according to their proximity to the Crown, not according to the title of their lordships; likewise, the other lords no longer enter into comparison with them since . . . some [of the Princes of the Blood] have come to the Crown . . . in the collateral line, . . . above all our great King Henry IV, who was twenty-one degrees removed from his predecessor. In such a fashion the Princes of the Blood now constitute without a doubt a separate body and an order of supreme dignity and surpass by much all the other dignities of France.[34]

Written less than four decades after the promulgation of Henry III's edict, Loyseau's words are one gauge of the preeminence of the Princes of the Blood; the high regard in which Loyseau was held undoubtedly did much to make his interpretation the one generally accepted. Other late sixteenth- and early seventeenth-century writers likewise made statements implicitly glorifying the dynastic principle. The princes were to take precedence over prelates, they were to have a deliberative voice in the Parlement of Paris, they were exempt from duels, and, along with the king, they were exempt from excommunication.[35] Furthermore, they were specifically chosen to represent the old Peers of France at the coronations. Perhaps the final step in the development of royal blood mysticism was taken in 1711, when an edict attempted to provide that Louis XIV's legitimized sons and their male descendants should represent the old peers at the coronations, "after and in default of the Princes of the Blood," an edict that evoked the full ire of the duke of Saint-Simon, peer of France.[36]

The coronations following the edict of 1576 certainly provide proof of the triumph of the absolutist principle of dynastic right as incorporated in the Princes of the Blood. Three of the four adult Princes of the Blood represented old lay peers at Henry IV's coronation in 1594; the only one who did not was Charles, cardinal of Bourbon, who had barred himself from representation by his active attempt to gain the crown for himself.[37] At Louis XIII's coronation in 1610 all three of the adult princes represented peers, but when Louis XIV was crowned in 1654, only Monsieur, the king's brother, represented a peer; the other three adult Princes of the Blood (Gaston d'Orléans, the prince of Condé, and the prince of Conti) were probably prevented from taking an active part in the coronation by their important roles during the revolt of the Fronde.[38] At Louis XV's coronation in 1722 all five of the adult Princes of the Blood represented peers (the Spanish Bourbons were excluded from the succession by the Peace of Utrecht), and all six of the old peers were represented by Princes of the Blood at Louis XVI's coronation in 1775.[39]

The aftermath of the quarrel between the Peers of France and the Princes of the Blood, in particular between the dukes of Guise and the duke of Montpensier, amply demonstrates the consequences of Henry III's decision. Yet Montpensier's role during the crucial phase of the squabble might be thought to have been characteristic of the great nobles of the sixteenth century, his struggle for precedence to have been part of some sort of "noble resurgence" that made civil war nearly inevitable. To describe noble incentives in this way explains little, however, for in each of the last centuries of the French monarchy historians have detected a noble recovery. The revolt of the Fronde has been seen as such, and it has been said that eighteenth-century France saw a great resurgence of the nobles;[40] one could equally argue that the war of the Ligue du Bien Public in the fifteenth century was indicative of such rehabilitation, or even that the activities of Charles VI's uncles during his minority and insanity marked an increased power of the "overmighty subject." For the reason that it was a noble against whom the duke of Montpensier asserted himself, this interpretation is further weakened—only if the two had made common cause against some nonnoble institution or class of people could Montpensier's actions possibly be viewed as part of a general trend on the part of the French nobility.

It is wiser to seek some personal ground or grounds for Montpensier's activity. He may have felt a personal antipathy to the dukes of Guise, he may have thought that the policy of the Guises was harmful to France, he may even have been constantly impressed by the fact that he, as a Prince of the Blood, stood a chance, however remote, of one day becoming the king of France; he may have been motivated by all of these. It is still more likely that Montpensier was attempting simply to acquire the greatest possible power and prestige for himself, which is what members of the other great families of the time—the Guises, the Montmorencys, the Colignys, the Bourbons—were doing; if they were more successful in the latter half of the century than the duke of Bourbon had been during the reign of Francis I, that achievement must be attributed more to a whole host of internal and external problems that France faced (including the problems of minor kings and a hesitant and vacillating government) than to any general activity peculiarly characteristic of the period after the death of Francis I.

Montpensier's dispute with the Guises certainly led to acrimonious feelings on both sides; both parties naturally sought aid from the most powerful figure in the land, the king, but the accident of blood relationship enabled Montpensier to enlist the argument from blood to his cause and to identify his personal interests with those of French kingship and, particularly, of the dynasty that governed it. The result of this, whatever the personal impulse behind Montpensier's suit, was obvious: a glorification of dynasticism and the royal blood.

When the Bourbons were restored to the throne in 1815, a new twist was given to the French monarchy: after the fall of the French Empire the upper house of the bicameral legislature was called the Chamber of Peers. At France's last royal coronation ceremony, that of Charles X in 1825, neither the twelve old Peers of France nor any of the new peers played any role as peers. The functions of the six representatives of the old lay peers were assumed by three men: not surprisingly, these three were the only adult Princes of the Blood,[41] the history of whose predecessors' contest with the Peers of France illuminates, perhaps more clearly than anything else associated with the coronation ceremony, France's gradual transition from the medieval to the modern monarchy. The new monarchy retained many elements of the old, though, but it was not stagnant, and it prepared the way for another form of state, the Empire.

PART FOUR

ARRIVAL AND DEPARTURE OF AN EMPIRE

.　.　.　.　.　.　.　.　.　.

11

ROYAL AND IMPERIAL IMAGERY

· · · · · · · · · · ·

1. The Coronation Entries at Reims

The modern French monarchy's dynastic bias was evident not only in the spectacular degree of precedence afforded to the Princes of the Blood, but occasionally also in the elaborate scenes associated with the king's precoronation entry into Reims, which was a flexible instrument for the expression of additional attitudes and concepts. Not every king was honored with a formal entry. Henry IV did not have one when he went to Chartres for his ceremony, and Louis XIV did not want an entry;[1] both rulers simply entered the respective cities with little pomp. We are also very poorly informed, or not informed at all, about the entries of several other kings. There are descriptions of enough of the entries, though, to enable us to trace from the fifteenth century to the end of the Old Regime much of the symbolism of French kingship.

The entries that are adequately documented serve as an interesting kind of barometer of French cultural fashions in a major provincial center rather than in the capital or in the court, although Reims was doubtless influenced by both of the latter. The themes of the fifteenth-century entries and the ways in which they were treated were distinctly medieval. In the course of the sixteenth century the allure of humanism with its classical motifs and allusions gave the entries a new coloration, although themes typical of the Middle Ages continued to find their places in the entries, and the only seventeenth-century entry, that of Louis XIII, was an amalgam of French and classical subjects. The two entries of the eighteenth century strongly reflected French neoclassicism—the entry of Louis XVI was so classically oriented that even the legend of the Holy Ampulla, the central fiction of the later medieval monarchy, was presented in a classical guise. Much of the symbolism in Reims sustained this sort of cultural change.

Two broad types of subject matter were displayed at the Reims entries. The first, dealing with topics of real or legendary French history, demonstrated a preoccupation both with medieval legends and with modern, legalistic kingship, whereas the second, which adapted classical Roman history and mythology to accord with French interests, not only used classical motifs to portray contemporary concern but also combined these motifs with longstanding currents of Frankish and French thought to elevate the French monarchy far above any other monarchy on earth, pointing at the same time toward France's postabsolutistic future.

2. French History

Because the French kingship had an inextricable religious bias, the consecration of the king at Reims was at least as important as his coronation, and it is to be expected that the legends connected with the consecration should be exhibited at the king's entry into the city. Of these legends, one in particular was associated solely with Reims, the legend of the Holy Ampulla, undeniably the most mysterious and most revered element of the cult of the French kings. Even though rationalists in the seventeenth and eighteenth centuries may have doubted the legend's truth, the churchmen at Reims never failed in their propagation of it, and the monarchs themselves put no obstacles in the way of popular devotion to it. The story of Clovis and the Holy Ampulla epitomized the divine institution of the French kingship so perfectly, was so central to French royalist theology, that visual representations of the legend at the precoronation entry acquired quickly and then maintained for over two hundred years a straightforward narrative form. Only at the last coronation before the Revolution was the legend presented symbolically rather than forthrightly.[2]

The pattern for most of the portrayals of the legend was established at the coronation of Charles VIII in 1484. A *tableau vivant* showed "the baptism and consecration of King Clovis, the first Christian king of the French," and the transmission of the Holy Ampulla. A verse accompanying the tableau said, "In the year of grace 500 King Clovis received from St. Remigius at Reims his baptism, crown, and consecration with the ampulla's chrism, which God had transmitted from heaven by his angel." Charles stopped when he saw the tableau and asked what it was. When he was told that it was the "mystery of the consecration" that he was to receive, he unbuttoned his mantle and removed his hat before passing on.[3]

The following kings either did not have a precoronation entry (Francis I and Henry IV) or their entries were not described extensively (Louis XII, Francis II, and Charles IX). The Holy Ampulla is not alluded to in the descriptions of the entries of Henry II and Henry III, so not before 1610 was the legend of Clovis's baptism again described. At Louis XIII's entry, the city of Reims erected a triumphal arch that contained a representation of Clovis, and accompanying Latin and French verses spoke of him as having acquired a kingdom and empire by his valor and the chrism. At one of the city gates a painting depicted the ampulla borne above an altar by a white dove; accompanying the painting was a device taken from Luke 1:78: ORIENS EX ALTO, "The dayspring from on high," a device that had reference not only to the sending of the ampulla from heaven but that also carried the connotation of the rising sun.[4]

The representation of the legend was similar at the coronation of Louis XV (Louis XIV had no coronation entry), but at the coronation of Louis XVI the legend was presented in a novel fashion. A cartouche showed Numa Pompilius, the legendary successor of Romulus to the Roman kingship, receiving a buckler from heaven. In the cartouche, Numa, under the direction of the "Nymph Egeria," was outlining the order of ceremonies for expiatory sacrifices to free "the cradle of the Roman Empire" from the plague; at this moment a thunderbolt opened the heavens and deposited a bronze buckler upon the altar. Egeria pointed to the buckler and "seemed to announce to him that it was a pledge of the protection of Heaven." The description concluded, "This event was regarded as a type of consecration that made him whom the gods protected in such a special manner respected and feared as their equal." Accompanying the cartouche was the device SACRAT, SACRUMQUE TUETUR, "He consecrates and maintains that that is consecrated." This cartouche, the only allusion at the entry of Louis XVI to the legend of the Holy Ampulla, thus served—even as late as 1775— as an expression of the belief in the divine right of the Bourbon king of France; it indirectly claimed a divine protection that was one of the basic elements of Bourbon kingship.[5]

Two other medieval legends received much less attention at the entries. The second major element of the royal cult, the king's efficacious touch for the "king's evil," received but scant attention at the entries, for it was depicted at the entries of only Charles VIII and Louis XV. This was not without reason: the myth itself was given concrete form as it was enacted in the course of the postcoronation ceremonies. The story of the miraculous origin of the royal fleurs-de-lys was not illustrated through any specific treatment at the entries, although the device itself played a prominent role at the entries throughout the period covered by this study.[6]

The elements of the royal cult so far discussed accentuated the mystical and even liturgical nature of French kingship, but another theme, introduced at the entry of Charles VIII, emphasized the legalistic kingship of the Renaissance. In resuscitating Frankish legends, it stressed the historical origins of French kingship and the antiquity of the French, at the same time coupling purely French elements with classical themes to portray another interpretation of kingship.

The new concept of the kingship was reflected in the revival of two older, phantom figures—Pharamond and Samothes. At Charles VIII's entry a tableau presented Pharamond, the mythical first king (as distinguished from the first Christian king) of the French and great-great-grandfather of Clovis, as a long-haired, bearded monarch with a sword in one hand and a scepter in the other. He was in the process of being crowned by a number of long-haired, bearded men "dressed as Turks and Saracens," who held a golden crown above his head. Before Pharamond were four bearded men dressed in doctoral robes; they were reading an epistle and were identified as Salagast, Uvisogast, Bosogast, and Uvidagast, the four lawgivers who gave Pharamond the Salic law. The history of Pharamond was briefly given in a verse: "The French, descended from the Trojans, pagans called Sicambrians, made Pharamond their first king; he created the Salic law for them and freed them from the Romans who ruled over all men at that time. This happened in the year of grace four hundred twenty."[7]

This tableau immediately followed one presenting the legendary Trojan origin of the French, and it immediately preceded a tableau picturing the baptism of Clovis. The three tableaux illustrated the three most important stages in the legendary history of the French: the Trojan origin of the French in an heroic age; the formation of the French kingship and the promulgation of the Salic law; and the baptism of the first Christian king of the French with the sacred balm from the Holy Ampulla. The Clovis legend had long been the mainstay of the French royal myth, so it is somewhat surprising to find that, with Pharamond placed before Clovis, attention was directed to the first king of the Franks, the man who supposedly gave them that Salic law that was considered to regulate the succession to the French throne.[8]

The history of Pharamond stressed law over the Church, and when the concept of fundamental law was invented in the sixteenth century, the Salic law associated with Pharamond was included among the fundamental laws of France. The law of succession did experience some difficulties in the course of the century, as we have seen,[9] but the general acceptance of the Salic law after the successful recognition of Henry IV, which lay at the heart of Bourbon dynasticism, partly accounts for the failure of the Pharamond legend to appear again at a coronation entry.

Sixteenth-century historiography and jurisprudence revived the legends of the early medieval historians and emphasized the antiquity of the French origins, an antiquity as great as that of the Romans. The genealogy of the French kings was extended back beyond Pharamond to Samothes, the first king of the Gauls and the first to govern the Gauls with law, and to Francus, the son of Hector and founder of the kingdom of Sicambria. Pharamond was only the first Frankish king, and the Franks were thought to be Gauls who had wandered in Germany and become mixed with the Germans. Pharamond's achievement paled in comparison with the much older achievements of Samothes and Francus, and this too helps to explain the disappearance of the revived Pharamond from the coronation entries.[10]

Samothes, like Pharamond, emphasized the role of law in the kingship, but Pharamond as a symbol of dynastic right came in 1610, at Louis XIII's coronation, to be embodied in Francus, the eponym of the French. As the son of Hector and son-in-law of Remus, Francus belongs not to French, but to classical history and mythology, which, impelled by Renaissance humanism, was called into the service of a changing kingship.

3. Classical History

Much of the Roman history in the coronation entries aimed at glorifying the French nation and its kingship. Numerous references to the Roman Empire (or to the Roman monarchy or republic with the imperial associations of later times) implied that the French king was as great as the Roman emperor, that he was a universal emperor to the same degree as the Roman ruler. Imperial pretensions of the French kings were centuries old by 1500. In their earlier stages they had been expressed by formulae like the one that claimed that "the king in his kingdom is the emperor of his kingdom," and these had been used as a vehicle for an assertion of independence from the Holy Roman emperor. Although Charlemagne had been canonized by an anti-pope at the behest of a German emperor, Frederick Barbarossa, the French also adhered to the cult of Saint Charlemagne. The French coronation sword, La Joyeuse, had been identified with and named after the weapon of the great conqueror, and when Charles V had the royal scepter refashioned, he had it surmounted by the figure of Charlemagne sitting in majesty. The medieval emperors were crowned with the closed crown "of Charlemagne" (now in the Imperial Schatzkammer in Vienna), but the French kings were also crowned with a closed "crown of Charlemagne" (a tiara that is no longer in existence). But, although Francis I actively sought the imperial election in 1519, and even later there could still be talk of similar candidature for other French kings, by the end of the sixteenth century the French monarchs' emphasis on universality ceased to be in competition with the Holy Roman emperor and began to imitate the ancient Roman emperors. The new direction was suggested at the coronation entry of Henry III into Reims in 1575, when one of the arches depicted Catholic Faith, under which a verse referred to "the three lilies of your empire."[11]

The creation of the classical history of French kingship was completed at the coronation entry of Louis XIII, at which it was possible to claim that "Rome still sighs for our kings" and that in anointing the kings with the Holy Balm the chrism promised them "the Empire of the world.[12] The main vehicle for conveying the new concept of empire was an old medieval legend of the Trojan origins of the Franks. The long-forgotten story, revived during the

Renaissance, alleged the Franks to be descended from the same Trojans who had founded Rome, and it implied that the French kings and their kingdom possessed an antiquity every bit as great as Rome's. According to the Reims version of the story, the family of Remus was evicted from Rome and founded the city of Reims,[13] and other Trojans, led by King Priam's grandson Francus, fled to Scythia and founded the kingdom of Sicambria. In the course of various difficulties over some fifteen centuries the latter gave rise to the Gauls and eventually the Franks.[14] The legend of the Trojan origin of the Franks had been thoroughly discredited by the more critical of the sixteenth-century historians, but it was again revived in the early seventeenth century, and it enjoyed an Indian summer that lasted well into the eighteenth century.

The theme was announced at Louis XIII's entry on the first of the triumphal arches, which was capped by figures of Samothes, Remus, and Francus. Samothes, the first king of the Gauls and legendary son of Noah's son Japheth, was identified in a Latin verse that said, "This is the descendant of Japheth [*Hic satus Iapeto*] who uttered the name Durocortorum [the ancient Latin name for Reims] and founded the city of Reims with tower and walls and who stretches forth to you the Palladian olive branch."[15] A French verse asserted that "Samothes was the first to govern our ancient Gallic fathers with law; he bears the olive in his hand and peace on his face."[16]

The inscription under the second figure, Remus, said that he had founded Reims; depicted as placing the crown on Louis's head, he was obviously an expression of local pride. The third figure, Francus, is much more interesting. The son of Hector, he was king of the Germans; when he married the only daughter of Remus, the king of the Celts, he joined the two kingdoms. The verse accompanying him said, "Behold, the Hectorean child, the son-in-law of Remus, illustrious in arms, the glory of the French, also father to the French kings, brings to you the conquering laurel, O thrice greatest King [*Rex ter maxime*]!" Another verse accompanying Francus addressed Louis: "Of the noble blood of Troy mixed with Latin blood was born the great Caesar who marshalled under the eagle the Empire of almost all the earth and the sea. And you, being born of the blood of Troy and Remus, true Caesar of the French, you are predestined to submit the Empire of this world to the rule of the three lilies." One of the many hieroglyphs at this entry referred to this verse with the device UNDARUM, TERRAEQUE POTENS, "Power of lands and seas."[17]

Except for Remus, these figures and inscriptions had nothing to do with the coronation as such. The precoronation entry was essentially a means of using old legends and new attitudes toward the past to glorify Louis XIII. The figure of Samothes, the first to govern the Gauls with law, implied that Louis, his supposed descendant, would govern his kingdom in the same way, that is, with peace and wisdom. Francus, on the other hand, had already been made the subject of what was supposed to be the French national epic, Pierre de Ronsard's *La Franciade*. The poem, written in emulation of the Vergilian epic, drew a clear parallel between the national greatness of Rome and that of France. At Louis XIII's entry the role was again assigned to Francus, the eponym and genearch of the French kings, a man whose marital alliance with Remus foreshadowed the future greatness of France, just as Remus and Romulus were symbols of the future greatness of Rome. The prophecy of coming grandeur was to be fulfilled by a new king, a Caesar who would conquer land and sea alike, bringing them under the rule of the fleurs-de-lys.[18]

Louis XIII's entry certainly gives the impression of presenting a political goal for that monarch's reign. One of the triumphal arches was decorated with the figures of Hercules, Alexander, and Achilles. The accompanying sonnet addressed Louis as "Achilles of the French, more powerful at your birth than was the Grecian Hercules in his cradle." His future was also foretold: "You will be therefore one day the Gallic Alexander; your father very expressly did not put this entire universe under his laws in order that you might take it." Another hieroglyph continued the theme with a device taken from Vergil's *Aeneid* (I, 279): IMPERIUM SINE FINE DEDI, "Dominion without end have I bestowed."[19] This device had a double meaning. On the one hand, it had an obvious meaning in its own right. On the other, it combined the French ideal of the ancient empire with the mythical Trojan origin of France, for it was taken from the passage in the *Aeneid* in which Mars prophesied to Venus the coming greatness of the Rome to be founded by Romulus; thus was a pagan prophecy adapted to the Most Christian King of France.

Classical history and French mythology were cleverly intertwined at Louis XIII's entry. There was a mixture of medieval and Renaissance attitudes toward the past, a mixture that claimed a national greatness for France and a personal greatness for its monarch. Louis XIII himself did not fulfill the promise of his coronation entry, but his successor, who had no such entry, raised the prestige of the French kingship to heights never before attained and spent the greater part of his adult years attempting to create a French empire.

When the next coronation entry took place at the coronation of Louis XV in 1722, only seven years had lapsed since the death of Louis XIV and nine years since the Peace of Utrecht, which had brought to an end the Sun King's long devotion to the extension of French geopolitical power. The reaction to Louis XIV's long series of wars surely had much to do with the near absence of imperial aspirations and implied comparisons with ancient Rome in 1722. One verse said of the monarch, "LOUIS is my Caesar, my Triumph and my Glory," it is true, but Louise of Savoy had also referred to her son Francis, then count of Angoulême, as "my Caesar." Much more evocative was the figure of the city of Reims pointing to Julius Caesar's (or so they were called) Roman arches in the city; the accompanying lines asked and answered the question, "What ancient titles shall I renew, what arch of Caesar? You are all my glory, you call Caesar into being for me." Even here, though, the emphasis was not on imperial grandeur, but on a renewal, the dominant theme of this entry.[20]

The renewal theme, calling for the return of a golden age under the new monarch, was announced by a phrase from Virgil's *Eclogues* (IV, 6): REDEUNT SATURNIA REGNA, "The Saturnian regimen returns," and there were several allusions to the substitution of peace for war.[21] The monarch's solar device likewise was used to carry out this theme. Cupids were shown lighting their torches from the first rays of the rising sun; an explanation said that this denotes that "similar to the sun, the light of which succeeds the shadow of night, the King, in dissipating the horrors of war and making his virtues glisten, will be the joy of his people and the delight of the universe."[22] Other cupids in another painting were playing with martial weapons taken from the Temple of Mars; the inscription said ERUNT ALTERA BELLA, "There will be other wars." Like the previous inscription, this was taken from Vergil's fourth *Eclogue* (IV, 35), and it predicted that a new golden age would begin with Louis XV's accession. One of the imperial references quoted above stressed the renewal, which was implied in a passage that said that the world was being prepared "to receive Astraea, whom Heaven will send it in favor of our young Monarch."[23]

At Louis XVI's coronation entry, too, the renewal theme, which made extensive use of solar imagery, was important. At no other coronation entry did the sun play such a role as at this one. The sun was used to personify the king, Louis XVI, who had recalled the parlements as one of his first acts of state. A sundial was shown in the rays of the sun, which had been obscured by clouds. A device, UTILITATI PUBLICAE RESTITUTUS, "Restored to public utility," a French verse, and the description tell us that the sundial represented the Parlement of Paris. The clouds that obscured the sun were the dissolution of the French parlements in the last years of Louis XV's reign.[24]

Another sun was shown lighting the fruit-bearing countryside with its first rays while the constellation Virgo seemed to rise with it (Louis was born on 23 August 1754, the day on which the sun entered the zodiacal sign of Virgo). Vergil's *Aeneid* was called into use with the quotation SPONDEO DIGNA TUIS INGENTIBUS OMNIA COEPTIS, "Be sure that all shall be worthy of thy mighty enterprise." The "mighty enterprise" was apparently the return of the golden age represented by the twin rising of the sun and Virgo (or Astraea, the last goddess to depart from earth, and a symbol of the golden age). Astraea was also Justice (*Justitia*), and it was at the base of a statue of Justice that all this was presented; the poet put in the mouth of Justice the words "I announced the beautiful days whose dawn was blessed."[25] Still another sun was shown traversing the sign of the zodiac with the device REGIT QUA REGITUR, "He rules to the extent that he is ruled." This device was explained as expressing "the attachment that His Majesty has shown for the laws and customs of his kingdom." An accompanying verse said, "I regulate the seasons, I divide the days; the universe embellishes itself with my prolific light, and, faithful to the law that governs my heart, I am the benefactor of the world."[26]

The Middle Ages had occasionally associated solar imagery with kingship, and, as we have seen, the sixteenth century had sometimes equated the French king with the sun, but it was the Bourbons, beginning with the coronation entry of Louis XIII, who had increasingly resorted to the conceit that in most people's minds reached its zenith under Louis XIV with the selection of the sun as the ruler's personal symbol. Thereafter the equation of the sun and the king was not forgotten, and in 1775 the king as sun, to whom there was no equal on earth, would enlighten his fellow men and bring about a return to the greatness of the past. Such conceptions may strike us as the sheerest sort of arrogance, but, after the transformation of feudalistic kingship into absolutistic and dynastic kingship, the exaltation of the person who was head of the dynasty, of the individual who could in some ways be identified with the state, could utilize no better symbol for the king than the sun.

Accompanying French absolutism was a French "imperialism," for Louis XVI was also twice referred to at his entry as *Ludovicus Augustus* (the Latin translation of his baptismal name), that is, not just as king, but as a king who possessed at least some of the attributes of an emperor. France itself was called an empire in a verse describing a bas-relief showing a vestal virgin throwing drops of aromatics on the hearth of the sacred fire; the fire was said to express the "ardent love of the French for their sovereigns," and, in the words of an accompanying verse, "this sacred flame of the empire ought always to assure glory and prosperity." Associated with the verse was the device NUTRIMENTA DEDIT, "He laid dry fuel about," which was taken from the passage in the *Aeneid* that describes the haven of Aeneas and his followers after their flight from Troy. The whole tableau thus cautiously used the legend of the Trojan origin of the Franks to imply that France had as great a claim to empire as ancient Rome.[27]

Louis XVI's coronation was the last of the Old Regime—which itself was the result of numerous influences and survivals of many centuries—and his coronation entry reflects a little of the heterogeneity of the past. There is something of the miraculous kingship of the Middle Ages in the treatment of the legend of the Holy Ampulla, classicized though it was in 1775. There may even be something of the legalistic kingship of the Renaissance in the reference to the monarch's rule in accordance with law, and the extensive use of solar imagery carried on a tradition as old as the Bourbon monarchy, so the use, or even the revival, of imperial terminology belongs firmly to the traditions of the French monarchy. Many of the traditions had changed with the passage of time, but the new did not always completely displace the old. In the eighteenth century France was often called an empire, not in any sense of competition with the Holy Roman Empire, or with an empire like the Roman one, but, as nearly as one can determine, with some of the sense of the word we use to refer to any vast territorial agglomeration, though perhaps still with legal overtones. This new concept of empire was expressed in 1775 along with the other two, and France was referred to as an empire in this sense in several places. It was not only a "French empire" but also a "Christian empire" (which accords with the interpretation of Louis's coronation as marking the beginning of a religious renewal), and Louis's accession "signalled the first days of an empire" that officials in Reims even called the personal empire of the monarch (*votre Empire*) in a letter to the king.[28]

Where concepts are commingled, even purposely so, it would be unwise to make sharp distinctions, but one further use of imperial terminology in 1775 must be noted. The French cult of Charlemagne naturally turned its attention to Aachen, and Louis XI had made the cult obligatory in France and had established special relations with the German city. Within a month of his coronation Louis XVI carried this tradition to the end of the Old Regime. On 26 June a special French envoy presented to the chapter of the royal chapel at Aachen Louis XV's funeral pall with the statement that the Omnipotent "has placed [the king, my master] at the head of a great Empire" and that the king "has commanded me to present this royal pall to you to be placed on the tomb of the emperor Charlemagne, whose scepter and crown His Majesty bears." In responding to the French envoy's speech, the dean of the chapter markedly avoided saying anything that could possibly be interpreted as recognizing a French empire.[29]

Louis XVI was not destined to become the artificer of an empire new or old, Christian, French, Holy Roman, ancient Roman, or territorial. The Revolution of 1789 was followed by the abolition of the monarchy, and the National Convention proclaimed the Year One of the French Republic on 22 September 1792, and Louis himself was executed on 21 January 1793. The Directory, the first French republic to be formally instituted, came into being on 16 October 1795, and the coup d'etat of 18 Brumaire (9 November 1799) led soon to the establishment of the Consulate. The latter government's institutions included the three consuls, a tribunate, and a senate, all obviously emulating the institutions of republican Rome, and, in addition, there was a council of state, a borrowing from the monarchy of the Old Regime. With the advantage of historical hindsight, we might say that it should have been obvious to anyone who knew his ancient history that the Roman Republic was followed by the Roman Empire and that the creation of the Consulate was the next-to-the-last step in the formal realization of the French Empire and the return of monarchy to France.[30]

AFTER NAPOLEON, THE DENOUEMENT

· · · · · · · · · ·

Napoleon's coronation has been aptly termed the first step toward the restoration of the monarchy.[1] The truth of this is evident in the next two reigns, for the Restoration monarchy was, willy-nilly, a mixture of the old and the new, that of Louis XVIII more so than that of his successor. Napoleon's peculiar form of a knightly order, the Legion of Honor, was retained and added to the old orders of Saint Michael, the Holy Spirit, and Saint Louis, which were revived, and the Napoleonic nobility swelled the ranks of the Bourbon nobility that returned from exile. Napoleon had concluded his coronation ceremonies with the distribution of the eagles to his soldiery, and, perhaps in imitation of that, one of Louis XVIII's first acts was to make provision for decorating his outstanding soldiers with the Bourbon lily.

1. Louis XVIII

There was one important difference between France's old and new rulers, however: Napoleon had been consecrated and crowned, whereas Louis XVIII never realized his hope of participating in the rite. It was not that he did not intend to be crowned, for he sincerely wished a coronation, but various factors eventually shattered his plans. There were quite definitely plans for the coronation—at least two of them—and they spanned the whole first half of Louis's reign. In the early autumn of 1814 the king entrusted François Joseph Belanger, royal architect for fêtes and ceremonies, with the task of preparing the coronation. The correspondence of Belanger is at least partially preserved, and it shows the dominant concern of the government in its search for a conception of kingship.[2] The architect began his work by attempting to determine what had happened to the Holy Ampulla, which, as was well known, had been solemnly destroyed in 1793 when a special envoy of the Convention dashed it to pieces against the base of what had been the statue of Louis XV in Reims. Belanger, nonetheless, was not satisfied that that had ended the matter, for there were rumors to the contrary.

Belanger's correspondence turned up three versions of the disappearance of the Holy Ampulla. The first stated that a monk of Saint-Remi had prudently substituted a faked ampulla for the original one and that it was the former that had been broken; in order to lend veracity to the substitution the monk had placed some of the Holy Balm in the forgery, and pious citizens saved pieces of the latter to which some of the balm had adhered; unfortunately, the monk who hid the original ampulla had died before divulging its hiding place. The second version urged that it was intended to replace the true with a false ampulla, but that that had proved impossible; consequently, the congealed balm was removed, and bits of it were distributed to various people for safekeeping (although one of them had had the misfortune to lose his portion). The final version, the one that came to be officially adopted, recognized that the original ampulla had in fact been destroyed, but some pieces (with balm) were preserved as relics by pious citizens, who thus made it possible for a Restoration monarch to be consecrated with the very balm with which Clovis had been baptized nearly a millennium and one-half earlier.[3]

With the highest of spirits the elated Belanger wrote that the Holy Balm had been saved, and he proceeded with other plans for the coronation of Louis XVIII. The city of Reims was examined to determine the condition of its monuments, lodgings, and the like, and it was estimated that the cathedral church was capable of seating 6,000 spectators. A list was also drawn up of the regalia that had escaped the destruction of the royal treasury at Saint-Denis. Charles Percier, who with Pierre Fontaine had been responsible for so many of Paris's public structures during Napoleon's reign, drew up a set of designs for the decoration of the cathedral of Reims for Louis's coronation, and Belanger could write confidently of the "ceremony of imminent consecration [*cérémonie du sacre prochain*] of His Majesty."[4] Napoleon's return from Elba brought this coronation project to a dead halt.

When the monarch returned from his second exile, the new regime was initially buttressed by the presence of foreign troops on French soil, and, by the time the government had become fully stable and the king thought that a coronation would not greatly antagonize the antiroyalists, Louis XVIII was in no physical condition either to undertake the journey to Reims or to meet the exhausting demands of a lengthy coronation ceremony. Belanger died in May 1818, and his post was ably filled by two men who were to change the modern face of Paris even more than he, Jean Le Cointe and, above all, Jacques Ignace Hittorff. These two drew up a most curious and interesting plan of the church of Sainte-Geneviève in Paris (now called the Panthéon), and the architects, "indicating provisionally the dispositions projected for the consecration of His Majesty Louis XVIII," placed the altar at the extreme eastern end of the choir; the platform with the throne (itself elevated upon a platform upon the platform) was placed across the nave between the western pillars that support the dome, and the chair for the king during the ceremony was located near the western end of the choir, between the altar and the throne; most of the remainder of the structure was filled with seating for the spectators. The plan probably dates from 1819, in any case after Le Cointe's and Hittorff's joint appointment as royal architects for fêtes and ceremonies, a date substantiated by the *grand écuyer's* budget for 1819, which estimated the office's costs for a coronation.[5] Because no text accompanies the plan, we cannot divine what sort of ceremony was envisaged for this new locus of a coronation ceremony. Was the ceremony to be carried out by the archbishop of Reims or by the archbishop of Paris? Was the king to be consecrated with a revived Holy Balm or with a more ordinary chrism? What coronation oaths were intended? Although none of these questions can be answered, the projected coronation presents the impression of having been conceived not as Belanger had envisioned his project, but as a sort of middle way between the Old Regime's last coronations and that of Napoleon. Whatever Hittorff's and Le Cointe's own plans, however, when the two were charged with the decorations for the coronation of Charles X, they produced a decor that reflected contemporary artistic taste, but the ceremony itself was modeled as much as possible upon the previous Bourbons' coronations.

2. Charles X's Coronation

Louis XVIII's age and health—he was sixty when he finally came to the throne—may have helped to prevent his coronation from taking place, but his younger brother, although sixty-eight in 1825, had the health of a young man. Furthermore, he had no desire to play the role of a constitutional monarch, as is demonstrated by the form of his coronation ceremony and his hesitation over the coronation oath.[6] Charles's desires notwithstanding, conditions had changed since the last royal coronation in 1775, and the final coronation of a French head of state could not help but reflect the new situation. It was as though old wine were poured into new wineskins.

Charles and his ministers were not totally blind to the changes in France since the coronation of Louis XVI, and a commission was formed to study the coronation ceremony and to bring it into line with the constitutional monarchy.[7] In all fairness it must be admitted that the commission did a tolerably good job of modernizing the ceremony. If the result was somewhat ridiculous in the context of the nineteenth century, that was only on account of the inappropriateness of a medieval ceremony requiring medieval credulity in a society noted for political consciousness and enlightened scepticism. Except for a few ultra-royalists and clerics, the vast majority of Frenchmen probably viewed the resurrection of the legacies of the French monarchy with amusement, concern, or anger —depending upon the political viewpoint of the observer. The legend of the Holy Ampulla was revived, and Charles X touched for scrofula—fifty years after the introduction of James Watt's steam engine, twenty-seven years after Edward Jenner's first smallpox vaccination, and twenty-four years after the use of the metric system had been made compulsory in France.

Charles X's coronation ceremony may be said to have begun on Saturday, 28 May, when he approached the city of Reims. By that time he had narrowly avoided disaster when an honorary cannonade in a small town near Reims frightened the horses drawing his carriage. Charles escaped unharmed, but a number of other people in other carriages were not so fortunate; one even lost his eyes in the accident. As Charles approached Reims, the mayor of the city presented him with the keys to the city, and Charles handed them to the captain of the guards. There were a number of triumphal arches in and near the city. With only one exception they portrayed the trades and industry, thus reflecting the bourgeois influence on post-Revolutionary France. The one exception was a Gothic arch that portrayed the consecration of Clovis. Charles went directly to the church, heard vespers, and presented to the church a number of very costly gifts.[8]

On the day of the coronation the clerics did not appear at the church until 7:30 A.M. At 8:00 A.M. the Cardinals of Clermont-Tonnerre and La Fare went to the archiepiscopal palace to fetch the king. The door of the king's chamber was closed, and the grand cantor of the cathedral church knocked on the door. The grand chamberlain, represented by that facile *homme politique*, Charles Maurice de Talleyrand-Périgord,[9] raised his voice from within the chamber and asked, "Whom do you want?" The cardinal of Clermont-Tonnerre replied, "Charles X, whom God has given us for king." The guards (*huissiers*) opened the door, and the cardinals entered the chamber and saluted the king. The latter, who was accompanied by the three Princes of the Blood, the great officers of the crown, and the household officials, rose from his armchair and returned their salute. Most of the occupants of the room left for the church, but Charles did not do so until Clermont-Tonnerre had intoned a prayer.

After the arrival of the king at the church, the archbishop of Reims (Jean Baptiste de Latil) went behind the altar to put on his pontifical vestments for the ceremony. When he returned he brought the new Holy Ampulla in its reliquary with him and placed it on the altar.[10] When the time came for the preparation of the Holy Chrism, the archbishop picked up the ampulla himself, withdrew some of the Holy Balm from it, and mixed it with chrism in a golden dish.

Before this ritual was carried out, however, Charles took the coronation oath, which he swore with his hands on the open Gospels held before him by the archbishop: "In the presence of God, I promise my people to maintain and honor our holy religion, as it behooves the Most Christian King and the Eldest Son of the Church; to render honest justice to all my subjects; and, finally, to govern in conformance with the laws of the kingdom and the Constitutional Charter, which I swear to observe faithfully; may God and the Holy Gospel aid me in this."[11]

The grand chamberlain (Talleyrand) then placed the slippers on

Charles's feet, and the dauphin invested Charles with the spurs, which he immediately removed. The litany (performed while the king prostrated himself before the archbishop) and consecration followed the investiture of the sword, and the chancellor turned to the three Princes of the Blood and, saluting them, invited them to approach the king for the coronation. As under the Old Regime, these three supported the crown before it was placed on Charles's head by the archbishop. Only Reims and the three Princes of the Blood kissed Charles, who is reported to have taken the dauphin in his arms and embraced him at that time.[12]

When the archbishop of Reims kissed the king, he cried, "Vivat rex in aeternum." Thereupon, the doors of the church were opened to the public, those within the church shouted "Vive le roi!," bells were rung and the artillery fired salutes, a large number of small birds were released, and the heralds distributed silver coronation jettons. The coronation mass followed, and the king communicated in both species. By 11:30 A.M. the ceremony was finished, and Charles had left the church for his lodgings in the archiepiscopal palace. France's last royal coronation ceremony had ended.

The most obvious change in Charles's ceremony was the absence of the twelve Peers of France. Two of the ecclesiastical peerages, the bishoprics of Laon and Noyon, had been suppressed during the Revolution. What remained of the roles of the bishops of Laon and Beauvais was carried out by the cardinals of Clermont-Tonnerre and La Fare. Except for the truncated role of the archbishop of Reims, the duties of the other ecclesiastical peers were completely omitted.

The original six lay Peers of France had been represented by the higher nobility and Princes of the Blood at the coronation ceremonies during the Old Regime. The Constitutional Charter of Louis XVIII provided for an upper house in the legislature, the Chamber of Peers, the members of which were nominated by the king. A goodly number of these peers were present at Charles's coronation, but they did not have any part in the ceremony as peers. The shortened roles of the six old lay peers were played by three Princes of the Blood: the dauphin (Louis-Antoine, duke of Berry, son of Charles X), the duke of Orléans (Louis Philippe, son of Louis Philippe "Egalité" and king of the France of the July Monarchy), and the duke of Bourbon (Louis-Henri-Joseph, the last prince of Condé).

When the dauphin invested the king with the spurs, he was acting the part played by the representative of the duke of Burgundy,
the first of the old lay peers under the Old Regime. On this occasion, however, the dauphin was acting as a Prince of the Blood, not
as a Peer of France. It may truly be said that the Peers of France
had no role at Charles's coronation. Thus it was that the chancellor
called upon the Princes of the Blood, not the peers, to assist the
consecrator in crowning the king. There seems to have been a last
official assertion of Bourbon dynasticism in this emphasis on the
Princes of the Blood; it is the final reduction of the edict given at
Blois by Henry III in 1576.[13]

Another notable change was the severe shortening of the ritual
of the sleeping king. No longer was there a grand procession of the
bishops from the church to the palace. No longer did they knock
thrice on the door of the king's chamber, and the king was no
longer said to be sleeping. Commenting on the suppression of the
fictional sleep, an editor of the *Constitutionnel* wrote, "The moral
sense of that ceremony is evident. *The king is sleeping* and it is the
priests who awaken him; *the king is reposing* [*le Roi est couché*]
and it is the priests who raise him. Does this not express as clearly
as possible that the king is nothing if the priests have not done
something to him? [If this ceremony does not have this meaning],
if it had not consecrated an overly revolting usurpation of the kingship by the clergy, why would one have modified it?"[14]

The editor of the *Constitutionnel*, in discussing the deletion
of the ritual of the sleeping king, may be accused of anticlerical
and republican bias, but it must not be forgotten that his newspa-
per was one of the most widely read papers of the time and that he
was expressing a viewpoint held by many of his contemporaries.
Whether the reason he gave for the suppression of the ritual was
the right one is doubtful, though. As we have seen, the ceremony
probably had different meanings attached to it in the sixteenth,
seventeenth, and eighteenth centuries, and none of them corresponded with the interpretation of the *Constitutionnel*'s editor, who
was obviously speculating.[15] The ceremony appears to have been
suppressed simply because it was not understood; the only significant part of the old ritual used at Charles's coronation, the
only part of it that still had any meaning, was the statement that
Charles X was a man "whom God has given us for king." The
Constitutional Charter implied in its preamble that it had been the

free gift of a king by divine right. Charles X certainly considered himself such a king, and he may have emphasized that fact by retaining the sole reference to the God-given king in the coronation ceremony prior to the king's entrance into the church. Thus there appears here, too, a last flickering assertion of Bourbon dynasticism.

Of course the divinely appointed king of France could not be properly anointed except with the Holy Balm sent from heaven in the beak of a dove for the baptism of Clovis. Belanger's research in 1814 on the fate of the Holy Ampulla had not been forgotten, and in 1819 an official inquest had been held to determine the authenticity of the supposed remnants of the ampulla and its balm. At the inquest the former curate of the abbey of Saint-Remi declared that he had been warned that the ampulla was to be destroyed, that he had then removed as much of the balm as he could, and that he had given it to the archbishop of Reims to be placed in a new reliquary in the tomb of Saint Remigius. Belanger had already turned up a version of this story, which is noteworthy in the present context only to show a continued interest in the subject during Louis XVIII's reign. The official version of the preservation of the balm was less dramatic: pious citizens had rescued pieces of the shattered ampulla, some of the Holy Balm had adhered to these shards of glass, and the archbishop of Reims collected the relics. The old balm was mixed with new chrism in a ceremony that took place on 22 May 1825, a few days before Charles X's coronation; the resulting new balm was inserted into a new ampulla, which was placed in a large white and yellow gold reliquary fabricated for the purpose (the new ampulla and its reliquary are now on display in the Musée du sacre in the former archiepiscopal palace in Reims).[16] Charles's view of the kingship was mirrored in the revival of the legend of the Holy Ampulla by means of elaborate stories, *procès-verbaux*, and ceremonies. With the resurrection of the legend of the ampulla, stress was laid upon the continuity of Charles X with his royal ancestors and upon the religious nature of Charles's kingship.

The manner in which the new ampulla was handled differed very much from the corresponding ceremonies of the Old Regime, however. The abbey of Saint-Remi had been partially destroyed during the Revolution, and the French monasteries had been dissolved. The only institution left to take care of the ampulla was the archbishopric of Reims. Therefore the ampulla was not ceremonially brought to the church in procession, and the *O pretiosum munus* hymn was not sung. The elaborate handling of the ampulla during the ceremony was likewise omitted, and the archbishop of Reims simply brought it with him from behind the altar and handled it himself. The descriptions of Charles's coronation do not say what was done with the ampulla after the ceremony, something that was almost always mentioned in the texts of the Old Regime; we may assume that it was carried without ceremony back to its resting place.

One of the most discussed changes in the ceremony concerned the coronation oath. Would Charles X swear to uphold the Constitutional Charter, or would he not? No one knew the answer to this question until the oath was uttered by the king. He did, in fact, swear to uphold the charter; this was thought by many contemporaries to be the most important part of his coronation. Both the ecclesiastical oath and the old oath of the kingdom were omitted. The former would have been inappropriate because the canonical privilege, law, and justice of the bishops and the church no longer existed in 1825. Also, Charles could not swear to preserve peace for the Church or to expel heretics in a French state become officially tolerant. Two additions were made to Charles's oath with the references to the Most Christian King and to the Eldest Son of the Church. These were titles of the Old Regime, and the fact that they were coupled with the coronation oath to maintain the Constitutional Charter foreshadowed the coming cooperation of throne and altar. They also emphasized Charles's conception of the restored kingship in France, a kingship that would depend on the Church for its very existence. After this oath, called the oath of the kingdom, the king took another short oath as chief and sovereign grand master of the Order of the Holy Spirit, the Order of Saint Louis, and the Royal Order of the Legion of Honor (the latter founded by Napoleon in 1802). Finally, the oath to uphold the edicts against duels was omitted because dueling as such was not illegal at the time.[17].

Even the purely liturgical parts of the ceremony did not escape the changes of the new age. Some of the prayers were completely omitted, whereas others were shortened. The long prayer recited immediately before the sacring, for example, was reduced to nearly one-third of its original length.[18] Every possible reference to the election of the king by the bishops was carefully deleted, as was every reference to the king as protector of the Church and enemy of heretics and infidels. Also excised were almost all the passages that drew a parallel between the Hebrew kingship of the Old Testament and the French kingship.[19]

All the changes in Charles's coronation ceremony had the effect of shortening the ceremony considerably. The omissions in the liturgy contributed to this, as did the omission of most of the ceremonial processions. Of course, the assumption of the roles of the twelve Peers of France by three Princes of the Blood would alone have shortened the ceremony. Under the Old Regime the coronation ceremony began with the arrival of the clerics at the church at about 4:30 A.M., and the king was present at the ceremony (exclusive of the coronation banquet) for about seven hours, which must have been terribly fatiguing for a young monarch like Louis XIII. In 1825 the clerics did not go to the church until 7:30 A.M., the ceremony began at 8:00 A.M., and Charles had already left for the archiepiscopal palace by 11:30 A.M.[20]

3. The Reaction to the Reaction

Charles X's coronation ceremony was anything but universally popular. To be sure, there were those who agreed with the cardinal of La Fare when he said, "The Lord deigns to contract a new pact with the house of France! We say and repeat that if the consecration of Clovis drew the valiant nation of the Franks out of barbarity in order to bring it to the faith of Jesus Christ, today, by a redoubling of the favors of Providence, the Consecration of Charles X will in a way renew that conquest."[21] A more typical comment was made by Victor Hugo several years later, after he had turned from the monarchism of his youth to republicanism, when he solemnly observed, "There was a moment when Charles X . . . lay stretched at the feet of the archbishop. The Peers of France at the right, . . . the deputies at the left . . . watched him do it."[22] That sarcastic author wrote even more viciously that "the aged neophyte . . . , who always fled the view of a distant combat, armed his weak hand with the heavy sword of Charlemagne and weighted his septuagenarian brow with the heavy crown of that conqueror." He enlarged his target to include even the city of Reims: "Reims is the land of chimeras. It is perhaps for that reason that they crown the kings there."[23] One of the descriptions of the ceremony said, "The king received with the *main de justice* another one of those religious exhortations that remind the masters of earth that they will find in their turn an equitable and severe judge at the foot of the celestial throne. That exhortation was unnecessary for Charles X."[24] The writer continued somewhat ambiguously, "The throng . . . had contemplated with a sort of respectful dread the august abasement of the monarch before the altar of Christ. . . ."[25]

The public's loss of belief in the legends of the kingship is well documented by the number of people who turned up to be touched for scrofula. Louis XIV had touched over 2,500 sufferers of the king's evil at his coronation, Louis XV had touched some 2,000, and Louis XVI had touched about 2,400; all three of these kings had touched publicly, as had their predecessors. The monarchs themselves may have expressed scepticism of their healing powers since the mid-seventeenth century, when they changed the touching formula from the indicative, "The king touches you, God cures [*guérit*] you," to the optative, "The king touches you, may God cure [*guérisse*] you," but the public attendance of the ceremony demonstrates the credulity of Frenchmen in the later decades of the Old Regime.[26] Only 120–130 scrofulous people appeared on the scene to be touched by the last of the thaumaturgic kings, and he touched them in the relative privacy of a hospital. Then, as if to express further doubt in his own healing powers, Charles told the diseased, "My dear friends, I have brought you words of consolation; I most sincerely hope that you may be cured [*que vous guérissiez*]." Three months later a *procès-verbal* determined that five of the touched children—but none of the touched adults—had been cured, and no further attempt was made to follow the progress of those touched. Marc Bloch has pointed out in his excellent study of the thaumaturgic kings that this was the usual proportion of scrofulitics who became well naturally.[27]

One of the poets of the coronation wrote, "And the aged universe dreams that it will see a new golden age reborn."[28] It was an age that did not last long, though, for the Bourbon monarchy was driven out of France by the revolution of 1830. The descriptions of Charles's coronation often referred to him as the grandson (*petit-fils*) of Henry IV. This was somewhat appropriate because both were the only crowned kings of France officially to adopt religious toleration, but, in addition, the appellation implied the restoration of the Bourbon absolutism of the Old Regime. There was an unconscious irony in the term, however, in that Henry IV and Charles X were the first and last Bourbon kings, and the latter proved that absolutistic monarchy would not be restored in France. Perhaps the *Constitutionnel* most succinctly summed up the reasons for the failure of the restored Bourbon dynasty and its coronation ceremony with the words, "Whatever changes the coronation ceremony has been subjected to, it resembles the old ceremony more than the public today resembles that of the past."[29] The same might have been said of the kingship of Charles X.

As far as the intellectual thrust of the royal coronation ceremony is concerned, no great amount of time lapsed between the coronation of Charles V in 1364 and that of Louis XVI in 1775. Ages separated 1775 and 1825, and the abdication and flight of Charles X paved the way for a government that faithfully reflected the new age, the July Monarchy. The question of a coronation for Louis Philippe was never raised, and the bourgeoisie's king contented himself with his proclamation by the Chamber of Deputies and the swearing of an oath of fidelity to the Constitutional Charter as his sole inaugural rite. Upon the restoration of the Empire, on the other hand, there were again calls for a coronation, whose proponents conceived of it more as one modeled after that of the Old Regime or of Charles X than after that of Napoleon. Napoleon III himself does not appear ever to have wanted a coronation, but that did not prevent the special pleaders from continuing to call for one throughout almost the whole of his reign.[30]

New governments succeeded the flight of Napoleon III, leading shortly to the fall of the government of Adolf Thiers and to the White Flag Crisis of 1873. The central figure in the crisis was Henry, count of Chambord, the duke of Berry's posthumous son (b. 1820), who had accompanied his grandfather and other members of the Bourbon family in their flight into exile in 1830. The particular French mixture of Right and Left, with excesses on either side, usually brought a reaction to the faction that was in power. Such took place in the late 1860s and early 1870s, when there was an astonishing resurgence of the Right. After the count of Chambord's declaration that he would refuse to accept the tricolor, there was feverish activity on the part of his supporters, and for a few weeks in October of 1873 it seemed probable that the Bourbon monarchy would be restored and that the count of Chambord would officially become Henry V of France.[31]

Preparations were undertaken for the return of the exile, plans were laid for his entry into France and for his formal entry into Paris, and placards were printed. There was talk of the coronation coach, presumably the magnificent vehicle that had been made for Charles X's coronation and that, redecorated for Napoleon III, still exists in the Musée des voitures at Versailles.[32] We shall never know what the count of Chambord's own plans were for a coronation, for his will provided that his papers should be burned after his death; many have made such provisions, but in few cases have they been carrried out as effectively as they were upon the demise of Charles X's grandson. If one ignores whatever aspirations more recent supporters of the Legitimist and Orleanist factions might have, one perceives the history of the French coronation ceremony as coming fully to an end in 1825. The coronation of Charles X was the final service the ceremony was to render to French kingship.

PART FIVE

THE CORONATION IN HISTORY

.   .   .   .

13

METAMORPHOSES OF KINGSHIP

• • • • • • • • • •

1. Medieval Kingship

The late medieval and modern coronation ceremony had no counterpart in the early Frankish age, for there was no ecclesiastical involvement in the establishment of kings in the Merovingian monarchies—neither unction nor benediction—and whatever accession ceremony there was remained purely secular.[1] The seventh-century Visigoths did introduce anointment of the king by a bishop in emulation of the anointing of the biblical kings, but this innovation was probably unknown in (and it certainly was foreign to) Frankish lands until the advent of a Carolingian king. Pepin the Short was the first Frankish ruler to be anointed and crowned, but on that occasion and in the case of his immediate successors the ecclesiastical and the secular ceremonies of accession remained distinct, not only in time but also in the minds of contemporaries. The early Carolingians did not regard the anointing as a particularly exclusive rite because it was capable of being repeated, and it does not seem to have been necessary to the monarch's accession; at least the chroniclers do not mention a sacring of Charles the Bald upon becoming the West Frankish king in 840. By then, though, a precedent of real importance had been set when Louis the Pious was anointed at his coronation as emperor in 816; within three decades of Louis's death several of his fractious sons and grandsons were apparently anointed and crowned at the same time, occasionally as kings, but primarily as emperors.[2]

The combination of anointing and crowning in a single ceremony was given a clear form by Archbishop Hincmar of Reims (archbishop 845–882), the coronator of Charles the Bald as king of Lorraine in 869 and of Louis the Stammerer as king of West Francia in 877. For each of these ceremonies Hincmar composed a

liturgical order that carefully melded into one service the ecclesiastical and secular acts of accession. Charles was anointed and
subsequently invested with the secular symbols of authority: the
crown, the *palma*, and the scepter. Louis, on the other hand, first
made a promise (which later became the ecclesiastical oath) to
preserve the canonical privilege, due law, and justice of the bishops
and their churches; only then was he anointed and invested with
the crown and the scepter. The subsequent history of anointing and
crowning in all the kingdoms of western Europe built upon the
foundations of these two works of Hincmar; half of the prayers in
the *ordo* for the coronation of Charles the Bald were still in the
French ceremony when Charles X was crowned a millennium later,
and only one of the dozen or more benedictions pronounced at
Louis's coronation was not repeated in 1825.[3] Louis the Stammerer's promise to the bishops in 877 was made, with some modification and as far as we can determine, by every French king thereafter, including Louis XVI in 1775. In short, from the time of
Hincmar of Reims the French ceremony of accession ceased to be a
secular practice, for it had become a liturgical rite through which
the Church inextricably associated itself with the monarchy.[4]

Hincmar's influence was also to prevail in the greatest mystery
of French kingship: the legend of the Holy Ampulla, which came
to dominate the French ceremony after the first part of the thirteenth century. Hincmar used the legend in an attempt to buttress
the claims of the archbishop of Reims to primacy in the French
Church and to the exclusive right of coronation in Reims. Hincmar's successors failed to achieve the supremacy of Reims, and
they became the coronators of the French kings only after a long
struggle with the archbishops of Sens, so the legend tended to be
forgotten outside of Reims. Not until the coronation of Louis VII in
1131 is there any evidence that the legend was remembered at the
coronation of a king, but the definitive amalgamation of the story
with the ceremony did not take place until around 1230, when the
ordo of Reims devoted lengthy passages to the ampulla and its
handling.[5]

The *ordo*'s incorporation of the legend into the body of the ceremony may be explained by contemporary intermonastic competition with the abbey of Saint-Denis. The latter's special relationship to the kings was hardly new, but in the twelfth century its
claims began to extend beyond all previous bounds. The abbey's

long-established right to guard the royal insignia became exclusive, thanks to a royal charter; the crown and the sword also came to be associated with Charlemagne, of whose royal-imperial cult Saint-Denis considered itself the guardian. By means of a forged charter attributed to Charlemagne—the charter stated that Charlemagne's "successors, the kings of France, should be crowned nowhere but in the church of Saint-Denis"—the abbot of Saint-Denis directly challenged the coronation role that the archbishops of Reims had so long struggled to obtain. In the mid-thirteenth century Saint-Denis was to go so far as to claim that the king himself was a vassal of the abbey. It is no wonder, therefore, that the abbey of Saint-Remi (or the cathedral chapter or the archbishop of Reims or any combination of the three) should take vigorous steps to counteract the Dionysian claims, founding Reim's priority upon the miracle associated with the baptism of Clovis, whose role as the first Christian king of the Franks eclipsed that of even the greatest of the Carolingian rulers.[6]

The thirteenth-century alterations in the ceremony assured Reims a permanent and significant place at the center of the royal religion. While undoubtedly serving the interests of the kingship, they also immutably defined and affirmed its character. The French conception of the *sacre* as an eighth sacrament and the French king's special position in the Church (dramatized by having him and his queen communicate in both species, like the priesthood) made it impossible for a man to become king of France without the direct and immediate aid of the ecclesiastically administered Holy Balm.[7] That it was no longer a secular ceremony with meaningful constitutive significance was forcibly demonstrated by the lapse of a year between the death of Louis IX in 1270 and the coronation of his successor. It had become an instrument through which the Church cemented its firm bond to the monarchy and through which the kingship became more or less dependent upon the Church for its very essence.

This central characteristic of the late medieval and modern kingship made it impossible to abandon the coronation ceremony even in the Enlightenment. Joan of Arc, as we have seen, refused to recognize Charles VII as king until after the ceremony in Reims, and even some secular chroniclers of the fifteenth century looked upon it as a religious *mystère* and *fête*.[8] The legal view that the coronation was not constitutionally essential was summarized succinctly several decades later in Michel de l'Hôpital's remark that "the kingdom is never vacant, but . . . we have a king, we have a lord and master, without awaiting coronation, unction, or consecration."[9] The timing of L'Hôpital's comment is striking, for it was made just two years after the first appearance in the ceremony of the king's precoronation sleep, which, as it came to act out a theory of God-given kingship, helped to define Bourbon absolutist monarchy.

2. Absolutism

Throughout this study there has often been a certain vagueness in speaking of absolutistic, or modern, or dynastic kingship. That has not been accidental, for I have wished to gather data that could be used to contribute to a definition of absolutism, and I have characterized a particular conception as absolutistic only in order to signal its eventual utility for defining the concept.

Broad historical constructs—medieval, Renaissance, modern, feudal, absolute—are like all historical generalizations in that they are always somewhat dangerous. They are abstractions that cannot possibly be true in every case, and if they are taken as expressing truths, they are misleading. What is worse is that we occasionally succumb to the temptation to argue from the constructs: "this or that was done because it was characteristic of medieval man to act in such and such a way." At best such arguments are tautologies that explain nothing, and at worst they are Isidorian explanations that fit the facts into the preconceived scheme, that derive the particular from the general. There is a certain sense in which all history can be only a congeries of particular data, history as *histoire événementielle*, as the French describe it. This type of history alone is least subject to misinterpretation and error.

On the other hand, however, collections of data by themselves do not satisfy our intellectual impulses. One of the great wonders of the human mind is its ability to abstract and generalize, perhaps even the necessity that it do so (we are speaking of biological and physical, not of supernatural or philosophical necessity). The results of Tycho Brahe's endless years of precise astronomical observations were useless until Johann Kepler managed to transform them into three generalizations about planetary behavior, and Galileo Galilei's experiments with balls rolling down inclined planes would have been meaningless had they not been used to develop abstractions ("laws") describing the behavior of physical objects acting in a gravitational field. The best historians are fully aware of the necessity to generalize; Fernand Braudel, for example, one of this century's great practitioners of *histoire événementielle*, is also a master of medium- and long-term history. Generalizations and constructs therefore meet a real need. They enable us to perceive the otherwise incomprehensible, they liberate our minds by relieving us of the necessity of constantly retaining in active memory an extensive host of unrelated data, they create objects of thought that can lead to further understanding. Our study of the Middle Ages, for example, would be terribly burdened if we had to say and think something like a form-of-government-that-consists-of-a-ruling-consortium-of-king-and-great-barons- with- expressed-or-implied-mutual-obligations-of-service-and-protection- and- with-personal-loyalty-guaranteed- by- proprietary- and- judicial- considerations (one should go on in this manner) every time we wished to speak of feudalistic kingship. The shorthand of the latter is clearly preferable, and it makes little sense to argue, as has been done recently, that one cannot really speak of feudalism.[10] It does make sense, nevertheless, to attempt to define what one means by feudalism, or absolutism, or any of our other constructs, and to emphasize just what they are so that they do not lead to the mistaken belief that they perfectly describe historical reality.

Absolutism is far too vast a concept to be fully defined here. The subject of scores of books and articles, practically every historian who writes of the early modern period has something to say about it, and it took different forms in each country in the seventeenth and eighteenth centuries; we here concern ourselves only with France. The term is used primarily to refer to a type of government in which the king is not limited by some sort of institution outside the kingship itself. In the modern period one usually thinks of the Estates General as that limiting institution, whereas for the Middle Ages it is the barons of the kingdom who limit the king. The medieval monarchy is, therefore, not absolutistic, and the modern monarchy is, at least between the dissolution of the Estates General in 1615 and the assembling of the estates in 1789. Although such a simplistic view enables one to assign a beginning date to absolutism (and textbooks, at least in the United States,

often unfortunately do so), it does not say when feudalistic kingship came to an end, and there remains a period of two or three
centuries when the monarchy was neither clearly feudal nor clearly
absolutistic. It is hoped that the study of the royal coronation ceremony will have cast some light upon this period of transition.

Absolutism, it should be noted, is not a positive term, but essentially a negative one: it does not normally describe what absolutist
monarchy is, but what it is not. It is government by the king not
limited by the barons or the estates. It implies an all-powerful king
and does not say what the monarch is limited by. The coronation
ceremony can be used to contribute to a positive definition of absolutism.

Three further general points need to be made about absolutism.
First, although the word *absolutism* is a neologism of the nineteenth century, the concept of absolute monarchy is not.[11] Several
writers of the sixteenth century wrote of *la monarchie absolue*,
although Jean Bodin was the writer who did the most to make the
term popular. Their phrase was based in turn on the speculations
of medieval lawyers who discussed at length the Roman law maxim
that *princeps legibus solutus (est)*, "the Prince is freed from (or
above) the laws."[12]

Second, *absolutism* is one of the most misleading terms in
the history of political thought. Hundreds or thousands of textbooks and studies of early modern Europe speak of absolutism and
thereby instill, willy-nilly, in the minds of their readers many times
over a concept of government that never existed and that contemporaries never conceived to exist. For the western European languages that derive their abstract political and legal concepts from
Latin, *absolute* is used to denote that which is freed from all restrictions, which is without limitation or boundary, than which
there is nothing greater. English speakers commonly say "Absolutely!" in this way, as do French speakers with their "Absolu-
ment!" and an English-German dictionary will translate *absolute*
as *unumschränkt* or *unbeschränkt*. When Nicolas of Cusa wished
in the fifteenth century to distinguish the infinity of God from
the infinity of the temporal universe, he contrasted the "absolute
maximum (and minimum)" with the "relative maximum (and
minimum)." Is it any wonder that students of the seventeenth and
eighteenth centuries—and this includes not only secondary, college, and university students, but also many of us who know better,

but who let the power of a word sometimes warp the meaning of a construct—tend to conceive of absolutist government in that period as though it were some sort of precocious totalitarian monstrosity? The fault is not with the students, but with the terminology (and to some extent with the propaganda called forth by the late eighteenth-century revolutions). If the history of the terminology is known, it is nonetheless possible to understand how such a confusing word came to be widely used. Again it is necessary to look at Bodin.

Much unnecessary ink has been spilled in attempts to explain Bodin's political theory and to reconcile the contradictions within his thought. Bodin was astonishingly widely read and extremely knowledgeable, but he was not terribly original, nor was he very systematic, and it will probably be impossible ever to reduce his political thought to a rational system. Nevertheless, it should be tolerably easy to solve one of the major problems in his thought, the apparent conflict between absolute sovereignty and limited sovereignty, which has plagued Bodin's numerous commentators. As one of them wrote after explaining Bodin's conception of absolute sovereignty, "It appears, after all, that Bodin did not conceive of sovereignty as necessarily involving a strictly unlimited power, even in law."[13] When Bodin wrote of the sovereign as unlimited by laws, he was referring to a sovereign who is *legibus solutus* (to use the phrase so much discussed by the medieval civilians), not of a sovereign who is *juribus solutus*. Bodin's sovereign is not limited by human laws—*leges*—and in that respect he is absolute, but he is limited by certain immutable *jures*—natural law, divine law, fundamental law (for France), and perhaps also by some of the individual *leges* which are essential to them.[14] We no longer accept the concepts of natural or divine law, and for that reason we are puzzled when we find them imposing limits upon the absolutism of the sovereign. Bodin accepted those limits as inherent in life, so there was for him no conflict in the idea of an absolute sovereign who was limited. If we recognize this basic principle of Bodin's thought and apply it to our conception of early modern French absolutism, we find that absolutism means something truly different from what the word itself would seem to imply.

A final generalization about the concept of absolutism is that it was always an ideal, never a fully realized actuality—at least in France. That is why part 3 of this study is entitled "Striving toward Absolutism,"[15] and that is partially also why the study of something as superficially arcane as the history of the coronation ceremony can make a contribution to an understanding of absolutism. It would be impossible in a few words to give a comprehensive definition of two or three centuries of absolutism with all of its political, institutional, and social ramifications. The next few pages are intended only to bring together and to recapitulate the numerous strands of this study so that they may contribute to a clearer understanding of absolutistic kingship and how it came into being.

3. Absolutistic Kingship

The first thing that one must say about such kingship is that it was a limited kingship. The most extensive, and also the most amorphous, boundaries around the royal freedom were the restrictions placed upon the monarch by the kind of divine and natural law, however defined, assumed by Bodin and others in the late medieval and early modern periods. There is probably no government, however capricious it be, that does not voluntarily limit itself in some way, and from voluntary restrictions provided by vaguely defined law some more specific limitations may be derived. In France these had a variety of immediate sources—Roman and canon law, custom, misunderstanding of the past—but the specific selection made from such sources resulted from the influence of contemporary needs and aspirations upon general preconceptions.

The coronation oaths restricted the kings and are an example of limitations originating in historical custom. Because the oaths were vague and could be broadly interpreted, they could and did serve to increase the king's power, but their restrictive function was not forgotten, and when this appeared detrimental they could be changed. That seems to have been what happened at the coronation of Henry II in 1547. A dozen or so years after the Affair of the Placards (1534) France's religious turmoil was not lessened, and Henry seems to have wanted to avoid swearing to expel heretics from the kingdom (the fourth clause of the oath of the kingdom). In order to do so, he used an older oath (which lacked the clause) found in an archaic coronation *ordo*. (In that text, the *ordo* of 1250, the oath was preceded by a ritual consent of the people; because the manuscripts were not edited as carefully as they should have been, the *consensus populi* was reintroduced into the ceremony to play its historic role in sixteenth-century thought and politics.)[16] If the coronation oaths had not been considered to limit the king, it would not have been necessary to make the change in 1547. The eighteenth-century oaths to observe the edicts against dueling might seem not to have been observed, but repeated royal clemency cannot disguise the fact that the king's government haled hundreds or thousands before the royal courts in order to try and to sentence them for infringing the edicts: thus the coronation oath was observed in a sense. We have also seen how the coronation oaths, despite their want of specific wording to the effect, contributed to the rise of inalienability, another powerful limitation upon the king. The practical effect of inalienability is not yet known, unfortunately, because no one has studied the effects of the law of nonalienation upon the practical political life of the Old Regime. We may note simply that inalienability was equivocal in that, while restraining the king, it also strengthened him by enabling him, even forcing him, to retain the legal and economic bases of his power.

The most striking limits upon the king are found in connection with the royal right of pardon. In the modern state we have become accustomed to the granting of pardon (which includes parole, a kind of pardon) for the most heinous of crimes, including even treason. It is astonishing, therefore, to find that the absolutist kings of France either found themselves increasingly limited, or voluntarily bound themselves, in the exercise of this most important mark of supreme political authority. Even when there was an apparent failure to observe the restrictions as pardons were granted to those guilty of crimes by law unpardonable, the machinery of government, which acted for the king and in his name, observed the limitations.[17]

Potentially the most severe restriction was the right to elect a king. From this right not only could the king have become the instrument of one or another of competing factions, but also from this other restrictions could have developed. The danger was clearly recognized in the second half of the sixteenth century, and Henry IV took every possible step to alleviate the threat. In doing so he completed the structure of dynasticism, the second major characteristic of absolutistic kingship.

Henry IV's success in getting himself recognized as the legitimate heir to the throne was crucial both to the destruction of the revived elective element of French kingship and to the acceptance of familial descent as a necessary component of succession. The family had always been central to the Capetian-Valois monarchy,[18] but the strongest emphasis upon blood relationship did not appear until sometime during the Hundred Years' War, when the Princes of the Blood made their first appearance. The rise of these princes eclipsed all other nobility by the end of the sixteenth century, and blood alone enabled Henry to succeed. (Blood alone did not make him king, of course, for contemporary political conditions and his conversion were likewise essential to his succession, but without the descent from Saint Louis, Henry could hardly have achieved his goal.) Consequently, upon Henry's death Louis XIII was called the living image of his father, and thenceforth the familial relationship by itself was sufficient to create a "king who never dies."[19] A mid-seventeenth-century writer was cognizant of this development when he argued that the coronation served only "to proclaim the kingship solemnly," and when from the old inthronization formula, *Sta et retine*, he selected for emphasis the phrases "by paternal succession" and "by hereditary right." The writer used words like *renewal, conservation,* and *confirmation* to characterize the ceremony, which was for him, therefore, truly a *sacre*. The religious element of the ceremony, strong ever since the age of Hincmar of Reims, thus fully dominated any possible remaining secular element.[20]

Not everyone in the modern age realized that the monarchy had been radically transformed since the Middle Ages. An extreme example of archaism may be found in the thought and writings of Saint-Simon, duke and Peer of France. Arguing constantly for the preeminence of his class of nobles, which he identified as possessing the same dignity and rights as the old Peers of France,[21] he viewed the modern Peers of France as an essential element in the government of the kingdom, which he conceived of in terms purely feudal.

> . . . the king cannot bear the great weight of the crown except with the aid of those who have placed it upon his head and who support it there. That is to say that the great affairs of the kingdom ought to be equally shared with them in

writing, in counsel, in power because they equally support
the Crown; that without them there is no important sanction,
no law, no new structure; that they are the instruments of all
that is great in the State and that they are those who come
closest to approaching and supporting the Crown and are
even the only ones who may place their hands upon it, that is
to say, who may join together with the king, establish laws
with the king, coexecute the most important things with him,
constitute, colegislate, and validate, authorize by their power,
by virtue of the whole nation residing in them, all that it
pleases the king to do with their concurrence.[22]

For Saint-Simon the peers demonstrate their right to create the
king by their role in the precoronation ritual of the sleeping king,[23]
by their bearing of the regalia, by their acclamation, by their role
at the postcoronation banquet.[24] Miffed by what he viewed as an
inexcusable slight upon the dignity of the peers at the coronation in
1722—he thought that they were the ones who should represent
the old peers in the ceremony—Saint-Simon refused to go to Reims
for Louis XV's coronation. He sometimes blamed the excessive role
given to the Princes of the Blood in 1722 upon the Regency in
general, but most particularly upon Louis XIV's edict of 1711.[25]
Apparently unaware of Montpensier's protracted struggle for precedence in the sixteenth century, Saint-Simon did not see that the
ceremony at Reims had become at least in part a display of dynasticism and its glory.

Michel de l'Hôpital's reference to the ceremony as a nonconstitu-
tive "solemnity," that is, as something that contributed to the grandeur of the kingship,[26] evokes a third characteristic of absolutistic
kingship, its grandiosity. A major part was here accorded to solar
symbolism, which played a central role already at the coronation
entry of Louis XIII in 1610, half a century before Louis XIV began
to resort to the conceit that identified him as the Roi Soleil, and
even earlier sun imagery had appeared in poetry produced for the
court of Charles IX. The grandeur and power of the king was also
expressed through the munificence of his largesse after the consecrator had exclaimed "Vivat Rex" and by the ceremonial pardon of
hundreds or thousands of prisoners after the coronation. Finally,
the greatness of the kingship was accentuated by various kinds of
imperial allusions. These changed with the passage of the centur-

ies: in the Middle Ages there was competition with and assertion of independence from the Holy Roman Empire, accompanied by occasional attempts on the part of the kings to have themselves actually elected to the imperial dignity; by the early seventeenth century this type of imperialism had come to be largely displaced by a sort of emulation of, and competition with, the greatest empire in the history of the western world, that of Rome; in the eighteenth century that in turn gave way to an empire *tout simple* or to a concept of French empire fraught with implications for the future.

The mutations in the expression of royal grandeur over the centuries reflect a fourth trait of absolutistic kingship: it was not created at any given point in time, but evolved gradually. This is true of each of the limitations upon kingship: the coronation oaths, inalienability, the limits placed upon the right of pardon, the development of the theory that the kingship was elective. It is also true of dynasticism, for the Princes of the Blood required more than a century to acquire their precedence over the Peers of France. If one had to point to a specific reign as marking the termination of the transition from feudal to absolutist kingship, one would have to say that it was the reign of Henry IV. If a more exact date were required, it would have to be 1610, when a series of three major ceremonies—the first inaugural *lit de justice*, the last of the Renaissance royal funerals, and the coronation of Louis XIII—expressed in their various ways the central concepts of the next two centuries of French kingship, concepts that had the effect of rendering inappropriate a government by king and Estates General before the latter institution made its next-to-the-last appearance on the French political scene.[27] Such temporal exactitude is misleading, of course, and one must recognize that absolutistic kingship came only haltingly into existence over the whole of the two and one-half centuries that separate the coronation of Charles V from that of Louis XIII. Even then, the old was not fully replaced by the new. At the coronation in 1610 there was an unresolved conflict between a kind of physical dynasticism that assured the succession by blood right and, on the other side, a kingship established by God alone. The disparity was expressed in the peculiar form of the dialogue devised for the fiction of the sleeping king on that occasion; Louis XIII as the dynastic successor was twice said to be sleeping, and only when he was called upon as God-given King was it admitted that he was not asleep.[28] The anonymous writer of the mid-century perhaps provided a theoretical solution to the conflict when he conceived of the coronation ceremony as confirming and renewing the dynasty; in other words, the religious consecratory element was constitutive of dynasticism, and thereby still another aspect of the kingship was seized for the Church.[29]

Religion, therefore, formed an essential element of the kingship. Already in the fourteenth century Jean Golein had stressed the religious nature of the institution: "And when the king removes his garments for his consecration, that signifies that he relinquishes his previous worldly estate in order to assume that of the royal religion, and if he does that with the devotion with which he should, I think that he is washed of his sins just as much as whoever newly enters orthodox religion."[30] Just as there is no way of avoiding the recognition that the ceremony was essentially religious, so must we admit that the kingship was likewise. The *religion royale* had many of the marks of a true religious sect, as Golein unambiguously demonstrates. The ceremony constantly emphasized the cult's miraculous elements, above all the legend of the Holy Ampulla and its balm that never needed replenishing. The postcoronation touching for scrofula was a mark of the suprahuman power of the anointed king, and his communion in both species and the coronation garments as tunicle, dalmatic, and chasuble were the marks of priesthood. The kings were thus at the center of a religion at the same time that their institution was attached to another cult, that of orthodox Catholic Christianity. Some writers of the late sixteenth century claimed that one of the monarchy's fundamental laws was that the king must be Catholic; it is indeed difficult to see how a French king could have been Protestant.[31]

Absolutist kingship was unable to escape its medieval past, which must be taken into account if the modern institution is to be appreciated. The last coronation of the Old Regime gives proof of the extent to which old conceptions were still at work. Not long after the death of Louis XV in May of 1774, Turgot, a Physiocrat and man of the Enlightenment, was named controller general of finances and minister of state.[32] As he became aware of the probable cost of a coronation in Reims, some 7 million livres, he suggested that tradition be abandoned and that the ceremony be moved to Paris in order to reduce costs, a proposal that was repulsed. He then urged alterations in the ceremony itself, arguing that the coronation oath to expel heretics from the kingdom be removed because it conflicted with religious freedom of conscience, natural law, and the political interest of the state; he also wished to delete most of the religious or ecclesiastical references in the ceremony. These recommendations were likewise rejected, and it was decided to stage a ceremony exactly like its predecessors. This decision was not simply the result of a determination to cling to tradition, though, for it harbored a whole politico-religious program.

For over a decade numerous court sermons had described what their authors considered a French religious crisis, which they associated with the crisis of state. This association was made particularly strongly after Louis XV's demise, and court preachers called upon the new king to restore religion and morals to their rightful place. The bishop of Senez hoped that it would be possible to give to the new king the title of *Restaurateur des moeurs*, which would be vastly superior to Francis I's title of *Restaurateur des lettres*. The bishop emphasized the relationship of the kingship to religion: ". . . by a prerogative peculiar to the French monarchy," he declared, "the Faith has been preserved without interruption in the hearts of you kings from the first who bent his head victoriously under the yoke of Jesus Christ to him who is about to mount the throne of Louis."[33] Just a few of the numerous examples expressing this view of the kingship and the coronation may be quoted. The latter was characterized as a "great spectacle of temporal power, ennobled and consecrated by Religion." "The king is the anointed of the Lord, His lieutenant, His image. His sacred person tenders us a second majesty; the submission that we render to him is a type of religion." The origin of royal authority "is none other but God Himself; it is in the authority of God that that of kings has its source; a king is the image of the Divinity; Sovereigns are the Gods of the Earth; independent of all created Power, their Crown only enhances that of the King of Kings."[34] Louis XVI himself revived the practice of touching for scrofula, which had lapsed nearly forty years before. His coronation in accordance with the old rites was to be the signal for a concomitant revival of religion and state. The use of the renewal theme at Louis XVI's precoronation entry into Reims is more, then, than simply an emulation of the renewal theme at Louis XV's precoronation entry in 1722 because, although couched in the guise of eighteenth-century classicism, the crux of its reference centered on medieval Christianity and *its* kingship.[35]

The king as the image of God takes us far back into the past, not just into the High Middle Ages, but to the first of the Carolingian kings. Throughout Frankish and French history since the later eighth century there was sporadic recurrence of the conception of the king as the *imitatio Christi*, which was similar to the *christomimesis* of the Byzantine imperial cult.[36] A systematic examination of the phenomenon has yet to be made, but a few instances will illuminate the tradition.

The first is the famous triad in the royal *laudes* from the reign of Charlemagne: CHRISTUS VINCIT, CHRISTUS REGNAT, CHRISTUS IMPERAT, "Christ is victorious, Christ reigns, Christ rules" or, more literally and without capitals, "the anointed one is victorious, the anointed one reigns, the anointed one rules." The important word is of course *christus*, the anointed one. Its very ambiguity served to confound the anointed king with the founder of Christianity. On account of the verb *imperare*, the triad has been interpreted as expressing an imperial aspiration of the Carolingian court before the coronation in Rome, but, although it may have done so very late in the eighth century, that must not have been its original intention. Ernst Kantorowicz, the authority on the royal *laudes*, was not able to say whether the triad dated from the reign of Charlemagne or of Pepin the Short. The latter is more likely. In the eighth century *imperare* still meant "to lead an army" or "to govern" as much as "to rule an empire."[37] The last of the Merovingian kings could in no sense have been said to *imperare*, but only to *regnare*, "to reign." Because Pepin did both, was the first Frankish king in over a century to do so, and was the first to be anointed, the triad surely applies to him rather than to Charlemagne, and the first Frankish *rex christus*, anointed king, was the first to whom we may attribute the confusion of the anointed one and the Anointed One.

The *Christus vincit* triad was not to be exclusively Carolingian, though. It was commonly used in the fourteenth century; one of Charles V's coins bore the legend, and Jean Golein twice referred to it in his *Traité du sacre*.[38] About 1300 there was a lengthy discussion of the king as a type of Christ.[39] There was also a clear parallel between the king and his twelve peers and Christ and His

twelve apostles; in the seventeenth century this parallel was explic-
itly noted.[40] It is even possible that the number thirteen, chosen for
the coins offered by the king at his coronation, was based upon a
like notion.[41] The sixteenth century presented an image fraught
with implications in the form of a *chant royal* by Clement Marot
(1496–1544). In each verse Marot speaks of a different object, and
each verse ends with the identification of that object as "the worthy couch upon which the king rests" (*La digne couche où le Roy
reposa*); the last verse, which closes with the same refrain, is devoted to the Virgin Mary![42]

The French came as close as possible to completing the deifica-
tion of the monarch in the seventeenth century. One of Rubens's
famous Marie de Médicis paintings in the Louvre, "The Apotheosis
of the King Henry IV and the Regency," depicts the late monarch in
the process of being transported to the realm of the immortal gods,
among whom one may distinguish Mercury, Jupiter, Venus, and
Eros. The General Assembly of the Clergy declared in 1625 that
"kings are ordained by God, but not only that: they are themselves
gods"; Bossuet repeated that statement in 1662 in a sermon in
which, speaking of kings in general, he told Louis XIV that "you
are gods" (*vous êtes des dieux*). In the meantime the advocate
general, Omer Talon, had declared at the Sun King's first *lit de
justice* (1643), "The seat of Your Majesty represents to us the
throne of the living God."[43] One supporter of the Fronde picked up
the living image metaphor, which had previously been an instrument for proclaiming dynastic succession, and called the king the
"living image of God," as though the king were descended from the
Divinity in the same way as from his earthly father.[44] This image
leads directly to a remarkable ode composed by the Jesuits on the
occasion of Louis XIV's coronation:

> JESUS et LOUIS Couronnés
> Tous deux nous sont des DIEU-DONNEZ.
> L'un est le FILS AISNE, l'autre EXPOUX de l'Eglise;
> Et pour parachever cette grande Union,
> Par le Titre commun d'une mesme devise
> Qu'ils ont de fils de DIEU: sont frères d'Onction.[45]

These astonishing declarations bring us back to the "Sovereigns
[who] are the Gods of the Earth" in the years immediately preceding Louis XVI's coronation.

Nevertheless, there was another France in 1775, the one reflected in the inattention of most who attended the ceremony, by
the failure of as many as expected to go to Reims for the event,
or by the count of Artois's exclamation, "Ah diable!" as his crown
fell from his head when he entered the cathedral.[46] This was the
France represented by Turgot when he suggested abandoning or altering the ceremony. The watchword for this France was given
by Condorcet, who asked Turgot whether he did not also believe
"that, of all useless expenses, the most useless and the most ridiculous would be the coronation."[47] There were others also who
thought that it would be worthwhile to abolish "cette absurde cérémonie," and some who attended the coronation described it as a
theater, a spectacle, an opera.[48] Condorcet's grounds for dispens-
ing with a coronation ceremony in 1775 have a prophetic ring: "In
a time of peace the presumptions [of the ceremony] are only puer-
ile; in a time of trouble they may have terrible consequences, and
prudence requires that one choose a time to attack them when they
are still not dangerous."[49]

The two attitudes toward kingship go far to summarize the intellectual crisis at the end of the Old Regime. On the one hand there
was the royal-ecclesiastical view that was firmly rooted in a long
Frankish-French tradition that went as far back as Pepin the Short
and the introduction of royal anointing into occidental monarchy,
as far back as Hincmar of Reims and his assimilation of the kingship by the Church. On the other hand there was the Enlightenment's anticlerical, antiecclesiastical, and rational outlook that saw
the clergy as working "to strike at the king and to make him dependent upon the clergy."[50] The French monarchy was simply incapable of stripping its kingship from the conceptual baggage of
the past. As Schramm so aptly concluded his *König von Frankreich*, "It is just that that is so astonishing about France, that it
retained in the modern age so much that was medieval after it had
supplied in the Middle Ages so much of what is modern."[51]

What a contrast there was between France and England! A detailed comparative examination of kingship in the two countries
has yet to be undertaken—and it cannot be until the medieval
coronation texts are sorted out and presented in usable form;
this is extremely unfortunate, for such a study would reveal much
about the inner nature of kingship in both countries.[52] Nonetheless, a few points are worth making. The English were more flexi-

ble, more apt to change the ceremony as necessary, and English scholars therefore speak of four major versions, "recensions," of the coronation ceremony, whereas for France one can trace only the linear development of the ceremony from reign to reign.[53] The English were able to add important secular elements to the ceremony, as is evident in Edward II's oath in 1308 to preserve "the laws and the customs" of the kingdom or in Henry VIII's modification of the coronation oath.[54] The English have preserved anointing to the twentieth century, but they have never placed as much emphasis as the French upon the miraculous nature of kingship (except perhaps for James I and his supporters), and the English kings ceased to touch for the "king's evil" in the seventeenth century, whereas the French retained the practice until the nineteenth century. From the thirteenth century the English kings were limited by the increasing power of Parliament, and the English constitutional monarchy was forged on the anvil of political expediency. The French kings tended to be limited either by the vague and lofty conceptions that prevailed in the High Middle Ages and that survived into modern times, or by their own administrative system. For the English, therefore, the ceremony retained something of the nature of a constitutive act, but for the French the ceremony was a consecration of the monarch and his authority or of his dynasty. The consequence of all these differences is that the English speak of the coronations of their kings, and the French prefer to discuss the *sacres* of their monarchs.[55]

APPENDIX A

Dates of Births, Coronations, and Deaths

King	Birth	Coronation	Death
John (II)	26 Apr. 1319	26 Sept. 1350	8 Apr. 1364
Charles V	21 Jan. 1337	19 May 1364	28 Sept. 1380
Charles VI	3 Dec. 1368	4 Nov. 1380	21 Oct. 1422
Charles VII	22 Feb. 1403	17 July 1429	22 July 1461
Louis XI	3 July 1423	15 Aug. 1461*	30 Aug. 1483
Charles VIII	30 June 1470	30 May 1484	7 Apr. 1498
Louis XII	27 June 1462	27 May 1498	1 Jan. 1515
Francis I	12 Sept. 1494	25 Jan. 1515	31 Mar. 1547
Henry II	31 Mar. 1518	26 July 1547**	10 July 1559
Francis II	19 Jan. 1544	18 Sept. 1559	5 Dec. 1560
Charles IX	27 June 1550	15 May 1561***	30 May 1574
Henry III	19 Sept. 1551	13 Feb. 1575	2 Aug. 1589
Henry IV	14 Dec. 1553	27 Feb. 1594	14 May 1610
Louis XIII	27 Sept. 1601	17 Oct. 1610	14 May 1643
Louis XIV	5 Sept. 1638	7 June 1654	1 Sept. 1715
Louis XV	15 Feb. 1710	25 Oct. 1722	10 May 1774
Louis XVI	23 Aug. 1754	11 June 1775	21 Jan. 1793
Louis XVII	27 Mar. 1785	None	June 1793
Louis XVIII	17 Nov. 1755	None	16 Sept. 1824
Charles X	9 Oct. 1757	29 May 1825	6 Nov. 1836

*Feast of the Assumption.
**Feast of Saint Anne.
***Feast of the Ascension.

APPENDIX B

The Medieval Coronation Texts

A few brief notes on the eight texts mentioned in chapter 3, section 1, may prove useful to the uninitiated reader.

(1) The West Frankish *ordo* (also called the Erdmann *ordo*, after the man who rediscovered it in the twentieth century in an obscure seventeenth-century printed edition) was composed about 900. It may have been used still in the latter half of the eleventh century, and it is the basis of further development in France, although it does not play a role in the present study.[1]

(2) The Fulrad (or Ratold) *ordo*—the name depends upon whether one chooses to call it after its composer or its recipient—was written in the monastery of Saint-Vaast in Arras about 980. The most widely represented of the early French *ordines* in surviving manuscripts (it exists in at least thirteen), it probably displaced the West Frankish *ordo* from about 1100 until the first part of the thirteenth century.[2]

The next three *ordines* form a series that may now be associated with the reign of Saint Louis.

(3) The *ordo* of Reims was, as noted, a directory rather than an *ordo* proper. It is quite brief, just some four pages long in its only complete printed edition. It was composed after the confiscation of Normandy by Philip Augustus (Burgundy, rather than Normandy, is listed as the first of the peerages, which would not have been true before 1204), after the Fourth Lateran Council of 1215, and after the "formation" of the college of peers. Since it precedes the *ordo* of 1250, it probably dates from the early years of the reign of Louis IX; however, there is no evidence that might connect it with Saint Louis's own coronation in 1226. The *ordo*'s emphasis on the role of the Holy Ampulla and the abbey of Saint-Remi points to the latter as its place of composition. The text of the *ordo* survives in three ordinaries in Reims and in numerous copies in a French translation that formed a part of the early registers of the Chambre des Comptes in Paris.[3]

(4) The *ordo* of 1250 now exists in only one manuscript, although there have been others. The manuscript dates from 1250 or slightly before, as studies of its miniatures have demonstrated, and this is consistent with the script. The *ordo* is really a very poor compilation, the basis of which was formed by a now lost form of the German *ordo*, to which were added

unchanged passages from the *ordo* of Reims and extracts from two other manuscripts. Probably unused as such (its structure would have made it impossible to follow in a ceremony), the *ordo* nonetheless had a significant influence upon sixteenth-century coronations. It was previously known as the *ordo* of Louis VIII (Godefroy) or the Compilation of 1300 (Schramm).[4]

(5) The last Capetian *ordo* was formerly called the *ordo* of Sens on account of the manuscript from which it was printed in the eighteenth century, but it has nothing to do with Sens, and Schramm gave it an appropriate new name. Schramm's date (1300–1320) was wrong, however, for there is a manuscript of the *ordo* from the latter part of the reign of Saint Louis. Again, this manuscript may be dated by its miniatures and script.[5] There were at least fourteen widely dispersed manuscripts of the *ordo*, including two at Reims that have now disappeared and an official copy in one of the registers of the Chambre des Comptes.[6] Like the *ordo* of Reims, it was probably composed at the abbey of Saint-Remi, the role of which it tends to emphasize, although royal officials may have had a hand in its composition. The *ordo* contains all of the *ordo* of Reims as rubrics and some material from the *ordo* of 1250 (or its German predecessor), the texts of the prayers, benedictions, etc., and some additional material (it is over twelve folio columns long in Martène's printed edition). It was used for several coronations, probably from Philip III (1271) on.[7]

(6) The *ordo* of Charles V was the final medieval coronation work that was only an *ordo* (rather than a description or a treatise). It may have been used at the coronation of Charles VI, and although the original version thereafter went to England, a copy was preserved at the abbey of Saint-Denis, and that manuscript was consulted for the preparation of the ceremonies of Louis XI and Charles VIII. Upon the latter all the later ceremonies were founded.[8]

(7) The *Traité du sacre* of Jean Golein is not an *ordo*, but a brief treatise on the coronation inserted by the author in his translation of William Durandus's *Rational of Divine Offices*. The structural framework of the piece was provided by the *ordo* of Reims and the last Capetian *ordo*, both in manuscripts in Reims as well as in the Chambre des Comptes. The *Traité* provides useful information on the conceptions of kingship in the circle of Charles V.[9]

(8) Jean Foulquart, *proceurer syndic* of Reims, wrote a tract on the coronation and its costs; he included an *ordo* that was a mixture of the last Capetian *ordo* and the *ordo* of Charles V. Foulquart's work, though written only in 1478, provides reliable information on the coronation of Louis XI in 1461.[10] Thereafter, more or less long descriptions of the coronations exist, forming a different sort of source material.

NOTES

CHAPTER I

1. The several works of Percy Ernst Schramm (see the bibliography cited, ch. 3, n. 9) discuss many of the complex interrelationships among the French, English, and German ceremonies. Perusal of the bibliography of this study will also reveal the tendency of each of the three languages to use the one word or the other. The mentality is so well entrenched in each language that it may even extend back to Latin. For example, the work by Reinhard Elze, *Ordines coronationis imperialis*, could just as well have been entitled *Ordines consecrationis imperialis*, for the medieval texts are often entitled *Ordo ad consecrandum et coronandum regem*.

2. The most useful collection of French ceremonial material (up to the mid-seventeenth century) is Godefroy, *Le cérémonial françois*. I have consulted almost all of the Godefroys' sources, whether manuscript or printed, but because they are often difficult to obtain I cite the edition of the Godefroys (except for the *ordines*, which I cite from the manuscripts); all references are to vol. 1 of the work. See Haueter, *Die Krönungen der französischen Könige*, pp. 57–58, on the visitors to Reims in the modern period.

3. Paris, Archives Nationales P 2288; P 1228; O^3 424 (=O 1717, no. 3), no. 2. Haueter, *Die Krönungen der französischen Könige*, pp. 62–74, discusses the church's decorations. Many other figures survive, for example, in AN K 1714 and P 2288 as well as in other archival repositories. For Napoleon, see Masson, *Le sacre et le couronnement de Napoléon*, Gaubert, *Le sacre de Napoléon*, and Pinoteau, "Sacre et couronnements napoléoniens." See also Desportes, *Reims et les Rémois*, pp. 389–90, 533–34, who says that in the early fourteenth century just the archbishop's coronation expenses amounted to three or four times his annual temporal revenues.

4. The bulk of current scholarship denies that there was knowledge of the Visigothic anointing in eighth-century Francia, so one cannot speak of the former as influencing the latter. Nevertheless, Michel Rouche, *L'Aquitaine*, p. 102, n. 98, and p. 382, n. 344, thinks that the kings of Aquitaine were anointed in the eighth century, perhaps on the Visigothic model. He has suggested also (conversation of June 1980) that that in turn might have influenced the anointing of Pepin owing to the latter's connections with Aquitaine, although there is no evidence for such a borrowing. Rouche's thesis does have plausibility, but one may ask whether the Davidic connotation of Pepin's anointing was present in the Visigothic

ceremony. It should be noted too that some scholars think that anointing may have been introduced in Byzantium already in the eleventh century.

5. Bouman, *Sacring and Crowning*, is the standard work on the subject, but it should be supplemented by Schramm, *Kaiser, Könige und Päpste*, 2:140–248. The best study of Charlemagne's coronation is Folz, *Le couronnement impérial*, which is clear and thought-provoking even when one cannot always agree with the author's conclusions (now available also in English translation). See Folz, *L'idée d'Empire*, p. 37, for a discussion of the imperial coronation in 816, which Desportes, *Reims et les Rémois*, p. 48, n. 1, says was essentially religious. However, Folz's source (MGH *Poetae*, 2:36) says nothing of a sacring but speaks only of a coronation, so it may be that the two rites were not combined until the 840s. There is a good discussion of the coronation of Louis the Pious by Charlemagne in 813 in Kleinclausz, *L'Empire carolingien*, pp. 232–36; there was no sacring then, either. The whole history of the Carolingian coronations needs a careful review. Janet L. Nelson has begun this task, at least as far as the liturgical aspects are concerned, in a series of studies: "Ritual and Reality," "Kingship, Law and Liturgy," "Inauguration Rituals," and "The Earliest Surviving Royal *Ordo*." She presents original and interesting arguments, although I cannot always agree with them. Likewise, I am not entirely convinced by the study by Carlrichard Brühl, "Fränkischer Krönungsbrauch." Brühl attempted to demonstrate that the coronation was introduced into the Frankish world before Charlemagne—perhaps already during the reign of Pepin the Short—and that coronation and anointing took place at the same time; my reservations have led me to present the generally accepted opinion in this paragraph. See also ch. 13, section 1.

6. Practically every work that deals with the Frankish monarchy in the ninth and tenth centuries deals with the question of election versus inheritance, but they often fail to temper theory with the realities of political life. There is an interesting discussion in Schramm, *Der König von Frankreich*, pp. 70–77 (all references to this work are to vol. 1 with the understanding that the notes in vol. 2 are also intended), as well as in Ewig, "La monocratie," 2:57–105. For the period before the ninth century, see also Grierson, "Election and Inheritance," pp. 1–22. See also the discussion by Ernst Wahle in Grundmann, *Gebhardts Handbuch*, pp. 209–15, 284–86 (with literature). I return to election in ch. 7.

7. One or more examples of anachronism are to be found in almost every chapter of this study; a good one is in ch. 7 at n. 6.

8. Georges Tessier, *La diplomatique royale*, pp. 224–26; Schramm, *Der König von Frankreich*, pp. 110–11, 226–27.

9. Kantorowicz, *The King's Two Bodies*; he unfortunately missed the Shakespearian pun.

10. The rejected statue by Girolamo della Robbia is now in the Louvre. The one by Germain Pilon is still in the cathedral of Saint-Denis. See Terasse, *Germain Pilon*, pp. 37–60 (esp. pp. 52–53).

11. This paragraph is the briefest summary of Giesey, *The Royal Funeral Ceremony*. See also ch. 9, section 4.

12. A still greater reason for ceasing to practice the Renaissance funeral was the development of the inaugural *lit de justice*; see Hanley, *The* Lit de Justice.

13. But there is still controversy over the sincerity of Edward III's claim. See, for example, Le Patourel, "The Origins of the War," pp. 28–50, and Palmer, "The War Aims," pp. 51–74. On dynastic succession, see Giesey, *The Juristic Basis of Dynastic Right*, and Scheidgen, *Die französische Thronfolge*.

14. Godefroy, *Louis XIII^a*, p. 414. For the full citation of this and the other works cited from Godefroy, *Le cérémonial françois*, see the bibliography, Works Cited from Godefroy.

15. Remond, *Le sacre et couronnement*, sig. o$_3$^{v} and p. 42^v.

16. Hanley, *The* Lit de Justice, chs. 11 and 12. See also ch. 4 at nn. 15–17.

17. See chs. 5–8.

18. Quicherat, *Procès de condamnation*, 3:20.

19. A recent popular but thoughtful and convincing study is Cazaux, *Henri IV*; see my review in the *American Historical Review* 83 (1978): 1023.

20. Such is the implication of the view attributed to Mazarin that one should "rien négliger de ce qui pouvoit procurer ou accroître au jeune Souverain l'obéissance, le respect, et la vénération" (Aubery, *Histoire du Cardinal Mazarin*, 4:42). It is difficult, though, to know how much of this is Mazarin and how much is Aubery.

21. See ch. 12, section 1.

22. For details of the post-Napoleonic coronations, see ch. 12.

23. Schramm, *Der König von Frankreich*.

24. I discuss these and related problems in greater detail in my study "Une revue des textes et des problèmes des *ordines* de couronnement français au moyen âge" (forthcoming).

25. See ch. 3, and the discussion of the oath of inalienability in ch. 6.

26. The portrait is reproduced in Maumené and d'Harcourt, *Iconographie des rois*, 2:296, pl. XX. The authors catalogue similar examples for Louis XIV: p. 28, no. 20 (portrait by Henri Testelin in 1648 of the king in the royal mantle and with a scepter); p. 30, no. 24 (engraving in 1648 of the king in the royal mantle and with a crown at his feet); p. 26, no. 15 (engraving in about 1646 of the king in the royal mantle and with a scepter). Haueter, *Die Krönungen der französischen Könige*, p. 213, n.

20, notes a similar example for Louis XVIII. Rigaud's portrait in Versailles remains the best known of these, however.

CHAPTER 2

1. The rapid series of events in those crowded days is neatly summarized by Hanley, *The* Lit de Justice, ch. 12. The more general background is discussed by Mousnier, *L'assassinat d'Henri IV*.

2. Hanley, *The* Lit de Justice, chs. 11 and 12.

3. Giesey, *The Royal Funeral Ceremony*, pp. 180–83. All dates up to the adoption of the Gregorian calendar in France are Old Style, except that the new year is taken to begin on January 1 rather than Easter; this includes the records of the Parlement of Paris, which retained the Easter dating until 1 January 1577, more than a decade after the remainder of France had adopted 1 January.

4. This description is based on Godefroy, *Louis XIII*^{a}, *Louis XIII*^{b}, and *Louis XIII*^{c}.

5. On Saint Remigius and the Holy Ampulla, see ch. 3 at nn. 21–23, ch. 13 at n. 5.

6. See ch. 9, section 2.

7. *Cérémonie du sacre et couronnement du roi Louis XIV*, printed in Dumont, *Le cérémonial diplomatique*, pp. 212–21 (cited as Dumont, *Louis XIV*), p. 213. See also ch. 4 at n. 18.

8. See ch. 9, section 1.

9. At this point it was customary to offer the cathedral church a reliquary or other precious object. The reliquaries given by Henry II and Henry III and the massive silver candlesticks given by Charles X are now on display in the Musée du sacre in Reims. For a discussion of these gifts, see Darcel, "Le Trésor de la cathédral de Reims."

10. On the *haquenée*, see Leber, *Cérémonies du sacre*, pp. 181–94.

11. At the coronation of Henry IV the coronator, Nicolas de Thou, bishop of Chartres, swore before notaries that he would return the Holy Ampulla to the Abbey of Marmoutier (Godefroy, *De Thou's Henry IV*, p. 359).

12. De Thou (ibid., p. 362) wrote that the insignia had to be made anew in 1594 because they had been destroyed during the Wars of Religion; see Montesquiou-Fezensac and Gaborit-Chopin, *Le Trésor de Saint-Denis*, 1:19–31. On the preservation of the coronation insignia in the abbey of Saint-Denis, see Schramm, *Der König von Frankreich*, pp. 131–44, 204–17. Three crowns rather than two were used at Louis XVI's coronation (Pichon, *Journal historique*, pp. 43–44). On the coronation insignia, see this chapter nn. 15–16, 21–24.

13. Beginning with the coronation of Francis II in 1559 most of the kings placed their hands on a peculiar Slavic Evangel given to the church by the cardinal of Lorraine; it is now in the Bibliothèque Municipale in Reims. There is a good discussion of the manuscript in Cabrol and Leclercq, *Dictionnaire d'archéologie chrétienne et de liturgie*, 14.2, col. 2284–86. For the oaths, see chs. 5 and 6; for the consent of the people, ch. 8.

14. I discuss the garments briefly in my article "The Sleeping King," p. 526, nn. 5–6.

15. See Schramm, *Der König von Frankreich*, p. 160, on the royal slippers, and pp. 169, 195–96, and 255 on the spurs.

16. Godefroy, *Louis XIII^c*, p. 449, says that a small sword was substituted for the large sword on account of the monarch's tender age; after Louis had given it to La Châtre it was replaced by the large sword. On the history of the sword in the Middle Ages, see Schramm, *Der König von Frankreich*, pp. 59, 140–41, 167–69, 195–96.

17. See ch. 3 at n. 26, on the versicle.

18. According to Godefroy, *Francis I^a*, p. 250, Francis I underwent a scrutiny after the litany and before the anointing. The archbishop of Reims asked the king three questions: "Will you keep holy faith to the Catholic men entrusted to you? Will you be a protector and defender of the Holy Churches and the ministers of the Churches? Will you rule and defend your kingdom granted by God, according to the justice of your fathers?" Francis replied "I will" to each of the questions. After the last question he promised faithfully to do all asked by the archbishop. This is the only example of a scrutiny in the history of the French ceremony, and, fortunately, we do not need to attribute a great deal of credibility to the source. The scrutiny was copied from the *ordo* of 1250, the manuscript of which (Paris, BN latin 1246) was apparently already in the royal collection—it was also consulted for the coronation of Henry II (see ch. 8 at n. 10, ch. 13 at n. 16). The other description of Francis's coronation, Godefroy, *Francis I^b*, pp. 259–60, does not mention the scrutiny.

19. This is the prayer that begins *Omnipotens sempiterne Deus, gubernator caeli*. It contains the odd request that the king "may not abandon the royal throne, that is, the kingdom, of the Saxons, Mercians, Northerners, and Cimbrians" (*ut regale solium videlicet Saxonum, Merciorum, Nordan, Cimbrorum sceptra non deserat*). The passage requires a few words of explanation. Originating in the English Edgar *ordo* (see Schramm, "Ordines-Studien II," pp. 30–33), a version of it is found in some manuscripts of the Fulrad *ordo* (there are two major manuscript traditions of the *ordo*) and in the *ordo* of 1250. The word *nordan-chimbrorum* was corrupted in the last Capetian *ordo* into *nordan chymbrorum*, which it was to remain until the end of the monarchy; it is itself a

corruption of *northanhymbrorum* (Northumbrians). Just how confused the history of the medieval *ordines* is may be demonstrated by the fact that a fifteenth-century translation of the last Capetian *ordo* (printed in Godefroy, *Le cérémonial françois*, pp. 1–12) properly asks that the king "ne delaisse le throsne Royal, sçavoir est les Sceptres des François, Bourguignons et Aquitainiens." At a later date it was thought that the corrupted text denoted pretensions of the French monarchs to the English throne; see, for example, the discussion in Godefroy, *Le cérémonial fran-çois*, pp. 80–82, and the anonymous *Cérémonies et prières du sacre des rois* (a work based, without attribution, on Alletz, *Cérémonial du sacre*), p. 58.

20. Beginning with Charles IX, most of the descriptions say that the kings were anointed "sur l'estomac," rather than "sur la poitrine." This does not mean that they were anointed on the stomach, though, but only that the word *estomac* was used for *poitrine*, which had come to be considered vulgar (see *Le petit Robert*, p. 696, s.v. "Estomac," II, 1, and Littré, *Dictionnaire*, 2:1505, s.v. "Estomac").

21. Godefroy, *Henry II*, p. 288, says that Henry had the vestments made anew, which was not uncommon, for both Charles V and Henry IV did the same. On the vestments see Pinoteau, "Quelques réflexions sur l'oeuvre de Jean du Tillet," pp. 16–19 (= *Vingt-cinq ans*, pp. 132–35); Schramm, *Der König von Frankreich*, pp. 159–62; see also this ch., n. 14. On the *Ungantur manus istae* prayer, see ch. 9 at n. 31.

22. Numerous texts say that the purpose of the gloves, which first appeared in the *ordo* of Charles V (see ch. 3 at n. 34), was to prevent desecration of the Holy Balm. Godefroy, *Francis I^a*, p. 251, says that after Francis had worn the gloves for a little while, they were removed by two bishops, who wiped the king's hands with cotton, bread crumbs, and salt; they then washed the king's hands and their own hands, and the archbishop of Reims also washed his hands. Godefroy, *Francis I^b*, p. 264, likewise says that Francis's hands were wiped and washed, but that that took place after the return to the archiepiscopal palace. The latter description is probably more accurate since the gloves would have been removed at the time that the other garments that came into contact with the chrism were removed to be burned (see this ch. at n. 30).

23. On the ring, see ch. 6, section 4.

24. On the scepter and the *main de justice*, see Pinoteau, "Quelques réflexions sur l'oeuvre de Jean du Tillet," pp. 11–15 (= *Vingt-cinq ans*, pp. 125–31); Pinoteau, "La main de justice"; Schramm, *Der König von Frankreich*, pp. 210-15.

25. On the Peers of France, see ch. 10.

26. On the meaning of the peers' support of the crown, see ch. 10 at n. 7, ch. 13 at nn. 21–24.

27. On the throne, see Schramm, *Der König von Frankreich*, pp. 215–17, and Pinoteau, "Quelques réflexions sur l'oeuvre de Jean du Tillet," pp. 19–24.

28. On the jettons, see ch. 4, section 3; on the birds, ch. 7, section 1.

29. The thirteen pieces of gold were usually similar to the coronation jettons, but at Henry IV's coronation they were different (and would have had to be so because Henry was not crowned at Reims). The obverse of Henry's pieces bore a portrait of the king and the inscription HENRICUS QUARTUS FRANCORUM ET NAVARRAE REX MDXCIIII. The reverse depicted Hercules and Henry's device: IN VIA VIRTUTI NULLA EST VIA, "There is no path on the way to virtue." On the meaning of Henry's device, see Panofsky, *Herkules am Scheidewege*. The "loaves of bread" were actually in the form of bread (those given by Charles X are now on display in the Musée du sacre in Reims). They could be quite valuable; for example, an inventory of the cathedral treasury made in 1792 says that the two loaves given by Louis XVI weighed three marcs, two ounces, two *gros*, and a "pain de vermeil, du même sacre" weighed one marc, two *gros* (printed in Cerf, *Histoire et description de Notre-Dame de Reims*, 1:528).

30. Godefroy, *De Thou's Henry IV*, p. 379, and *Louis XIII^a*, p. 416, says that the ashes from the burned garments were to be used for Ash Wednesday.

31. On the order of the Holy Spirit, see ch. 5 at nn. 10–12.

32. On the touching for scrofula, see Bloch, *Les rois thaumaturges*; see also ch. 12 at nn. 26–27. Louis also pardoned a number of prisoners before leaving the city; see ch. 7 at nn. 5–7, 13–15.

CHAPTER 3

1. Richardson, "The Coronation in Medieval England," pp. 112–15.

2. Godefroy, *Charles VIII*, and *De Thou's Henry IV*.

3. *Rélation de la cérémonie du sacre et couronnement du roi Louis XV, faite en l'église métropolitaine de Reims, le dimanche 25 octobre 1722*, printed in Dumont, *Le cérémonial diplomatique*, pp. 221–34 (cited as Dumont, *Louis XV*). Pichon, *Sacre et couronnement de Louis XVI*.

4. On the *ordo* of Reims, see Appendix B, no. 3.

5. See Appendix B, no. 5.

6. Oppenheimer, *Frankish Themes*, and *The Legend of the Ste. Ampoule*. The errors in Oppenheimer's dating are incomprehensible because he often refers to Schramm, *Der König von Frankreich*.

7. Schramm, "Ordines-Studien II," p. 28.

8. Schramm briefly discussed the Schreuer-Büchner controversy, ibid., p. 5, n. 3. Bloch, *Les rois thaumaturges*, pp. 73, n. 1, 492–93.

9. There is a good bibliography of Schramm's works in *Festschrift Schramm*, 2:291–316. For the period before about 1000, nevertheless, Schramm's work has been superseded by the detailed study by Bouman, *Sacring and Crowning*.

10. I present the preliminary results of my research in my forthcoming study, "Une revue des textes." On the texts that follow, see Appendix B.

11. In addition to Jackson, "Les manuscrits des *ordines*," see introduction and notes in the edition by E. S. Dewick, *The Coronation Book of Charles V*; Schramm, "Ordines-Studien II," pp. 42–47; and ch. 6, n. 14.

12. For the complicated history of the *ordines* at the fifteenth-century coronations, see ch. 3, section 3.

13. See ch. 6 at n. 43 and Appendix B, no. 5.

14. Delachenal, *Histoire de Charles V*, 3:71.

15. On the autograph, see Schramm, "Ordines-Studien II," p. 42; see ch. 6, n. 14.

16. See ch. 6, section 2.

17. See ch. 9, section 2.

18. Strayer, "Defense of the Realm," pp. 288–96.

19. Schramm, "Ordines-Studien II," pp. 45–46, discusses the sources. There is manuscript evidence for the presence of most of these materials in both cities, but I was unsuccessful in my attempt to find in either city either the manuscript or the history of the manuscript of the Spanish *ordo*.

20. Sherman, "The Queen in the King's 'Coronation Book,'" is the first to have noticed the importance of the queen's *ordo* in this text.

21. Hincmar of Reims, *Vita Remigii episcopi Remensi*, in MGH *Scriptores rerum Merovingicarum*, 3:296–97, recounts the legend, and he discusses it on pp. 297–300 (with some passages that were taken from earlier texts, or that became parts of the coronation prayers). See Devisse, *Hincmar, archevêque de Reims*, 3:1004–54.

22. The grounds for the revival are discussed in ch. 13 at nn. 5–6.

23. Reims BM 328, fol. 72.

24. Bloch, *Les rois thaumaturges*; Roy, "Philippe le Bel," 383–88. The conception of the French royal consecration as an eighth sacrament has yet to be satisfactorily investigated.

25. Schramm, "Ordines-Studien II," p. 38.

26. An eleventh-century breviary of Reims (Paris, BN latin 17991) contains an old form of the hymn: "Gentem francorum inclita[m] simul cum rege nobili beatus Remigius sumpto [*sic*] cęlitus [*sic*] crismatę sacro sanctificavit gurgite atque spiritus sancti plene dictavit munere." On the manuscript, see Leroquais, *Les bréviaires manuscrits*, 3:349–50. The versicle may also have intentionally recalled the legitimacy of Charles as

king (and implied the illegitimacy of Edward III's claim), for one cannot help but be struck by the similarity of its first words and the opening words of the preface to the Salic law, "Gens Francorum inclyta, auctore Deo condita," which themselves sound suspiciously like the beginning of a hymn. The Salic law as determining the succession was first evoked during Charles V's reign; see Scheidgen, *Die französische Thronfolge.*

27. The last Capetian *ordo* (Paris, BN nouv. acq. latines 1202, fol. 126^v) says, "[Rex francie] solus inter universos reges terre hoc glorioso prefulget privilegio, ut oleo celitus misso singlerariter [*sic* for *singulariter*] inungatur." See this ch. at n. 23.

28. Jackson, "Les manuscits des *ordines*," pp. 70–71, 76, 78–79.

29. Details are presented in Jackson, "Une revue des textes" and in "Les manuscrits des *ordines*," passim.

30. See ch. 6 at nn. 33–34.

31. Quicherat, *Procès de condamnation,* 4:185–86.

32. Ibid., 5:129.

33. Jackson, "Charles IX's Coronation," p. 296: "Après, la Messe dicte, le Roy . . . est venu au grand Autel recevoir son createur, et de là retourner en son logis à huict heures du matin jusques à une heure après midy." Reims, BM 1491, no. 4, pp. 10–11, says that the Holy Ampulla arrived at the church at about 9:00 A.M. and that "le Saint Sacre faict et accomply, environ les unze heures de matin, est sailly ledict Grand Prieur dudict Cueur" to return the ampulla, so obviously he did not wait until the ceremony was finished. The same was true at the coronation of Francis II in 1559: "ledict Sacre faict et acomply [*sic*], environ l'heure de unze à douze heures du matin, est sailly ledict Grant Prieur dudict Cueur" (ibid., no. 5, p. 7). At Henry III's coronation in 1575, on the other hand, the ampulla left the choir "ledict sacre faict et accomply, environ l'heure de deux heures de relevée" (ibid., no. 6, p. 8), which must have been after the termination of the mass.

34. Quicherat, *Procès de condamnation,* 1:104: "Interroguée qu'elle fist à Rains des gans où son roy fut sacré: respond: 'Il y oult une livrée de gans pour bailler aux chevaliers et nobles qui là estoient. Et en y oult ung qui perdit ses gans'; mais ne dist point qu'elle les feroit retrouver."

35. Paris, BN français 8334 (see Appendix B, no. 8).

36. Chastellain, *Oeuvres,* 4:57–58.

37. This curious episode is fully discussed by Marlot, *Histoire de la ville,* 4:240–45, who included related documents on pp. 669–72. (Marlot's work was not published until 1843, but it was written in the seventeenth century.)

38. Chastellain, *Oeuvres,* 4:59. Marlot, *Histoire de la ville,* 4:212–14, discusses the coronation of Louis XI; based on material in Reims at the

time, apparently, it tends to bolster Chastellain's attribution of an inordinate role played by the duke of Burgundy, without requiring that we believe the improbable in Chastellain's description.

39. Godefroy, *Charles VIII*, p. 191.

CHAPTER 4

1. Schramm, *Der König von Frankreich*, and "Ordines-Studien II."
2. Fawtier, *The Capetian Kings*, p. 57.
3. Typical is the view of Schramm, *Der König von Frankreich*, p. 110: "So brachte er [Philipp August] das Prinzip der Mitherrschaft, das bei ihm selbst noch einmal in Kraft getreten war, zum Erlöschen. Damit fiel nun—bis auf die noch weiter vor der Krönung vom Reimser Erzbischof eingeholte Vollbort—auch die zum 'Beraten' verkümmerte Wahl weg. Daß auf den französischen König sein erstgeborener Sohn folge, war nunmehr durch Gewohnheit zu einem 'Fundamentalgesetz' der Monarchie geworden."
4. Lewis, "Anticipatory Association."
5. But see ch. 6 at nn. 51–53.
6. See ch. 2, nn. 22 and 30. See also Dewick, *The Coronation Book of Charles V*, pp. 32–33.
7. See ch. 3 at nn. 20–27.
8. Godefroy, *Charles VIII*, p. 195, where only the incipit is given. I translate from the version given in *Formulaire moderne qui s'observe au sacre et couronnement des roys de France . . . recueilly exprés pour servir au sacre du roy Louys XIII*, printed in Godefroy, *Le cérémonial françois*, p. 59. The hymn suffered an interesting alteration at the coronation of Henry IV, when it read, "O precious gift, O precious gem, whose invisible meaning we comprehend through the visible gift" (*cuius visibili dono invisibilia percipimus*), which despite its beginning was not only an entirely different antiphon, but also one that could hardly fail to imply that the royal unction was a sacrament, the most important definition of which was "a visible sign of an invisible grace"; at later coronations the older antiphon was restored to use (Godefroy, *De Thou's Henry IV*, p. 359, and *Anon. Henry IV*, p. 392).
9. Godefroy, *Charles VIII*, p. 195.
10. "Traicté du sacre des roys de France" (Paris, BN Baluze 112, fols. 74–95^v), fols. 84, 85^v.
11. Ibid., fol. 84^v. The scriptural passage is Ecclesiasticus 46:16. The final part of the quotation, in evoking some sort of election of the king, raises a host of questions with which we must eventually deal at greater length (see ch. 8).
12. Paris, BN nouv. acq. latines 1202, fol. 136^v; London, British Li-

brary Tiberius B.viii, fol. 59^v; Godefroy, *Charles VIII*, p. 203.

13. There was much discussion of this issue in 1594. Some material is printed in Godefroy, *Le cérémonial françois*, pp. 127–33, 401–402.

14. See ch. 3 at n. 37. See also Bloch, *Les rois thaumaturges*, p. 78, n. 2.

15. Godefroy, *Charles IX*, p. 314; Jackson, "Charles IX's Coronation," pp. 295–96; Godefroy, *Louis XIII^b*, pp. 431, 433, and *Louis XIII^c*, pp. 449–52. According to the last work, the king struck the duke of Elbeuf when giving him the kiss of peace and not the previous kiss of homage; for present purposes it is not important when the event took place.

16. Godefroy, *Louis XIII^a*, p. 414.

17. See ch. 1 at nn. 14–16.

18. Le Gras, *Procès-verbal*, p. 6, says that the coronation was postponed "pour des raisons à Nous inconnuës." As late as 13 May the ceremony was still planned for the end of the month, as is shown by the *lettres de cachet* sent to those invited to play roles in the ceremony; one such letter is quoted by Haueter, *Die Krönungen der französischen Könige*, p. 51, n. 182.

19. Paris, BN latin 13314, fols. 48^v–49: "[François] debuoit estre sacré le dimanche ensuivant [i.e., the 17 September], mais ledit Sacre fut differé jusques au lendemain xviiie dudit mois à cause de la fievre de monsieur le Duc de Savoye qui le tint le dimanche." See also Reims, BM 1489, no. 15, a drawing of Francis's coronation jettons, which is accompanied by a note, "L'indisposition du Prince de Piémont la fit defferer d'un jour." A marriage contract had been signed between the duke and Henry II's sister Margaret only a few weeks before, on 28 June 1559. On the jettons, see this ch., n. 21.

20. *Le chanson de Roland*, 647–702, 2471–68 (Bédier ed., pp. 50–54, 206–208).

21. Bie, *La France métallique*, plates 1–50 passim. On the jettons in general, see Blanchet, "Médailles et jetons," and *Médailles, jetons, méreaux.* Because Henry IV was not crowned at Reims, his jettons had to depart from the established pattern; see ch. 2, n. 29.

22. Godefroy, *Charles VIII*, p. 204.

23. Leber, *Des cérémonies du sacre*, pp. 422–37; Marlot, *Le théatre d'honneur*, pp. 687–88. Marlot seems to have been the first to associate the jettons with marriage (on which, see ch. 6, section 4.)

24. Reims, BM 328, fol. 72^v; Paris, BN nouv. acq. latines 1202, fol. 139^v; London, British Library Tiberius B. viii, fol. 63.

25. See ch. 10 at n. 9.

26. On Saint-Denis and its pretensions, see Schramm, *Der König von Frankreich*, pp. 131–44; Spiegel, "The Cult of Saint Denis"; see ch. 13 at n. 6.

27. Bromley, "The Decline of Absolute Monarchy," p. 139.

28. Kantorowicz, *"Oriens Augusti—Lever du Roi."*

29. I briefly discuss the Byzantine influences in my study "De l'influence du cérémonial byzantin sur les sacres des rois de France."

30. Godefroy, *Henry II*, p. 290.

31. Pseudo-Codinos, *Traité des offices*, pp. 254–55.

32. Ibid., pp. 270–71.

33. On the history of the manuscript, see Verpeaux's introduction, pp. 48–50, and the literature he cites. I have collated the manuscript with Verpeaux's edition, and there are no important variations in the passages cited.

34. Godefroy, *Henry II*, p. 236: "Ledit Seigneur . . . feit apporter devant luy en son Chastel de Sainct Germain en Laye, les ornemens estans en garde en l'Abbaye de Sainct Denys en France, destinez audit Sacre et Couronnement . . . , pour veoir en quel ordre lesdits ornemens estoient. Et pource que ledit Seigneur veit que lesdits [ornemens] . . . estoient jà deteriorez et usez par laps de temps, et pour avoir servuy à plusieurs, et autres Sacres et Couronnemens de ses predecesseurs, il voulut et luy pleut en faire faire de tous neufs."

35. For the latter, see ch. 9, sections 4–5.

36. I borrow the statement from Facinger, "A Study in Medieval Queenship," p. 31.

CHAPTER 5

1. David, *Le serment du sacre*, pp. 155–219.

2. London, British Library Tiberius B.viii, fol. 46^v: "Promitto vobis et perdono, quia unicuique de vobis, et ecclesiis vobis commissis, canonicum privilegium, et debitam legem, atque justiciam conservabo, et deffensionem quantum potuere exhibebo, Domino adjuvante, sicut rex in suo regno, unicuique episcopo et ecclesie sibi commisse, per rectum exhibere debet."

3. See ch. 8.

4. For the Latin text, see ch. 6, n. 17.

5. It is not necessary here to say much about the development and validity of both oaths, which have been studied at length by David, *Le serment du sacre* and *La souveraineté*, and by Buisson, *Potestas und Caritas*, pp. 270–98, 307–15.

6. In the High Middle Ages the oath was not necessarily sworn as quoted this ch., n. 2, because that served essentially as a model that was altered as necessary, as is demonstrated by the oath sworn by Philip I in 1059. See Bouman, *Sacring and Crowning*, pp. 141–47.

7. Guenée and Lehoux, *Les entrées royales*, p. 84.

8. Schramm, *Der König von Frankreich*, pp. 199–200.

9. Le Noble, *Histoire du sacre*, p. 41; Haueter, *Die Krönungen der französischen Könige*, pp. 138–46.

10. See ch. 8 at nn. 9–10, and ch. 13 at n. 16.

11. I use *demeaning* here not only in its lexicographical sense, but also to imply "stripped of meaning."

12. *Cérémonies observées en la reception du Collier*, in Godefroy, *Le cérémonial françois*, pp. 582–83; Godefroy, *Anon. Henry IV*, p. 397, *Louis XIII^a*, p. 417, *Louis XIII^b*, p. 435, and *Louis XIII^c*, p. 456; *Le sacre et couronnement de Louis XIV*, sigs. C$_8$^{v}, H$_3$–H$_5$; Dumont, *Louis XIV*, pp. 215, 220, and *Louis XV*, p. 225. Pichon, *Journal historique*, pp. 40–43, quotes all five of the oaths taken by Louis XVI. See also *Cérémonies et prières*, p. 40.

13. Dumont, *Louis XV*, p. 225. Louis XVI's oath omitted the word *inviolably* toward the end of the oath.

14. Pichon, *Journal historique*, pp. 42–43. See also Haueter, *Die Krönungen der französischen Könige*, pp. 132–38.

15. That was the duel between Guy Chabot, sieur de Jarnac et de Montlieu, and François de Vivonne, sieur de la Châtaigneraie, that resulted in the death of the latter and gave the French language the phrase *coup de Jarnac* for a perfidious blow; see Letainturier-Fradin, *Le duel*, pp. 29–30, 136–44. Clausel de Cousserges, *Developpmens de la proposition*, pp. 9–10, says that there was one authorized duel under Henry III, but he does not give any details; is it possible that he erred, attributing to the reign of Henry III the duel of 1547?

16. See Godefroy, *Le cérémonial françois*, sig. e$_3$, where the writer says that he is publishing his collection for that very reason.

17. Montesquiou, *Étude sur la suppression du duel*, p. 42.

18. Chatauvillard, *Essai sur le duel*, pp. 218–482, published a collection of edicts and decrees that includes quite a few materials not found in the great collections of French laws like Isambert, *Recueil général*. Most of his material appears to have been taken from the *Recueil des édits* of 1689, which (pp. 393–441) includes the whole of the ordinance of 1679 (the text of that ordinance in Isambert, 19:209–17, is incomplete). I should add that I have not managed to find a satisfactory history of dueling and its ramifications, although there is a good survey of the ecclesiastical and French law by L. Falletti, "Duel," in Naz, *Dictionnaire du droit canonique*, 5:cols. 23–37.

19. Paris, BN nouv. acq. françaises 21708–712.

20. Paris, BN nouv. acq. françaises 21708, fols. 1–2 and case nos. 6, 7, 34, 88, 251, and 297 were duels. Nos. 16, 40, 55, 69, 83, 91, 95, 136, 154, 186, and 275 were various other crimes. No. 161 was deleted.

21. The figure is given by *Le sacre et couronnement de Louis XIV*, sig. H₆ ("en nombre de plus de six mille"), but see a possible downward revision of that number, ch. 7 at n. 10.

22. This figure may be a little high, but it is close enough for our purposes. See Reinhard, Armengand, and Dupaquier, *Histoire générale de la population*, pp. 174–96, who suggest that the population of all of France within the boundaries of the end of the seventeenth century may have amounted to 19.3 million and that the amplitude of population variations did not exceed 20 percent during the whole century.

23. L'Estoile, *Registre-Journal*, part ii, p. 514: ". . . il se vérifiera, par les registres des chancéleries seulement, que depuis l'avénement de nostre Roy à la couronne, jusques à la fin de l'an passé 1608, en ont esté sellées et expediées sept mille grâces."

24. Pasquier, *Rapport fait par M. le baron Pasquier*, p. 9n.

25. It is impossible to know what percentage of duelers decided to avail themselves of the king's pardon in 1654. If as many as 10 percent did so —admittedly a purely speculative figure—the incidence of dueling would have been 20.85 per 100,000 of the general population per year, a terribly high figure that compares well (or ill) with the murder rate in a modern American city like Houston or, worse, Detriot (respectively 20.9 and 49.4 murders per 100,000 in 1972–73), particularly when one considers that the figures for dueling do not include all other forms of homicide.

26. Isambert, *Recueil général*, 17:275, and *Recueil des édits*, p. 440.

27. *Le sacre et couronnement de Louis XIV*, sigs. C₇ᵛ–C₈ᵛ, quotes the ecclesiastical oath and the oath of the kingdom and notes the oath of the order of the Saint-Esprit.

28. My thesis here is nicely supported by a text that was found by Haueter, *Die Krönungen der französischen Könige*, p. 134. In November 1722, *after* the coronation of Louis XV on 25 October, a master of ceremonies was still trying to determine the supposed text of Louis XIV's oath.

29. Louis de Montmorency, comte de Bouteville, and François de Rosmadec, comte des Chapelles, were beheaded on 22 June 1627. See Letainturier-Fradin, *Le duel*, pp. 159–67, and Anselme de Sainte Marie, *Histoire généalogique*, 3:588.

30. Paris, BN nouv. acq. françaises 21708, no. 411, and Paris, Bibliothèque de l'Assemblée Nationale 1388, no. 134.

31. Brillat-Savarin, *Essai historique*, p. 32, for example, wrote in 1819 that he had not found a single case among the best-known sentences in which the sentence was applied; Billacois, "Le Parlement de Paris et les duels," pp. 41–47, makes a similar remark.

32. Paris, Bibliothèque de l'Assemblée Nationale 1387–1388.

33. These three cases are nos. 28, 237, and 241. The other three are nos. 5, 34, and 90.

34. No. 34.

35. Billacois, "Le Parlement de Paris et les duels."

36. Clausel de Coussergues, *Développmens de la proposition*, p. 26: "Mais dans le cours de sa longue vie, ce prince [Louis XIV] n'accorda la grâce à aucun de ceux qui s'en étaient rendus coupables. Ils furent obligés de s'expatrier, et aucun ne rentra en France, si ce n'est après son règne." To this one should add that, judging from the records of the pardons in 1654 and 1722, a good many duelers were condemned to the galleys.

CHAPTER 6

1. London, British Library Tiberius B.viii, fol. 46^v; for the Latin , see this ch., n. 17. It is nearly impossible to render easily into English the words "superioritatem, jura, et nobilitates," for each of them has broad implications, and each overlaps the others. I intend to prepare a much longer study of the rise of inalienability in France, but I thought it wise to present some of my findings here in truncated form because the coronation plays such a large role in the issue. I am most grateful to Elizabeth A. R. Brown for carefully reading and commenting on this chapter.

2. Godefroy, *Le cérémonial françois*, pp. 76, 197; Riesenberg, *Inalienability of Sovereignty*; Hoffmann, "Die Unveräusserlichkeit."

3. On inalienability in general, see, in addition to Riesenberg and Hoffmann, Kantorowicz, "Inalienability," in *Selected Studies*, pp. 138–50, and *The King's Two Bodies*, pp. 212–23, and Index, s.v., "Inalienability"; Post, *Medieval Legal Thought*, pp. 415–33. For the sixteenth century, see also Doucet, *Les institutions*, 2:545–48, and Zeller, *Les institutions*, pp. 82–84. The best study of the fundamental laws is Church, *Constitutional Thought*.

4. See ch. 8.

5. Kantorowicz, "Inalienability"; Hoffmann, "Die Unveräusserlichkeit," pp. 399–400, 468–69; Sweeney, "The Problem of Inalienability," pp. 235–51. For an extract from the decretal, see this ch., n. 29.

6. Such is the conclusion of Andrew W. Lewis in his recent book, *Royal Succession in Capetian France*. It is supported in part by Kienast, *Untertaneneid und Treuvorbehalt*, pp. 170–71, who was impressed by the extent to which the French king "nur ein Lehnsherr neben anderen Lehnsherren war, fast ohne Sonderrechte als König."

7. Fawtier, "Comment le roi de France," pp. 65–77.

8. Hoffmann, "Die Unveräusserlichkeit," pp. 450–51. I say theoretical in part because I am not sure that contemporaries knew precisely where

the frontier of France was, although there is still considerable disagreement over the matter.

9. Isambert, *Recueil général*, 3:179–82, 294–96; a list of the legislation after 1322 is given in ibid., 5:217, n. 1. See also Riesenberg, *Inalienability of Sovereignty*, pp. 18–19, 105–12, 124–26; Esmein, *Cours élémentaire*, pp. 327–34; Declareuil, *Histoire générale*, pp. 410–21. Charles IV's revocation may well have been the direct result of the inquest into alienations that was begun in March 1321; see Bloch, *Rois et serfs*, pp. 125–26.

10. Isambert, *Recueil général*, 4:837. On the relationships of the Hundred Years' War to French territoriality, see Le Patourel, "The Treaty of Brétigny" and "The Origins of the War," and Palmer, "The War Aims"; all three articles cite further literature.

11. For details, see the studies cited in the previous note.

12. Isambert, *Recueil général*, 5:130–31: ". . . videlicet, quando nobis presenti vita functis, dictus primogenitus noster in regno successor extiterit, ad quod nunc consolidandum jubemus, et ad hoc ipsum, quantum possumus, obligamus, cum insignia coronacionis suscipiet, prestans tunc juramentum quod numquam per ipsum inter tam sic unita et conjuncta, aliqua generabitur divisio seu scissura . . . [et] nos et futuros successores nostros reges Francie obligamus et volumus esse astrictos, ac dum insignia coronacionis recipient, ad predicta juramenta renovenda per eosdem modo et forma predictis. . . ." There is no provision for a similar oath for Burgundy, Champagne, or Toulouse (which were simply declared united with the crown) because, no doubt, they did not share Normandy's dangerous position.

13. Jackson, "Les manuscrits des *ordines*," pp. 75, nn. 26, 85.

14. Fol. 74^v: "Ce livre du sacre dez Rois de France est à nous, Charles le Ve de Notre nom, Roy de France, et le fimes Coriger, ordener, Escrire et istorier l'an MCCCLXV. Charles." The autograph is reproduced in Dewick, *The Coronation Book*, pl. 39, in Bond and Thompson, *Facsimiles*, 3:77 (pl. 148), and elsewhere.

15. John Selden first published the manuscript in the second edition of his *Titles of Honor* (London, 1631), pp. 222–55 (pp. 177–206 in the third edition [London, 1672]).

16. Jackson, "Les manuscrits des *ordines*," pp. 69–71.

17. The remainder of the oath reads: "Item, ut omnes rapacitates et omnes iniquitates omnibus gradibus interdicam.

"Item, ut in omnibus judiciis equitatem et misericordiam precipiam, ut mihi et vobis indulgeat per suam misericordiam clemens et misericors Deus.

"Item, de terra mea ac juridicione mihi subdita universos hereticos ab ecclesia denotatos pro viribus bona fide exterminare studebo; hec omnia supradicta firmo juramento" (London, British Library Tiberius B.viii, fols. 46^v–47). For a translation, see this ch. at n. 4.

18. Hoffmann, "Die Unveräusserlichkeit," p. 453, n. 17, suggested that the erasure might have been made in order to insert the clause containing heretics. A careful count of minims and study of abbreviations in the manuscript shows that this was not the case, but the evidence is too complicated and lengthy to be presented here. Examination under ultraviolet light proved fruitless (I should like to express my thanks to my former student, Dianna P. Evans, for having undertaken the examination, and to the curators of the British Museum for having aided her). Professor T. J. Brown of the University of London carefully examined the manuscript from a palaeographical viewpoint, and I should like to thank him for his time and effort.

19. On the distinction and the lists, see ch. 10 at n. 11.

20. The evidence for the use of the newer oath (but without the clause concerning heretics) in 1328 is presented this ch. at n. 34. The clause was noted already in the *ordo* of Reims (see ch. 5 at n. 9). The marginal addition of the older oath is in Reims BM 342, fol. 70.

21. Jackson, "Les manuscrits des *ordines*," pp. 78–84.

22. Ibid., pp. 77–78; see ch. 3, section 3, but see also this ch. at nn. 27–30.

23. Charles's revocation is printed in Isambert, *Recueil général*, 5:217–18, and John's letters in 5:112–13.

24. Chaplais, "The Opinions of the Doctors of Bologna," pp. 51–78.

25. Perroy, *The Anglo-French Negotiations*, p. 57; quoted also in Hoffmann, "Die Unveräusserlichkeit," p. 454.

26. *Somnium viridarii*, in Goldast, *Monarchia*, 1:189; *Le Songe du Vergier*, in *Revue du moyen âge latin*, 13:177–78, 14:107. On the authorship of the work, see Zeller, "Les rois de France candidats," p. 305. For the arguments at Vincennes, see this ch. at nn. 42–44.

27. Paris BN français 2700, fol. 41, no. 46: "lequel le Roy print pour son sacre 5 jour d'octobre l'an mil iiii.^{xx} [*sic* for 4 October 1380]."

28. Isambert, *Recueil général*, 7:10–11; printed also in *Ordonnances des rois*, 8:484. The ordinance, despite its brevity, makes two further references to the oath and gives the impression of insisting too much on its actuality.

29. See this ch. at n. 5. The pertinent passage from *Intellecto* (Friedberg, *Corpus Juris Canonici*, 2:373) reads: ". . . nos . . . eidem regi dirigimus scripta nostra, ut alienationes praedictas, non obstante juramento, si quod fecit de non revocandis eisdem, studeat revocare, quia, quum teneatur, et in sua coronatione juraverit etiam, jura regni sui et honorem

coronae illibata servare, illicitum profecto fuit, si praestitit de non revocandis alienationibus hujusmodi juramentum, et propterea penitus non
servandum."

30. The *ordonnance Cabochienne* of 1413 mentions the oath with revocation (Isambert, *Recueil général*, 7:296) and, according to Jean Juvénal des Ursins (*Histoire de Charles VI*, 2:550–51), one of the French
negotiators in 1419 also believed that his king had sworn an oath of nonalienation.

31. Marot, "L'expédition de Charles VII," p. 145.

32. Paris, BN français 2701, fol. 30ᵛ. Peter S. Lewis has begun the
publication of his edition of Jean Juvénal des Ursins' political works
(*Écrits politiques*, 1), but I had already had to work with the manuscripts,
and the edition has been published only in part, so I cite the manuscripts.

33. Paris, BN français 17,512, fols. 13, 32ᵛ.

34. Paris, BN français 2701, fol. 47. In concluding his quotation, the
author did not quote the clause concerning the heretics for reasons that
are not yet clear. He had just quoted the ecclesiastical oath.

35. See ch. 3, section 3.

36. Isambert, *Recueil général*, 10:386, 467.

37. Paris, BN français 8334, fols. 54–54ᵛ; see Appendix B, no. 8.

38. Dupuy, *Traité de la majorité*, pp. 232–33, prints the oath as registered in the Parlement on 22 April 1482. According to Duchesne, *Les
antiquitez et recherches*, p. 408, Monstrelet (i.e., a continuator) also referred to the registration, but I was not able to find the Monstrelet reference in any of three sixteenth-century editions (1512, 1572, and 1595),
nor was I able to find the oath in the registers of the Parlement of Paris.

39. Godefroy, *De Thou's Henry IV*, p. 362.

40. Archives Departmentales d'Eure et Loire, C, c.1.b, no. 84.

41. I exclude references to the oath in manuscripts written after the
first publication of Tiberius B.viii.

42. *Libellus D. Bertrandi, Cardinalis Sancti Clementis, adversus Ma-
gistrum Petrum de Cugneriis*, in Durand de Maillane, *Les libertez de
l'église gallicane*, 3:456–57. On the circumstances of the meeting, see
Olivier-Martin, *L'assemblée de Vincennes*.

43. [Pierre Roger], *Oratio electi Senonensis summaria Philippi probi*,
in Durand de Maillane, *Les libertez de l'église gallicane*, 3:477–78.

44. Ibid.; *Responsio Cardinalis Bertrandi ad Orationem Petri de Cugneriis*, in Durand de Maillane, 3:482.

45. *Somnium viridarii*, in Goldast, *Monarchia*, 1:189.

46. *Le songe du vergier*, in *Revue du moyen âge latin* 13:177–78.

47. Ibid., pp. 109–10.

48. Chaplais, "The Opinions of the Doctors of Bologna," pp. 51–78.

49. Printed in Mayer, *Des États Généraux*, 10:195–96.

50. Isambert, *Recueil général*, 12:51.

51. Godefroy, *Henry II*, p. 288.

52. Paris, BN nouv. acq. latines 1202, fols. 132ᵛ–133; London, British Library Tiberius B.viii, fols. 57–57ᵛ. Schramm, *Der König von Frankreich*, p. 239, wrote of the ring in Charles V's *ordo* that "durch ihn der König mit seinem Königreich vermählt werde"; many writers since have based similar statements upon Schramm's.

53. Kantorowicz, *The King's Two Bodies*, p. 222, n. 84. In the second edition of *Der König von Frankreich*, 2:21 (note to p. 205), Schramm recognized Kantorowicz's argument.

54. Paris, Bibliothèque de Sainte-Geneviève 3036, fol. 16: "Oultre plus mondict Seigneur le Legat en continuant les benedictions et oraisons luy mist et posa au premier doict de la main dextre ledict aneau sponsal signiffiant et denotant qu'elle espousoit et prenoit possession . . . du royaulme de France. . . ." On what follows, see also Hanley, *The* Lit de Justice, ch. 4.

55. Gratian wrote of it in his *Decretum*, 30, 5, 7 (Friedberg, *Corpus Juris Canonici*, 2:97), and some of Gratian's sources may be traced back to antiquity.

56. Bouchart, *Les grandes chroniques*, fol. 68ᵛ (fols. 58–59 in the 1541 edition).

57. Grassaille, *Regalium Franciae*, p. 217.

58. Lucas de Penna, *Commentaria in tres libros codicis*, pp. 563–64, as quoted by Kantorowicz, "Mysteries of State," in *Selected Studies*, pp. 390, n. 48, and 391, n. 56.

59. See this ch. at n. 51. Grassaille's book was republished in 1545, seven years after the first edition.

60. Kantorowicz, *The King's Two Bodies*, pp. 221–22. See also Kantorowicz, "Mysteries of State," in *Selected Studies*, pp. 388–89, and Giesey, *The Juristic Basis of Dynastic Right*, pp. 12–17.

61. Cappel, *Plaidoyez*, p. 11ᵛ.

62. Papon, *Recueil d'arrests*, p. 107ᵛ.

63. Bodin, *La république*, liv. 6, ch. 2, p. 631 (*The Six Bookes of a Commonweale*, p. 652); *Recueil de tout ce qui s'est negotié*, pp. 101–3.

64. For example, the Chambre des Comptes even worked the theory into a remonstrance in 1593; see Zeller, *Les institutions*, p. 83. See also Kantorowicz, "Mysteries of State," in *Selected Studies*, p. 389, n. 40.

65. Choppin, *Traité du domaine*, in *Oeuvres*, 2:171. The *Lex Julia* is to be found in Digest 48, 5, and in Codex 5, 13, 15. Viollet, *Histoire du droit*, pp. 796–97, discusses the spread of the Roman law principle in medieval France (without giving specific dates, however).

66. The treaties of Madrid and Crépy are discussed in Lavisse, *Histoire de France*, 5,2: 50–51, 116–17. On Henry's objection to Crépy, see Dupuy, *Traitez touchant les droits*, pp. 269–70.

67. See ch. 4. n. 34.

68. Godefroy, *De Thou's Henry IV*, p. 369.

69. La Guesle, *Remontrance*, p. 3.

70. This paragraph is based on Olivier-Martin, "La réunion de la Basse-Navarre," pp. 253–72. The edict of 1607 is printed in Isambert, *Recueil général*, 15:328. Renewed French interest in the issue of inalienability also derived from the speculations of such lawyers as Guillaume Budé or Andrea Alciati on the delegation of *merum imperium*; see Gilmore, *Argument from Roman Law*, pp. 46–57. Late in the century, of course, the problem was to take a new orientation with the work of Jean Bodin and Charles Loyseau (ibid., pp. 106–7, 110–11).

71. Godefroy, *Louis XIIIᵃ*, p. 412, and *Louis XIIIᵇ*, p. 430. In the seventeenth and eighteenth centuries the marriage metaphor was given a different interpretation, which need not concern us here; see Lacour-Gayet, *L'éducation politique*, p. 329, and Haueter, *Die Krönungen der französischen Könige*, pp. 310–11.

72. See ch. 1 at n. 12.

73. Isambert, *Recueil général*, 14:185–89. It would be redundant to say anything about the edict's statement that the king had sworn alienation and revocation.

74. Ibid., 14:452–54.

75. Dupuy, *Traitez touchant les droits du roy*, p. 272: "Il est certain que l'Estat de cette Couronne consiste principalement en la conservation du Domaine Royal, qui est dedié à l'entretenement de la paix, pour fournir aux frais de la guerre, pour soulager les peuples, pour servir au repos et à la tranquillité publique. De là vient que l'on tient le Domaine sacrosainct et inaliénable; de là aussi le serment solemnel que les Rois font à leur Sacre, qui est tel, qu'il semble qu'ils prennent la Couronne à cette condition. Voicy ce qu'il porte, *Superioritatem, iura, et nobilitates Coronae Franciae inviolabiliter custodiam, et illa nec transportabo, nec alienabo.*"

76. Navigation maps were produced earlier, of course, exactly because they were useful and meaningful, which lends support to the argument here presented.

77. These terms were certainly used in the fourteenth century, but they did not then appear to have the territorial implications of modern usage. The edict of Moulins (Isambert, *Recueil général*, 14:186, art. 2), for example, defines the domain as consisting partly of "that that has been expressly consecrated to, united with, and incorporated into the Crown,"

which would include the great medieval fiefs like Champagne, Normandy, or Brittany.

CHAPTER 7

1. Paris, Bibliothèque de l'Assemblée Nationale 1387, fols. 1–49ᵛ. It is usually impossible to give precise locations in this and in manuscript 1388 (the second volume of the records) because most of the folio numbers were cut off when the manuscripts were bound.

2. For the unpardonable crimes, see this ch. at n. 57.

3. Dumont, *Louis XV*, p. 233.

4. Lacointa, *Du sacre des rois*, pp. 136–37; Millon, *Cérémonial du sacre*, p. 107 (apparently based on Lacointa).

5. See this ch. at n. 14.

6. Menin, *Traité historique*, p. 314, n. 1. See also Doucet, "Pierre du Chastel," p. 25, and Anselme de Sainte Marie, *Histoire généalogique*, 8:266.

7. See this ch. at nn. 13–15.

8. Millon, *Cérémonial du sacre*, p. 108n, copied from Menin, *Traité historique*, p. 316.

9. See ch. 5, n. 21.

10. See ch. 5 at nn. 19–23.

11. Millon, *Cérémonial du sacre*, p. 108; Haueter, *Die Krönungen der französischen Könige*, p. 265.

12. Pichon, *Journal historique*, p. 49.

13. Godefroy, *Louis XIII ᵇ*, p. 432. No other description of the ceremony speaks of the episode.

14. Remond, *Les cérémonies observées*, pp. 25–26.

15. I was no more successful than Haueter, *Die Krönungen der französischen Könige*, pp. 219–22, in finding details of the freeing of birds at later coronations. At least one writer in 1722 did interpret the ceremony correctly though: "Les oiseleurs lachèrent ensuite un grand nombre de petits oiseaux, qui par le recouvrement de leur liberté, signifioient l'effusion des grâces de leur souverain pour les prisonniers qui devoient être élargis, à l'ocassion de cette Sainte Cérémonie" (Chantilly, Musée Condé 1022, "Relation du voyage de Louis XV. à Rhains pour son sacre et son retour à Versailles," p. 111). And M. de Coppier, mayor of Saint-Maximin, wrote a treatise, "Sacre des rois et des reines de France," in 1774 in which he mixed the type of interpretation given by Pichon with the older one: "Ce recouvrement de liberté est un augure favorable qui présage la liberté dont les Français jouiront dans le règne du nouveau monarque. Il

est de plus l'avant coureur de l'élargissement que S. M. à l'occasion de son sacre va accorder aux prisonniers" (Reims, BM 1482, p. 226–27).

16. Jousse, *Traité de la justice*, 2:400–404; La Roche-Flavin, *Treze livres des parlemens*, p. 753, no. 18.

17. Sermet, *Le droit de grâce*, p. 82; Rozès, *Un récidiviste*, p. 18.

18. Bloch, *Rois et serfs*, pp. 48–49.

19. Sermet, *Le droit de grâce*, pp. 60–69.

20. Lewis, "Anticipatory Succession."

21. Isambert, *Recueil général*, 4:819–20, and 5:14–15, 69; Sermet, *Le droit de grâce*, pp. 77–78.

22. Sermet, *Le droit de grâce*, pp. 80–81. Laboulaye and Dareste, *Le grand coutumier*, pp. 100–101 (liv. I, ch. 3): "Item à luy [le roy] seul et pour le tout appartient la vérification et entérinement de toutes grâces, pardons et rémissions par lui faictes à quelconques personnes, de et [*sic*] sur quelque cas de crisme ou excès. . . ."

23. Isambert, *Recueil général*, 5:54, no. 289, and 9:228, par. 67.

24. Ibid., 6:546, and 10:782–83, no. 242. Leber, *Des cérémonies du sacre*, pp. 118–19.

25. Isambert, *Recueil général*, 11:353–54, art. 70, and 11:514, art. 253.

26. Sermet, *Le droit de grâce*, p. 75.

27. Ibid., pp. 69, 76. In the first half of the sixteenth century the right was not necessarily exercised only by the king himself. In the edict of Villers-Cotterêts (August 1539) Francis I allowed the *gardes des sceaux*, the royal chancelleries, and the sovereign courts to grant pardon or remission to homicides of certain sorts, like those who had killed in self-defense, but at the same time the *gardes des sceaux* were forbidden to grant either pardon or remission in cases in which the capital punishment was required (Isambert, *Recueil général*, 12:635–36, arts. 168–69, 172). In England certain aspects of the royal pardon are amply discussed by Hurnard, *The King's Pardon for Homicide*, who briefly treats of pardon for crimes other than homicide (pp. 245–47). Pardoning was made an exclusive royal right much earlier in England than in France, although there were some exceptions (pp. 214–15). As in France, all homicides, including accidental and excusable ones (self-defense, for example), had to seek the king's pardon. I have not come upon a similar study of the French practice, but I have not been able to consult Brissaud, *Le droit de grâce en France*, brought to my attention by Jean-Michel Mehl.

28. Bouchel, *La bibliothèque*, 1:804, s.v. "Remission"; Menin, *Traité historique*, p. 315, n. 1.

29. Seneca, *De clementia*, book II.

30. Leber, *Des cérémonies du sacre*, p. 114; Sermet, *Le droit de grâce*, p. 50.

31. Gobron, *Des sources du droit*, pp. 64–68. Not even Mommsen's great *Römisches Strafrecht*, pp. 452–56, is of much help in tracing the development of the Roman practice.

32. Bodin, *La république*, liv. I, ch. 10, pp. 173–77.

33. Bouchel, *La bibliothèque*, 1:15–16; Le Bret, *De la sourveraineté*, pp. 586–87; Godefroy (ed.), *Codex Theodosianus*, 3:293; Gobron, *Des sources du droit*, pp. 66–68. Godefroy is probably quite close to the truth, for the Theodosian Code 9, 38, 8 (Godefroy ed., 3:302) is a law of Valentinian (A.D. 385) that lists the irremissible crimes nearly as they are listed in seventeenth-century France; see this ch., section 4.

34. See this ch. at n. 22.

35. Sermet, *Le droit de grâce*, pp. 80–81.

36. Jousse, *Traité de la justice*, 2:400, 405, and *Nouveau commentaire*, pp. 403–407; Legoux, *Du droit de grâce*, pp. 131, 134–35, 149; Allard, *Histoire de la justice*, pp. 366–68 (a good summary of the procedure to be followed when *lettres de grâce* were accorded); La Roche-Flavin, *Treze livres des parlemens*, p. 751. Much of the procedure was prescribed already by Louis XII in an edict published at Blois in March 1499 (Isambert, *Recueil général*, 11:368–69, arts. 126–28). The requirement that nobles present themselves bare-headed was promulgated by Charles IX in an edict of Amboise in January 1572 (ibid., 14:250, art. 9).

37. See this ch. at nn. 1–3. There is no record of the advertising before 1722, but it must have been done in 1654, for there is no other way to account for the large number of prisoners involved.

38. Sermet, *Le droit de grâce*, p. 78. Sermet asserted that Philip VI had declared in 1349 that he would not pardon merchants who frequented the fairs of Champagne and Brie, but that is false (see Isambert, *Recueil général*, 4:547–48, art. 2). He also says that in 1354 John forbade recognition of *lettres de grâce* that debtors to the king might have acquired, but what John's letters in fact say (ibid., 4:698, no. 208) is that they were not valid unless confirmed by the king and approved by the Chambre des Comptes; furthermore, the act refers only to Toulouse and the officials *in partibus Occitanis*.

39. Isambert, *Recueil général*, 4:819–20, art. 6.

40. Ibid., 5:74.

41. Ibid., 14:198, art. 34, and 14:246, art. 1.

42. Ibid., 14:426, art. 190.

43. Ibid., 12:635, art. 168; see also this ch., n. 27.

44. Ibid., 14:427, arts. 194–95.

45. Bodin, *The Six Bookes of a Commonweale*, pp. 171–72, 174–75 (liv. I, ch. 10, fifth mark). See ch. 13 at nn. 13–14.

46. See Chanteur, "L'idée de loi naturelle dans la République de Jean Bodin."

47. *The Six Bookes of a Commonweale*, p. 174. Bodin again refers to this biblical passage in liv. I, ch. 6 (McRae ed., p. 779). In liv. I, ch. 8, he says that transgressors of the law of God are guilty of high treason to divine majesty and of making war against God (p. 92) and that theft and murder are against the law of God and nature (p. 104).

48. Bouchel, *La bibliothèque*, 1:15–16, s. v. "Abolition."

49. La Roche-Flavin, *Treze livres des parlemens*, pp. 751, no. 1, and 754, no. 20. On the royal edicts he cites, see this ch. at nn. 41–43.

50. Le Bret, *De la souveraineté*, p. 589.

51. Isambert, *Recueil général*, 18:403–4, tit. XVI, art. 4.

52. See this ch. at n. 57.

53. Paris, BN nouv. acq. françaises 21708-21712. References are to volume and case number, except for vol. 5, for which references are to folio number.

54. See ch. 5 at nn. 17–18. Perhaps this judgment is too harsh considering the legal complications caused by the events of the previous six years. Was it not simpler to clear the slate of all such past crimes and to begin a clean one?

55. The records are not complete enough to determine completely the grounds for refusal.

56. Bouchel, *La bibliothèque*, 2:804, s.v. "Remission," copied (without attribution) from Papon, *Nouvelle et cinquième édition du recueil d'arrests*, pp. 1392–93. This procedure was in effect at least as early as 1532.

57. Paris, Bibliothèque de l'Assemblée Nationale 1387 (no folio number possible; see this ch., n. 1).

58. My interpretation of the crime for which pardon was refused is subject to correction; the records themselves do not specify the crime. I obtained these figures from the alphabetical lists at the end of each of the volumes (1387 and 1388). Manuscript 1388, fols. 256–69, lists the names of only 486 prisoners to whom pardon was accorded, and fols. 281–288^v list the names of 79 prisoners refused pardon. There are additional lists in manuscript 1390, which also concerns other occasions on which pardon was granted.

59. La Roche-Flavin, *Treze livres des parlemens*, p. 751, no. 5.

60. See, for example, *France-Soir* (19 June 1969), pp. 1, 6. The headline declared in bold type, "1er acte du président Pompidou: l'amnistie," but in fact he had to exercise his *droit de grâce* in the form of a parliamentary law.

CHAPTER 8

1. Bernard, *Procès-verbaux des Etats Généraux*, discusses the background of the meeting in his preface, pp. xxxi–lii; Mayenne's declaration is printed on pp. 30–40.

2. Giesey, *The Juristic Basis of Dynastic Right*. For much of what follows, the reader may profitably consult the general studies of sixteenth-century political thought, e.g., Allen, *A History of Political Thought*; Church, *Constitutional Thought*; Mesnard, *L'essor de la philosophie politique*; Weill, *Les théories sur le pouvoir royal* (a study that is particularly useful for present purposes); Skinner, *Foundations of Modern Political Thought* (with an extensive, up-to-date bibliography).

3. Masselin, *Journal des Etats Généraux*, pp. 146–49.

4. Craig, *The Right of Succession*, p. 22: "Yea I know 'tis controverted among some learned men, especially some Lawyers, whether the Election of a New King is not preferable to the Order of Succession, by which the next in Blood is advanced to the Government of the Kingdom. I remember to have heard this Question much toss'd and disputed at *Paris*, when I was a student there, among the candidates for their degree in the University. . . ." According to Aeneas Mackay in the *Dictionary of National Biography*, 12:449, Craig studied law in Paris from 1555 to 1561.

5. *Francogallia* (Cologne, 1574), pp. 43, 47, 97–100. On Hotman, particularly as an historian, see Giesey, "When and Why Hotman Wrote the Francogallia," and "The Monarchomach Triumvirs"; Kelley, *Foundations of Modern Historical Scholarship*, and *François Hotman*.

6. *Francogallia* (Frankfurt, 1665), 1:286–87, 294; these passages were first added in the edition of 1586. Such variations are now easy to detect in the variorum edition and translation by Giesey and Salmon.

7. *L'histoire de France*, p. 19; cf pp. 123–24, where Du Haillan repeats this assertion in almost identical words. Du Haillan's agreement with Hotman is emphasized in the passage in which he says that "nous avons monstré que ce droict de creer et deposer les Rois appartenoit à l'assemblee des trois Estats, de façon qu'il ne fault croire que en Pepin seul les François eussent voulu mespriser leur droict ancien et immemorial" (p. 129). On Du Haillan's position in the sixteenth-century historiographical tradition, see Kelley, *Foundations of Modern Historical Scholarship*, pp. 233–38.

8. Du Haillan, *Histoire de France*, p. 124.

9. Godefroy, *Henry II*, p. 287. One might note the interesting phrase, "Serment au Royaume," instead of the more usual "serment du royaume"; it may or may not have notable significance.

10. The pertinent passage of the *ordo* of 1250 (Paris, BN latin 1246, fols. VIII–IX) reads: "Postea [the ecclesiastical oath] inquirant alii duo

Episcopi [who are not otherwise identified] assensum populi, quo habito cantent *Te Deum*. Et prosternat se usque ad finem *Te Deum*. Cantato *Te Deum laudamus*, erigatur rex de solo ab episcopis et hec promittens dicat: *Hec tria populo Christiano et michi subdito in Christi nomine promitto*." The fact that the first two words in Henry II's oath of the kingdom also began with *Haec tria* is a clear demonstration of the origin of this portion of Henry's ceremony; all the recorded oaths from the time of Charles V began with the words *Haec populo Christiano*, and in fact there were four, not three, clauses to the oath (see ch. 5, section 1). See also ch. 2, n. 18, and ch. 13 at n. 16, where other evidence of the influence of the *ordo* of 1250 is discussed.

11. It should be clear by now that the coronation ceremony often developed fortuitously. In this case, though, one may explain how the change came about (see ch. 13 at n. 16). The same sort of haphazard development of ceremonial has been noted in other contexts by Giesey, *The Royal Funeral Ceremony*, and Hanley, *The Lit de Justice*. For an extended example of this process, see ch. 9.

12. Beza, *Du droit des magistrats* and *De iure magistratuum*. On the circumstances and role of this tract, see the introductions to Kingdon's and Sturm's editions, and Giesey, "The Monarchomach Triumvirs."

13. Beza, *Du droit des magistrats*, pp. 39–41, and *De iure magistratuum*, pp. 61–63. Cf. the translation of the quoted passage in Franklin, *Constitutionalism and Resistance*, p. 121.

14. Beza, *Du droit des magistrats*, p. 50, and *De iure magistratuum*, p. 72.

15. Beza, *Du droit des magistrats*, p. 9, and *De iure magistratuum*, p. 34. The anonymous author of *Le politique*, in Goulart, *Mémoires de l'estat*, 3:72^r–73^v, argues at length that the ancient Hebrew kingship was both elective and successive.

16. *Vindiciae*, p. 76: "Ostendimus antea, Deum Reges instituere, Regna Regibus dare, Reges eligere. Dicimus iam, Populum Reges constituere, Regna tradere, electionem suo suffragio comprobare." I do not wish to say anything about the authorship of this work, particularly in the light of the study by Mastellone, "Aspetti dell'antimachiavellismo," pp. 376–415, who argues for the authorship of Innocent Gentillet and Hubert Languet. See the remarks by Franklin, *Constitutionalism and Resistance*, pp. 138–39, and by Giesey, "The Monarchomach Triumvirs," p. 42, n. 2.

17. *Vindiciae*, p. 88: ". . . Populum universum in omni Regno, urbéve legitimè repraesentant, qui quidem vulgo, Regni, non Regis Officiarii censentur." For examples of definitions of the *people*, see the *Vindiciae*, pp. 46–47, 83, 88–89, 90, 95–96, 214–15.

18. Ibid., p. 96: "Habet praeterea Regnum Francicum suos sive Pares, tanquam Regis consortes, sive Patricios, tanquam Reipublicae Patres, sin-

gulos à singulis Regni Provinciis denominatos quibus Rex inaugurandus, tanquam universo Regno, fidem dare solet."

19. Ibid., p. 164.

20. Ibid., pp. 103–104: "Vulgatum est, nullam fisco praescriptionem nosere; multò verò minus Populo universo, qui rege potior est, cuiusque gratia Princeps id privilegium habet. Cur enim alioqui, cum fisci Princeps administrator tantum sit, Populus verò, ut inferius probabitur, verè proprietarius? Deinde: an non scitum est illud; libertati nulla, ne diutissima quidem servitute, violentia praescribi posse? Quod si verò reges à populo constitutos fuisse, qui ante D. fortè annos vivebat, non ab eo, qui hodie extat, obiicias: at, inquam ego, etsi moriuntur reges, populus interim, ut neque ulla alia Universitas, nunquam moritur." On *nulla praescriptio currit contra fiscum*, see Kantorowicz, *The King's Two Bodies*, p. 165, n. 226. On *universitas non moritur* and *le roi ne meurt jamais*, see ibid., pp. 302–13, and Giesey, *The Royal Funeral Ceremony*, pp. 177–83.

21. Boucher, *De justa Henrici tertii abdicatione*. In some places Boucher's work is only a slight paraphrase of the *Vindiciae*; see, for example, Boucher, fol. 27ᵛ, and *Vindiciae*, pp. 96, 164.

22. *De justa reipublicae*, fols. 28ᵛ, 31–34. (On the authorship of this see Salmon, *The French Religious Wars*, p. 75.) The author of *De la puissance des roys*, pp. 106–7, argued that the French kingship had been elective, thereby implying that it still was; he seems to have drawn his argument from Hotman or Du Haillan, rather than from the *Vindiciae*, and he argued that it would have been unnecessary for the father to crown the son co-king if the kingdom had not been elective.

23. *Discours par lequel*, p. 59. The author is referring to the assembly—which could hardly be called an Estates General—at which a marriage alliance was the primary topic of discussion; see Major, *Representative Institutions*, pp. 122–25. Labitte, *De la démocratie*, p. 229, believed that the author of the *Discours* was a jurist, Pierre Saint-Julien.

24. *Discours*, pp. 11–17 (where the writer quotes a long passage from Du Haillan to support his argument against Salic law), 26–37.

25. Ibid., p. 60. This is an interesting interpretation of the practice of having the old lay peers represented at the coronation ceremony (see ch. 10, the last paragraph of section 2.)

26. *Discours*, p. 61, where the tract concludes, "Joint que mauvaises coustumes n'aquierent droit: et ne doivent tant estre dictes coustumes, que corrupteles, diuturnitez d'erreur, et inveterez abus."

27. See Bernard, *Procès-verbaux des Etats Généraux*, passim, and pp. 736–50 (where Bernard prints and discusses the Parlement's decision and Mayenne's reaction).

28. See this ch. at nn. 5–8.

29. Le Caron, *Pandectes*, pp. 143–44; see also pp. 3, 5.

30. *De gli stati*, pp. 31–32, 40–41. This work was also published ten years later in a French translation, *Des estats de France*.

31. *De l'excellence du gouvernement royal*, fols. 26^v–27.

32. Ibid., fol. 28^v: "Mais sans autrement revoquer en doubte les histoires anciennes, escrittes la plus part par moynes ignorans, ou estrangers envieux, il est certain que la longue experience a monstré estre meilleur, et plus seur, que le Royaume de France, sans forme d'election, aille tousjours de masle en masle, au plus prochain du lignage: tellement que le Roy ne meurt jamais, comme on dit: et que les puisnez soient honnestement apanagez." This latter statement bears out the contention of Giesey, *The Royal Funeral Ceremony*, p. 177, that Bodin was not the first to use the maxim that the king never dies (see this ch., n. 20), but now there is a much earlier example of use of a very similar phrase; see Saenger, "Burgundy and the Inalienability of Appanages," pp. 16–17.

33. *La république*, pp. 722–25 (liv. VI, ch. 5).

34. *Les memoires et recherches*, pp. 143–45: "Ces mots de l'election estans en ladite vieille forme et demeurez en la nouvelle des sacres et couronnemens des rois, doivent estre prins et entendus pour declaration, acceptation et submission au roy esleu, destiné et predestiné de Dieu qui l'a conservé et fait le plus proche de la couronne, non pour aucun droict aux sujets de donner le royaume par voix ou election. Car il a esté tousjours hereditaire, tant durant le Paganisme que Christianisme, et tel l'ont transferé à leur posterité ceux qui par la providence divine (à laquelle seule appartient de mettre et oster les rois) y ont fait ces mutations que Agathie confesse."

35. *Les grandes annales*, 1: preface (sigs. A$_1$^{r}–B$_4$^{r}). The quotation is from sig. B$_3$^{r}.

36. Ibid., fols. 1^{r-v}, 2^v–3^v. The quotations are from fol. 3^v.

37. Belloy, *Apologie catholique*. On *le mort saisit le vif*, see ch. 9, n. 40.

38. Belloy, *Examen du discours*, pp. 257–67. Church, *Constitutional Thought*, p. 91, n. 30, says that this was a response to an apparently lost, anonymous pamphlet, *Discours sur la maison royale*. In turn it elicited a response, *Sommaire responce à l'examen d'un heretique*.

39. Godefroy, *De Thou's Henry IV*, p. 361: "Non que cette acception se prenne pour eslection, ayant ce Royaume esté tousjours hereditaire, et successif au plus prochain masle: mais pour declaration de la submission, obeyssance, et fidelité qu'ils luy doivent comme à leur souverain Seigneur de l'expresse ordonnance de Dieu." See the passage from Du Tillet quoted this ch., n. 34.

40. *Dialogue d'entre le Maheustre et le Manant*, fols. 9^{r-v}, 11^r–13^r, 29^r–30^r. On this curious work, see Salmon, "The Paris Sixteen," and Peter Ascoli's introduction to his edition.

41. Boucher, *Apologie pour Jehan Chastel*, pp. 35–36. I can make no

sense of Boucher's assertion that there was a triple request unless the fact that he was in exile at the time forced him to work from faulty memory. This is as appropriate a place as any to note the comments of Ullmann, *Principles of Government and Politics*, pp. 202–3: "Nothing illustrates the sagacious alertness of the French kings better than the step they took in eliminating this element of Recognition [i.e., what I call the *consensus populi*] altogether; it was absent in all French coronation *ordines* after the so-called *ordo* of Rheims of *circa* 1270. . . . The monarchy in France perfectly clearly realized the potentialities of this populist remnant and cut it out altogether. The concomitant strengthening of French theocratic kingship was not only a by-product, but was, it seems clear, also the motivating driving force behind the excision of the Recognition. No such populist element was henceforth to mar the coronation of the *rex christianissimus*." See also Ullmann's *The Carolingian Renaissance*, p. 109, where this statement is repeated.

42. Coquille, *Institution au droict*, p. 1 (p. 1 *double* in *Oeuvres*, 2); Duchesne, *Les antiquitez et recherches*, p. 385, which paraphrases the Du Tillet passage quoted this ch., n. 34 (without attributing it to Du Tillet, however); Baricave, *La defence de la monarchie*, pp. 669–72. Baricave's method is essentially to quote the French translation of the *Vindiciae* and then to answer it; much of his work is inept, and his scholarship leaves very much to be desired.

43. See Haueter, *Die Krönungen der französischen Könige*, p. 308. Aubery, *Histoire du Cardinal Mazarin*, 4:50–54, discusses at length the *consensus populi* in connection with the coronation of Louis XIV, and there is a long discussion of the issue in Lacour-Gayet, *L'éducation politique*, pp. 301–15, 325–28.

44. Haueter, *Die Krönungen der französischen Könige*, pp. 337–38. On the peculiar views of Saint-Simon and election by the Peers of France, see ch. 9 at n. 45.

45. The comments by Salmon in the preface to his *French Religious Wars*, p. v, are as germane here as there: "Political institutions are seldom constructed from a system of abstract beliefs: rather do they grow from the countless responses which individual men are compelled to make to the demands of transient situations. Nevertheless, it would be foolish to affirm that in their reactions to the practical problems which confront them men are uninfluenced by political principles. There can be no fixed boundary line between theory and event. The terms in which the last political crisis has been rationalized are the presuppositions which are brought to the solution of the next. In this study I have often been unable to distinguish between political theory and political history."

CHAPTER 9

1. The following description is based upon Godefroy, *Louis XIII*^{a}, *Louis XIII*^{b}, and *Louis XIII*^{c}.

2. Godefroy, *Louis XIII*^{c}, p. 446, also adds censers, but the other two descriptions do not mention them. We know that one or more censers appeared in the procession at previous coronations.

3. Godefroy, *Louis XIII*^{a}, pp. 407–8: "Arrivez à la Chambre du Roy, et l'ayant trouvée fermée, ledit sieur Evesque de Laon frappa à la porte par trois diverses fois; à toutes lesquelles Monsieur le Duc d'Esguillon, Grand Chambellan de France, demanda, *Que voulez-vous*: L'Evesque respondit, *Louys XIII. fils de Henry le Grand*. A quoy repartit ledit sieur Grand Chambellan, *Il dort*: Puis frappant pour la seconde fois, disant la mesme chose, fit pareille response. Et à la troisiesme, demandant encore ce qu'ils vouloient, ledit sieur Evesque dit, *Louys XIII. que Dieu nous a donné pour Roy.*"

4. The word *parade* was introduced into the French language in the sixteenth century from the Spanish *parada*, a stopping or assembling for exercise (primarily for displays of horsemanship); it has retained some of its original meaning in French, but it also came to mean a displaying. The term *lit de parade* was not used in the descriptions of the bed until the coronation of Charles IX in 1561; it may have been a corruption of *lit de parement*, the term most commonly used for the bed until the mid-seventeenth century. See Giesey, *The Royal Funeral Ceremony*, p. 4, n. 15, and Index, s.v. "Bed of State."

5. Various representations depict both of these garments as reaching nearly to the king's ankles; see, for example, Dewick, *The Coronation Book of Charles V*, pl. 7–16; Pichon, *Sacre et couronnement de Louis XVI*, pp. 92–93. I have preferred to call the second garment a camisole rather than a tunic or tunicle—despite the fact that some descriptions of coronations call it a tunic (e.g., Godefroy, *Charles VIII*, p. 194)—in order to avoid confusion with the tunicle of a subdeacon, which was put on the king after his sacring. The camisole is always described as red, crimson (*cramoisi*), or hyacinth in color.

6. Charles VIII and Francis I wore a robe of white damask, furred with sable (Godefroy, *Charles VIII*, p. 194, and *Francis I*^{a}, p. 246). The robe of silver cloth first appeared at the coronation of Henry II in 1547 (Godefroy, *Henry II*, p. 285). It is to be expected that a white robe would be introduced as the apparel of a *candidatus* prior to the coronation, but one can say only with some ambiguity that it was introduced between 1365 and 1484. Some of the kings before Louis XIII, and all of the kings after him, also wore a toque of black velvet, which came to be richly decorated.

7. The incipit of the prayer is not given in any of the three descriptions

of this coronation, but there is no reason to doubt that it was this one.

8. Godefroy, *Louis XIII^a*, p. 408: "Lesdits sieurs Evesques . . . sous-leverent le Roy de dessus son lict, l'un par le costé dextre, et l'autre par le senestre, avec toutes exhibitions d'honneur, comme à leur Prince souverain, representant en terre la divine Majesté, et souveraine puissance. . . ." As far as it is possible to tell, the two bishops kissed their hands at only three coronations, those of Henry II (Godefroy, *Henry II*, p. 285), Henry IV (Godefroy, *De Thou's Henry IV*, p. 356, and *Anon. Henry IV*, p. 391), and Louis XIII. One kisses one's own hands to do reverence to a person as is shown in Godefroy, *Louis XIII^c*, p. 447: "ils [the bishops] luy [to the king] eurent baisé les mains." This custom seems to have been quite common in the sixteenth and seventeenth centuries; see Selden, *Titles of Honor*, p. 31: "For, adoring simply is often taken only for a man to kiss his own hand or fore-finger with a bending of his body." The question is discussed at some length by Leber, *Des cérémonies du sacre*, pp. 403–13.

9. Both first appeared in the French ceremony in the *ordo* of 1250. The response, which begins "Ecce ego mitto angelum meum, qui praecedat te," is based on Exodus 20:20–23. It is not to be confused with the *adventus* chant based on Malachi 3:1 ("Ecce ego mitto angelum meum, et praeparabit viam ante faciem meam"), Matthew 11:10, Mark 1:2, and Luke 7:27. For the latter, see Kantorowicz, "The 'King's Advent.' "

10. Bévy, *Histoire des inaugurations*, pp. 519–20 (note to p. 408), asserted that fatigue caused the kings to sleep when sought by the peers. The relaxation of the night vigil is betokened in the *ordo* of Charles V, which says, "Et debet rex intempeste noctis silencio venire in ecclesiam orationem facturus, et ibidem in oratione aliquantulum si voluerit vigilaturus" (London, British Library Tiberius B.viii, fol. 43^v).

11. The pertinent section of the *ordo* of Mainz, printed in Schramm, "Die Krönung in Deutschland," pp: 310–11, reads, "Primum, exeunte illo [rege] thalamum, unus episcoporum dicat hanc orationem: *Omnipotens, sempiterne Deus*. . . . Postea suscipiant illum duo episcopi dextera laevaque, honorifice parati, habentes sanctorum reliquias collo pendentes; ceteri autem clerici sint casulis adornati. Praecedente sancto evangelio et duabus crucibus cum incensu boni odoris, ducant illum ad ecclesiam, canentes responsorium: *Ecce mitto angelum meum*. . . . Versus: *Israel, si me audieris* . . . cuncto cum vulgo sequente." The antecedents of the *ordo* of Mainz probably include the Gregorian and Gelasian sacramentaries and early Christian practices of initiation, but they have no direct bearing on the problem of the sleeping king.

12. On the *ordo* of Reims and the *ordo* of 1250 (i.e., Schramm's "Compilation of 1300"), see Schramm, "Ordines-Studien II," pp. 24–28, 30–33. The pertinent portion of the English Edgar *ordo* of 973 is printed in

Legg, *Three Coronation Orders*, p. 53 (with variant readings on p. 163).

13. London, British Library Tiberius B.viii, fols. 44–44ᵛ.

14. Daniel, *Histoire de la milice*, 1:74–76. One may ask whether the ceremony ever took place in this fashion. The whole text is so pervaded by the literary ideal that it may be but an invention of courtly literature. Of course, that would not prevent the ideal from having an effect upon later ceremonies of knighting. On the ceremonies of initiation into knighthood, see Gautier, *La chevalerie*, pp. 245–340; Selden, *Titles of Honor*, pp. 451–59, 636–79; La Curne de Sainte-Palaye, *Mémoires sur l'ancienne chevalerie*, l:passim; Erdmann, *Die Entstehung des Kreuzzugsgedankens*, pp. 62–63, 74–82, 253–65; Luyn, "Les *milites*," pp. 217–20, 237–38.

15. Richardson, "The Coronation in Medieval England," p. 198. This is the *ordo* commonly known as the *Forma et modus*; it is printed in Richardson and in Legg, *English Coronation Records*, pp. 172–82. Legg attributed it to the late fourteenth century, as did Schramm, "Ordines-Studien III," pp. 369–70, but Richardson has shown that it basically stems from the later thirteenth century. The royal seat (*sedes regalis*) seems to have served the English kings to a certain extent as the bed of state was to serve the French kings; it was used at the same time in the ceremony. Professor Reinhard Elze has told me that he thinks that the Burgundian *ordo* may be quite a bit older than its oldest manuscript (mid-thirteenth century), as does Bouman, *Sacring and Crowning*, p. 158. The first part of the ceremony seems to be a later addition, though, and it is hard to date. There is an unsatisfactory edition of the *ordo* in Martène, *De antiquis ecclesiae ritibus*, 2: cols. 634–36.

16. Richardson, "The Coronation in Medieval England," pp. 113–15, 192. The French translation of the *ordo* of Reims precedes Charles V's *ordo* in London, British Library Tiberius B.viii and in other manuscripts no longer in existence; see Jackson, "Les manuscrits des *ordines*," pp. 70–78.

17. The use of the word *suscipere* shows the influence of baptismal ceremonial on the *ordo* of Mainz (see this ch., n. 11); cf. Du Cange, *Glossarium*, s.v. "suscipere": "Suscipere, dicuntur Patrini, qui baptizandum ad fontem deducunt, et baptizatum de fonte excipiunt, et inde Susceptores appellati. . . ." The initiation into knighthood was often considered a sort of baptism and confirmation; see La Curne de Sainte-Palaye, *Mémoires sur l'ancienne chevalerie*, 1:119, n. 11, and Gautier, *La chevalerie*, pp. 24–25.

18. Godefroy, *Charles VIII*, p. 191.

19. Ibid., p. 194. The existing evidence does not show that any of the French kings prior to Charles VIII was raised from a bed of state. The significance of the verb *lever* (or *soulever*) will become clear this ch. at nn. 54–55.

20. Francis I may not have been fully lying on his bed; Godefroy, *Francis I^b*, p. 255, says that he was "acoudé sur le bord du lict," but Godefroy, *Francis I^a*, p. 246, says that the bishops "trouverent ledit Seigneur ainsi comme gisant sur sa couche." Godefroy, *Le cérémonial françois*, p. 310, quotes Jean Sleidan to the effect that Henry II was reclining (*decumbentem*), but the description of Henry's coronation (Godefroy, *Henry II*, p. 285), which is much more detailed and appears to be more accurate, says that "sur lequel lict le Roy estoit couché" and that he had a richly embroidered pillow of crimson velvet under his head. The confusion here probably derived from the custom of sleeping in a half-sitting position.

21. Godefroy, *Charles IX*, p. 312: "Où est nostre nouveau Roy, que Dieu nous a donné pour nous regir, et gouverner?" "Il ese ceans." "Que fait-il?" "Il repose." "Esveillez le, afin que nous le salüions, et luy faisions la reverence." The text continues, "Cela fait, ils attendirent quelque peu à la porte, puis ledit grand Chambellan leur ouvrit, disant qu'il est esveillé. . . ."

22. Ibid., pp. 312–13.

23. Dom Bévy, *Histoire des inaugurations*, pp. 519–20, erroneously asserted that it was a common practice for all the peers to go to the king's chamber; for further evidence of the unreliability of Bévy's scholarship, see this ch., n. 10.

24. Jackson, "Charles IX's Coronation," p. 292.

25. *Troezieme livre de l'histoire du President de Montagne* (Paris, BN français 15494), fol. 4. A passage in a memoir written before the coronation, "Ce qu'il faut pour le sacre du Roy Charles IX," shows that the precoronation ritual was planned at least in part, for it lists among the king's garments and regalia, "La Robbe de nuit en laquelle Messeigneurs les pairs Ecclesiastiques trouverent le Roy sur son Lit enrichie de pierreries" (Paris, Archives Nationales KK 1439[1], fol. 94^v).

26. "Michiel Surian, Venetian Ambassador in France, to the Doge and Senate" (report of 2 May 1561), in *Calendar of State Papers, Venetian*, 7:310. This discussion is based mainly on Lavisse, *Histoire de France*, 6, 1:27–54.

27. "Michiel Surian, Venetian Ambassador in France, to the Doge and Senate" (report of 3 May), in *Calendar of State Papers, Venetian*, 7:311–12.

28. "Michiel Surian, Venetian Ambassador in France, to the Doge and Senate" (report of 14 May), in ibid., 7:313.

29. Here, as elsewhere in this study, relationships and genealogies (up to ca. 1725) are taken primarily from Anselme de Sainte Marie, *Histoire généalogique*, vols. 1–3 passim.

30. Representing the lay peers at this coronation (according to Godefroy, *Charles IX*, p. 312) were Monsieur, the duke of Orléans, brother of

the king; Antoine de Bourbon, king of Navarre; François de Lorraine, duke of Guise; François de Cleves, duke of Nevers; the duke of Montpensier; and Claude de Lorraine, duke of Aumale. Representing the ecclesiastical peers were Charles de Guise, cardinal of Lorraine and archbishop of Reims; Charles, cardinal of Bourbon and archbishop of Rouen; Odet de Coligny, cardinal Châtillon and bishop of Beauvais; Louis de Lorraine, cardinal of Guise; Claude de Longuy, cardinal of Givry and bishop of Langres; and Jerome Burgensis, bishop of Châlons. Jackson, "Charles IX's Coronation," pp. 292–93, mentions the seating of the bishop of Noyon rather than the bishop of Châlons, but this would have been erroneous because Jean de Hangest, bishop of Noyon, was in either Italy or Germany at this time (according to Anselme de Sainte Marie, *Histoire généalogique,* 2:420). Political affairs seem to have brought about another change in the ceremony at Charles's coronation. At previous coronations, the peers had delegated the bishops of Laon and Beauvais to go seek the king. The bishopric of Laon was vacant, so it was necessary that someone be found to represent the missing bishop. The bishop of Beauvais was present, but he was Odet de Coligny, a leader of the reformers and suspected of having celebrated Holy Communion according to the Genevan rite on Easter day itself. Such a man, good Catholics must have thought, was not the proper person to play the important role of conducting the king to the church for the consecration and coronation of the Most Christian King. So it seems that his role in this part of the ceremony was played by either Louis de Guise or Charles de Bourbon, both staunch Catholics. It is not known which of the two represented Beauvais at this time, but the other would have represented the bishop of Laon. (Less than two years later Odet de Coligny was deprived of his benefices and excommunicated by Pius IV.)

31. London, British Library Tiberius B.viii, fol. 55. A French translation of this prayer in one of the descriptions of Francis I's coronation (Godefroy, *Francis I^b,* p. 260) gives the last words almost exactly as they appear at the precoronation ritual of Charles IX: "soient enoinctes ces mains de l'huile sanctifiée, dont furent enoincts les Roys et Prophetes, si comme Samüel enoignit David en Roy, afin que vous soyez benit, et constitué Roy en ce Regne, que Dieu nostre Seigneur vous a donné à regir, et gouverner."

32. The crux of the argument of Leber, *Des cérémonies du sacre,* pp. 163–76, consists of the sleep of the king as a symbol of his minority. Leber wrote (p. 169), "En un mot, *le roi dormait,* suivant l'expression de nos vieux chroniqueurs; et de-là cette coutume de faire coucher le monarque au moment où il va commencer la cérémonie qui doit accomplir ses destinées; de figurer le repos de la minorité, avant l'acte que l'on considérait autrefois comme le réveil ou l'apparition du souverain dans toute

sa puissance. De-là cette formule de réponse trois fois répétée: *le roi dort.*" Unfortunately for our purposes, Leber thought that the fiction of the sleeping king antedated the *ordo* of Charles V and that it had lost its raison d'être by the end of the fourteenth century: "Dès-lors [1403], on ne s'est plus imaginé que le roi dormait, parce qu'il n'était pas couronné ou majeur. Le fond a disparu, mais les formes sont restées . . ." (pp. 171–72).

33. For Louis XIII's ceremony, see this ch., section 1.

34. Quoted by Young, *Drama of the Medieval Church*, 1:92, from Martène, *De antiquis ecclesiae ritibus*, 3rd ed. (1788), 3:72 (this dialogue is not to be found in the second edition of Martène, which I use).

35. *Missale mixtum*, in Migne, *Patrologiae Latinae*, 75:391[a–b]. On the position of this ritual in the development of liturgical drama, see Hardison, *Christian Rite*, pp. 109–28, esp. pp. 113–14.

36. This French version of the Navarrese ceremony is given by Lagrèze, *La Navarre française*, 2:27.

37. For the complete dialogue, see this ch., n. 3.

38. See ch. 1 at n. 11.

39. "Harangue de Michel de l'Hôpital," in Dupuy, *Traité de la majorité*, p. 363.

40. Loyseau, *Des offices*, I.x.58, p. 153. On the maxim *le mort saisit le vif*, see Giesey, *The Royal Funeral Ceremony*, pp. 181–82, and *The Juristic Basis of Dynastic Right*, pp. 10–11.

41. Giesey, *The Royal Funeral Ceremony*, pp. 177–83. Kantorowicz, *The King's Two Bodies*, esp. pp. 7–23, discusses the English fiction of the king's two bodies as expressed by the terms "body politic" and "body natural."

42. Ibid., pp. 401–9, emphasizes the carefulness of the English to distinguish between the king and the King.

43. See this ch. at n. 40.

44. Aubery, *Histoire du Cardinal Mazarin*, 4:54.

45. Saint-Simon, *Mémoire succint sur les formalités*, pp. 221–22.

46. "Epithalame sur le mariage du roy et de tres-noble et tres-excellente princesse Loyse de Lorraine," in *Advertissement du sacre*, pp. 17, 19: "What is it that Phoebus does not gild, what is it that he does not color? Who among kings does not know that the king this day bends beneath the laws of your son Hymeneus? Who does not know that the arrows covered with the sparks of your amorous son are in the form of a flame secreted within the soul of this generous king? . . . May his praises be carried to the foreign lands, and his reputation that gleams as does the night-chasing sun by the plain of the desert of Cyrene. O happy day, Hymen, O Hymeneus!" Grassaille, *Regalium Franciae*, p. 2, asserts, "Et dicitur [rex Franciae] secundus sol in orbe terrarum," and he cites Baldus

de Ubaldi's similar assertion about the emperor.

47. Ronsard, "Cartel pour le Roy Charles IX, habillé en fome de soleil," in *Oeuvres complètes*, 1:1017, and "Comparaison du soleil et du roy, recitée par deux joueurs de lyre," in ibid., 1:1015–17. On p. 1127 (note to p. 1017) Cohen asks whether Ronsard might have been responsible for "la tradition du Roi-Soleil," but in view of the earlier example of Grassaille that could hardly have been the case.

48. Marlot, *Le theatre d'honneur*, pp. 541–42: "Seated on this dry stone, I live on the freshness of the water, and Phoebus harms my verdure when he uses his hottest torches. But today I am having peradventure a happy change in my nature; for, if the excessively cruel ardor of Phoebus harms and kills me, I again come to life in seeing the splendor of *LOUIS*, Sun of France." The cement joining the two stones is most likely a reference to Louis, either as the cement that would bring the two religious factions of France together, or as the product of the marriage of Henry IV and Marie de Médicis.

49. Ibid., p. 546.

50. Le Noble, *Histoire du sacre*, p. 471: "Previously my beautiful clear days seemed to become darkened in falling into their primeval night. But the rising of my sun, a star with a peerless countenance, changes this night into light."

51. Favyn, *The Theater of Honour*, p. 166 (p. 278 in the French edition of Paris, 1620). On p. 299 Favyn discusses briefly the calling forth of the king but says only that the ceremony "is remarkeable, for remembrance of the dead, and may serve as a Spurre to the Sonne, for imitation of his Fathers valour."

52. Ibid., p. 172 (pp. 287–88 in the French edition).

53. A further implication of the solar symbolism in 1610 should be noted. If the fiction of the king's sleep was meant to connect the king with the sun, the word *thalamus* in the coronation *ordo* would have brought into play the song of the Psalmist (Psalm 18:6–7; 19:4–6 in the AV): "In sole posuit tabernaculum suum; Et ipse tanquam sponsus procedens de thalamo suo. Exsultavit ut gigas ad currendam viam; A summo caelo egressio eius. Et occursus eius usque ad summum eius; Nec est qui se abscondat a calore eius." In other words, if the king was the same as the sun, he was "as a bridegroom coming out of his chamber." Thus the king was about to become a spouse, and this part of the ceremony would have added weight to another part of the ceremony, the bestowal of the ring, by which the king in the sixteenth century was considered to marry his kingdom; see ch. 6, section 4. Many other examples of solar imagery are listed in Hennequin, *Les oraisons funèbres*, 4:249–53 (but only in the version of the *thèse d'Etat* deposited in French university libaries, for most of the

extremely useful appendices were deleted from the printed edition of the study).

54. Kantorowicz, "*Oriens Augusti—Lever du Roi,*" pp. 119–77.

55. Danchet, *Le sacre du Roy,* tableau I (no pagination). Danchet wrote the text of this work, which was produced by a number of scholars and artists in collaboration. The tableau has been reproduced in part in Pichon, *Sacre et couronnement de Louis XVI,* p. 95, and in Millon, *Cérémonial du sacre;* the reproductions in the latter work, the text of which is based on Pichon, are of very poor quality, for which there is little excuse because the original printing plates still exist in the Louvre, where new originals may be purchased at reasonable cost.

56. See this ch. at nn. 48–50.

57. Pichon, *Sacre et couronnement de Louis XVI,* pp. 95–96, reproduces the engraving entitled *Lever du roi* from Danchet, but without the SURGENS CORUSCAT device at the bottom; the explanation is altered only enough to apply to Louis XVI rather than Louis XV.

58. See ch. 12 at n. 14.

CHAPTER 10

1. The ordinance is printed in Godefroy, *Le cérémonial françois,* pp. 295–97, and in Du Tillet, *Recueil des rangs,* pp. 94–95. That the dispute did not arise suddenly on the day before the coronation is demonstrated by a royal request to the Parlement of Paris asking to be given the dates of the origin of the various peerages. This information was sent to Henry on 6 July by Jean du Tillet, *Greffier* (clerk) of the Parlement (Godefroy, *Le cérémonial françois,* pp. 294–95). See also Giesey, *The Juristic Basis of Dynastic Right,* p. 39, n. 151. The count of Nevers had been raised to the peerage by Charles VII in 1459 (and raised to duke by Francis I in 1538) and the duke of Guise in 1527; the count of Montpensier had been raised to duke and peer early in 1539. On the distinction between the old and the new peers, see this ch. at n. 11.

2. This was recognized in the sixteenth century by Du Tillet, *Recueil des roys,* p. 315 ("le rang des representez estoit gardé, non des represen-tans"), and *Recueil des rangs,* p. 16.

3. It is worth quoting the definition of Prince of the Blood that Charles Loyseau gave in his *Des ordres et simples dignitez,* VII, no. 12, p. 103: "[Princes are those] qui sont de la lignee de nos Roys, à sçavoir que la coronne est destinee à chacun d'eux en son rang et degré de consan-guinité: destinee dis-je par voye d'heredité, qui transfere le droit du de-funct au plus proche heritier, et par consequent le charge de ses faits et

promesses, comme representant sa personne. . . ."

4. Du Tillet, *Recueil des rangs*; Loyseau, *Des ordres et simples dignitez*. The subject is mentioned also in the work of the able lawyer, Le Caron, in his *Pandectes*, I, xxi, p. 120.

5. For a partial listing of the peers and the regalia borne by them, see Choppin, *Traité du domaine*, in *Oeuvres*, 2:425 (III, viii, no. 1).

6. Guy Coquille, who ought to have known better, speaks in his *Institution au droict*, in *Oeuvres*, 2:5, col. 2, of "le serment que le Roy prête à son sacre és mains des Pairs."

7. Choppin, *Traité du domaine*, in *Oeuvres*, 2:425 (III, viii, no. 1): "Or d'autant que la principale charge des Pairs de France consiste au devoir et assistance, à laquelle ils sont obligez au Sacre et Couronnement du Roy, pour luy rendre toutes soubmissions et devoirs de serment de fidelité, comme les premiers vassaux du Royaume. . . ." There are occassional implications that the peers swore a special oath to the king either at his coronation or at other times. Schramm, *Der König von Frankreich*, pp. 173–74, argued that the peers acted as representatives of the people when they supported the crown, but he did recognize (p. 202) that the kiss was the kiss of homage. Cf. the comments of Jean Golein: "Adonc vient larcevesque par devant et le [le Roy] baise. et apres les pers evesques. et apres les autres pers seculiers. et cest en demonstrant quil li font hommage et quil ont avec lui union paisible et amiable" (Jackson, "The *Traité du sacre* of Jean Golein," p. 317). On the kiss of homage, see Mitteis, *Lehnrecht und Staatsgewalt*, pp. 497–500.

8. This is not the place to get into the vexing problem of the origin of the peers. One of the best studies of the subject is still Lot, "Quelques mots sur l'origine des pairs." I tend to agree with Lot on the origin of the ecclesiastical peers, although I should like to suggest that it is significant that all of the five bishops, with the exception of the bishop of Langres, were suffragan bishops of the archbishop of Reims; why Langres, then, should have also been selected cannot be fully explained. Lot's explanation of the origin of the lay peers is inferior to that given by Holtzmann, *Französische Verfassungsgeschichte*, p. 233. See also the discussion by Labatut, *Les ducs et pairs de France*, pp. 41–56.

9. Reims, BM 328, fols. 70ᵛ–72ᵛ.

10. Loyseau, *Traité des seigneuries*, V, no. 4, p. 64, and VI, nos. 46–60, pp. 82–85. The best sixteenth-century discussion of the peers as judges is Budé, *Annotationes in pandectas*, fol. lxiʳ⁻ᵛ (on *Digest*, 1, 9, 12, 1, "Senatores autem accipiendum"). More recently Chéruel discussed the rights of the peers in his *Dictionnaire historique*, 2:922–23, s.v. "Pairs."

11. This brief survey of the early history of the Peers of France is based on Holtzmann, *Französische Verfassungsgeschichte*, pp. 231–35; Schramm, *Der König von Frankreich*, pp. 170–76; Chéruel, *Dictionnaire*

historique, 2:920–22; Viollet, *Histoire des institutions politiques*, 3:301–8. Viollet, 3:305, asserts that in 1386 no distinction was made between the old peers and the new, and that the same was true in 1458. However, the source he quotes (Du Tillet, *Recueil des rangs*, p. 65) for the latter occasion demonstrates just the opposite, that a distinction was indeed made. See also this ch. at n. 14. The old were distinguished from the new peers as early as the reign of Charles V; a list of the peers in the British Library's Tiberius B.viii, fol. 42^V (see ch. 6 at n. 19), obviously differentiates when it uses the words *ces pers anciens*.

12. The "Doléance des Etats" is printed in Isambert, *Recueil général*, 9:108–9: "*Item*, qu'aux grans affaires de ce royaume, le roi devroit appeler les princes de son sang, plus que nuls autres; et qu'ainsi se doit faire raisonnablement, veu leur grand intérêt; et ainsi est accoutumé de faire par les très-chrétiens roys de France, ses progéniteurs." For examples of the earlier phrases from the reign of John, see ibid., 5:105, 156; after that such phrases are quite common (e.g., ibid., 5:213, 270–71, 277, 329; 8:641 [in the Treaty of Troyes of 1420], 731); I have not searched for earlier examples. One of the best lawyers at the end of the Renaissance, Charles Loyseau, recognized that the term "Princes of the Blood" was not as old as commonly thought, but he did not indicate when he thought the phrase came into use (*Des ordres et simples dignitez*, VII, no. 29, p. 105). On the conception of *prince*, see Pacaut, "Recherche sur les termes 'Princeps, principatus, prince, principauté'," which supports my contention.

13. Du Tillet, *Recueil des roys*, p. 316; *Recueil des rangs*, p. 15. Loyseau, *Des ordres et simples dignitez*, VII, nos. 31–32, p. 106, saw the dispute among Princes of the Blood as beginning already in 1380. One must be cautious about reading into Giesey, *The Juristic Basis of Dynastic Right*, p. 39, the implication that "Princes of the Blood" was a well-developed concept by the fifteenth century.

14. Du Tillet, *Recueil des rangs*, 65–66; Parlement's refusal, as quoted in Du Tillet, said, "La cour n'y a peu deliberer pour le present, pource qu'il y a procés appoincté en droict en ladite Cour en pareil cas, et seroit la deliberation de cet article en effect la decision du procés." This implies that an otherwise unknown case was being deliberated, but one still has the impression that the refusal was related to the trial of the duke of Alençon. Giesey, *The Justistic Basis of Dynastic Right*, p. 39, says aptly that by the decision of 1458 "we see an equilibrium of the passing feudal monarchy and the rising dynastic monarchy"—as we shall see, it was an equilibrium that lasted for more than another century.

15. For this information I rely upon the great authority in such matters, Hervé Pinoteau, "Les armoiries et la symbolique de Jeanne d'Arc."

16. Godefroy, *Le cérémonial françois*, pp. 173, 228, 232–33, and

Charles VIII, p. 193; Le Noble, *Histoire du sacre*, pp. 264, 285, 309. It was at this last coronation that a member of the house of Lorraine (René, duke of Lorraine) first represented one of the old peers. Members of the house of Lorraine—or of the house of Guise, which descended from it— were to represent peers at every coronation from 1498 to 1575. No fewer than four members of the house were to do so at the coronation of Charles IX—the Princes of the Blood were not better represented (see ch. 9 at n. 30). Du Tillet, *Recueil des roys*, p. 315, erred when he wrote that all of the peers were represented by Princes of the Blood at Louis XI's coronation; the count of Eu, who represented the count of Toulouse, was not a Prince of the Blood.

17. Masselin, *Journal des États Généraux*, pp. 124–25 (speaks of the Princes of the Blood as *principes*), 140 ("principibus regii sanguinis"), 144 ("regii sanguinis viros"). In a speech at the Estates General, Jehan de Rély often used the term *princes du sang* (ibid., pp. 166–217).

18. Le Noble, *Histoire du sacre*, p. 316; Anselme de Sainte Marie, *Histoire généalogique*, 1:315–16. For Francis's entry, see Godefroy, *Le cérémonial françois*, pp. 272–73.

19. Du Tillet, *Recueil des roys*, p. 315, and *Recueil des rangs*, pp. 12– 13, 79–80. Whether the lay peers should precede the ecclesiastical peers was another issue that had not yet been settled; for later examples of this dispute, see Dumont, *Le cérémonial diplomatique*, 4:34. The prince of La Roche-sur-Yon (Louis I de Bourbon) was the father of Louis II de Bourbon, duke of Montpensier, who was to play such an important role in the struggle over precedence from 1547 on (see this ch., section 4). Louis de Bourbon, cardinal of Vendôme (or of Bourbon) was, as bishop of Laon, a Peer of France; he was the younger brother of Charles, duke of Vendôme (the father of Antoine de Bourbon, king of Navarre).

20. Du Tillet, *Recueil des rangs*, pp. 14, 15, 80, 91–92. Charles, duke of Alençon, was the last survivor of the nearest of the cadet lines.

21. The composition of a genealogy of all the male heirs of Saint Louis was an important portion of the research for this chapter; the genealogy impressively and graphically portrays the disappearance of line after line in the fifteenth and sixteenth centuries.

22. Le Caron, *Pandectes*, p. 120, wrote, "Aussi tousjours leur [the princes'] authorité, comme un rayon de la Majesté Royale, a esté grandement honorée, estans Conseilleurs nez du Roy . . ." (Le Caron's terminology suggests solar symbolism, which I discuss ch. 9, section 5). See also Coquille, *Institution au droict*, in *Oeuvres*, 2:2; Du Tillet, *Recueil des roys*, p. 314; Loyseau, *Des ordres et simples dignitez*, VII, nos. 80–81, pp. 114–15. Jacques Auguste de Thou, *Historiarum sui temporis*, 7:105 (XXVII, 23), says, "Non eadem ratio in regii sanguinis principibus habita, quippe qui absque ullis titulis et patriciorum privilegio gaudent et

patricios omneis natalium praerogativa non patriciatus ratione praecedunt; quoniam dignitatis atque adeo personae regiae, quae cunctas alias exsuperat, pars ipsi quodammodo consentur"; one French edition (The Hague, 1740), 3:47, translates this, "Cette préséance n'est pas un appanage de leurs Pairies, s'ils en ont; c'est un privilége attaché à leur auguste naissance, qui les fait considerer comme faisant partie de la personne sacrée du Roi, dont la dignité éminente surpasse incontestablement toute autre dignité." (On the editions of de Thou, see Kinser, *The Works of Jacques-Auguste de Thou*.)

23. Paris, Archives Nationales manuscript *Table de Lenain*, 22:317, quoting from the *Registres du Parlement*, 40:266ᵛ (10 September 1551), says, "En l'absence du Roy, les Pairs, Princes du Sang, et non autres entrerent en la Cour avec l'espeé. Le Roy l'a mandé." Du Tillet, *Recueil des roys*, pp. 314–15.

24. Loyseau, *Des ordres et simples dignitez*, XI, no. 8, p. 160: "les Princes du sang . . . soient vrais Princes, pource qu'ils sont seuls capables de la vraye Principauté et souveraineté"; *Traité des seigneuries*, V, no. 74, p. 73; Saint-Gelais, *Histoire de Louys XII*, p. 47.

25. For the dispute in 1547, see this ch., section 1. One must not confuse the Bourbon dukes of Montpensier with the former Bourbon counts of Montpensier, the last of whom (Charles de Bourbon, constable of France) was killed during the sack of Rome in 1527 (by Benvenuto Cellini, if one were to believe that writer's laudatory account of his role in defending the person of the pope). Louis II de Bourbon, duke of Montpensier, was, through his mother, a nephew of the constable, but he was more distantly related through the male line, which was all that counted as a Prince of the Blood.

26. Du Tillet, *Recueil des rangs*, pp. 93–94. On the ceremony of presentation of the roses, see Chéruel, *Dictionnaire historique*, 2:1049, s.v. "Redevances féodales."

27. Du Tillet, *Recueil des rangs*, pp. 15, 95–99. Henry II's letter patent is printed in Godefroy, *Le cérémonial françois*, pp. 297–98. That the issue on the last occasion was argued between Montpensier and Guise as peers does not really hide the essential nature of the struggle.

28. Du Tillet, *Recueil des rangs*, pp. 15, 100–101, 104; Du Tillet gives a number of similar examples from the 1550s. Henry II may have avoided ending the strife between Montpensier and his opponents in order to keep the issue as confused as possible and, thus, to help prevent either party from becoming overly powerful; obviously such a policy did not work. On the other hand, Henry might simply have taken a dislike to Montpensier, who does strike one as having been an unpleasantly aggressive sort of individual.

29. Both of these coronations remain enigmatic; no very credible rec-

ords of Francis II's coronation survive, so we are forced to rely on the word of later writers, and the sources for Charles IX's coronation conflict. For Francis II, see Jacques Auguste de Thou, *Histoire*, 3:256 (XXVII, 9); Loyseau, *Des ordres et simples dignitez*, VII, no. 33, p. 106; Fauchet, *Origines des dignitez*, p. 48; Giesey, *The Juristic Basis of Dynastic Right*, p. 39, n. 153; one wonders whether the king's youngest brother was dressed as a peer on this occasion. For Charles IX's coronation, see Thou, *Histoire*, 3:256 (XXVII, 9); *Du sacre dudit Roy Charles IX. et de ce qui s'y passa pour le regard des pairs*, in Godefroy, *Le cérémonial françois*, p. 318; Godefroy, *Charles IX*, p. 312; Jackson, "Charles IX's Coronation," pp. 292–93. Because the latter two works list Montpensier after Guise and Nevers, whereas the former two list Montpensier before Nevers, it is impossible to determine whether Montpensier preceded or followed Nevers in 1561.

30. Du Tillet, *Recueil des rangs*, pp. 105–6.

31. Giesey, *The Juristic Basis of Dynastic Right*, pp. 39–40. The compact is printed in full in Bourbon de Parme, *Le traité d'Utrecht*, pp. 247–48, and in Cenival, "La succession de Charles IX," pp. 223–24. As far as I can determine, the only Princes of the Blood who did not sign the agreement were Charles de Bourbon (the fourth surviving son of Louis, prince of Condé), who was born in 1566 and was consequently still a minor, and Henri de Bourbon (the grandson of Montpensier and the last of the Bourbon dukes of Montpensier), who was born in 1573 and may not have been born at the time of the agreement (22 August).

32. *Requeste presentée au Roy par Monsieur le Duc de Montpensier*, in Godefroy, *Le cérémonial françois*, pp. 332–33: "Toutesfois encore que en vostre Royaume les Pairries Layes soient confuses en vostre personne, Sire, et que nul de vos sujets n'en pût faire representation, sinon par idée ou imagination . . . , Monsieur de Guise, qui sous pretexte que ses predecesseurs se sont fait à croire qu'ils representent les Pairs du Duché de Bourgongne . . . és Sacres de Henry II. François II. et Charles IX. . . . veut de present par tels moyens induire une consequence . . . contre les Suppliant. . . ." Montpensier's request was probably made between 13 February (the date of Henry's coronation) and 17 April (the date of the *arrêt* ordering the Parlement to investigate Montpensier's demands). Montpensier does not seem to have played any role at Henry's coronation, although he was present for Henry's wedding the next day; see *Brief, et sommaire discours de l'entrée, sacre et couronnement de Henry III*, in Godefroy, *Le cérémonial françois*, p. 327. Was he excluded from acting as one of the old peers on this occasion? Francis, duke of Alençon (Henry's younger brother), acted for the duke of Burgundy at Henry's coronation, thus playing the role taken by Henry himself at the previous coronation (ibid., p. 325). Henry of Navarre represented Normandy, and the duke of Guise

represented Guyenne on both occasions (see the sources cited this ch., n. 29).

33. The documents relative to this decision are printed in ibid., pp. 332–46. The most important portion of the edict is printed in Loyseau, *Des ordres et simples dignitez*, VII, no. 34, p. 106; in Le Caron, *Pandectes*, I, xxi, p. 120; and in Giesey, *The Juristic Basis of Dynastic Right*, p. 40, n. 155. Godefroy, pp. 334–36, quotes from the registers of the Parlement the report of Montpensier's verbal request and gives as the date 15 March 1575; internal evidence demonstrates that the year was 1576, which was the last year that Parlement began the new year with Easter, for the registration of the edict is dated 1577 (the remainder of France had begun the new year on 1 January since 1565; cf. Isambert, *Recueil général*, 14:176, n. 1).

34. *Des ordres et simples dignitez*, VII, nos. 36–37, p. 107. Loyseau discussed the limitations of the edict in no. 35 and the continuing problems of precedence in nos. 63–66, pp. 111–12.

35. Du Tillet, *Recueil des roys*, p. 316; Le Caron, *Pandectes*, I, xxi, p. 120; Loyseau, *Des ordres et simples dignitez*, VII, nos. 81–83, 104–5, pp. 115, 119.

36. Loyseau, *Traité des seigneuries*, VI, no. 60, p. 85; Isambert, *Recueil général*, 20:566–67. For the Saint-Simon sources, see ch. 13, n. 25.

37. He is not to be confused with his uncle Charles II, cardinal of Bourbon (1523–1590), who was the League's nominal king "Charles X" after the assassination of Henry III. This Charles III, cardinal of Bourbon (born ca. 1560), formed a third party of Catholics with the intention of obtaining the crown for himself (would he have been Charles XI?), and Henry IV seems to have formed a particular dislike for him. In any case, he could not have acted as a peer at Henry's coronation because he was bedridden during the last year of his life (he died on 30 July 1594). See Michaud, *Biographie universelle*, 5:273–74.

38. Gaston d'Orléans was exiled to his estates in Blois from 1652 until his death in 1660. Louis, prince of Condé (the Great Condé) turned against the French and fought for the Spanish until pardoned in 1660, after the Peace of the Pyrenees; he had a son eleven years old at the time of Louis XIV's coronation, and he might have acted as a peer, except that he naturally shared his father's fortune. The prince of Conti, on the other hand, was reconciled to Cardinal Mazarin in 1653 and married to the cardinal's niece in 1654, so he could have represented a peer, except that his changing policies during the troubles of the Fronde probably led to his being passed over in favor of more stalwart supporters of the king. Aubery, *Histoire du Cardinal Mazarin*, pp. 47–48, offers two other explanations for Conti's absence, neither of which is very convincing: "On a peine à deviner au vrai le motif qu'eut le Prince de Conti de ne se trouver

point à la ceremonie. . . . Il ne peut avoir en cela que deux vuës. L'une le service du Roi, qui l'appelloit promptement vers les Pyrenées: et l'autre, la crainte, que sa présence ne signalât et ne fit remarquer davantage l'absence de Monsieur le Prince, son frere. La derniere paroît la plus vraisemblable."

39. For listings of the representatives of the old Peers of France from Henry IV to Louis XVI, see Le Noble, *Histoire du sacre*, pp. 440, 480, 504, 506, 538, 569–70. See Giesey, *The Juristic Basis of Dynastic Right*, pp. 40–42, for a brief characterization of the role of the Princes of the Blood after the Bourbons came to the throne in France.

40. See, for example, Wolf, *Louis XIV*, p. 365: "However, in the sixteenth and seventeenth centuries a new feudality struggled to establish itself out of the disorders of the 'religious' war and the rebellions of the first half of the seventeenth century." Palmer, *A History of the Modern World*, p. 335: "The noble order . . . had enjoyed a great resurgence since the death of Louis XIV in 1715." But see, for the eighteenth century, the contrary view argued by Doyle, "Was There an Aristocratic Reaction?"

41. Siret, *Précis historique*, p. 68 and passim; see also ch. 12 at nn. 12–13.

CHAPTER II

1. According to Dumont, *Louis XIV*, p. 212, there was no entry at his coronation because he "did not want one." *Le sacre et couronnement de Louis XIV*, sig. A$_6$^{v}, says that the inhabitants of Reims would have prepared an official entry "if a contrary order had not put limits on their zeal."

2. On the Clovis legend and its history, see Schramm, *Der König von Frankreich*, pp. 145–50; Bloch, *Les rois thaumaturges*, pp. 224–29; Oppenheimer, *The Legend of the Ste. Ampoule*; Pange, "Doutes sur la certitude"; above all, Tessier, *Le baptême de Clovis*.

3. Godefroy, *Charles VIII*, p. 189.

4. Godefroy, *Louis XIII*^{b}, pp. 422, 424–25. The ORIENS EX ALTO device could have referred not only to the ampulla "from on high" but also to the sunrise by means of the word *oriens*; *altum* may mean either high or deep (see Kantorowicz, "*Oriens Augusti—Lever du Roi*"). See also ch. 9 at nn. 54–55.

5. For Louis XV, see Guimond de la Touche, *Explication des emblèmes*, pp. 10–11; for Louis XVI, Pichon, *Journal historique*, pp 12–15. On Numa Pompilius and the buckler, see Plutarch, *Numa*, XIII, and Dionysius of Halicarnassus, *The Roman Antiquities*, II, 71. These are the only

two classical authors I could find who discuss the legend of the buckler. The statement that the cartouche at Louis XVI's coronation is the only reference to the Holy Ampulla is true unless one wishes to agree with Pichon, *Journal historique*, pp. 10–11, that a statue of religion with an olive branch in her right hand meant that the fruit of the olive was "le symbole de l'huile sainte qui devoit couler sur le front de nos Rois" and that the branches of the olive represented "la paix dont l'Eglise se promet de jouir toujours sous le Règne de notre sage et vertueux Monarque."

6. Godefroy, *Charles VIII*, p. 189; Guimond de la Touche, *Explication des emblèmes*, p. 13.

7. Godefroy, *Charles VIII*, pp. 187–89. The historical Sicambrians were a tribe of Salian Franks; the historical Clovis, who was supposedly the great-great-grandson of Pharamond, was the king of the Sicambrians. The legendary Sicambria was the kingdom founded by Francus (see this ch. at nn. 12–14) after his flight from Troy. On the significance of this tableau in the history of Salic law, see Giesey, *The Juristic Basis of Dynastic Right*, pp. 18, n. 64, 20.

8. On the Trojan origins of the Franks, see this ch. at nn. 12–18. For the history of Salic law, see Scheidgen, *Die französische Thronfolge*, and Giesey, *The Juristic Basis of Dynastic Right*, pp. 17–22. One should note here that Giesey demonstrated that the French law of succession was much more complicated than a simple reliance upon Salic law.

9. See ch. 8.

10. On Samothes and Francus, see this ch. at nn. 13–16.

11. On the French "crown of Charlemagne," see Pinoteau, "L'ancienne couronne française." For Henry III, see Godefroy, *Le cérémonial françois*, p. 322. On the canonization of Charlemagne and the use of his cult by the French, see Guenée, *L'Occident aux XIVe et XVe siècles*, pp. 127–30; Folz, *Le souvenir et la légende de Charlemagne*, pp. 208–13, 304–7, and "La chancellerie de Frédéric Ier." For an extended discussion of imperial imagery toward the end of the fifteenth century, see Scheller, "Imperial themes in art and literature."

12. Godefroy, *Louis XIII^c^*, p. 425.

13. The foundation of Reims by descendants of Remus was portrayed at the entries of Charles VIII (Godefroy, *Charles VIII*, pp. 187–88) and Henry III (Godefroy, *Le cérémonial françois*, p. 323).

14. On the history of the legend of the Trojan origin of France, see Huppert, "The Trojan Franks."

15. Godefroy, *Louis XIII^b^*, p. 421. The first three words, "Hic satus Iapeto," may have a double meaning; Ovid, *Metamorphoses*, I, 82, used "satus Iapeto" as an appellation of Prometheus, the bringer of fire. Also, the last line of the verse, "et tibi Palladiae ramum praetendit olivae,"

must have referred to the queen mother and regent, Marie de Médicis, as the temporary successor to Samothes; because the olive branch was called "Palladian," the sacredness of the olive tree to Minerva was recalled. A medallion struck in 1611 to commemorate the accession of Louis had on the reverse a represenation of Marie, the queen mother, as Minerva holding an olive branch in her raised right hand (see Kantorowicz, "*Oriens Augusti—Lever du Roi*," p. 167, and fig. 42b). One of the triumphal arches at Louis's entry bore the device PARNASSIA LAURUS, "The laurel of Parnassus" (Godefroy, *Louis XIII*[b], p. 423). This was taken from Vergil, *Georgics*, II, 19–20: "etiam Parnassia laurus / parva sub ingenti matris se subicit umbra" ("the laurel of Parnassus, too, springs up, a tiny plant, beneath its mother's mighty shade," as translated by H. Rushton Fairclough in Loeb Classical Library). This obviously referred to Louis and his mother, Marie de Médicis.

16. Godefroy, *Louis XIII*[b], p. 422.

17. Ibid., pp. 421–23.

18. See also this ch. at nn. 27–29.

19. Godefroy, *Louis XIII*[b], p. 423.

20. Guimond de la Touche, *Explication des emblèmes*, p. 5; Zeller, "Les rois de France candidats," p. 501.

21. Guimond de la Touche, *Explication des emblèmes*, pp. 6, 8, 14–15.

22. Ibid., p. 15. For additional sun imagery at the coronation of Louis XV, see ch. 9 at nn. 55–56.

23. Ibid., pp. 6, 14; see this. ch. at n. 20.

24. Pichon, *Journal historique*, pp. 13–14.

25. Ibid., p. 13. The Vergilian device is from the *Aeneid*, IX, 296; it does not seem to recall any allusions from its context (the translation used here is that of J. Rushton Fairclough in the Loeb Classical Library). On Virgo-Astraea-Justice and the golden age, see Yates, "Queen Elizabeth as Astraea." Yates discusses Astraea as an imperial symbol on pp. 34–56 and 76–82, and she notes the association of Astraea with Henry IV of France on p. 81.

26. Pichon, *Journal historique*, p. 13.

27. Ibid., pp. 15–17. As elsewhere, the translation from Vergil (*Aeneid*, I, 176) is by H. Rushton Fairclough.

28. Ibid., pp. 18 ("Empire Chrétien"), 23 ("les premiers jours d'un Empire"), 24 ("la gloire de votre Empire"), and 20 ("l'Empire françois"); Zeller, "Les rois de France candidats," p. 529.

29. On the cult of Charlemagne at Aachen see ibid., p. 311. The relevant documents for 1775 are printed in Pichon, *Journal historique*, pp. 117–24.

30. Zeller, "Les rois de France candidats," p. 529, recognized that Napoleon fitted nicely into the historical framework of the French monarchy,

although he did not press the point. For the fifteenth century, see now also Scheller, "Imperial Themes in Art and Literature."

CHAPTER 12

1. In the funeral oration for Pope Pius VII: "Pie VII ne consacra pas l'usurpation, il rétablit la souveraineté; il n'institua point une monarchie nouvelle, il renouvela l'ancienne pour servir d'appui et de fondement à toutes les autres; il ne couronna point le fils de la Révolution, mais l'instrument et le vicaire de la Légitimité" (quoted in Masson, *Le sacre et le couronnement de Napoléon*, p. 272). Or, as Masson himself wrote, "[I]l se disait que le Sacre était un pas vers la contre-Révolution, et il avait raison" (ibid.). I should like to express my thanks to Professor Alan Spitzer for his comments on this chapter.

2. Rouen, BM Martainville 256, nos. 1–2, 5–7.

3. See this ch. at n. 16.

4. Rouen, BM Martainville 256, nos. 3–4, 6.

5. Paris, Archives Nationales O^3 525, a manuscript kindly brought to my attention by Baron Hervé Pinoteau. The grand ecuyer's budget is in Paris, AN O^3 424 ($=O$ 1717, no. 3), no. 1; it is not as detailed as that office's budget for 1825 (ibid., no. 2).

6. See this ch. at n. 17.

7. Siret, *Précis historique*, p. 7. The commission, formed two weeks after the death of Louis XVIII, was composed of the ministers of Finance, the Interior, and the Royal Household, the archbishop of Reims, the first gentleman of the Chamber, the captain of the Service Guards, and the grand master of ceremonies.

8. This discussion of Charles's coronation is based on Siret, *Précis historique*, and two anonymous works, *Promenade à Reims* and *Sacre de S.M. Charles X*. These descriptions are basically alike, so they will not be cited individually except when they differ. Siret, p. 38, describes the arch of Clovis; the representation of Clovis's baptism was very similar to equivalent representations prior to 1775; see ch. 11, section 2.

9. Talleyrand had already assisted at the coronations in 1775 and 1804; see Haueter, *Die Krönungen der französischen Könige*, p. 37, n. 86.

10. See this ch. after n. 16.

11. "En présence de Dieu, je promets à mon peuple de maintenir et d'honorer notre sainte religion, comme il appartient au Roi très-chrétien et au fils aîné de l'église, de rendre bonne justice à tous mes sujets; enfin, de gouverner conformément aux lois du royaume et à la charte constitutionnelle, que je jure d'observer fidèlement; qu'ainsi Dieu me soit en aide et le saint évangile" (Siret, *Précis historique*, p. 70). See also this ch. at n. 17.

12. Ibid., p. 73, says that Charles embraced all three of the Princes of the Blood, but both *Promenade à Reims*, pp. 131–32, and *Sacre de S. M. Charles X*, fol. 16ᵛ, say that Charles embraced only his son.

13. See ch. 10 at n. 33.

14. Quoted in Millon, *Cérémonial du sacre*, p. 36, n. 2, and in Haueter, *Die Krönungen der französischen Könige*, p. 100.

15. For the older interpretations, see ch. 9, sections 3–5.

16. The official version of the rescue of the remnants of the Holy Ampulla and the Holy Balm is given by Siret, *Précis historique*, p. 122, n. 19; on p. 28 he discusses the ceremony of 22 May. *Cérémonies et prières*, pp. 107–8, presents the version of the story told by the curate.

17. Garnier, *Le sacre de Charles X*, pp. 52–57, discusses the decision to swear to uphold the Constitutional Charter, and on pp. 66–72 he treats of the coronation oaths. Haueter, *Die Krönungen der französischen Könige*, pp. 138–46, does likewise.

18. This was the *Omnipotens sempiterne Deus, gubernator caeli* prayer; see ch. 2, n. 19.

19. Garnier, *Le sacre de Charles X*, pp. 73–97, discussed in detail the liturgical aspects of Charles's coronation and the grounds for the changes made; it is unnecessary to repeat his work here.

20. The times are given in Siret, *Précis historique*, p. 78, and in Garnier, "Le sacre de Charles X," pp. 646–47, 652.

21. Quoted by Garnier, *Le sacre de Charles X*, p. 51; the citation Garnier gives is false, and I have not found his source.

22. Hugo, "A Reims," p. 455; quoted also in Garnier, "Le sacre de Charles X," p. 660.

23. Quoted in Garnier, "Le sacre de Charles X," p. 661. The irony of Hugo's remarks is that he had been one of the poets chosen to write the official coronation ode.

24. *Sacre de S. M. Charles X*, fol. 15ᵛ.

25. Ibid., fol. 16.

26. Haueter, *Die Krönungen der französischen Könige*, p. 250, n. 8, which complements Bloch, *Les rois thaumaturges*, pp. 399–405.

27. Ibid., p. 424, discussed the investigation of the effectiveness of Charles X's touch; on pp. 401–4 Bloch described the attitude of Charles's contemporaries to the monarch's thaumaturgic power. Siret, *Précis historique*, p. 95, quotes the king's words to the ill.

28. Lamartine, *Le chant du sacre*, as quoted in Garnier, *Le sacre de Charles X*, p. 116: "Et l'Univers vieilli rêve qu'il voit renaître / Un nouvel âge d'or."

29. Quoted in Garnier, "Le sacre de Charles X," p. 660.

30. As late as 1868 the Abbé Quéant published his *Étude sur le sacre* in the apparent attempt to convince Napoleon III to go to Reims for his

coronation; see also Haueter, *Die Krönungen der französischen Könige*, pp. 369–70.

31. On the background and events of the *crise du drapeau blanc*, see Brown, *The Comte de Chambord*.

32. On this coronation coach, see Wackernagel, *Der französische Krönungswagen*, pp 291–319. The coronation coach first appears late in the history of the ceremony, in the eighteenth century.

CHAPTER 13

1. I say "whatever" because I am not convinced that we know enough about Merovingian accession rites to assert anything specific about them. For this and what follows on the ceremony before 1000, see Bouman, *Sacring and Crowning*, and Schramm, *Der König von Frankreich*, pp. 1–90.

2. I am purposely being vague about names and dates because we lack sufficient information about the accessions during the first half of the ninth century, and what evidence does survive needs to be reexamined. See Schramm, *Der König von Frankreich*, pp. 16–20; also see ch. 1, n. 5.

3. Hincmar's texts are printed in MGH *Capitularia*, 2:337–41, 363–65, 425–27, 453–58, 461–62.

4. See ch. 4, section 1, and ch. 5 at n. 6. If I understand Walter Ullmann correctly, the same view is presented in his "Der Souveränitätsgedanke."

5. Schramm, *Der König von Frankreich*, pp. 112–20, 145–48. See also Appendix B, no. 3, on the *ordo* of Reims.

6. Ibid., pp. 130–37. See also ch. 4 at n. 26 for another example of the intermonastic rivalry.

7. This was the conclusion of Schramm also (ibid., p. 150): in evaluating the destruction of the ampulla in 1793, he wrote, "Damit wurde zugleich der Kirche ein Mittel genommen, das jahrhundertelang ihrer Herrschaft gedient hatte."

8. See ch. 1 at n. 18, and Wolff, "Le mystère et la fête," read at the Colloque International d'Histoire sur les Sacres et Couronnements Royaux, Reims, October 1975. Wolff's paper is still unpublished, although there is a brief resumé of it in *Bulletin du Comité du folklore champenois*.

9. See ch. 9 at n. 39. See also Hanley, *The* Lit de Justice, ch. 8.

10. Brown, "The Tyranny of a Construct."

11. See the remarks by Durand, *États et institutions*, pp. 275–80, translated also as part of "What is Absolutism?" pp. 18–23.

12. In addition to the works cited ch. 8, n. 2, the reader may consult

Carlyle and Carlyle, *Medieval Political Theory*, and Gilmore, *Argument from Roman Law*.

13. Allen, *A History of Political Thought*, p. 416. The best study of Bodin is Franklin, *Jean Bodin and the Rise of Absolutist Theory*.

14. On Bodin's conception of divine law, see ch. 7 at nn. 45–47.

15. I had selected the phrase long before I read exactly the same words in the translation of Durand, "What is Absolutism?" p. 21.

16. See ch. 8 at nn. 9–10.

17. See ch. 7 at nn. 59–60.

18. See Lewis, "Anticipatory Association."

19. See ch. 1 at nn. 14–16 and ch. 4 at nn. 15–17.

20. See ch. 4 at n. 11.

21. Saint-Simon, *Mémoire succint sur les formalités*, pp. 233–37.

22. Ibid., p. 224.

23. See ch. 9 at n. 45.

24. Ibid., pp. 221–29.

25. Saint-Simon, *Mémoires*, 7:261–63, and Boutaric, "Un mémoire inédit," p. 540. See ch. 10 at n. 36.

26. See ch. 9 at n. 39.

27. Giesey, *The Royal Funeral Ceremony*, pp. 183–84, and Hanley, *The* Lit de Justice, chs. 11 and 12.

28. See ch. 9 at nn. 37–43.

29. See ch. 4 at n. 11.

30. Jackson, "The *Traité du sacre* of Jean Golein," p. 315.

31. It would be hard to imagine a Protestant king satisfactorily acquitting himself even in the coronation ceremony with its presupposed confession and absolution, participation in the mass, communion, and the like. On the requirement that the king be a Catholic, see Church, *Constitutional Thought*.

32. For much of what follows I rely upon the outstanding article by Weber, "Das *Sacre* Ludwigs XVI.," a model of the way in which kingship ought to be studied within the context of the times, and upon Haueter, *Die Krönungen der französischen Könige*, p. 10.

33. "Oraison funèbre de Louis XV" by the Bishop of Senez on 27 July 1774, as quoted in Weber, "Das *Sacre* Ludwigs XVI.," p. 548.

34. These and numerous similar texts are quoted in ibid., pp. 549–51, and in Haueter, *Die Krönungen der französischen Könige*, pp. 68–69, 339–42.

35. See ch. 11 at nn. 20–27.

36. On the latter, see Kantorowicz, "*Oriens Augusti—Lever du Roi*," and Treitinger, *Die oströmische Kaiser- und Reichsidee*.

37. Pacaut, *Les structures politiques*, p. 110; Folz, *L'idée d'Empire*, pp. 26, 194; Kantorowicz, *Laudes Regiae*, pp. 21–31. On the meaning of *im-*

perare, see, in addition to Kantorowicz, Du Cange, *Glossarium*, 4:304–5, s.v. "Imperatoris."

38. Jackson, "The *Traité du sacre* of Jean Golein," pp. 310–11, 324.

39. Strayer, "France: The Holy Land," pp. 307, 311–12.

40. Rebuffi, *De Christianissimi atque invictissimi regis Franciae muneribus et eius praerogativis tractatus*, fol. 2, in *Tractatus varii*: "Plus ex praedictis infero, illos reges nostros esse aequiparandos quibusque consanguineis, sive cognatis, quos Christus habuerit: Cùm in jure nostro appellatione cognatorum veniant grandes, et perfecti amici: imò eis preferuntur." Villette, *Les raisons de l'office*, pp. 190–91 (10, no. 11): "Ce nombre de douze Pairs, my Clercs, my Laiz, nombre d'universelle perfection en l'Eglise, monstre la grandeur nonpareille, et du Clergé, et de la Noblesse de France sur une mesme eschaffaut, c'est à dire, ne faisans qu'un mesme corps conspirant à la gloire de Dieu, et Majesté de son Roy. Ce nombre de douze, nombre d'assemblee de Dieu, comme les douze Patriarches, douze enfans de Jacob, douze Tribuz, douze Prophetes, douze Apostres, douze Royaumes Chrestiens, monstrent la grandeur du Conseil du Roy aux affaires de son Royaume, estre reglee par la Loy divine, ordonnee de Dieu: au jugement duquel, les Rois estrangers ont obey, comme en l'an mil cent vingt-deux, le Roy Jean d'Angleterre, ayant tué de sa main un forçat, fut adjourné par le Roy de France Philippes Auguste à la Cour de ses Pairs, et y fut condamné." (One wonders where the writer got that story of an event that took place six years after John's death!)

41. See ch. 4 at nn. 23–25.

42. Marot, "Chant royal de la conception," in *Oeuvres*, 1:357–59. See also Pasquier, *Les recherches de la France*, in *Les oeuvres*, 1:697.

43. Rébelliau, "Bossuet et les débuts de Louis XIV" (15 Nov. 1927), pp. 319–20, 323; Lacour-Gayet, *L'éducation politique*, p. 356. Haueter, *Die Krönungen der französischen Könige*, pp. 299, 313–16, gives a number of similar examples.

44. Saint-Joseph, *Catéchisme des partisans*, in *Choix de Mazarinades*, 1:278; quoted also in ibid., p. 300, n. 9. See ch. 1 at nn. 14–16 and ch. 4 at nn. 15–17. Several other examples of the "living image" are given in Hennequin, *Les oraisons funèbres*, 4:186–87.

45. "Jesus and Louis crowned are both to us the God-given; the one is the Eldest Son, the other the Spouse of the Church; this great union is achieved by the common rank of sons of God, which they have from the same title: they are brothers in unction" ("Ode au Roy sur son sacre," in *Le lys sacré*, p. 13 [= Reims, BM 1492, fol. 11]); quoted also in Haueter, *Die Krönungen der französischen Könige*, p. 314, n. 5.

46. Quoted in Haueter, *Die Krönungen der französischen Könige*, p. 277, n. 11.

47. Ibid., pp. 10, 339–40.

48. Ibid., pp. 68–69, 340; the decor of the church was described as theatrical in 1825 also (ibid., p. 73).

49. Quoted in ibid., pp. 340–41.

50. Bachaumont, *Mémoires secrets*, 8:90–91; quoted also in Weber, "Das *Sacre* Ludwigs XVI.," p. 549. See also this ch., section 1.

51. *Der König von Frankreich*, p. 266.

52. In his works Schramm often compared kingship in the two countries, but he did not do so systematically. A very good example of how such a study could be undertaken is Wood, "Queens, Queans and Kingship."

53. A good edition of the collected *ordines* in both countries is still wanting. Professor John Brückmann of the University of Toronto was working on the English texts, but his recent early death brought that project to an end; I am preparing an edition of the French ones (see Appendix B, n. 2.) Both countries were much influenced by the German *ordines*, though, and those too need to be presented systematically. In short, the work that Schramm began so well nearly half a century ago needs to be completed.

54. Schramm, *Geschichte des englischen Königtums*, pp. 204–7, 214–17; Richardson, "The English Coronation Oath"; Legg, *English Coronation Records*, pp. 240–41; and above all Hoyt, "The Coronation Oath of 1308."

55. The distinction was neatly put in the seventeenth century by Antoine Aubery, *Histoire du Cardinal Mazarin*, pp. 60–64. After discussing the two points of the body on which the king of the Romans was anointed, he urged, "Cela est bien éloigné de sept ou neuf Onctions que nos Monarques reçoivent en de pareilles Cérémonies. Aussi cette sorte de solemnité, en la personne des Rois de France, est qualifiée un vrai Sacre, et en la personne des autres Souverains, ne passe que pour un simple Couronnement."

APPENDIX B

1. See Bouman, *Sacring and Crowning*, pp. 15–17, 155–56, 168–69, and Schramm, "Ordines-Studien II," pp. 17–18.

2. For this and the *ordines* that follow, see my "Une revue des textes." Paul L. Ward, "An Early Version," pp. 345–61, presented a good critical edition of the text, but he did not note the variant readings in Reims, BM 342, which, with its marginal additions, was the version used at the French coronations; therefore I cite from this manuscript. Also, I cannot agree with Ward that the Fulrad *ordo* represents a version of the Anglo-Saxon ceremony. For one reason or another, I am not satisfied with any

printed edition of any of the medieval *ordines*, so I quote from the best manuscripts. I am in the process of preparing an edition of the texts.

3. I quote from the oldest of the three manuscripts of the *ordo*, Reims, BM 328.

4. Paris, BN latin 1246, from which I quote. There are some excerpts from the *ordo*, representing what appears to be a separate manuscript tradition, in a sixteenth-century manuscript, Paris, BN latin 12080, fols. 9ᵛ–10.

5. The *ordo* says that the peers should be called "a cancellario, si praesens est," a condition that might or might not have been expressed after 1271. Also, the transformation of the king's offering from the "thirteen gold coins" of the *ordo* of Reims to the "thirteen gold bezants" of the last Capetian *ordo* points to Louis IX's reign (see ch. 4 at nn. 22–26). I am grateful to François Avril, Conservateur au Cabinet des Manuscrits of the Bibliothèque Nationale, for confirming my dating of the miniatures in Paris, BN nouv. acq. latines 1202, from which I quote.

6. For details about this manuscript, sewn at the end of the register called *Croix*, which was destroyed in the fire of 1737, see my study "Les manuscrits des *ordines*," pp. 70–71.

7. That it was used in 1328 is shown by Pierre Roger's discussion of the coronation oath of Phillip VI (see ch. 6 at n. 43). There is no good reason for believing that the *ordo* was not used at the other coronations (in 1271, 1285, 1314, 1317, and 1322) after its completion.

8. Jackson, "Les manuscrits des *ordines*," passim.

9. Edited by Jackson, "The *Traité du sacre* of Jean Golein," pp. 308–24, from which I quote.

10. Paris, BN français 8334, fols. 22–77, from which I quote because it has never been published in full. NOTE: Certain of the above remarks concerning the *ordines* will be modified in the author's forthcoming study "Une revue des textes."

BIBLIOGRAPHY

MANUSCRIPTS

This list includes most of the manuscripts that deal with the French coronation ceremony in all periods, although it does delete a number of manuscripts not in France because I have not been able to see them. Some additional manuscripts for the period after 1654 are listed in Haueter, *Die Krönungen der französischen Könige*, pp. 371–74, and there are a few more in Saffroy, *Bibliographie généalogique*, 1:679–719. Together, those two lists, the documentation in my forthcoming edition of the medieval French coronation orders, and this one compose a fairly complete list of the relevant manuscripts. In my notes Archives Nationales, Bibliothèque Municipale, and Bibliothéque Nationale are abbreviated AN, BM, and BN, and the manuscripts I cite are here preceded by an asterisk.

Champaign-Urbana
University of Illinois Library: *Ordo ad consecrandum et coronandum regem Franciae*

Chantilly
Musée Condé: *1022, 1104, 1129, 1148, 1149, 1246

London
British Library: Additional 32097, Arundel 149, Egerton 931, *Tiberius B.viii

Orléans
Archives Departmentales d'Eure et Loire: *C,c.1.b
Bibliothèque Municipale: 144

Oxford
Bodleian Library: Ashmolean 842

Paris
Archives Nationales: *K 1714, *KK 1439[1], KK 1442, L 866, O^3 121, O^3 231, O^3 241, O^3 242, O^3 287–88, *O^3 424, *O^3 525, *P 2288, *Table de Lenain*
Bibliothèque de l'Arsenal: 676, 2001, 2002, 4227, 4228, 5027
Bibliothèque de l'Assemblée Nationale: 195, *1387, *1388, 1389, *1390
Bibliothèque Mazarine: 2036 (nos. 4–5)
Bibliothèque Nationale: fonds Baluze *112, 379
fonds français 176, 437, 931–32, 994, *2700, *2701, 2758 (no. 29),

2833, 2883, 4316 (nos. 38, 42, 44), 4399, 4596, *8334, 10279, 11195, 11221, 12814, 14371, *15494, 16600, 17299, *17512, 17909, 18513, 18540, 18648, 19894, 21716, 21722, 24049, 31994
nouvelles acquisitions françaises 7232, *21708–12
grec *1786
latin 943, 945, 953, 1223, *1246, 3968, 9430, 11743, 12052, *12080, 13313, *13314, 13315, 17333, 17335, *17991
nouvelles acquisitions latines 306, *1202
Bibliothèque de Sainte-Geneviève: 148, *3036

Reims
Bibliothèque Municipale: *328, 329, 330, *342, 348, 943, *1482, 1485, 1487, 1488, *1489, *1491, *1492, 1497, 1500, 1510, 1511

Rome
Biblioteca Vaticana: Chigi C VI 182, latini 4733

Rouen
Bibliothèque Municipale: A20, A34, *Martainville 256

Saint-Omer
Bibliothèque Municipale: 98

Sens
Bibliothèque Municipale: 9, 11, 70

Troyes
Trésor de la Cathédrale: 4

WORKS CITED FROM GODEFROY

This bibliography presents the full citations of the descriptions printed in the Godefroys' *Le cérémonial françois.* Most of the works were published separately, but I use the Godefroy edition for the reason given above, ch. 1, n. 2.

Cy-aprés s'ensuit la venuë du roy Charles huictiesme de ce nom à Rheims, pour recevoir son sainct sacre et couronnement; et les choses qui y furent faites, pp. 184–208. Cited as Godefroy, *Charles VIII.*

L'ordre du sacre du roy en ce que j'en ay peu voir et entendre, pp. 245–53. Cited as Godefroy, *Francis I^a.*

L'ordre du sacre et couronnement du Roy Tres-Chrestien nostre Sire, François de Valois premier de ce nom: fait en l'Eglise Nostre-Dame de Rheims, le jeudy vingt-cinquiesme jour de Janvier, l'an mil cinq cens et quatorze, pp. 253–64. Cited as Godefroy, *Francis I^b.*

Le sacre et couronnement du roy Henry deuxième de ce nom, pp. 279–93. Cited as Godefroy, *Henry II.*

L'entree, sacre, et couronnement du roy Charles IX faits en la ville de Rheims, le mercredy 14 et le jeudi 15 jour de may Feste de l'Ascension, l'an 1561, pp. 312–14. Cited as Godefroy, *Charles IX.*

Thou, Nicolas de. *L'ordre observé au sacre et couronnement du roy Henry le Grand, l'an 1594*, pp. 346–82. Cited as Godefroy, *De Thou's Henry IV.*

L'ordre des ceremonies du sacre, et couronnement du Tres-Chrestien Roy de France et de Navarre, Henry IV du nom, fait en l'Eglise Nostre-Dame de la ville de Chartres, le dimanche vingt-septiesme jour de fevrier 1594, pp. 383–97. Cited as Godefroy, *Anon. Henry IV.*

Les ceremonies du sacre, et couronnement du Tres-Chrestien Roy de France, et de Navarre Louys XIII par le Cardinal de Joyeuse, à Rheims, le dimanche 17 octobre 1610. Plus son entrée dans ladite ville de Rheims, et son retour à Paris, pp. 404–19. Cited as Godefroy, *Louis XIII^a.*

Sieur D. L. R. *Le voyage de Rheims, avec l'entiere et tres-exacte description, tant des ceremonies de la confirmation, sacre, couronnement, et reception en l'Ordre du S. Esprit, que du touchement des malades du roy Louys XIII l'an 1610*, pp. 419–37. Cited as Godefroy, *Louis XIII^b.*

Discours manuscrit, pp. 437–58. Cited as Godefroy, *Louis XIII^c.*

GENERAL BIBLIOGRAPHY

Advertissement du sacre, couronnement, et mariage du très chrestien roy de France et de Pologne Henry III. Lyons, 1575.

Allard, Albéric. *Histoire de la justice criminelle au seizième siècle.* Ghent, Paris, and Leipzig, 1868.

Allen, J. W. *A History of Political Thought in the Sixteenth Century.* London, 1960.

[Alletz, Pons Augustin]. *Cérémonial du sacre des rois de France.* Paris, 1775.

Anselme de Sainte Marie [=Pierre de Guibours]. *Histoire généalogique et chronologique de la maison royale de France.* 9 vols. Paris, 1726.

Ascoli, Peter, ed. *Le dialogue d'entre le Maheustre et le Manant.* Geneva, 1977.

Aubery, [Antoine]. *Histoire du Cardinal Mazarin.* New ed. 4 vols. Amsterdam, 1751.

Bachaumont, [Louis Petit de]. *Mémoires secrets pour servir à l'histoire de la république des lettres en France, depuis 1762 jusqu'à nos jours, ou journal d'un observateur.* 24 vols. London, 1777–84.

Baricave, Jean. *La defence de la monarchie françoise, et autres monarchies: Contre les detestables et execrables maximes d'estat d'Estienne Junius Brutus, et de Louys de Mayerne Turquet, et leurs adherans.* Toulouse, 1614.

Bayard, Jean-Pierre. *Le sacre des rois.* Pleins Feux, no. 2. Paris, 1964.

Belleforest, François de. *Les grandes annales, et histoire générale de France, dès la venue des Francs en Gaule, jusques au règne du roy très-chrestien Henry III.* 2 vols. Paris, 1579.

[Belloy, Pierre de]. *Apologie catholique contre les libelles declarations, advis, et consultations faictes, escrites et publiées par les Liguers perturbateurs du repos du royaume de France.* N.p., 1585.

———. *Examen du discours publié contre la maison royalle de France, et particulièrement contre la branche de Bourbon, seule reste d'icelle, sur la Loy Salique, et succession du royaume.* N.p., 1587.

Bernard, Auguste, ed. *Procès-verbaux des États Généraux de 1593.* Collection de documents inédits sur l'histoire de France. Paris, 1842.

Bévy, Dom Charles Joseph de. *Histoire des inaugurations des rois, empereurs, et autres souverains de l'univers, depuis leur origine jusqu'à présent.* Paris, 1776.

Beza, Theodore. *Du droit des magistrats.* Edited by Robert M. Kingdon. Les classiques de la pensée politique, no. 7. Geneva, 1971.

———. *De iure magistratuum.* Edited by Klaus Sturm. Texte zur Geschichte der evangelischen Theologie, no. 1. Neukirchen, 1965.

Bie, Jacques de. *La France métallique contenant les actions célèbres tant publiques que privées des rois et reynes.* Paris, 1636.

Billacois, François. "Le Parlement de Paris et les duels au XVIIe siècle." In *Crimes et criminalité en France sous l'Ancien Régime: 17e–18e siècles,* pp. 33–47. Cahiers des Annales, no. 33. Paris, 1971.

Blanchet, Adrien. *Manuel de numismatique française.* 3 vols. Vol. 3, *Médailles, jetons, méreaux.* Paris, 1930.

———. "Médailles et jetons du sacre des rois de France." *Études de numismatique* 1 (1892): 191–220.

Bloch, Marc. *Rois et serfs: Un chapitre d'histoire capétienne.* Paris, 1920.

———. *Les rois thaumaturges: Étude sur le caractère surnaturel attribué à la puissance royale particuliérement en France et en Angleterre.* Publications de la Faculté des Lettres de l'Université de Strasbourg, no. 19. Strasbourg, 1924.

Bodin, Jean. *Recueil de tout ce qui s'est negotié en la compagnie du tiers Estat de France, en l'assemblée générale des trois Estats, assignez par le Roy en la ville de Bloys, au XV. Novembre 1576.* N.p., 1577.

————. *The Six Bookes of a Commonweale*. Facsimile reprint of the English edition of 1606. Edited by Kenneth Douglas McRae. Cambridge, Mass., 1962.

————. *Les six livres de la république*. Paris, 1578.

Bond, E. A.; and Thompson, E. M., eds. *The Palaeographical Society: Facsimiles of Manuscripts and Inscriptions*. 3 vols. London, 1873–83.

Bouchart, Alain. *Les grandes chroniques de Bretaigne*. Edited by H. Le Meignen. Rennes, 1886.

Bouchel, Laurens. *La bibliothèque ou thresor du droict françois*. 2 vols. Paris, 1615.

[Boucher, Jean]. "François de Verone." *Apologie pour Jehan Chastel, Parisien: Exécuté à mort, et pour les pères et escolliers de la Societé de Jesus, bannis du royaume de France*. In *Mémoires de Condé*, 6.

————. *De justa Henrici tertii abdicatione e Francorum regno*. Paris, 1589.

Bouman, Cornelius A. *Sacring and Crowning: The Development of the Latin Ritual for the Anointing of Kings and the Coronation of an Emperor before the Eleventh Century*. Bijdragen van het Instituut voor Middeleeuwse Geschiedenis der Rijks-Universiteit te Utrecht, no. 30. Groningen, 1957.

Bourbon de Parme, Prince Sixte. *Le traité d'Utrecht et les lois fondamentales du royaume*. Paris, 1914.

Boutaric, E. "Un mémoire inédit du duc de Saint-Simon." *Revue des questions historiques* 16 (1874): 532–42.

Brillat-Savarin, J. A. *Essai historique et critique sur le duel*. Paris, 1819.

Brissaud, Yves. *Le droit de grâce en France aux XIVe et XVe siècles*. Thèse de Droit. Poitiers, 1971.

Bromley, J. S. "The Decline of Absolute Monarchy (1683–1774)." In *France: Government and Society*, edited by J. M. Wallace-Hadrill and John McManners, pp. 134–60. London, 1957.

Brown, Elizabeth A. R. "The Tyranny of a Construct: Feudalism and Historians of Medieval Europe." *American Historical Review* 79 (1974): 1063–88.

Brown, Marvin. *The Comte de Chambord: The Third Republic's Uncompromising King*. Durham, N.C., 1967.

Brühl, Carlrichard. "Fränkischer Krönungsbrauch und das Problem der 'Festkrönungen.' " *Historische Zeitschrift* 194 (1962): 265–326.

Budé, Guillaume. *Annotationes in quatuor et vigenti pandectarum libros*. Paris, 1530.

Buisson, Ludwig. *Potestas und Caritas: Die päpstliche Gewalt im Spätmittelalter*. Forschungen zur kirchlichen Rechtsgeschichte und zum Kirchenrecht, no. 2. Cologne and Graz, 1958.

Cabrol, Fernand; and Leclercq, Henri. *Dictionnaire d'archéologie chré-

tienne et de liturgie. 15 vols. in 30. Paris, 1924–53.

Calendar of State Papers and Manuscripts Relating to English Affairs, Existing in the Archives and Collections of Venice, and in Other Libraries of Northern Italy. Vol. 7. Edited by G. C. Bentinck.

Capitularia regum Francorum. Edited by Alfred Boretius and Victor Krause. Monumenta Germaniae Historica: Legum sectio II, 2. Hannover, 1897.

Cappel, Jacques. *Plaidoyez de feu maistre Jacques Cappel.* Paris, 1561.

Carlyle, R. W.; and Carlyle, A. J. *A History of Mediaeval Political Theory in the West.* 6 vols. Edinburgh and London, 1962.

Cazaux, Yves. *Henri IV ou la grande victoire.* Paris, 1977.

Cenival, P. de. "Un document relatif à la succession de Charles IX." *Bibliothèque de l'École des Chartes* 72 (1911): 222–25.

Cérémonie du sacre et couronnement du roi Louis XIV. Printed in Dumont, *Supplement au corps universel,* 4: 212–21. Cited as Dumont, *Louis XIV.*

Cérémonies et prières du sacre des rois de France, accompagnées de recherches historiques. Paris, 1825.

Cerf, Charles. *Histoire et description de Notre-Dame de Reims.* 2 vols. Reims, 1861.

Le Chanson de Roland. Edited by Joseph Bédier. Paris, 1922.

Chanteur, Janine. "L'idée de loi naturelle dans la République de Jean Bodin." In *Jean Bodin: Verhandlungen der internationalen Bodin Tagung in München,* edited by Horst Denzer, pp. 195–212. Munich, 1973.

Chaplais, Pierre, ed. "The Opinions of the Doctors of Bologna on the Sovereignty of Aquitaine (1369): A Source of the Songe du verger." In *Some Documents Regarding the Fulfillment and the Interpretation of the Treaty of Bretigny, 1361–1369,* pp. 51–78. Camden Miscellany, no. 19, 1. London, 1952.

Chastellain, Georges. *Oeuvres.* Edited by Kervyn de Lettenhove. 8 vols. Brussels, 1863–66.

Chatauvillard, Comte de. *Essai sur le duel.* Paris, 1836.

Chéruel, A. *Dictionnaire historique des institutions, moeurs et coutumes de la France.* 5th ed. 2 vols. Paris, 1880.

Choppin, René. *Oeuvres.* 5 vols. Paris, 1662.

———. *Traité du domaine de la couronne de France.* In *Oeuvres,* vol. 2.

Church, William Farr. *Constitutional Thought in Sixteenth-Century France: A Study in the Evolution of Ideas.* Harvard Historical Studies, no. 47. Cambridge, Mass., 1941.

Clausel de Coussergues, Jean Claude. *Développmens [sic] de la proposition de M. Clausel de Coussergues, député de l'Aveyron, sur le duel.* Chambre des Députés, impressions ordonnées, no. 4, 49. Paris, 1818.

_____. *Du sacre des rois de France, et des rapports de cette auguste cérémonie avec la constitution de l'État aux différens âges de la monarchie.* Paris, 1825.

(Pseudo-) Codinos. *Traité des offices.* Edited by Jean Verpeaux. Paris, 1966.

Coquille, Guy. *Institution au droict des François.* Paris, 1607.

_____. *Institution au droict des François,* in *Oeuvres,* vol. 2. Bordeaux, 1703.

Corpus Juris Canonici. Edited by Aemilius Friedberg. 2 vols. Leipzig, 1879. Reprint: Graz, 1959.

Craig, Thomas. *The Right of Succession to the Kingdom of England.* London, 1703.

Danchet, Antoine, et al. *Le sacre du roy [Louis XV].* Paris, 1732.

Daniel, Gabriel. *Histoire de la milice françoise.* 2 vols. Amsterdam, 1724.

Darcel, Alfred. "Le Trésor de la cathédrale de Reims." *Gazette des Beaux-Arts* 23 (1881): 97–111, 293–304.

David, Marcel. *Le serment du sacre du IXe au XVe siècle, contribution à l'étude des limites juridiques de la souveraineté.* Strasbourg, 1951. Reprinted from *Revue du moyen âge latin* 6 (1950): 5–272.

_____. *La souveraineté et les limites juridiques du pouvoir monarchique du IXe au XVe siècle.* Annales de la Faculté du Droit et des Sciences Politiques de Strasbourg, no. 1. Paris, 1954.

Declareuil, J. *Histoire générale du droit français des origines à 1789.* Paris, 1925.

De justa reipublicae christianae in reges impios et haereticos authoritate. Paris, 1590.

Delachenal, Roland. *Histoire de Charles V.* 5 vols. Paris, 1909–31.

De la puissance des roys, et droict du succession aux royaumes. Paris, 1590.

Desportes, Pierre. *Reims et les Rémois aux XIIIe et XIVe siècles.* Paris, 1979.

Devisse, Jean. *Hincmar, archevêque de Reims, 845–882.* 3 vols. Geneva, 1976.

Dewick, E. S., ed. *The Coronation Book of Charles V of France (1338–1380).* Henry Bradshaw Society, no. 16. London, 1899.

Dialogue d'entre le Maheustre et le Manant: Contenant les raisons de leurs debats et questions en ces presens troubles au royaume de France. N.p., 1594. See also Ascoli, Peter.

Discours par lequel il apparoistra que le royaume de France est electif, et non hereditaire. N.p., 1591.

Discours sur la maison royale de France, et particulièrement contre la branche de Bourbon. 1587.

Doucet, Roger. *Les institutions de la France au XVIe siècle.* 2 vols. Paris, 1948.

———. "Pierre du Chastel, Grand Aumônier de France." *Revue historique* 133 (1920): 212–57, and 134 (1920): 1–57.

Doyle, William. "Was There an Aristocratic Reaction in Pre-revolutionary France?" *Past and Present* 57 (1972): 97–122.

Du Cange, Charles du Fresne. *Glossarium mediae et infimae latinitatis.* 7 vols. Paris, 1840–50.

Duchesne, André. *Les antiquitez et recherches de la grandeur et majesté des roys de France.* Paris, 1609.

Du Haillan, Bernard. *Histoire de France.* Paris, 1576.

Dumont, Jean. *Louis XIV.* See *Cérémonie du sacre.*

———. *Louis XV.* See *Rélation de la cérémonie.*

———. *Supplément au corps universel diplomatique du droit des gens.* 5 vols. Vol. 4, *Le cérémonial diplomatique des cours de l'Europe.* Amsterdam and The Hague, 1739.

Dupuy, Pierre. *Traité de la majorité de nos rois, et des régences du royaume.* Paris, 1655.

———. *Traitez touchant les droits du roy très-chrestien sur plusieurs estats et seigneuries possedées par divers Princes voisins.* Paris, 1655.

Durand, Georges. *États et institutions, XVIe–XVIIIe siècles.* Collection U. Paris, 1969.

———. "What is Absolutism?" In *Louis XIV and Absolutism,* edited by Ragnhild Hatton, pp. 18–36. Basingstoke, 1976.

Durand de Maillane, Pierre Toussaint. *Les libertez de l'église gallicane.* 5 vols. Lyons, 1771.

Du Tillet, Jean. *Les memoires et recherches.* Rouen, 1578.

———. *Recueil des rangs des grands de France.* N.p., 1606. Bound with Du Tillet, *Recueil des roys.*

———. *Recueil des roys de France, leurs couronne et maison.* Paris, 1618.

Elze, Reinhard. *Ordines coronationis imperialis.* Fontes iuris Germanici antiqui in usum scholarum ex Monumentis Germaniae Historicis, no. 9. Hannover, 1960.

Erdmann, Carl. *Die Entstehung des Kreuzzugsgedankens.* Forschungen zur Kirchen- und Geistesgeschichte, no. 6. Stuttgart, 1935.

Esmein, Adhémar. *Cours élémentaire d'histoire du droit français.* 4th ed. Paris, 1901.

Ewig, Eugen. "La monocratie dans l'Europe occidentale du Ve au Xe siècle." In *La monocratie,* 2:57–105. Recueils de la Société Jean Bodin pour l'histoire comparative des institutions, nos. 20–21. Brussels, 1969–70.

Facinger, Marion F. "A Study of Medieval Queenship: Capetian France,

987–1237." *Studies in Medieval and Renaissance History* 5 (1968): 1–47.

Falletti, L. "Duel." In *Dictionnaire de droit canonique*, edited by R. Naz, 5: cols. 3–39. 7 vols. Paris, 1935–65.

Fauchet, Claude. *Origines des dignitez et magistrats de la France*. Paris, 1600.

Favyn, André. *The Theater of Honour and Knighthood or a Compendious Chronicle and Historie of the Whole Christian World*. London, 1623.

———. *Le théatre d'honneur et de chevalerie, ou l'histoire des ordres militaires des roys, et princes de la chrestienté, et leur généalogie*. Paris, 1620.

Fawtier, Robert. *The Capetian Kings of France: Monarchy and Nation (987–1328)*. Translated by Lionel Butler and R. J. Adam. London, 1965.

———. "Comment le roi de France, au début du XIVe siécle, pouvait-il se représenter son royaume?" In *Mélanges offerts à M. Paul-E. Martin, par ses amis, ses collègues et ses élèves*, pp. 65–77. Geneva, 1961.

Folz, Robert. "La chancellerie de Frédéric Ier et la canonisation de Charlemagne." *Le moyen âge* 70 (1964): 13–21.

———. *Le couronnement impérial de Charlemagne*. Trente journées qui ont fait la France. Paris, 1964.

———. *L'idée d'Empire en Occident du Ve au XIVe siècle*. Paris, 1953.

———. *Le souvenir et la légende de Charlemagne dans l'Empire germanique médiéval*. Publications de l'Université de Dijon, no. 7. Paris, 1950.

Franklin, Julian H. *Constitutionalism and Resistance in the Sixteenth Century*. New York, 1969.

———. *Jean Bodin and the Rise of Absolutist Theory*. Cambridge, 1973.

Friedberg, Aemilius. See *Corpus Juris Canonici*.

Garnier, Jean-Paul. "Le sacre de Charles X." *Revue des deux mondes* 37 (1937): 634–62.

———. *Le sacre de Charles X et l'opinion publique en 1825*. Paris, 1927.

Gaubert, Henri. *Le sacre de Napoléon Ier*. Paris, 1964.

Gautier, Léon. *La chevalerie*. Paris, 1895.

Giesey, Ralph E. *The Juristic Basis of Dynastic Right to the French Throne*. Transactions of the American Philosophical Society, no. 51, no. 5. Philadelphia, 1961.

———. "The Monarchomach Triumvirs: Hotman, Beza and Mornay." *Bibliothèque d'Humanisme et Renaissance* 32 (1970): 41:56.

————. *The Royal Funeral Ceremony in Renaissance France*. Travaux d'Humanisme et Renaissance, no. 37. Geneva, 1960.

————. "When and Why Hotman Wrote the Francogallia." *Bibliothèque d'Humanisme et Renaissance* 29 (1967): 581–611.

Gilmore, Myron P. *Argument from Roman Law in Political Thought, 1200–1600*. Harvard Historical Monographs, no. 15. Cambridge, Mass., 1941.

Gobron, Louis. *Des sources du droit de grâce dans la législation romaine*. Paris, 1893.

Godefroy, Jacques, ed. *Codex Theodosianus cum perpetuis commentariis*. 6 vols. Lyons, 1665.

Godefroy, Théodore; and Godefroy, Denis. *Le cérémonial françois*. 2 vols. Paris, 1649.

Goulart, Simon. *Mémoires de l'estat de France*. 2nd ed. 3 vols. N.p. 1578.

Grassaille, Charles de. *Regalium Franciae libri duo*. Paris, 1545.

Grierson, Philip. "Election and Inheritance in Early Germanic Kingship." *Cambridge Historical Journal* 7 (1941–43): 1–22.

Grundmann, Herbert, ed. *Gebhardts Handbuch der deutschen Geschichte*. 9th ed. Vol. 1, *Frühzeit und Mittelalter*. Stuttgart, 1970.

Guenée, Bernard. *L'Occident aux XIVe et XVe siècles: Les Etats*. Nouvelle Clio, no. 22. Paris, 1971.

————, and Lehoux, Françoise. *Les entrées royales françaises de 1328 à 1515*. Paris, 1968.

Guimond de la Touche, C. *Explication des emblèmes héroïques, inventées par M. le chevalier D***, pour la décoration des arcs de triomphe erigés aux portes de Reims, lors de la cérémonie du sacre de Louis XV*. [Reims, 1722].

Hanley, Sarah. *The* Lit de Justice *of the Kings of France: Constitutional Ideology in Ceremonial, Legend, and Discourse*. Princeton, 1983.

Hardison, O. B., Jr. *Christian Rite and Christian Drama in the Middle Ages: Essays in the Origins and Early History of Modern Drama*. Baltimore, 1965.

Haueter, Anton. *Die Krönungen der französischen Könige im Zeitalter des Absolutismus und in der Restauration*. Zurich, 1975.

Hennequin, Jacques. *Les oraisons funèbres d'Henri IV: Les thèmes et la rhétorique*. Thèse Paris, 1975. 4 vols. in 2. Lille, 1978.

Hoffmann, Hartmut. "Die Unveräusserlichkeit der Kronrechte im Mittelalter." *Deutsches Archiv für Erforschung des Mittelalters* 20 (1964): 389–474.

Holtzmann, Robert. *Französische Verfassungsgeschichte von der Mitte des neunten Jahrhunderts bis zur Revolution*. Berlin, 1910. Reprint: Munich, 1965.

Hotman, François. *Francogallia*. Cologne, 1574.

———. *Francogallia*. Frankfurt, 1665.

———. *The* Francogallia *of François Hotman*. Variorum Latin text by Ralph E. Giesey. English translation by J. H. M. Salmon. Cambridge Studies in the History and Theory of Politics. Cambridge, 1972.

Hoyt, Robert S. "The Coronation Oath of 1308: The Background of 'les leys et les custumes.' " *Traditio* 11 (1956): 235–59.

Hugo, Victor. "A Reims: 1825–1838." *La revue de Paris* 6, vol. 5 (September–October 1899): 449–61.

Huppert, George. "The Trojan Franks and Their Critics." *Studies in the Renaissance* 12 (1965): 227–41.

Hurnard, Naomi D. *The King's Pardon for Homicide before A.D. 1307*. Oxford, 1969.

Isambert, François André, et al., eds. *Recueil général des anciennes lois françaises*. 29 vols. Paris, 1822–33.

Jackson, Richard A. "De l'influence byzantin sur les sacres des rois de France." *Byzantion* 51 (1981): 201–10.

———, ed. "A Little-known description of Charles IX's Coronation." *Renaissance Quarterly* 25 (1972): 289–96.

———. "Les manuscrits des *ordines* de couronnement de la bibliothèque de Charles V, roi de France." *Le Moyen Age* (1976): 67–88.

———. "Une revue des textes et des problèmes des *ordines* de couronnement français au moyen âge." Forthcoming.

———. "The Sleeping King." *Bibliothèque d'Humanisme et Renaissance* 31 (1969): 525–51.

———, ed. "The *Traité du sacre* of Jean Golein." *Proceedings of the American Philosophical Society* 113 (1969): 305–24.

Jousse, Daniel. *Nouveau commentaire sur l'ordonnance criminelle de mois d'août 1670*. New ed. Paris, 1763.

———. *Traité de la justice criminelle de France*. 4 vols. Paris, 1771.

Juvénal des Ursins, Jean. *Écrits politiques de Jean Juvénal des Ursins*. Edited by Peter S. Lewis. Vol. 1. Société de l'Histoire de France. Paris, 1978.

———. *Histoire de Charles VI*. Edited by J. F. Michaud and J. J. F. Poujoulat. Nouvelle collection des mémoires, Ière série, no. 2. Paris, 1836.

Kantorowicz, Ernst H. "Inalienability: A Note on Canonical Practice and the English Coronation Oath in the Thirteenth Century." *Speculum* 29 (1954): 488–502. Reprinted in Kantorowicz, *Selected Studies*, pp. 138–50.

———. "The 'King's Advent' and the Enigmatic Panels in the Doors of Santa Sabina." *Art Bulletin* 26 (1944): 207–31. Reprinted in Kantorowicz, *Selected Studies*, pp. 37–75.

————. *The King's Two Bodies: A Study in Mediaeval Political Theology*. Princeton, 1957.

————. *Laudes Regiae: A Study in Liturgical Acclamations and Mediaeval Ruler Worship*. University of California Publications in History, no. 33. Berkeley and Los Angeles, 1946.

————. "Mysteries of State: An Absolutist Concept and Its Late Mediaeval Origins." *Harvard Theological Review* 48 (1955): 65–91. Reprinted in Kantorowicz, *Selected Studies*, pp. 381–98.

————. "*Oriens Augusti—Lever du Roi.*" *Dumbarton Oaks Papers* 17 (1963): 119–77.

————. *Selected Studies by Ernst H. Kantorowicz*. Edited by Michael Cherniavsky and Ralph E. Giesey. Locust Valley, N.Y., 1965.

Kelley, Donald R. *Foundations of Modern Historical Scholarship: Language, Law, and History in the French Renaissance*. New York, 1970.

————. *François Hotman: A Revolutionary's Ordeal*. Princeton, 1973.

Kienast, Walther. *Untertaneneid und Treuvorbehalt in Frankreich und England: Studien zur vergleichenden Verfassungsgeschichte des Mittelalters*. Weimar, 1952.

Kinser, Samuel. *The Works of Jacques-Auguste de Thou*. International Archives of the History of Ideas, no. 18. The Hague, 1966.

Kleinclausz, Arthur. *L'Empire carolingien, ses origines et ses transformations*. Revue Bourguignonne de l'Enseignement Supérieur, 12, nos. 2, 3, and 4. Dijon and Paris, 1902.

Labatut, Jean-Pierre. *Les ducs et pairs de France au XVIIe siècle: Étude sociale*. Publications de la Sorbonne, N. S. Recherches, no. 1. Paris, 1972.

Labitte, Charles. *De la démocratie chez les prédicateurs de la Ligue*. 2nd ed. Paris, 1865.

Laboulaye, Édouard; and Dareste, R., eds. *Le grand coutumier de France*. Paris, 1868.

Lacointa, Félix. *Du sacre des rois de France, de son origine et de la Sainte-Ampoule*. Paris, 1825.

Lacour-Gayet, Georges. *L'éducation politique de Louis XIV*. Paris, 1898.

La Curne de Sainte-Palaye, Jean Baptiste. *Mémoires sur l'ancienne chevalerie*. 2 vols. Paris, 1759.

Lagrèze, M. G. B. *La Navarre française*. 2 vols. Paris, 1882.

La Guesle, Jacques de. *Remontrance de messire Jacques de la Guesle Procureur Général du Roy, prononcée le vingt-neuviéme juillet mil cinq cens quatre-vingt-onze au Parlement lors séant à Tours*. N.p., n.d.

Lamartine, Alphonse de. *Le chant du sacre, veille des armes*. Paris, 1825.

La Roche-Flavin, Bernard de. *Treze livres des parlemens de France.* Bordeaux, 1617.

Lavisse, Ernest. *Histoire de France dès origines à la Révolution.* 9 vols. in 18. Paris, 1900–11.

Leber, Jean M. C. *Des cérémonies du sacre, ou recherches historiques et critiques sur les moeurs, les coutumes, les institutions et le droit public des Français dans l'ancienne monarchie.* Paris, 1825.

Le Bret, Cardin. *De la souveraineté du roy.* Paris, 1632.

Le Caron, Louis Charondas. *Pandectes ou digestes du droit françois.* Lyons, 1596.

Legg, John Wickham. *Three Coronation Orders.* Henry Bradshaw Society, no. 19. London, 1900.

Legg, Leopold G. Wickham. *English Coronation Records.* Westminster, 1901.

Legoux, Jules. *Du droit de grâce en France comparé avec les législations étrangères.* Paris, 1863.

Le Gras, Simon. *Procès-verbal du sacre du roy Louis quatorze du nom.* Soissons, 1694.

Le Noble, Alexandre. *Histoire du sacre et du couronnement des rois et reines de France.* Paris, 1825.

Le Patourel, John. "The Origins of the War." In *The Hundred Years War,* edited by Kenneth Fowler, pp. 28–50. London, 1971.

———. "The Treaty of Brétigny, 1360." *Transactions of the Royal Historical Society* 5th ser. 10 (1960): 19–39.

Leroquais, Abbé Victor. *Les bréviaires manuscrits dans les bibliothèques publiques de la France.* 5 vols. Paris, 1934.

Le Roy, Louis. *De l'excellence du gouvernement royal.* Paris, 1575.

L'Estoile, Pierre de. *Registre-Journal de Henri IV et de Louis XIII.* Edited by Champollion-Figeac and Aimé Champollion. Nouvelle collection des mémoires, IIme série no. 1. Paris, 1837.

Letainturier-Fradin, Gabriel. *Le duel à travers les ages.* Paris, 1892.

Lewis, Andrew W. "Anticipatory Association of the Heir in Early Capetian France." *American Historical Review* 83 (1978): 906–27.

———. *Royal Succession in Capetian France: Studies on Familial Order and the State.* Cambridge, Mass., 1982.

Littré, Émile. *Dictionnaire de la langue française.* 4 vols. Paris, 1876.

Lot, Ferdinand. "Quelques mots sur l'origine des pairs de France." *Revue historique* 104 (1894): 34–59.

Loyseau, Charles. *Cinq livres du droict des offices.* Paris, 1620.

———. *Traité des ordres et simples dignitez.* Paris, 1620. Bound with Loyseau, *Cinq livres du droit des offices* and *Traité des seigneuries.*

———. *Traité des seigneuries.* Paris, 1620. Bound with Loyseau, *Cinq livres du droit des offices* and *Traité des ordres et simples dignitez.*

Luyn, P. van. "Les *milites* dans la France du XIe siècle." *Le Moyen Age* 77 (1971): 5–51, 193–238.

Le lys sacré roy des fleurs ou le sacre de Louys XIV. N.p., 1654. In Reims Bibliothèque Municipale 1492.

Major, J. Russell. *Representative Institutions in Renaissance France, 1421–1559.* Studies Presented to the International Commission for the History of Representative and Parliamentary Institutions, no. 22. Madison, 1960.

Marlot, Dom Guillaume. *Histoire de la ville, cité et université de Reims.* 4 vols. Reims, 1843–46.

————. *Le theatre d'honneur, et de magnificence, preparé au sacre des roys.* Reims, 1643.

Marot, Clément. *Oeuvres complètes de Clément Marot.* Edited by Abel Grenier. 2 vols. Classiques Garnier. Paris, n.d.

Marot, Pierre. "L'expédition de Charles VII à Metz (1444–1445): Documents inédits." *Bibliothèque de l'École des Chartes* 102 (1941): 109–55.

Martène, Edmond. *De antiquis ecclesiae ritibus.* 2nd ed. 4 vols. Antwerp, 1736.

————. *De antiquis ecclesiae ritibus.* 3rd ed. 4 vols. Venice, 1788.

Masselin, Jehan. *Journal des États Généraux de France tenus à Tours en 1484 sous le règne de Charles VIII.* Edited and translated by A. Bernier. Collection de documents inédits sur l'histoire de France. Paris, 1835.

Masson, Frédéric. *Le sacre et le couronnement de Napoléon.* Paris, 1908.

Mastellone, Salvo. "Aspetti dell'antimachiavellismo in Francia: Gentillet e Languet." *Il Pensiero Politico* 2 (1969): 376–415.

Maumené, Charles; and d'Harcourt, Comte Louis. *Iconographie des rois de France.* 2 vols. Archives de l'art français, nouvelle période nos. 15–16. Paris, 1928–31.

Mayer, Charles Joseph, ed. *Des États Généraux, et autres assemblées nationales.* 18 vols. The Hague, 1788–89.

Mémoires de Condé, ou recueil pour servir à l'histoire de France. 6 vols. London and The Hague, 1743.

Menin, Nicolas. *Traité historique et chronologique du sacre et couronnement des rois et des reines de France.* Paris, 1723.

Mesnard, Pierre. *L'essor de la philosophie politique au XVIe siècle.* 3rd ed. De Pétrarque à Descartes, no. 19. Paris, 1969.

Migne, J. P. *Patrologiae cursus completus latinae.* 221 vols. Paris, 1844–64.

[Millon, Charles]. *Cérémonial du sacre des rois de France*. La Rochelle, 1931.

Mitteis, Heinrich. *Lehnrecht und Staatsgewalt: Untersuchungen zur mittelalterlichen Verfassungsgeschichte*. Weimar, 1933. Reprint: Weimar, 1958.

Mommsen, Theodor. *Römisches Strafrecht*. Handbuch der deutschen Rechtswissenschaft, I, no. 4. Leipzig, 1899.

Montesquiou, Léon de. *Etude sur la suppression du duel*. Paris, 1899.

Montesquiou-Fezensac, Blaise de; and Gaborit-Chopin, Danielle. *Le Trésor de Saint Denis: Inventaire de 1634*. 3 vols. Paris, 1973–77.

Moreau, C., ed. *Choix de Mazarinades*. Société de l'histoire de France. 2 vols. Paris, 1853.

Moreri, Louis. *Le grand dictionnaire historique*. 18th ed. 8 vols. Amsterdam, 1740.

Mousnier, Roland. *L'assassinat d'Henri IV: 14 mai 1610*. Trente journées qui ont fait la France. Paris, 1964.

Nelson, Janet L. "The Earliest Surviving Royal *Ordo*: Some Liturgical and Historical Aspects." In *Authority and Power: Studies on Medieval Law and Government Presented to Walter Ullmann on His Seventieth Birthday*, edited by Brian Tierney and Peter Linehan, pp. 29–48. Cambridge, 1980.

———. "Inauguration Rituals." In *Early Medieval Kingship*, edited by Paul Sawyer and Ian Wood, pp. 50–71. Leeds, 1977.

———. "Kingship, Law and Liturgy in the Political Thought of Hincmar of Rheims." *English Historical Review* 92 (1977): 241–79.

———. "Ritual and Reality in the Early Medieval *Ordines*." *Studies in Church History* 11 (1965): 41–51.

Olivier-Martin, François. *L'assemblée de Vincennes de 1329 et ses conséquences: Etude sur les conflits entre la juridiction laïque et la juridiction ecclésiastique au XIVe siècle*. Travaux juridiques et économiques de l'Université de Rennes, 1er supplément. Rennes, 1909.

———. "La réunion de la Basse-Navarre à la couronne de France." *Anuario de historia del derecho español* 9 (1932): 249–89.

Oppenheimer, Sir Francis. *Frankish Themes and Problems*. London, 1953.

———. *The Legend of the Ste. Ampoule*. London, 1953.

Ordonnances des rois de France de la troisième race. 21 vols. Paris, 1723–1849.

Pacaut, Marcel. "Recherche sur les terms 'Princeps, principatus, prince, principauté' au moyen-âge." In *Les principautés au moyen-âge*, Actes des Congrès de la Société des Historiens Médiévistes de l'Enseignement Supérieur Public (1973), pp. 19–27. Bordeaux, 1979.

————. *Les structures politiques de l'Occident médiéval.* Collection U. Paris, 1969.

Palmer, John. "The War Aims of the Protagonists and the Negotiations for Peace." In *The Hundred Years War*, edited by Kenneth Fowler, pp. 51–74. London, 1971.

Palmer, R. R. *A History of the Modern World.* 2nd ed. New York, 1956.

Pange, Jean de. "Doutes sur la certitude de cette opinion que le sacre de Pépin est la première époque du sacre des rois de France." In *Mélanges d'histoire du moyen âge dédiés à la mémoire de Louis Halphen*, pp. 557–64. Paris, 1951.

Panofsky, Erwin. *Herkules am Scheidewege.* Studien der Bibliothek Warburg, no. 18. Leipzig, 1930.

Papon, Jean. *Nouvelle et cinquième édition du recueil d'arrests notables des cours souveraines de France.* Lyons, 1569.

————. *Recueil d'arrests notables des courts souveraines de France.* Paris, 1565.

Pasquier, Estienne. *Les oeuvres d'Estienne Pasquier, contenant ses Recherches de la France.* 2 vols. Amsterdam, 1723.

Pasquier, Etienne Denis. *Rapport fait par M. le baron Pasquier, député de la Seine, au nom de la Commission chargée de l'examen de la proposition relative à la répression du duel.* In Chambre des Députés, inpressions ordonnées, no. 4, 152. Paris, 1818.

Penna, Lucas de. *Commentaria in tres libros codicis.* Lyons, 1582.

Perroy, Edouard, ed. *The Anglo-French Negotiations at Bruges, 1374–1377.* Camden Miscellany, 19, no. 2. London, 1952.

Pichon, Thomas Jean. *Journal historique du sacre et du couronnement de Louis XVI, roi de France et de Navarre.* Paris, 1775.

————. *Sacre et couronnement de Louis XVI, roi de France et de Navarre à Rheims le 11 juin 1775.* Bound with Pichon, *Journal historique*, as pp. 92–147.

Pinoteau, Hervé. "L'ancienne couronne française dite 'de Charlemagne', 1180?–1794." *Bulletin du Vieux Papier* 243–45 (January–July 1972): 305–12, 351–62, 381–99. Also printed separately Paris, 1972, and reprinted in Pinoteau, *Vingt-cinq ans*, pp. 375–430.

————. "Les armoiries et la symbolique de Jeanne d'Arc et de ses compagnons." *Les Amis de Jeanne d'Arc* 96 (1979): 5–13, and 97 (1979): cover 2 and pp. 1–8.

————. "La main de justice des rois de France; essai d'explication." *Bulletin de la Société nationale des Antiquaires de France, 1978–79*, pp. 262–65. Paris, 1982.

————. "Quelques réflexions sur l'oeuvre de Jean du Tillet et la symbolique royale française." *Archives héraldiques suisses* 70 (1956): 1–24. Reprinted in Pinoteau, *Vingt-cinq ans*, pp. 100–140.

_____. "Sacre et couronnements napoléoniens." In Pinoteau, *Vingt-cinq ans*, pp. 271–94.

_____. *Vingt-cinq ans d'études dynastiques*. Paris, 1982.

Le politique: Dialogue traitant de la puissance, authorité, et du devoir des princes. In Simon Goulart, *Mémoires de l'estat de France*, 2nd ed., 3. N.p., 1578.

Post, Gaines. *Studies in Medieval Legal Thought: Public Law and the State, 1100–1322*. Princeton, 1964.

"1ᵉʳ acte du président Pompidou: l'amnistie." *France-Soir*, 19 juin 1969, pp. 1, 6.

Promenade à Reims, ou journal des fêtes et cérémonies du sacre, précédé d'une introduction historique sur les sacres des rois de France; suivi de la relation circonstanciée des fêtes qui ont eu lieu à Paris, à l'occasion du retour de S. M. Charles X. Paris, 1825.

Quéant, Abbé Constant C. *Étude sur le sacre*. Paris, 1868.

Quicherat, Jules, ed. *Procès de condamnation et de réhabilitation de Jeanne d'Arc, dite La Pucelle*. Société de l'histoire de France. 5 vols. Paris, 1841–49.

Rébelliau, Alfred. "Bossuet et les débuts de Louis XIV." *Revue des deux mondes* 7ᵉ période, 97ᵉ année, 38ᵉ vol. (15 October 1927 = 1927:5): 826–59; 42ᵉ vol. (1 November 1927 = 1927:6): 117–41, and (15 November 1927 = 1927:6): 306–28.

Rebuffi, Pierre. *Tractatus varii*. Lyons, 1600.

Recueil des édits, declarations, arrests, et autres pièces concernant les duels et rencontres. Paris, 1689.

Reinhard, Marcel R.; Armengaud, André; and Dupaquier, Jacques. *Histoire générale de la population mondiale*. 3rd ed. Paris, 1968.

Rélation de la cérémonie du sacre et couronnement du roi Louis XV. faite en l'église metropolitaine de Reims, le dimanche 25 octobre 1722. Printed in Dumont, *Supplément au corps universel*, 4: 221–34. Cited as Dumont, *Louis XV*.

Remond, Charles de. *Les cérémonies observées au sacre et couronnement du roy Loys XIII*. Paris, 1610.

_____. *Le sacre et couronnement du roy Loys XIII*. Paris, 1610.

Richardson, H. G. "The Coronation in Medieval England: The Evolution of the Office and the Oath." *Traditio* 16 (1960): 111–202.

_____. "The English Coronation Oath." *Speculum* 24 (1949): 44–75.

Riesenberg, Peter N. *Inalienability of Sovereignty in Medieval Political Thought*. Columbia Studies in the Social Sciences, no. 591. New York, 1956.

Robert, Paul. *Dictionnaire alphabétique et analogique de la langue française* (=*Le petit Robert*). Paris, 1979.

Ronsard, Pierre de. *Oeuvres complètes*. Edited by Gustave Cohen.

2 vols. Bibliothèque de la Pléiade, no. 45. Paris, 1950.

Rouche, Michel. *L'Aquitaine des Wisigoths aux Arabes, 418–781: Naissance d'une région*. Paris, 1979.

Roy, Émile. "Philippe le Bel et la légende des trois fleurs de lis." *Mélanges de philologie et d'histoire offerts à M. Antoine Thomas*, pp. 383–88. Paris, 1927.

Rozès, Joseph. *Un récidiviste au quinzième siècle: François Villon*. Toulouse, 1898.

Sacre de Sa Majesté Charles X, dans la métropole de Reims, le 29 mai 1825. Paris, 1825.

Le sacre et couronnement de Louis XIV roy de France et de Navarre. Paris, 1654.

Saenger, Paul. "Burgundy and the Inalienability of Appanages in the Reign of Louis XI." *French Historical Studies* 10 (1977): 2–26.

Saffroy, Gaston. *Bibliographie généalogique, héraldique et nobiliaire de la France*. 4 vols. Paris, 1968–78.

Saint-Gelais, Jean de. *Histoire de Louys XII, roy de France*. Edited by Théodore Godefroy. Paris, 1622.

[Saint-Joseph, Pierre de]. *Catéchisme des Partisans, ou Résolutions théologiques touchant l'imposition, levée et emploi des finances, dressé par demandes et par réponses, pour plus grande facilité*. In *Choix de Mazarinades*, edited by C. Moreau, 1:277–89. Société de l'histoire de France. 2 vols. Paris, 1853.

Saint-Simon, Louis de Rouvroy, duc de. *Mémoire succint sur les formalités desquelles nécessairement la renonciation du Roy d'Espagne tant pour luy que pour sa postérité doit estre revestue en France pour y estre justement et stabilement validée*. In *Ecrits inédits de Saint-Simon*, edited by M. P. Faugère, II, 1, pp. 179–408. Paris, 1880.

_____. *Mémoires*. Edited by Gonzague Truc. Bibliothèque de la Pléiade. 7 vols. Paris, 1961.

Salmon, J. H. M. *The French Religious Wars in English Political Thought*. Oxford, 1959.

_____. "The Paris Sixteen, 1584–94: The Social Analysis of a Revolutionary Movement." *Journal of Modern History* 44 (1972): 540–76.

Scheidgen, Helmut. *Die französische Thronfolge (987–1500): Der Ausschluss der Frauen und das salische Gesetz*. Dissertation Bonn. Bonn, 1976.

Scheller, Robert W. "Imperial Themes in Art and Literature of the Early French Renaissance: The Period of Charles VIII." *Simiolus: Netherlands Quarterly for the History of Art* 12 (1981–82):5–69.

Schramm, Percy Ernst. *Festschrift Percy Ernst Schramm*. Edited by Peter Classen and Peter Scheibert. 2 vols. Wiesbaden, 1964.

———. *Geschichte des englischen Königtums im Lichte der Krönung.* Weimar, 1937.

———. *Kaiser, Könige und Päpste.* 4 vols. in 5. Stuttgart, 1968–71.

———. *Der König von Frankreich: Das Wesen der Monarchie vom 9. zum 16. Jahrhundert.* 2nd ed. 2 vols. Weimar, 1960.

———. "Die Krönung in Deutschland bis zum Beginn des Salischen Hauses (1028)." *Zeitschrift für Rechtsgeschichte, kan. Abteilung* 24 (1935): 184–322.

———. "Ordines-Studien II: Die Krönung bei den Westfranken und den Franzosen." *Archiv für Urkundenforschung* 15 (1938): 3–55.

———. "Ordines-Studien III: Die Krönung in England." *Archiv für Urkundenforschung* 15 (1937): 305–91.

Scriptores rerum Merovingicarum. Vol. 3, *Passiones vitaeque sanctorum aevi Merovingici et antiquiorum aliquot,* edited by Bruno Krusch. Monumenta Germaniae historica. Hannover, 1896.

Selden, John. *Titles of Honor.* 2nd ed. London, 1631. 3rd ed. London, 1672.

Sermet, Ernest. *Le droit de grâce.* Toulouse, 1901.

Sherman, Claire Richter. "The Queen in Charles V's 'Coronation Book': Jeanne de Bourbon and the 'Ordo ad Reginam Benedicendam.' " *Viator* 8 (1977): 255–309.

Siret, C. J. Ch. *Précis historique du sacre de S. M. Charles X.* Reims, 1826.

Skinner, Quentin. *Foundations of Modern Political Thought.* 2 vols. Cambridge, 1978.

Sommaire responce à l'examen d'un hérétique, sur un discours de la loy Salique. N.p., 1587.

Somnium viridarii. In *Monarchia S. Romani Imperii,* edited by Melchior Goldast, vol. 1. Hannover and Frankfurt, 1612.

Le songe du vergier. In Pierre Dupuy, *Traitez des droits et libertez de l'église gallicane,* edited by Jean Louis Brunet, vol. 2. [Paris], 1731. Photomechanically reprinted in *Revue du moyen âge latin* 13–14 (1957–58).

Spiegel, Gabrielle M. "The Cult of Saint Denis and Capetian Kingship." *Journal of Medieval History* 1 (1975): 43–69.

Strayer, Joseph R. "Defence of the Realm and Royal Power in France." In *Studi in onore de Gino Luzzatto,* 1:288–96. 4 vols. Milan, 1949–50.

———. "France: The Holy Land, the Chosen People, and the Most Christian King." In *Medieval Statecraft and the Perspectives of History: Essays by Joseph R. Strayer,* pp. 300–314. Princeton, 1971.

Sweeney, James Ross. "The Problem of Inalienability in Innocent III's Correspondence with Hungary: A Contribution to the Study of the

Historical Genesis of *Intellecto*." *Mediaeval Studies* 37 (1975): 235–51.

Terrasse, Charles. *Germain Pilon*. Paris, 1930.

Tessier, Georges. *Le baptême de Clovis*. Trente journées qui ont fait la France. Paris, 1964.

――――. *La diplomatique royale française*. Paris, 1962.

Thou, Jacques Auguste de. *Histoire universelle*. 11 vols. The Hague, 1740.

――――. *Historiarum sui temporis libri CXXXVIII*. 7 vols. London, 1733.

Thou, Nicolas de. *De Thou's Henry IV*. See above, Bibliography of Works Cited from Godefroy.

Treitinger, Otto. *Die oströmische Kaiser- und Reichsidee nach ihrer Gestaltung im höfischen Zeremoniell*. Jena, 1938.

Ullmann, Walter. *The Carolingian Renaissance and the Idea of Kingship*. London, 1969.

――――. *Principles of Government and Politics in the Middle Ages*. 2nd ed. London, 1966.

――――. "Der Souveränitätsgedanke in den mittelalterlichen Krönungsordines." In *Festschrift Percy Ernst Schramm*, edited by Peter Classen and Peter Scheibert, 1:72–89. 2 vols. Wiesbaden, 1964.

"Verone, François de." See Boucher, Jean.

Villette, Claude. *Les raisons de l'office et cérémonies qui se font en l'église catholique, apostolique et romaine*. Rouen, n.d. Also printed in Paris, 1611.

Vindiciae, contra tyrannos: sive, de principis in populum, populique in principem, legitima potestate. Edinburgh [actually Basel], 1579.

Viollet, Paul. *Histoire des institutions politiques et administratives de la France*. 3 vols. Paris, 1890–1903.

――――. *Histoire du droit civil français*. 2nd ed. Paris, 1893.

Wackernagel, Rudolf H. *Der französische Krönungswagen von 1696–1825: Ein Beitrag zur Geschichte des repräsentativen Zeremonienwagens*. Neue Münchener Beiträge zur Kunstgeschichte, no. 7. Berlin, 1966.

Ward, Paul L. "An Early Version of the Anglo-Saxon Coronation Ceremony." *English Historical Review* 57 (1942): 345–61.

Weber, Hermann. "Das *Sacre* Ludwigs XVI. vom 11. Juni 1775 und die Krise des Ancien Régime." In *Vom Ancien Régime zur französischen Revolution: Forschungen und Perspektiven*, edited by Ernst Hinrichs, Erberhard Schmitt, and Rudolf Vierhaus, pp. 539–65. Veröffentlichungen des Max-Planck-Instituts für Geschichte, no. 55. Göttingen, 1978.

Weill, Georges. *Les théories sur le pouvoir royal en France pendant les guerres de religion*. Paris, 1891. Reprint: New York, [1966].

Wolf, John B. *Louis XIV*. New York, 1968.

Wolff, Hélène. "Le mystère et la fête: les sacres royaux racontés par les chroniqueurs du XVe siècle." *Bulletin du Comité du folklore champenois* 119–21 (1976): 1–4.

Wood, Charles T. "Queens, Queans and Kingship: An Inquiry into Theories of Royal Legitimacy in Late Medieval England and France." In *Order and Innovation in the Middle Ages: Essays in Honor of Joseph R. Strayer*, edited by William C. Jordan, Bruce McNab, and Teofilo F. Ruiz, pp. 385–400. Princeton, 1976.

Yates, Frances A. "Queen Elizabeth as Astraea." *Journal of the Warburg and Courtauld Institutes* 10 (1947): 27–82.

Young, Karl. *The Drama of the Medieval Church*. 2 vols. Oxford, 1933.

Zampini, Matteo. *Des estats de France, et de leur puissance*. Paris, 1588.

———. *De gli stati di Francia, et della lor possanza*. Paris, 1578.

Zeller, Gaston. *Les institutions de la France au XVIe siècle*. Paris, 1948.

———. "Les rois de France candidats à l'Empire: Essai sur l'idéologie impériale en France." *Revue historique* 173 (1934): 273–311, 497–534. Reprinted in Gaston Zeller, *Aspects de la politique française sous l'Ancien Régime*, pp. 12–89. Paris, 1964.

INDEX

Aachen, 186
Aaron, 4
Ableiges, Jacques d', 99–100
Absolutism, 65–66, 113, 126–27, 185, 206–16
Acclamations, 21, 39, 95–97, 193, 213
Achilles, 182
Admiral of France, 119. *See also* Coligny, Gaspard de
Aeneas, 185
Aimoin, 116, 118, 125
Alciati, Andrea, 244 (n. 70)
Alençon, Charles, duke of, 162–63
Alençon, John, duke of, 161
Alexander the Great, 182
Alsace, 61
Amnesty, 60, 102, 114
Ampulla, the Holy: legend of, 13, 31–32, 176–78, 204–5; handling of, 19, 35, 192, 195–96; Louis XI and, 37–38; liturgy and, 43; in the Restoration, 188–89
Andrew II of Hungary, 70
Anjou, Francis, duke of Alençon, 120, 126, 266 (n. 32)
Anne of Brittany, 86, 100
Anointing, 3–5, 20, 37, 42–43, 203–4, 218
Antoine de Bourbon, king of Navarre, 139–41, 163–64, 166
Appanages, 91
Aquitaine, duchy of, 84
Aquitaine, kingdom of, 226 (n. 4)
Aragon, 71
Artois, Charles, count of. *See* Charles X
Artois, county of, 89
Astraea, 184
Aubery, Antoine, 146, 276 (n. 55)
Aumale, Claude de Lorraine, duke of, 141-42

Balm, the Holy, 19, 22, 189. *See also* Ampulla, the Holy
Bane, Jacques de, 65, 110
Banner, 32–33
Banquet, coronation, 22, 213
Baptism, 135
Barbatia, Andreas, 107
Baricave, Jean, 126
Bath, 134–35
Beauvais, bishop of, 17–18, 28, 119, 131–32
Bed of state, 28, 131, 133–38, 152
Bedford, John, duke of, 75
Bedrene, Jean, 109–10
Belanger, François Joseph, 188–89, 195
Belleforest, François de, 123–24
Belloy, Pierre de, 124–25
Berry, Charles, duke of, 160
Berry, Jean, duke of, 34, 73, 100
Beza, Theodore, 118–19
Bezants. *See* Jettons
Bie, Jacques de, 49
Birds, 21, 96–98, 193
Bloch, Marc, 25, 198
Bodin, Jean, 88, 101–2, 106–7, 112, 123, 209, 244 (n. 70)
Bologna, school of law at, 76, 83–84
Borgia, Caesar, 144–45
Bosogast, 178
Bossuet, Jacques Bénigne, 218
Bouchart, Alain, 86–87
Bouchel, Laurens, 101–3, 107, 112
Boucher, Jean, 120, 125–26
Bourbon, Charles II, cardinal of, 137, 140–42, 169
Bourbon, Charles III, cardinal of, 267 (n. 37)
Bourbon, Louis de Bourbon, cardinal of, 163
Bourbon dynasty, 153, 170, 188, 195, 198–200